THE VULCAN STORY

XM599

THE VULCAN STORY

1952–2002

TIM LAMING

Left: XM599 at high altitude delivering a full payload of 1,000lb high-explosive bombs on a weapons range. (MoD)

A Cassell Book

Published in 2002 by Silverdale Books
An imprint of Bookmart Ltd
Registered Number 2372865
Trading as Bookmart Limited
Desford Road
Enderby
Leicester LE19 4AD

ISBN 1-85605-701-1

This book was designed for Cassell & Co
Wellington House, 125 Strand
London WC2R 0BB
by DAG Publications Ltd

Printed and bound in Slovenia

CONTENTS

Introduction	6
1. **The Need for a Nuclear Deterrent**	9
2. **Design Genesis**	23
3. **Testing the Delta**	43
4. **Into Service**	60
5. **Arming the Vulcan**	87
6. **Working on the Vulcan**	100
7. **Training and Flying**	110
8. **Displaying the Vulcan**	120
9. **Into Battle – and Beyond**	132
THE AIRCREW MANUAL	155
Vulcan Production, Service and Disposals	217
Vulcan Deployment	227
Index	229

INTRODUCTION

Thus it may be that we shall, by a process of sublime irony, have reached a stage in this history where safety will be the sturdy child of terror, and survival the twin brother of annihilation.'

— Sir Winston Churchill

Ask any casual observer to identify an aircraft design, and chances are they would be spectacularly unsuccessful. Despite the astonishing variety of aircraft patterns and the fundamental part they are likely to play in our lives, surprisingly few have managed to earn themselves a place in history as true icons. Notable among the exceptions are classic aircraft such as the Spitfire and Concorde, and of course the Vulcan.

Anyone who has watched the mighty Vulcan seemingly leap into the air will admit that it's an experience never to be forgotten. The sheer size of the huge four-engined monster, combined with a noise which one Vulcan pilot described as 'a dinosaur during rutting season', make the Vulcan's departure a truly memorable event. Equally impressive, however, is the Vulcan's remarkable agility and performance. It seems incredible that it is now some forty years since test pilots Roly Falk and Jimmy Harrison first demonstrated the Vulcan's ability to barrel roll almost effortlessly, something which even today's Lancer and Spirit pilots would

Above: *VX770, the Avro 698 prototype. (via Mick Coombes)*

Left: *Vulcan 698 prototype VX770. Oblique sunlight reveals the wrinkled skinning over the intake area. (British Aerospace)*

be very reluctant to attempt, even if they were allowed to try.

Yet despite the Vulcan's charisma and undeniable beauty, it is somewhat ironic to remember that the aircraft was designed to kill. A classic example of what we now refer to as a Weapon of Mass Destruction, the Vulcan was created to fulfil a simple but deadly task – to deliver a single thermonuclear weapon to the heart of the Soviet Union. Undoubtedly, the Vulcan was more than capable of performing such a task, and the very fact that it was never called upon to do so suggests that the doctrine of nuclear deterrence really did work. The concept of Mutually Assured Destruction persuaded the Soviet Union to accept that nuclear war was not a practical military or political option, even though the history books now reveal that there were a few occasions when the so-called balance of terror very nearly tipped us all into oblivion.

The Vulcan's presence during the bleakest of the Cold War years gave the Royal Air Force a destructive power of almost unimaginable scale. Prepared to make rapid 'scramble' take-offs from dispersals all around the United Kingdom, the Vulcans were earmarked as the spearhead of the RAF's striking force, destined to hit the Soviet Union hard and decisively, long before America's Strategic Air Command's bombers could reach European skies.

When Britain's nuclear deterrent was handed to the Royal Navy in 1970, the Vulcan could easily have been written-off as redundant. But a long service career still remained ahead, both in the low-level tactical nuclear strike role, and as a conventional HE (High Explosive) bomber. It was in this latter role that the Vulcan was finally called upon to fly in anger, just weeks before its scheduled retirement, when Argentina invaded the Falkland Islands in 1982. Even after this remarkable turn of events, the Vulcan's operational history was not over, and a handful of aircraft were rapidly modified to become refuelling tankers, supporting RAF forces around the world.

When the Vulcan's RAF career did finally end, the Royal Air Force was surprisingly reluctant to let the now-obsolete bomber go. Two examples were retained by the RAF simply to entertain and delight the public, performing at air shows around the United Kingdom. Like the Battle of Britain Flight and the famous Red Arrows, the Vulcan had become part of British history, and the public wanted to see (and hear) the mighty jet bomber. Sadly, cost finally ended the Vulcan's annual series of air show performances and the RAF sold its much-loved aircraft to a civilian buyer. This might well have concluded the Vulcan's long and fascinating history, but even now, the story doesn't seem to be completely at an end. If present plans continue for the full restoration of the RAF's last Vulcan, a team of dedicated enthusiasts may well succeed in getting this aircraft back into the air, and new generations of appreciative spectators will be able to witness the unmistakable and unforgettable Vulcan experience first-hand.

At the time I wrote the original edition of *The Vulcan Story*, it seemed fairly certain that the retirement of the RAF's last Vulcan really did mean that we would never again see or hear a Vulcan in the air. CAA (Civil Aviation Authority) approval for the operation of former military aircraft was then restricted to relatively simple jet types such as the Jet Provost and Hunter. The sheer complexity of the Vulcan's systems suggested that there was not even a chance that the CAA would ever allow a four-engined jet bomber to operate under civilian ownership. But the perseverance and dedication of owner David Walton, together with his team of volunteers, has finally persuaded the CAA that a Vulcan can be maintained and operated safely, and if the aircraft's restoration is completed to the CAA's satisfaction, XH558 will fly once again.

CAA approval, naturally, is only part of the story, and the main factor dictating XH558's future is of course cost. Although a great deal of money has been dedicated to the Vulcan project, surprisingly few British companies have offered any significant support. Although one might have expected a positive rush of potential sponsorship deals, British businesses evidently cannot quite comprehend the attention-grabbing potential of the Vulcan. Unless the situation improves, history may well record that it was not technical failure or CAA reluctance which kept the Vulcan firmly on the ground, but rather a simple lack of cash. What a disappointment and sheer waste that would be. And what an insult to the countless people who designed, built and operated this magnificent machine.

As ever, I must thank the many people who have helped me in the preparation of this book. In addition to all those who contributed so generously to the first edition of *The Vulcan Story*, I must add my thanks to Ray Deacon, Andy Leitch, Steve Oddy and Craig Jackson, and Barry Holmes. Understandably, lack of space prevents me from including every available Vulcan photograph, and every snippet of relevant information in this new edition. Indeed, in the case of the Vulcan, the difficulty is to decide what to leave out, rather than what to include. Let me take this opportunity, however, to include a 'plug' for another book entitled *V-Bombers* (written by myself) which goes some way to explaining the wider concept of the RAF's V-Force, beyond the more specific story of the Vulcan's development. Ideally, I would have enjoyed the luxury of delaying completion of this second edition until the fate of XH558 was secured; but publishing deadlines must be met, and so, like countless others, I shall now be watching the progress of XH558 very carefully, keeping my fingers firmly crossed!

Tim Laming
Sheffield
January 2002

__Below:__ A Vulcan B.2 with a Blue Steel missile under its fuselage; the missile's ventral fin is extended. The pastel-shade RAF markings are augmented by the pink lightning bolts of No. 617 Squadron, whose badge appears in full colour on the nose. (British Aerospace)

1. The Need for a Nuclear Deterrent

The origins of the Avro Vulcan can be traced back to 1940, when Winston Churchill's Cabinet first examined the possibilites of developing a nuclear bomb. An Austrian scientist, Otto Frisch, and a German scientist, Rudolf Peierls, working at the University of Birmingham, produced a report during 1940 which indicated that uranium 235 could be separated from uranium 238, thus initiating a 'chain reaction' necessary to produce an atomic bomb. Their calculations illustrated the awesome power which could be produced by such a weapon, and as it was known that Nazi Germany was already looking at the same possibilities, the British Government wasted no time in setting up the Maud Committee, a group of scientists who quickly agreed that an atomic bomb was a practical proposition. They concluded that a usable weapon could be developed and constructed by the end of 1943, at an estimated cost of £5 million. Their estimate was somewhat optimistic. However, they also predicted (accurately) that an atomic bomb would probably create an explosive force equivalent to around 1,800 tons of TNT, and that radio-active fall-out would also be produced, rendering large areas of land totally uninhabitable for a long time. Churchill realized that a usable bomb might not be developed until after the end of World War Two; nevertheless the Maud Committee concluded that development and production of an atomic bomb should still be pursued, because 'no nation would care to risk being caught without a weapon of such decisive possibilities'.

American scientists were greatly impressed by reports from the Maud Committee, and they succeeded in persuading President Roosevelt to set up the famous Manhattan Project, in anticipation of full collaboration with Britain; indeed, Roosevelt wrote to Churchill to propose a joint project. Britain, however, was less than enthusiastic at the prospect of divulging nuclear secrets to the USA. There was great concern that America would be either unable or unwilling to 'keep nuclear

Below: *Roy Chadwick, creator of the immortal Lancaster and the genius behind the equally outstanding Vulcan, photographed beside an Avro 534 Baby in 1919. (British Aerospace)*

secrets', and an equally great unease about Roosevelt's neutrality with regard to the war in Europe. Likewise, the British Government wanted to maintain its lead in nuclear know-how, envisaging a great post-war political superiority over other countries. However, following the Japanese attack on Pearl Harbor, America's neutrality collapsed overnight, and Roosevelt quickly allocated huge resources to the Manhattan Project. War-ravaged Britain was suddenly placed at a distinct disadvantage, being unable to match America's financial support for atomic bomb development. Ironically, Britain was now required to seek the co-operation of a reluctant United States, and Churchill was forced to make great diplomatic efforts to persuade Roosevelt to sign the 1943 Quebec Agreement, which permitted British scientists to join their American counterparts at Los Alamos in New Mexico, where the first atomic weapon was to be developed.

Unfortunately for Britain, the Manhattan Project was far from being a truly 'joint' programme for the two participating countries. British scientists working at Los Alamos were 'compartmentalized', being permitted to work purely on specific aspects of the bomb, rather than the project as a whole. General Groves, who was in charge of the Manhattan Project, later stated that Britain's contribution was not vital to the successful development of a bomb; however, he also commented that, in his opinion, there would probably have never been an atomic bomb to drop on Hiroshima (thus ending the war) without 'active and continuing British interest'. Certainly the Americans could have been accused of exploiting the British scientists, but it is also fair to say that British nuclear know-how also benefited greatly from the Manhattan Project. As Lord Chadwick, chairman of the post-war atomic committee which reported to the Ministry of Supply, noted, British scientists could not be expected 'to take amnesia tablets before returning home'.

After the end of World War Two, the relationship between Britain and the USA worsened. The 1944 Hyde Park Memorandum, signed by Roosevelt and Churchill, outlined plans for full nuclear collaboration after the defeat of Japan. It was conveniently 'lost' and later forgotten. America appeared to be moving towards isolationism once again, and although President Truman was somewhat sympathetic to Prime Minister Attlee's position, Congress was deeply suspicious of Britain's new socialist government. The 1946 McMahon Bill made all exchanges of nuclear information between the USA and another country illegal, Britain included, regardless of wartime treaties which had been signed by both USA and Britain. Attlee was furious and sent a telegram to Truman making a final plea for 'an exchange of information which will give us, with all proper precautions with regard to security, that full information to which we believe we are entitled, both by the documents and by the history of our common efforts in the past'. Truman did not even bother to acknowledge receipt of the telegram.

Thus the British Government was forced to 'go it alone' and design a purely

Left: Sir Roy Dobson, Managing Director of A. V. Roe & Co when the Vulcan was designed and manufactured. (British Aerospace)

Right: Stuart Davies, Manager of Avro's Projects Department, and later the Chief Designer when Roy Chadwick became Technical Director. Chadwick and Davies were the two people primarily responsible for the design of the Vulcan. (British Aerospace)

British atomic bomb, based on knowledge gleaned from participation in the Manhattan Project. Attlee was eager to ensure that Britain could defend herself independently, should the USA become an isolationist nation once more, and under the control of scientist William Penney (who the Americans had wanted to stay with their atomic bomb team after completing the Manhattan Project), the development and production of an atomic bomb was begun. As Attlee later admitted, the decision to proceed with a British atomic bomb was based largely on the desire to maintain a strong political position in relation to the USA. However, the Berlin blockade, the war in Korea and the news of the first Russian atomic explosion in 1949 served to reinforce an ever-growing fear of a full-scale war with Russia, and prompted a great sense of urgency on the part of the bomb's design team. Relations with America continued to deteriorate, and although talks to discuss atomic co-operation had been resumed, and USAF B-29 Superfortress bombers (all nuclear capable) were now being based in England, Truman was still making great efforts to prevent Britain from manufacturing atomic bombs, on the basis that the weapons might be 'captured', presumably by Russia. When Klaus Fuchs, a British-naturalized spy (who had worked at Los Alamos), was arrested in 1950, it became clear that there was absolutely no possibility of any further co-operation between Britain and America.

During 1952 the Chiefs of Staff met to discuss the future of Britain's defence strategy, and concluded that America could not be trusted to enter into a conflict with any country which did not directly threaten the USA. Equally, it was understood that without a nuclear capability, Britain would be little more than an unfortunate bystander in any future war. Although Britain was suffering great economic problems, the Chiefs of Staff called for a doubling in plutonium output, and a programme to build up the Royal Air Force's bombing capability. On 3 October 1952 Britain's first atomic device was detonated at 09:15am on the Monte Bello Islands, off North West Australia. Similar to the 'Fat Man' weapon dropped on Nagasaki, the British bomb was basically a gun-like assembly of two subcritical pieces of plutonium which, when compressed, became the supercritical mass which created the explosion. Thus Britain finally joined America and Russia as an embryonic nuclear power.

However, although the device, code-named 'Hurricane', was a success, it was far from being an operational bomb, and as development continued, attention was also devoted to the means of delivering the weapon to its target. Although a decision had been made on the height and speed at which the operational bomb (code-named

Above: *Wing Commander Roland Falk, test pilot for the Avro 707 series (apart from the prototype, which was flown by Flight Lieutenant Eric Esler) and the Avro 698 Vulcan. (British Aerospace)*

'Blue Danube') would be carried, nobody yet knew the precise dimensions of the weapon, as these would be dictated by the high-explosive supercharge, required to compress the fissile plutonium. It was assumed that the bomb would be roughly 10ft in diameter, 30ft long and weigh around 10,000lb; these dimensions were based largely on the 'Grand Slam' ten-ton bomb used towards the end of World War Two. Initially studies into weapons delivery centred around ballistic missiles, following a proposal made in 1945 by Dr Alwyn Crowe, the Comptroller of Projectile Development. He suggested that captured German V-2 rockets should be test-launched as part of an experimental programme to determine the possibilities of developing the rocket into a usable British weapon. Unfortunately, as far as atomic warfare was concerned, the V-2 was a long way from being a capable nuclear missile. The V-2's maximum payload was 2,150lb, whereas the Blue Danube would weigh 10,000lb, and there was absolutely no prospect of a smaller and lighter bomb being developed in the near future. Range would also be a problem because, for the V-2 to fly from even Germany to Moscow, the rocket's range would have to be multiplied by six. Clearly there was no way that even an 'upgraded' V-2 could form the basis of a British atomic missile, and in 1948 the Ministry of Supply decided to abandon rocket development for the foreseeable future. Consequently the Blue Danube would be carried by a long-range bomber aircraft.

As the first atomic bomb was dropped over Hiroshima in 1945, the RAF's concepts of bomber operations were instantly rendered obsolete. The devastation caused by just one bomb, delivered by one aircraft, demonstrated the revolutionary effect which nuclear technology would have upon military thinking. While the RAF was equipping its bomber squadrons with Avro Lincolns (developments of the earlier Lancaster design), a new and infinitely more destructive weapon had been developed, which the Lincoln was incapable of carrying. Consequently, attention quickly switched towards the design of a totally new aircraft which would be able to carry a Blue Danube bomb. The first specification for an all-new jet-powered aircraft was issued by the Ministry of Supply on 7 January 1947. It was based on the Air Staff's Operational Requirement 229 of 17 December 1946 and called for an aircraft capable of carrying a 10,000lb weapon load over a still-air range of 3,350 nautical miles, at 500 knots, and with an over-the-target height of 50,000 feet. Additionally, the specification required the aircraft to carry a 20,000lb bomb load over shorter ranges. The specialist research departments in the Ministry of Supply then examined OR.229 in detail, and determined that a practical aircraft design could be manufactured to meet the requirement, resulting in Air Ministry Specification B.35/46.

Having already established the dimensions of the Blue Danube bomb, Spec. B.35/46 required the new aircraft to incorporate a weapons bay that measured at

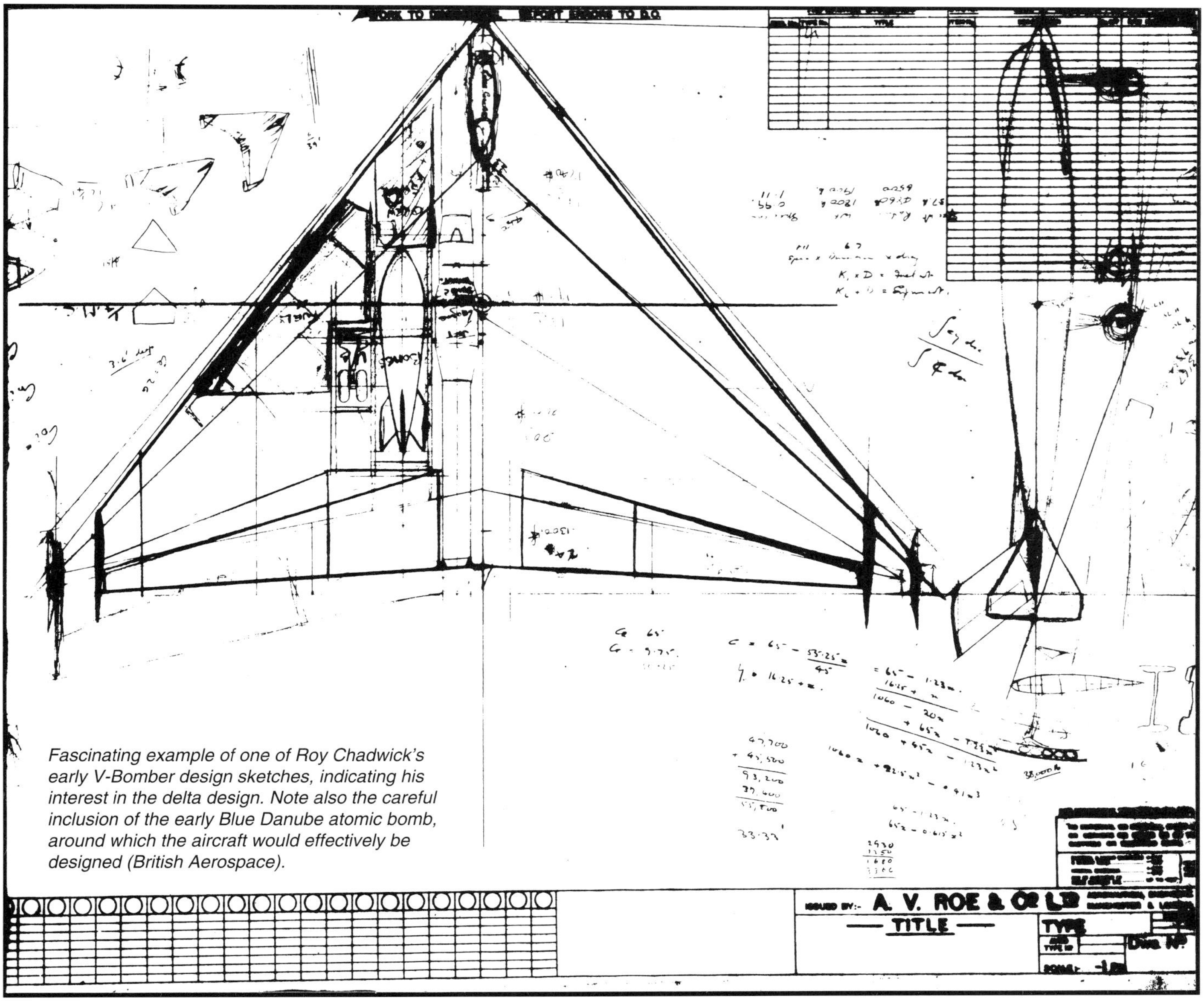

Fascinating example of one of Roy Chadwick's early V-Bomber design sketches, indicating his interest in the delta design. Note also the careful inclusion of the early Blue Danube atomic bomb, around which the aircraft would effectively be designed (British Aerospace).

least 25ft by 5ft in order to accommodate it. The four-engined aircraft would have a five-man crew, seated in a cabin pressurized to 9psi, which is equivalent to an altitude of 8,000ft above sea-level when flying in cruising configuration at 45,000ft. Over the target area, pressurization would be reduced to 3.5psi to avoid the risk of an explosive cabin decompression, if hit by enemy fire. In addition to these very demanding requirements, it was also envisaged that the crew would not be expected to make individual parachute exits in the event of an emergency; the entire cabin section would therefore form a jettisonable capsule. Initially the all-up weight limit was to be 100,000lb, as the RAF's airfields would not be able to support anything heavier, but after discussions with the aircraft industry the weight limit was raised to 115,000lb. As the requirements of the new bomber became clear, it also became increasingly evident that the RAF's next long-range bomber would be something more than the latest in a series of design developments. It would have to be totally new and radically different in terms of both configuration and capability.

On 9 January 1947 Avro, Armstrong Whitworth, Bristol, English Electric, Handley Page and Short Brothers were invited to submit tenders based on Spec. B.35/46. Despite the extremely ambitious performance figures required, each company confidently set to work on a wide variety of designs, culminating in the submission of formal tenders in May 1947 (the submissions deadline). The advanced and largely unknown nature of these fairly radical design proposals led the Ministry of Supply to refer the whole subject to the Royal Aircraft Establishment at Farnborough, where an Advanced Bomber Project Group was set up under the chairmanship of Morien Morgan, the head of Farnborough's Aerodynamic Flight Section. Eighteen aerodynamicists and structural engineers were appointed to the group, and together they examined the various proposals in an effort to determine which design should be chosen.

The group had an unenviable task: the performance requirements of Spec. B.35/46 were essentially mutually exclusive of each other. The speed could be achieved, the payload and range too, but to achieve all three objectives with one aircraft seemed like an impossible task. Range was the major concern, as the group felt that an aircraft could be designed to carry the required payload to 50,000 feet at 500 knots, but to achieve a range of more than 3,000 miles seemed to be an insurmountable problem. Likewise, the all-up weight limit of 115,000lb seemed to create additional design problems, in that it imposed a restriction on the design altitude. A bigger wing would enable the aircraft to fly at higher altitude, thanks to lower wing loading, but the bigger wing would increase the aircraft's all-up weight. Eventually the RAF accepted that the solution would be to build longer and stronger runways, specifically to accommodate the new bomber, thus removing the weight restriction.

After a great deal of consideration, the group produced a proposal to proceed with no fewer than three designs in an effort to remove the risk of a single design failing to meet expectations. The Handley Page H.P.80 was thought to offer the best performance in terms of altitude over the target, albeit at the expense of manoeuvrability. The group also recommended that the H.P.80 beredesigned to incorporate a conventional tailplane (the original proposal featuring wingtip-mounted control fins), in order to minimize the predicted effects of aeroelastic distortion. In addition, the group proposed the adoption of the Avro 698 which, while unable to match the H.P.80's altitude of 52,000 feet (the Avro design being expected to achieve 48,500 feet), was able to offer much improved manoeuvrability. Both designs clearly offered advantages, but the group was reluctant to decide in favour of just one, because of insufficient aerodynamic data on which to base their decision. It was felt that a basic flaw might be found in one of the designs at some stage, and it would be better to proceed with both. Indeed, the group recommended spreading the risks still further, by proceeding with a 'design intermediate between the two extremes'. However, the need for such an aircraft had already been recognized by the RAF, which understood the risks involved with the production of either the Handley Page or Avro designs, and the fairly long time-scale which would probably be required to put the aircraft into production. Consequently Specification B.14/46 was issued in August 1947 to Short Brothers, who designed a 'conventional' aircraft with a lower speed and altitude capability. Designated S.A.4, the Sperrin first flew on 10 August 1951.

THE DELTA
A Tried and Proven Design.
by J. A. R. Kay, F. R. Ae.S.
A 1955 Paper Written by Director, A. V. Roe & Co., Limited.

In less than ten years the hitherto unusual triangular shape for aircraft wings has become an accepted part of the aeronautical scene. That this should be so is due to the pioneering efforts of A. V. Roe & Co., Limited, in Great Britain and Convair in America. Both companies started where the German, Professor Lippisch, left off at the end of the war. His only product, a tailless delta glider for low speed research, was completed under American supervision.

Since then so much air has flowed over the triangular wings of many different deltas that the protagonists of the design are no longer concerned with refuting their critics. Their case has been proved for them by hundreds of hours of successful flying and large scale production orders. The sceptics must surely have been convinced when the Douglas Skyray landed on an aircraft carrier shortly after capturing the world's speed record over 3 kilometres. Such a speed range has not yet been demonstrated by any other configuration.

Now why should the delta have risen to popularity so rapidly? As it has been chosen for a variety of aircraft for many differing roles, it must obviously have characteristics which suit many varying requirements. The concern of this article, however, is the choice of the tailless delta for a high altitude bomber, the Avro Vulcan.

The introduction of a radically new design is usually accompanied by a much longer period of development than that associated with variations of the conventional. This has not been the case with the Avro Vulcan which has a remarkable record of steady and impressive progress unmarred by a crop of major or even minor changes to the design. This has been due to the extensive programme of research flying carried out by the company with the Avro 707 series of deltas. The only change of note was the lengthening of the nose-wheel to improve take-off. This modification was found necessary on the 707B and introduced on the Vulcan before detail design had been fixed.

At this point it is necessary to emphasise that every aircraft is a compromise because every specification consists of a number of requirements, many of them in conflict with others. The basic requirements of the specification, to meet which the Vulcan was designed, were high altitude, high speed and long range. In our view, and after a most intensive study of several designs, the tailless delta appeared to be the best compromise. In meeting the performance requirements it will be obvious that we also had to provide ease of handling and embody the simplest possible structure. The latter, naturally, eases manufacture and simplifies maintenance. A noteworthy fact which followed the choice of the delta planform from performance considerations was the bonus of a simplified structure providing a large internal volume within the wing for engines, undercarriage and fuel.

Let us, then, look at the delta wing layout with reference to its aerodynamic characteristics. The delta has a high lift/drag ratio at high sub-sonic speed because it incorporates a number of desirable features which delay the rise in drag due to compressibility effects. These are:

1. Sweepback
2. Thickness:chord ratio.
3. Wing Loading
4. Aspect Ratio.

1. Sweepback. This can be defined as the angle by which the quarter chord line of the wing lies behind the normal to the centre line of the aircraft. Sweeping the wing back 45° may delay the critical Mach number by as much as 0.1 beyond a straight wing equivalent. While the critical Mach number can be said to depend on the geometric sweepback of a wing, it is more correct to interpret this as a dependence on the sweep of the isobars, or lines of constant pressure, along the wing. In order to make sure the isobars adopt a large relative angle of sweep the position of maximum thickness of the aerofoil section on the Vulcan is further forward at the wing root than at the tip, thus ensuring the maximum effective sweepback for the entire wing.
2. Thickness:chord ratio. This is a measure of the slenderness of the aerofoil section used for the wing. Thickness: chord ratios as high as 20% have been used in the past on low speed aircraft, but compressibility considerations have more than halved this value on present high speed types. In practice wing tip sections can have rather lower thickness: chord ratios than sections at the root. The minimum thickness: chord ratio at the tip is related to that required to give satisfactory cruising lift co-efficient and low speed stalling characteristics.
3. Wing loading. A low wing loading is a most important feature in an aircraft which must fly at high altitudes and high sub-sonic Mach numbers. The lift coefficient is thus kept at a small value and the drag increases associated with high lift coefficient at high Mach numbers kept to a minimum.
4. Aspect ratio. At high subsonic Mach numbers a valuable postponement of compressibility effects is obtained by the use of low aspect ratio. In addition, the lower aspect ratio wing has very much better handling characteristics near the stall and in manoeuvres. By comparison most highly swept aircraft with normal aspect ratios have a tendency to pitch nose up at the stall or to get an unacceptable tightening up when applying "g". A typical comparison of this is shown below. In either condition the aircraft may get into a dangerous attitude or lose considerable height before control can be regained.

ASPECT RATIO ON DRAG GRAPH

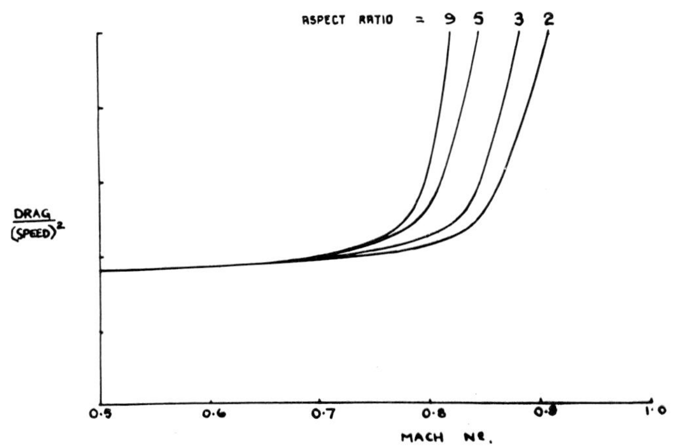

Owing to the aerodynamic qualities of the delta wing, it is an established fact that a tailplane is no longer necessary for normal flight manoeuvres. It is, in some cases, a disadvantage. Adequate damping is provided in the longitudinal plane by the concentration of wing area near the root. The control surfaces fitted to the trailing edge of a delta wing retain their power up to very high incidences.

Static stability is ensured by arranging the centre of gravity to be a suitable distance in front of the aerodynamic centre of the aircraft. The allowable range of centre of gravity movement is comparable with that of conventional aircraft. Furthermore the deletion of the tailplane offsets the increase in skin friction drag due to the relatively large area of the delta wing.

All long range high altitude bombing aircraft will be flying near their minimum drag speed at which the profile drag and the induced drag or "drag due to lift" are equal. A bomber design must make a compromise between these two and the aspect ratio must be chosen so that this compromise is obtained between the two types of drag. In this respect, it is important to remember that the drag due to lift factor of a delta wing is very close to unity whereas for a conventional swept wing this factor is appreciably greater than unity so that the effective aspect ratio of the swept wing is considerably less than its geometric aspect ratio. It should also be remembered that by avoiding the need for a tailplane and its associated interference drag, there is a reduction in profile drag which again enables the lower aspect ratio which is efficient at high subsonic Mach number to be adopted.

One criticism which has been directed at the tailless delta is the supposed difficulty of obtaining directional stability owing to the short moment arm available for the fin. This difficulty has been offset to a great extent owing to the proximity of the fin and rudder to the delta wing, the end plate effect of which increases the effective area of the vertical surfaces by up to 60%.

In practice a normally proportioned fin and rudder provides satisfactory stability and control characteristics throughout the required speed range.

Aeroelastic effects

A problem which has come to light only during the last few years is that of aeroelasticity in airframes. It is an accepted fact that any structure will deflect when a working load is applied to it. The manner in which it deflects and its subsequent oscillations about its final position should not in any way detract from the performance of the task for which it is designed. This is a relatively easily achieved state of affairs in a stiff structure whose final deflected form is very similar to that of its initial unloaded condition. However, it is not the case when a straight high aspect ratio, swept back, wing deflects. Increased loading of a wing of this type causes it to bend and twist relative to the airstream. Thus the alteration of the wing loading by a manoeuvre such as a pull-out, decreases the angle of attack of the outboard part of the wing to such an extent as to alter the longitudinal trim of the aircraft considerably. Clearly the change of trim in this case will be nose up, thus increasing the applied rate of pull-out. This can be interpreted by the pilot as a loss of stability or, more correctly, as a reduction of manoeuvre margin, which is measured as control movement per "g", this is a most undesirable feature.

The delta wing layout, owing to its geometric shape and inherent stiffness, does not suffer from this change of manoeuvre margin. Thus, there is no tendency to "tighten up" in turns or pull-outs. The large cross-sectional area of the wing, which is to some extent responsible for this advantage, also puts the aileron reversal speed well beyond the maximum diving speed of the aircraft.

The oscillations set up in a structure following any change of loading are of great interest to the aircraft designer, the phenomenon being known as "flutter". It is clear that for an airframe to be satisfactory these oscillations must die away quickly. There should be no possibility of their reaching dangerous amplitudes following any disturbance which might occur in flight.

The possibility of such oscillations becoming established in an airframe greatly depends on the distribution of mass and the stiffness inherent in the structure. Naturally the main distribution of mass is likely to be dictated by the basic design and shape of the aircraft, so that flutter criteria are in the form of stiffness requirements which may involve a severe weight penalty in a high aspect ratio swept wing aircraft.

The delta wing has very low aspect ratio and considerable depth, owing to its large root chord. These give a structure of this type ample inherent stiffness to be stable under conditions which might otherwise excite dangerous vibrations.

Structures

Present day trends in aircraft design often lead to stringent structural requirements. The combination of great structural strength and stability which is necessary is not easily achieved by classical methods of aircraft construction. High aspect ratio wings have their own special problems, the most crucial of which is probably flutter. Care must be taken in designing such wings to ensure that dangerous modes of vibration cannot occur.

From a purely structural point of view, low aspect ratio wings have always held some great advantages. However, it is only recently that the aerodynamic and aeroelastic advantages at high speed have been fully realised with the result that low aspect ratio wings are being used extensively.

For a long time the flying wing has been looked upon as the best long range aircraft configuration. The deletion of the tailplane, a much sought after ideal, has become a practical possibility with the evolution of the delta. The fuselage is, at last, only a thickened and extended part of the wing. The structure has in fact become blended rather than pieced together. This results in a stiff airframe to meet the strict requirements enforced by such elements as flutter, and manoeuvring stability.

The adoption of low aspect ratio wing structures together with low wing loading has led to some interesting structural developments. These represent great advances on the accepted designs of the past few years. It will be possible to make compression and shear structures stabilised to an unusual degree. They will also lead to lighter and cleaner structures if present trends in these developments are followed.

Conclusion

From the foregoing comments it will be clear that the tailless delta has some very useful qualities which have already been turned to good account. They show why the delta is so popular and there can be no doubt that the configuration has a large development potential. After all, it is only five and a half years since the first Avro delta flew.

To sum up its application to a high altitude bomber such as the Vulcan which must fly fast and far, we can translate these characteristics into aerodynamic terms as (a) low wing loading, (b) high critical Mach number and (c) high lift/drag ratio at cruising speed. A tailless delta has been shown to combine these qualities in a simple, efficient and elegant manner. At the same time its low speed behaviour is most satisfactory and is achieved without the use of flaps or nose droop. Aircraft with higher wing loadings require these high-lift devices and therefore need a tailplane to provide adequate trimming power. The inclusion of a tailplane cannot help the ultimate performance at high altitude and the complexity of high-lift devices makes their use undesirable.

A. V. Roe & Co., Limited,
Manchester.(1955)

DELTA DESIGN
by Mr. Stuart Davies (chief designer of A. V. Roe at the time of the Vulcan project)

"It was obvious from the start that no conventional aircraft, as we then knew them, would do the job the Air Staff were asking for. We knew something about swept-back wings even in those days – we gathered quite a lot from the Germans on that scene – and it was obvious that any successful bomber would have to have a fair amount of sweep-back on its wings. We went ahead with our preliminary sketches, and it became increasingly obvious that we were going to exceed the maximum all-up weight by a considerable amount.

The first idea we produced was an aircraft three times as big as the machine the Air Staff wanted – and we could still not see how we could get the performance they required. The next stage in our thinking turned against the Air Staff's requirements. Are they ridiculous? Have they made a mistake to ask for all these qualities in one aircraft? These were the sort of questions we asked ourselves.Then we started to think again and studied projects emboyding thin swept-back wings and low wing loading in various configurations. The high specified cruising speed more or less fixed these design features at values which for a conventional aircraft meant more structure weight than we could afford, and as this meant a corresponding reduction in payload the concept was rendered quite uneconomical.

Stalemate seemed to have been reached until, as our next step, we investigated the possibility of utilising the tips of our highly swept wing for longitudinal control. This seemed to be a move in the right direction for it meant elimination of weight and drag of the tailplane. But we were still faced with a wing design which seemed too large and too heavy for what it had to do. It didn't all come at once. This initial groping for a solution took the men of Avro's Project Department between four and five weeks work. They drew on knowledge gained from working on designs for a jet-engine civil transport – the Brabazon 3 project – which was never carried through, and they used the German data showing the benefits of a swept-back wing at high speeds.

The outstanding difficulty was the excessive weight of the wing, and a series of exercises was undertaken to reduce the span of the wing and so the weight. At the same time we had to make sure we did not upset unduly the inter-relation of other factors, including sweepback, thickness, and wing area. So we reduced the weight by reducing the span, and, as this reduced the area, which we didn't want to do, we put the area back by filling in the space between the swept-back wing and the fuselage. The result of all this logical thinking was the delta.

Calculations began to show that there was every likelihood of the aircraft meeting the Air Staff requirements. A. V. Roe's management then took a courageous step. They backed their projects team in putting forward the preliminary design of a revolutionary aircraft to the Air Ministry. The Ministry were interested, and the Projects Department went on to produce documents on the structure of the new machine, and to prepare the official tender for the job. The Avro team worked throughout 1947 on the new design. It was a fateful year for the company marred by the crash at Woodford, in which Roy Chadwick, their technical director, was killed. In the autumn of that year the facts and figures of the projected delta bomber were in the hands of the Air Staff and Ministry of Supply experts. It was their job to 'shoot the thing down' if they could. Experts in all branches of aeronautical science examined our documents, and word came through to the company at the end of 1947 'Go ahead and build a prototype.'

It was a bold decision, and I believe the Air Staff at that time showed foresight in demanding the high performance in their requirements; and courage in placing the order when no previous delta-wing aircraft had flown.

As soon as the order was placed, we proposed building a model, a small research aircraft which would test our theories. This eventually became the first of the 707 series. It flew well and confirmed many of our theories before it was unfortunately lost in an accident. A second small delta, the 707B was built and flown to investigate the slow-flying characteristics of this wing shape. And the 707A followed for high-speed research. Every second those three 707s have flown, automatic recording gear has been piling up information about the delta-wing flying. These aircraft were invaluable for the information they provided before the 698 was ready, and the success of our design is perhaps best illustrated by the fact that very few changes – none of them major alterations – had to be made in the 698 bomber as a result of test flying with the 707s. During 1948, work on the small 707s occupied the projects department, but men were already working on designs for the bomber. It was, however, not until the end of 1949 that the first full-scale "mock-up" of the cockpit was completed. In the spring of 1950 the outside dimensions of the aircraft were fixed, and certain basic information about sizes and shapes of new parts was issued to the men in the shops so that a production line could be prepared.

The work now spread to other parts of the factory. Two hundred draughtsmen began to make detailed drawings of the innumerable parts of the 698. Behind them were another 100 technical men working out calculations on specialised sections of the design. It took us 28 months to build the 698. That's really quite a short time in which to build a prototype of such a revolutionary aircraft. While this was going on we were gaining still more information from the 707 series – and we are still learning from those machines. When the 698 made its first flight from Woodford we had a good idea of the way it should behave. In the few flying hours the aircraft has so far put in, we have confirmed much of the data found on the 707s. And I don't think I'm giving anything away when I say that so far we are extremely pleased with the first results we have obtained. After its maiden flight from Woodford with Wing Commander Roland Falk at the controls, the 698 went to the Farnborough Air Display with the two small deltas.

Throughout the display flying the automatic recording gear was keeping a constant watch on all aspects of the aircraft's performance. The large amount of information obtained from the recordings needs to be analysed, and such is the extensive nature of the instrumentation on a modern aircraft that a team of analysts is fully employed on this work.

What it can do in the way of speed? How far it can fly? At what height and with what bomb load aboard? These are questions to which only Avro's and the Air Ministry have the answers. The prompt ordering of the aircraft before the first flight had been made showed the confidence the present Air Staff had in the aircraft backed by their predecessors five years ago, when the first Avro plans for a delta-bomber were being considered.

Sir Roy Dobson, managing director of the company, told the world at Farnborough his company was already working on a civil version of the bomber. Sir Miles Thomas, chairman of British Overseas Airways Corporation, has announced that his experts are already examining the new Avro project with a view to its possible use on world air routes.

So far other countries are following Britain's lead slowly in taking up the delta-wing shape for military aircraft, but Mr. Davies and the Avro designers are sure this machine has a performance far in advance of any other comparable aircraft flying in the world today. Whatever the future of the delta – in either civil or military form – the men of A. V. Roe's will take pride in the fact that here in Manchester the world's first practical aircraft was designed and built."

Many people, and not only those connected with the aircraft industry are speculating on the reason for A. V. Roe & Co. Limited designing and building the 707 series of Delta Research Aircraft, the first of which appeared at the 1949 S.B.A.C. Show. After all, the name of Avro is closely associated with very much larger aircraft, such as the Lancaster, Lincoln and Shackleton in the military field and the Tudor in the Civil field. The little 707's seem to be a complete departure from this tradition. The reason is partly explained by the fact that the aircraft are research aeroplanes and are intended to find out more about the flying qualities of this sort of an aeroplane which is known as a Delta because of the close similarity between the wing plan form and the Greek letter Delta.

We, like other large aircraft concerns, cannot afford to stagnate and merely produce the same basic type with miscellaneous detailed alterations and improvements as the years go by. The advent of the jet engine has raised the performance levels of all military aircraft and also long range commercial aircraft, and with the radical change in power plant must come equally radical changes in the airframe to match it. Considering that a military bomber or commercial transport is essentially an aircraft designed to carry pay loads for relatively long distances, the basic aerodynamic problems are rather similar and just as from a military point of view the highest possible cruising speed is necessary, so in the case of a transport aircraft, it has been proved that high cruising speed can lead to overall economy and the lowest overall cost per passenger/mile. From an economical point of view there is a limit to the cruising speed which, as is well known, is set by the so called "barrier" of the speed of sound. Some aircraft have flown faster than the speed of sound, but it is not yet an economical proposition to attempt to cruise for long distances at these speeds. However, the nearer one can get to it the better, and it is this consideration which starts the designer thinking on radical lines.

In order to fly economically the aircraft must have the minimum possible drag and in order to keep the drag down at speeds approaching that of the speed of sound it is necessary for technical reasons to sweep the wings back at a very pronounced angle to the fuselage. Also it is necessary to keep the thickness of the wing as low as possible in terms of the chord; that is to say, whatever the wing chord is at any particular point along the span, the thickness should be kept down to a value of 10% of the chord or even less. Furthermore, if you want to fly at a high true air speed and go as far as possible with an economical fuel load, it is well known that you must go as high as possible where the air is less dense. Unfortunately, the speed of sound drops with increasing altitude and, therefore, as you design to fly higher, you must not only take the steps mentioned previously but in addition you must keep the angle between the wing and the flight path (known as the angle of incidence) low or else the drag will rise rapidly. In order to keep the angle of incidence low it is necessary to keep the wing loading low, or in other words, for a given gross weight of aircraft the wing area must be larger than we have become accustomed to in the last 15 years.

Another factor to be borne in mind, is that on a commercial aircraft or long range bomber, if you want to fly long distances you utilise wings of high aspect ratio; that is the span is large relative to the chord; the ratio varying from say, 9 up to 14. This is necessary in order to keep down that part of the drag (known as the induced drag) which is the penalty we pay for the wing lift.

Now you can get a broad picture of what the designer of a large load carrying, long range aircraft is faced with, if he wants to fly at speeds comparable with the speed of sound. He has at one and the same time to sweep the wings back, make them thinner, increase the area and keep up the span. This poses very great structural problems, and in fact to try to keep a really high aspect ratio and do all the other things simultaneously is economically impossible. One solution is to reduce the aspect ratio, in order to keep the structure weight down, and let the induced drag rise with the hope that so much saving can be made on the rest of the drag that the total will still not be too high. If you combine what is structurally desirable with what is necessary aerodynamically you soon arrive at the solution that the best thing to do is to taper the wings very drastically so that in the limit the plan form becomes triangular in shape.

A little thought will show that with such a wing the required sweep back is achieved and large area can be automatically obtained at the lowest possible structure weight, since the area out at the tip which causes the big bending loads on the wing structure is reduced to a minimum and, therefore, such a wing of large area can be obtained with the minimum possible structural penalty. Furthermore, our aim of keeping the wing at the centre portion nearest the fuselage is quite large in terms of feet and inches.

We now find that as an interesting by-product of the theme we have got a relatively large usable volume in the wing that can be used for packing away the engines, undercarriage, fuel etc., so that the excrescences hitherto so evident on the wing of an otherwise clean aeroplane have completely disappeared. Furthermore, the thickness of the wing at the centre is sufficiently large as to absorb the fuselage almost entirely so that it is reduced virtually to a streamlined projection ahead of the apex of the triangle.

Another by-product of this type of wing with its low loading is that no special devices such as slots or flaps are necessary to keep the landing speed down. The wing loading is sufficiently low as to enable quite normal take-offs and landings to be done on existing aerodromes. Once we have abolished the need for landing flaps, which produce big changes of trim that have to be balanced out by the tail, the very need for the tail itself becomes questionable. The large wing chord of the Delta type of wing enables us to fit elevators at the trailing edge of the wing and these elevators have sufficient power to enable the aircraft to be flown through all normal manoeuvres.

We thus, by fairly logical process, arrive at an aircraft capable of high cruising speeds for long distances with a respectable payload and consisting of nothing more than a smooth wing, streamlined fuselage nose and vertical fin and rudder to look after directional control. If we have done our calculations properly we have now reduced the drag to the absolute minimum possible, and, therefore, have achieved, whether by military or commercial standard, the highest possible cruising efficieny.

Technically, therefore, the case for the Delta on paper is proved provided that in fact it flies in a respectable manner and does not suffer from hidden vices which have been overlooked in thinking only of the performance. Any aircraft Company interested in the large type of aircraft cannot afford to ignore the possibilities of the Delta configuration. It is one thing, however, to prove a theoretical case on paper and it is another to sell it to the customer. What more obvious step, therefore, to take than to build a small one and fly it and this the Avro Company have done.

This, however, is only the beginning of the story; to translate this rather hopeful lesson into a large and intricate piece of hardware such as a bomber or a transport aircraft requires an enormous amount of investigation into the engineering details and it is here where the designer's Art is more important than his Science, where time is dictated by the speed with which materials can be obtained, fabricated and assembled, equipment provisioned and tested, all of which adds up to a process which can run into many years. (1952)

DELTA ORIGINS

A Paper written during 1956 by J. R. Ewans, Chief Aerodynamicist at A. V. Roe during the development of the Mk 1 Vulcan, and responsible, as Chief Designer, for the concept and development of the Mk2.

Introduction

So far as can be ascertained, the idea of using a triangular planform for aircraft wings, now known as the delta wing, was first put forward in 1943 by Professor Lippisch, who will be remembered for his association with the Messerschmitt Company. His studies had led him to think that this planform was most suited for flight at speeds in the region of the speed of sound, where conventional aircraft designs were already known to be in trouble. By the end of the war, he had a number of Delta wing projects in hand, including an unpowered wooden glider which was intended to explore the low speed properties of the Delta wing. This was by then partly built, and was later completed under United States orders.

The idea of the Delta wing was studied by many other aeronautical experts and a strong recommendation for its use was given, for instance, by Professor Von Karman, of U.S.A., at the 1947 Anglo-American Aeronautical Conference in London.

At the time of writing, three British Delta aircraft and two American are known to have flown, and it is pretty certain that others are on the way. In the date order of their first flight, these are:-

Consolidated-Vultee	XF-92
A. V. Roe	707
Boulton Paul	P111
Douglas	XF-3D
Fairey	FD-1

With the exception of the last named, which is fitted with a small fixed tailplane for the first flights, all the above aircraft are tail-less.

The following notes are intended to give a logical explanation of why there is this considerable interest in the Delta wing, and just what advantages it promises the aircraft designer. To do this, we must consider the type of aircraft the designer is trying to produce.

The Designer's Aim

Right at the beginning, it must be said that the Delta wing is of value only for very high speed aircraft, and at the present stage of engine development, this implies the use of jet engines. When projecting his high speed aircraft, the designer will attempt to produce an aircraft carrying the greatest pay-load for the greatest distance, at the highest speed, and for the least expenditure of power (i.e. using the least amount of fuel). This applies to all types of aircraft, whether bombers in which the pay-load is bombs, or civil aircraft in which the pay-load is passengers or cargo, or fighters, in which the pay-load is guns and ammunition.

Problems of High Altitude and High Speed Flight

The most fundamental factor determining what is achieved is the height at which the aircraft flies. At higher altitudes, the density of the air reduces so that the aircraft drag is less and it is possible to fly at a given speed at say 40,000 feet, for an expenditure of only one quarter of the power required at sea level.

It has been shown in theory, and found in practice, that the speed of sound occupies a fundamental position in the speed range of aircraft. The speed of sound is actually 760 miles per hour at sea level, and falls off to a value of 660 miles per hour at heights above 30,000 feet. Because the speed of sound is of such importance aeronautical engineers relate aircraft speeds to the speed of sound, using the term MACH NUMBER defined as the ratio of the speed of an aircraft to the speed of sound at the same height. As an aircraft approaches the speed of sound – in fact for conventional aircraft when a speed of about 70% of the speed of sound (i.e. a Mach Number of 0.7) is reached – the effects of compressibility become important and the characteristics of the air-flow round the aircraft change fundamentally. There is a very large increase in the air resistance or drag, and an excessive expenditure of power becomes necessary to increase the speed any further.

For transport and bomber aircraft the speed at which the drag starts to increase (known as the "drag rise" Mach Number) becomes the maximum cruising speed since if the aircraft is flown at higher speeds, the disproportionally higher thrust required from the engine means excessive fuel consumption and loss of range. At a rather higher Mach Number there will be changes in the stability of the aircraft and in its response to the pilot's control – leading possibly even to complete loss of control.

In order to progress along the speed range to higher speeds it is therefore necessary to design aircraft so as to postpone and/or overcome these effects.

We have noted that with an "old fashion" type of aircraft design, i.e. thatof jet propelled aircraft current in 1945, the limiting speed in steady cruising flight is likely to be a Mach Number of 0.7 (higher speeds have, of course, already been achieved and a number of aircraft have exceeded the speed of sound, but only for short periods, either by diving or by use of rocket power). From the knowledge available, however, it appears possible by careful aerodynamic design of an aircraft, to postpone the rise in drag until a Mach Number in the region of 0.9 is reached and this figure is likely to be the practical limit of cruising speed for transport aircraft of all types for many years to come. The designer of a civil aircraft, a bomber, or a long range fighter, will, therefore, bend all his energies to achieving a Mach Number of this order without any drag rise. In addition he must pay attention to the changes of stability or lack of control which might occur in this region, and this will occupy his attention to the same extent as the purely performance aspect of the drag rise.

Design for High Mach Number

It is quite easy to design a fuselage shape which is relatively immune from Mach Number effects. It is the design of wings which is difficult particularly since a wing that is suitable for high speed must also give satisfactory flying properties at low speeds, e.g. for take-off and landing.

As the air flows past a wing its speed is increased over the upper surface to a considerable extent and over the lower surface to a lesser extent so that there is greater suction on the upper surface than on the lower surface. This difference gives rise to the lift which enables the wing to sustain the weight of the aircraft. Thus, whatever speed an aircraft is flying, the speed of the air around the wing will, in fact, be higher. In the case of an aircraft flying at Mach Number of 0.8 the speed around its upper surface will be equal to, or may easily exceed the speed of sound. At this stage, the air-flow pattern around the wing will be considerably changed, and it is, in fact, this change which gives rise to the drag and stability effects mentioned above. It is essential, therefore, to keep the velocity above the wing as little in excess of the speed of the aircraft as possible.

There are four ways of improving the high Mach Number behaviour of the wings. They are different methods, all of which can be applied simultaneously, of keeping down the air velocities round the wing. They are:-

a) Sweepback
b) Thinness
c) Low wing loading
d) Low aspect ratio

We will consider each of these effects in turn.

Sweepback

The amount of sweepback is measured by the angle by which the tip of the wing lies behind the centre line. The extent of the gains possible from sweepback is very considerable, and sweeping a wing back may easily lead to a postponement of the compressibility effects by a Mach Number of 0.1. The drag rise of the former occurs at 0.7 and the latter is 0.83.

Thinness

Keeping a wing thin leads to a reduction in the amount of air that must be pushed out of the way by the wing. This helps the passage of the wing through the air. The thickness of a wing is measured by the thickness/chord ratio, which is the maximum depth of the wing divided by its length in the line of flight. In the past, the thickness/chord ratios of an aircraft wing have ranged from 21% down to perhaps 12%. Now values of 10% down to 7% are becoming common.

Low Wing Loading

The wing loading is the weight of aircraft carried by a unit area of wing, measured in pounds per square foot. Mach Number effects are postponed by keeping the wing loading as low as possible, i.e., by supporting the weight of the aircraft with a large wing area. This is particularly important for flight at high altitudes where the low air density puts a premium on keeping the wing loading low. In fact, flight at high altitudes becomes virtually impossible unless this is done.

Low Aspect Ratio

Aspect ratio is the ratio of the span of a wing to the average chord. For moderate speeds, a high aspect ratio, i.e., a large span relative to the chord, gives greatest efficiency. At high Mach Numbers this consideration is no longer important, in fact, some alleviation of compressibility effects is given by reducing aspect ratio.

There is another reason for choosing a low aspect ratio. One of the disadvantages of sweeping a wing back is that the flying characteristics at low speed become worse. A typical symptom is that the wing tip of a swept back wing stalls, giving violent behaviour if the speed is allowed to fall too low. Research has, however, shown that this bad characteristic of highly swept back wings may be overcome relatively easily. Fig. 6 is a graph of sweepback versus aspect ratio, compiled from a very large number of tests of wings of various planforms. Each of these planforms has been classified as giving good or bad characteristics. It will be noted that although almost any aspect ratio can be accepted with an unswept wing, for wings of 45° sweepback an aspect ratio of little over 3 is the most satisfactory.

There is yet a third reason for choosing a low aspect ratio – the behaviour (as regards stability etc) in the high Mach Number region. For reasons which it is not possible to go into here, compressibility effects are minimised and a transition from speeds below that of sound to the speed of sound and above is much more readily accomplished if the aspect ratio is low, say in the order of 2 to 4.

The Delta Planform

Put the above requirements together and the result is an aircraft with a highly swept back, thin wing, a moderately large wing area and a low aspect ratio. A little consideration of geometrical properties and possible planform of wings leads to the conclusion that the Delta wing is the only form which satisfies these requirements. It possesses high sweepback and low aspect ratio. The wing area will, of necessity, be generous for the size of the aircraft and for reasons which will be detailed later, it is easy to build it with a low thickness/chord ratio.

We must see how the Delta planform, indicated from considerations of aerodynamic performance, lines up with practical design requirements, and in particular the over-riding necessaity for keeping weight and drag low in order to obtain a maximum performance. A preliminary question is whether a tailplane is necessary.

To Fit or Not to Fit a Tailplane

From the earliest days of flying, the question has been raised as to whether aircraft can be flown satisfactorily without a tailplane. Confining our attention only to the case of high speed jet aircraft, we will examine each of the functions of a tailplane in turn, in relation to the Delta wing aircraft. A tailplane performs the following functions:

a) To trim out changes of centre of gravity position according to the load carried and the consumption of fuel.

Investigation shows that a control surface at the trailing edge of the wing, provided that the latter has a large root chord (as has the Delta), can cater for all but the extreme c.g. movements.

b) To deal with trim changes due to landing flaps etc.

With the low wing loading associated with the Delta wing, take-off and landing speeds are moderate without the use of flaps, and this question does not, therefore, arise.

c) To provide damping of pitching oscillations.

The reduction of damping of the pitching oscillation has led to difficulty on some tail-less aircraft but it does not arise on the Delta since the large chord near the root gives adequate damping.

d) To deal with loss of stability on control power consequent on distortion of the wing structure at high speed (Aerolastic Distortion).

At very high speeds, all aircraft structures distort to a greater or lesser extent under the high loads imposed, and this distortion alters the aerodynamic form. In extreme cases this leads to a loss of stability or control power, making the aircraft dangerous or impossible to fly at high speeds. An aircraft with a high aspect ratio sweptback wing would need a tailplane to deal with this, but the shape of the Delta wing makes it extremely stiff, both in bending and in torsion, and a tailplane does not appear necessary.

e) To provide for spin recovery

Although this point has not been proved, it is expected that the controls on a tail-less Delta wing would not be powerful enough to ensure recovery from a fully developed spin. A tailplane appears to be the only way of dealing with this. This restriction is of no significance for transport or bomber type aircraft for which spinning does not arise, but on fighter or trainer aircraft, a tailplane would appear to be a necessity. It is, therefore, concluded that for a Delta wing aircraft of the transport type, a tailplane is unnecessary. Its deletion leads immediately to a considerable saving of weight and drag, and to a major gain in performance.

Reduction of Mechanical Complexity

Compared with a conventional aircraft, the Delta wing aircraft will therefore be simpler by the omission of the following items:- the tailplane, the rear fuselage necessary to carry the tailplane, wing flaps and other high lift devices such as the drooped wing leading edge. There is a considerable saving of weight, of design and manufacturing effort, and of maintenance when the aircraft is in service. These economies will have considerable bearing on the initial cost and the manpower necessary to produce and maintain a number of aircraft.

Value of the Large Internal Volume

Because of its shape and the large root chord, the Delta wing provides a large internal volume in relation to its surface area, even when using the thin wing sections which, as we have seen above, are essential for high speed aircraft. Simple calculations show that for the same wing area, the Delta wing has 33% more internal volume than an untapered wing, while if the inboard half of the wing only is considered, as this represents a more practical case from the point of view of the aircraft designer, the internal volume of the Delta wing is more than twice that of the corresponding untapered wing.

It is found that without exceeding a wing thickness of as little as 8% to 10% it is possible on a moderate sized Delta wing aircraft to bury completely the engines, undercarriage, and sufficient fuel tanks for a very considerable range. The fuselage also has a tendency to disappear into the wing at the root. The result is the attainment of an aircraft consisting only of a wing, a fin and a rudimentary fuselage, representing a degree of aerodynamic cleanliness which has never before been reached. In fairness, it must be pointed out that this is achieved at the expense of a rather larger area than usual, but investigation shows that the drag of this is considerably less than that due to a conglomeration of items such as engine nacelles, tailplane, etc.

The Structural Design of the Delta Wing
From the design point of view, the shape of the Delta wing leads to an extremely stiff structure without the use of thick wing skins, and strength becomes the determining feature rather than structural stiffness. This avoids the inefficiency of conventional sweptback wings where the wing has to be made stronger than necessary in order that it shall be stiff enough. It is found that the Delta wing lends itself to conventional design techniques, and to conventional methods of construction.

Summary
Summarising the above, we have seen that in order to meet the requirements of large loads for long range, at high speeds, the high performance transport or military aircraft of the future will cruise at a considerable altitude, at a speed not much below that of sound. The delta wing provides the only satisfactory solution to these requirements, for the following reasons:-

1. It meets the four features necessary for avoiding the drag rise near the speed of sound, i.e., it is highly swept back, it can be made very thin, the wing loading is low, and the aspect ratio is low.
2. Extensive wind tunnel and flight tests have shown that the low aspect ratio Delta wing gives minimum change in stability and control characteristics at speeds near the speed of sound.
3. In spite of being thin, the internal volume is large, so that the engines, undercarriage, fuel and all the necessary equipment can be contained within the wing and a rudimentary fuselage.
4. Adequate control can be obtained by control surfaces on the wing, thus eliminating the need for a conventional tailplane. Together with item 3, this leads to considerable reduction in the drag of the aircraft, and, therefore, to high performance.
5. Auxiliary devices such as flaps, nose flaps, slots and the all-moving tailplane are unnecessary, thereby saving weight and design effort, and simplifying manufacture and maintenance.
6. The Delta wing is very stiff and free from distortion troubles.
A.V. Roe & Co.

Below: *RAF Scampton – A Vulcan B.2 salutes an older Avro design which has since been removed to make way for a car park. (D. Haller)*

2. Design Genesis

By the time the Sperrin made its first flight, it was already clear that this 'interim' bomber would not be required. Although Vickers' Chief Designer, George Edwards, had proposed a design to meet Spec. B.35/46, it was rejected on the grounds that it did not fully meet the required performance figures. Edwards later turned this inescapable fact to his advantage however, by convincing the Ministry of Supply that the Vickers Type 660 would offer the RAF a long-range high-performance bomber without any risk of design failure, within a much shorter time-scale. As the Type 660 relied on proven aerodynamics rather than theory, the Advanced Bomber Group were instructed to consider the proposal. They concluded that it would be a viable proposition if the RAF felt that such an aircraft was urgently needed. Thus the Type 660, later named the Valiant, became the true 'interim' design, with a new specification (B.9/48) written around it; it flew for the first time on 18 May 1951. The Sperrin was redundant, and only two prototypes were built, chiefly to secure jobs at the Short factory in Northern Ireland. However, the two Sperrins did provide a great deal of aerodynamic test data, one machine being used to drop dummy Blue Danube bombs during trials. The Valiant went on to enjoy a very successful career with the RAF.

Design work on the Avro 698 began in January 1947 at A. V. Roe's Projects Department at Chadderton in Manchester. The six-man team, under the leadership of Chief Designer Stuart Davies and Technical Director Roy Chadwick, was at that time heavily committed to the continuing development of the Anson, design of the Shackleton, the Athena advanced trainer, and the Tudor airliner. The 698, however, was to be something totally different, a radically new design, based on some very advanced (for that time) aerodynamic theories. A great deal of knowledge had been obtained from the Germans, who had produced a huge amount of aerodynamic data during World War Two, some of which had begun to be applied to practical designs towards the end of the war. Walter and Reimar Horten in Bonn had produced a number of all-wing tailless aircraft, beginning in 1932 with their H-1 glider, and culminating in the Ho 9 fighter-bomber, which would have become the Go 229 production model had the war in Europe not ended. Much of Horten's development drawings and models were destroyed before the Allies could capture them, but from what did remain, it was estimated that the Go 229 would have been capable of achieving almost 600mph at sea-level, a ceiling of 52,000ft, and an initial climb rate of over 4,000ft/min, with a 4,400lb bomb load and four 30mm cannon.

Dr Alexander Lippisch was another leading German designer, famous for the creation of the Messerschmitt Me 163 rocket fighter. His interest in all-wing designs extended to triangular delta wing planforms which were tested in supersonic wind tunnels (a facility which only Germany possessed during World War Two). Lippisch was working on a delta-winged glider known as the DM-1 as the war ended, and after the American forces had captured his factory at Wiener Wald in 1945, the aircraft, together with its designer, was transferred to the USA. Following a period of wind-tunnel tests, Convair and Lippisch produced the XF-92A, the world's first delta-winged jet aircraft to fly (during 1948), later leading to the famous F-102 Delta Dagger fighter. Outside Germany some investigation into all-wing aircraft design had also been undertaken. In Britain it was Armstrong Whitworth which pioneered research in this field, with the construction of an all-wing research glider, the A.W.52G (first flown on 3 March 1945). Two larger powered aircraft were also built later; when one of these crashed during 1949, its test pilot, Jo Lancaster, became the first British pilot to use the ejection seat as an escape system. Meanwhile Northrop in the USA developed the XB-35, a huge 'flying wing' bomber which, although later abandoned by the USAF, proved the design as a viable aerodynamic concept. All the initial British and American design work was undertaken before the end of the war, and it was only during the immediate post-war period that the detailed and extensive German data became available. Unfortunately for Britain, most of the material was acquired by the Americans, thanks largely to the route taken by the advancing American forces, which led them across central and southern Germany, where most of the research facilities had been located. However, a sizable amount of aerodynamic data and hardware (in the form of captured aircraft) was assembled at Farnborough, and a series of reports compiled by the RAE staff, together with translations of German data, was circulated to British aircraft manufacturers.

Avro's Roy Chadwick was convinced that the all-wing design would prove to be the ultimate in both aerodynamic and structural efficiency, but he was also aware that the radical design would probably be a little too exotic to be adopted as a serious contender for Spec. B.35/46. Certainly, it was accepted that on the basis of German data a swept-wing design was necessary, and the preliminary Avro drawings looked remarkably similar to an earlier design submitted by Bristol (their Type 172), ahead of Spec. B.35/46. Likewise, Blackburn also submitted a pre-B.35/46 design, the B.66, which was probably the first long-range jet bomber to be drawn up as a workable design; it was also a delta. Like Bristol's 172, the early Avro design

EARLY DELTA DESIGN FOR THE AVRO 698

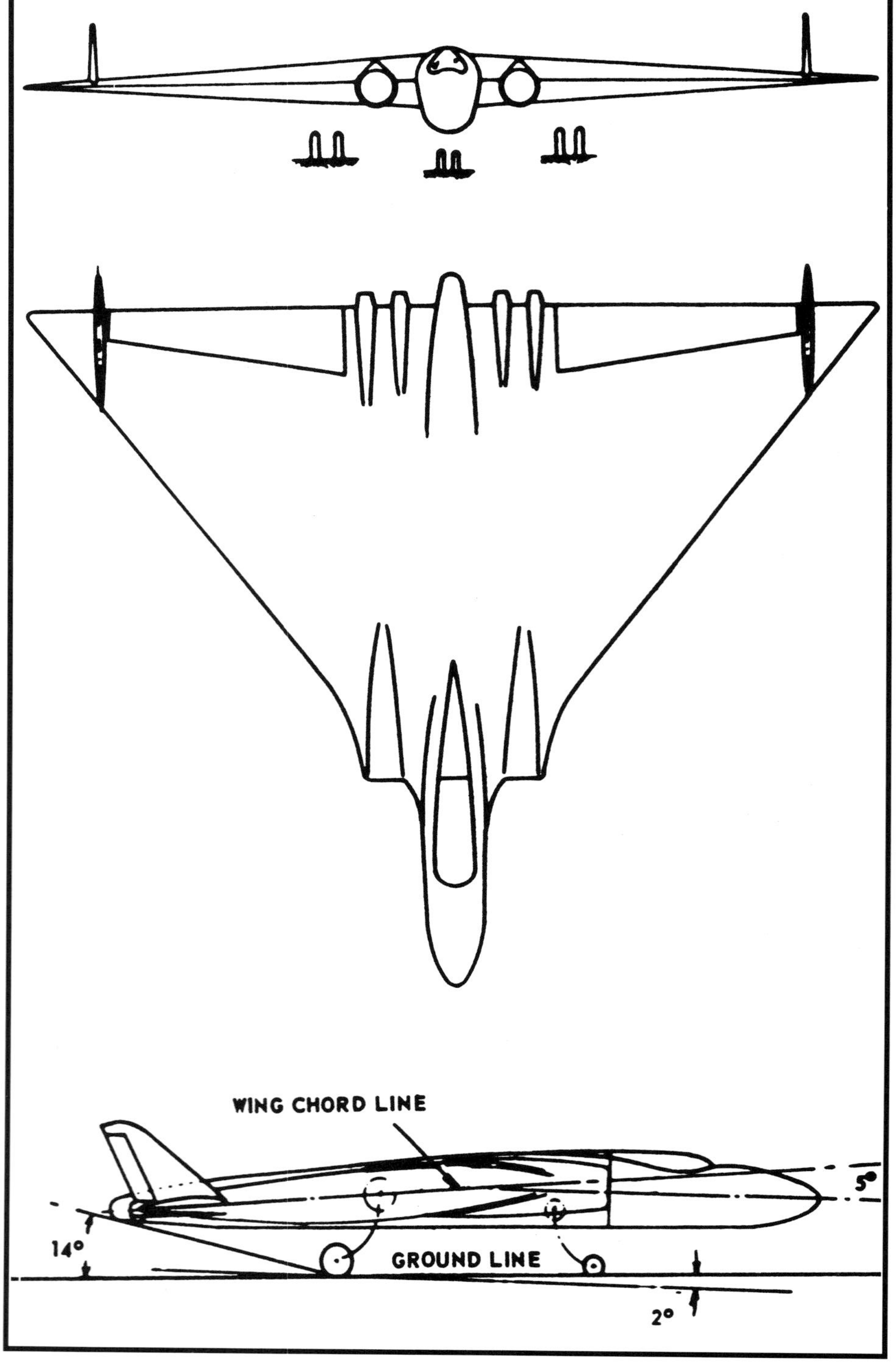

also exceeded the all-up weight limit by a wide margin, the gross figure being estimated at around 193,000lb. Attempts to make the wing thinner simply pushed the weight figure still higher. The specified cruising speed effectively fixed the design features to such an extent that the structure's weight would always be too high, and a corresponding reduction in the payload reached a stage where the overall design was no longer practical. It was only at this stage that the design team looked at the possibility of using the wingtips for longitudinal control, thus making the entire tail section redundant and saving a great deal of drag and weight. The 'flying wing' began to look like the most logical solution.

With 45deg wing sweep, combined elevators and ailerons (elevons) and small fins and rudders placed at the wingtips, the gross weight dropped to 137,000lb, and both Stuart Davies and Robert Lindley (head of the Projects Office, and later a leading participant in McDonnell's Mercury space capsule project) believed that they had identified the best design configuration, after conducting over a month of detailed studies. Drawing on German data, Armstrong Whitworth's experience, and Northrop's continuing development of the XB-35 (which was now being converted into the jet-powered YB-49), an all-wing design seemed practical, but still too heavy. The obvious way to make the wing lighter would be to make it deeper, but in order to achieve high subsonic speed, the thickness/chord ratio had to be kept as low as possible, and so the root chord was increased. Attempts to reduce the wing span while maintaining the wing sweep, thickness and area, meant that the 'missing' wing area was re-located in the space between the wing's trailing edge and the fuselage. By March 1947, after following this design process to its logical conclusion, the team had, of course, produced a delta. Roy Chadwick, who had been ill, returned to Avro, and was immediately delighted with the design configuration, especially because it was so close to his personal liking for all-wing aircraft.

More weeks were spent investigating the properties of the delta, and it was quickly realized that with a root chord of 70ft, the wing still had a high-speed section, but was sufficiently deep to incorporate the engines, fuel tanks, undercarriage and weapons payload. Designated the Type 698, the basic delta layout was established, but it was a long way from what was to become the Vulcan. At this stage, for example, there was to be no true nose section as such: the crew compartment was to be located at the apex of the leading edges. The engines, fed by two large circular intakes, were to be positioned in superimposed pairs, in much the same way as the Lightning, with the upper engines ahead of the lower ones and their exhausts emerging through the upper surface of the wing at about 70 per cent chord. The lower engine exhaust pipes emerged in a cut-back inner section of the wing trailing edge. The atomic bomb was to be housed in a weapons bay, outboard of the port wing engine, with a similar-sized bay under the starboard wing, for the carriage of fuel cells or (when carrying conventional bombs) half the total bomb load.

Although early interest was shown in a bicycle-style undercarriage with wing outriggers (similar to that of the Boeing B-47), the delta wing layout suggested a what is now a fairly conventional tricycle arrangement, with twin-wheel main gears retracting forward into wells located outboard of the weapons bays. However, after an extensive series of wind-tunnel tests at Farnborough, it was suggested that the thickness/chord ratio of the wing be reduced in order to meet the required cruising speed, and after much discussion the Avro design team agreed. The new wing left insufficient space for the engines, which were repositioned and now placed side by side. With the engines now occupying more wing space, there was insufficient space for the two weapons bays, so a single bomb bay was placed directly under the aircraft centre-line. The crew compartment was also revised, and a new nose section was designed, emerging ahead of the wing to house the crew, the radar system and fuel. The large circular intakes remained in their original position, either side of the nose. Avro also considered the possibility of using movable wingtips to achieve lateral control, with the fins moved inboard of each tip, in order to house the power and drive units which would be required. By September the idea had been abandoned, after concluding that individual inboard elevators and outboard ailerons could be fitted to the wing trailing edge, which meant that the vertical stabilizer had to be mounted on the aircraft centre-line. Furthermore, there was some doubt as to the longitudinal stability of the design, and it was felt that a conventional central fin would make a convenient mount for a tailplane, if such a feature proved necessary. The resulting configuration would have looked strikingly similar to a scaled-up version of the Gloster Javelin fighter, had it not been for the decision to eliminate also the circular engine intakes in

Below: *Early Avro 698 model illustrating the original plan for two bomb bays, either side of the four engines, and small wing-tip fins in place of a more conventional tail. (British Aerospace)*

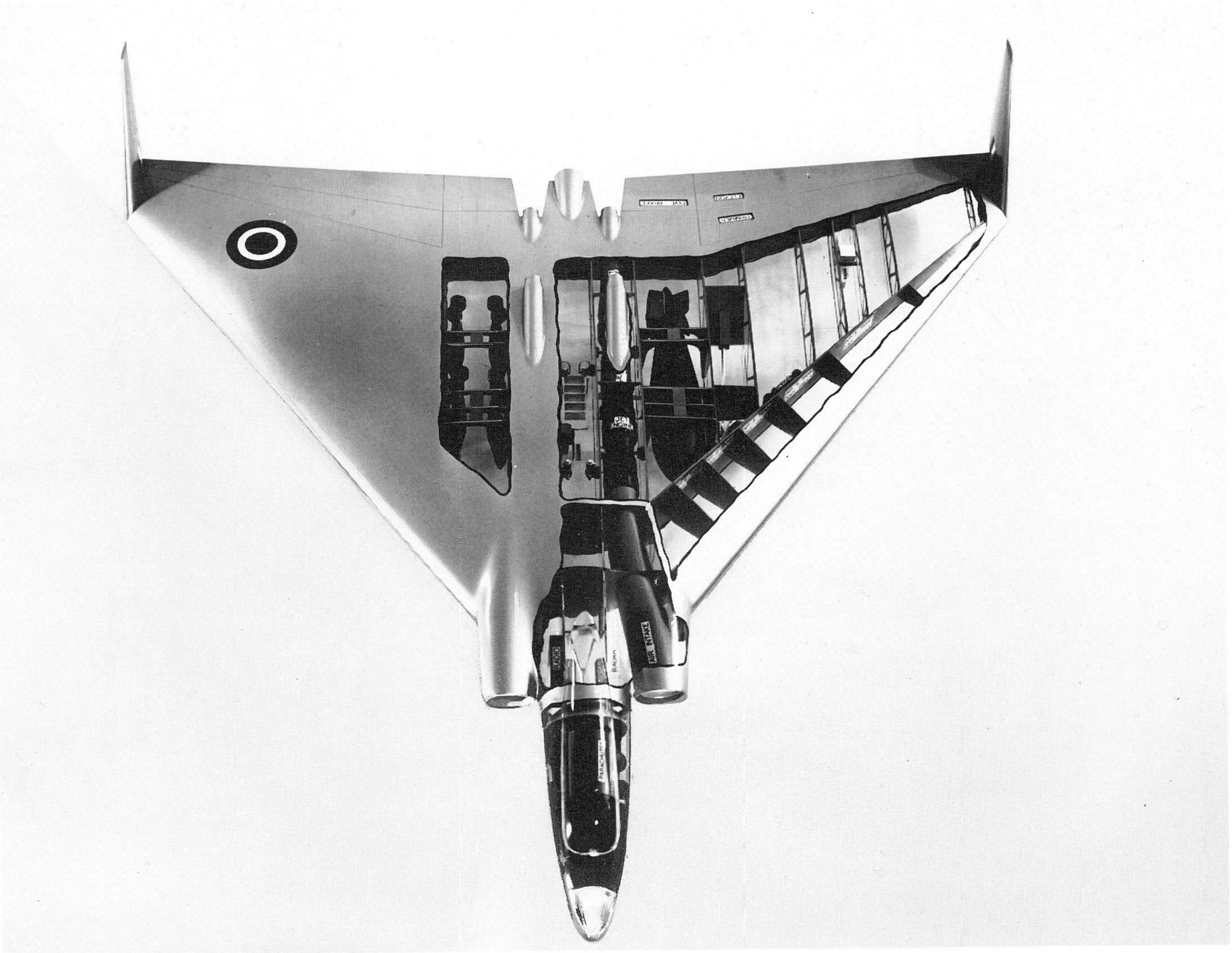

favour of an extension of the wing leading edges, into which horizontal 'letter-box' intakes were inserted. Like many other aspects of the Avro design, the aerodynamic qualities of this type of intake were largely unknown.

During the summer of 1947, Roy Chadwick had a series of meetings with Ministry of Supply officials, and having been responsible for the design of the wartime Lancaster bomber, his reputation counted for a great deal. Clearly a man who could produce an aircraft like the Lancaster would not give his wholehearted support to the new bomber unless he was convinced that it would be successful. On 28 July a tender design conference at the Ministry of Supply reviewed the progress which was being made by all the companies which had submitted designs for Spec. B.35/46. Effectively the choice was between the Handley Page and Avro designs. Tragically Chadwick was killed on 23 August when the Tudor 2 prototype crashed on take-off from Avro's airfield at Woodford. The aileron control cables had been connected the wrong way round. The shock of Chadwick's death was quickly replaced by a growing fear that without his enthusiastic backing, the Avro 698 would not be accepted. Indeed, Ministry of Supply interest in the Avro 698 did begin to diminish somewhat, chiefly because the Ministry felt that development work might also be affected by Chadwick's absence. However, William Farren was appointed as Avro's new Technical Director, and as a former director of RAE Farnborough, he also possessed a formidable reputation in the aeronautical world. On 19 November Handley Page were awarded a contract to produce a prototype of their (more conventional) H.P.80, but after a further week the Avro proposal was also accepted.

Instruction to proceed with the construction of two Avro 698 prototypes was received in January 1948, and although this obviously fell short of a full-scale contract, at least the 698 design could be converted into flying hardware. There was still a considerable lack of information on the flying characteristics of a delta aircraft, in both high and low speed configurations, and at altitudes of up to 50,000ft where the new bomber would be excpected to operate. The Avro team decided that some research should be made

AVRO 710 LAYOUT (NOT CONSTRUCTED)

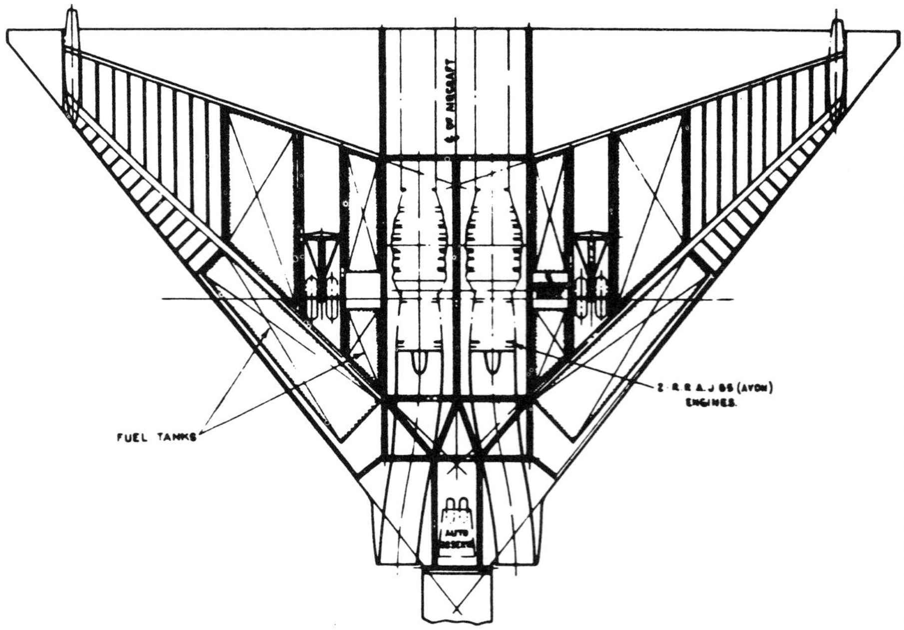

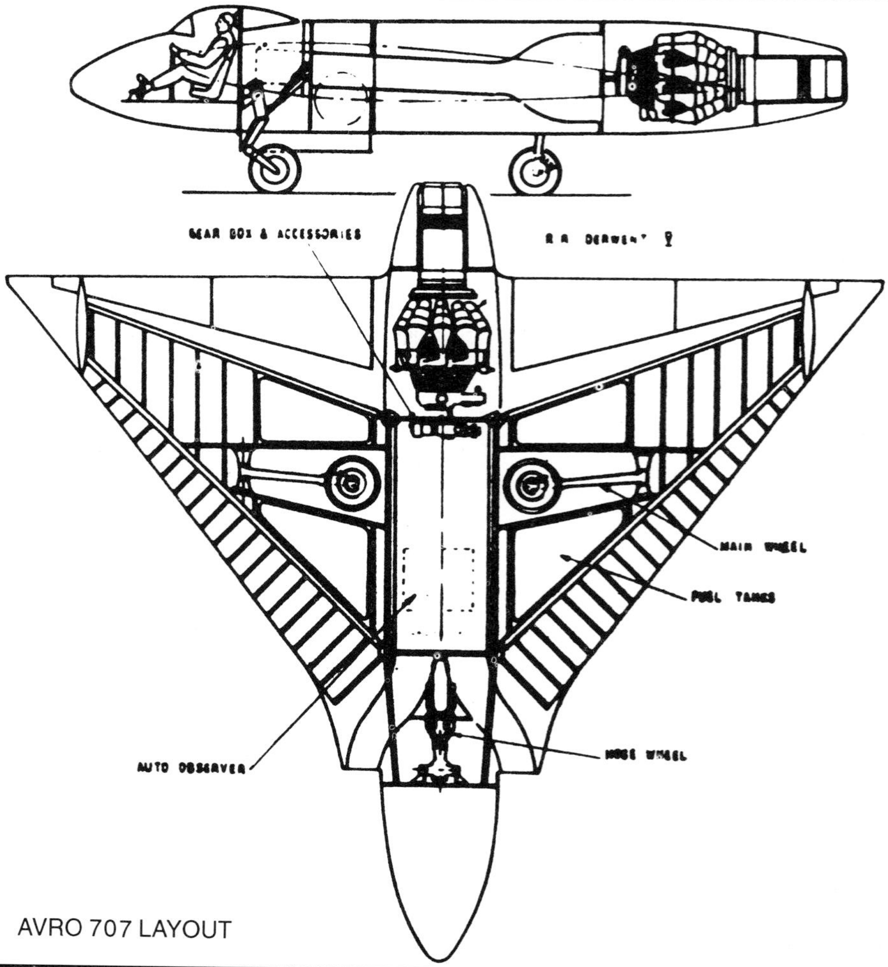

AVRO 707 LAYOUT

Above: *Early Avro 698 design model illustrating the huge circular intakes that were part of the initial design for some time. (British Aerospace)*

Below: *Rear view of an early Avro 698 design showing the unusual engine arrangement which was first considered. (British Aerospace)*

with a flying scale model. During 1947 thought had been given to the possibility of building a delta glider which could be towed into the air and used to gather data on low speed handling characteristics. However, by the time that the order for the two 698 prototypes was received, opinion favoured a powered aircraft, and after discussions with the MoS, it was agreed to build a one-third scale research aircraft. Powered by a single Rolls-Royce Derwent engine, this machine, with the company designation Avro 707, would be used to investigate low-speed characteristics. In addition, a high-speed research aircraft (the Avro 710) would be constructed. Powered by two Rolls-Royce Avons, it was to be capable of exploring the flight envelope up to 60,000ft and Mach 0.95. By September 1948 confidence in the 698 design had increased considerably, and it was felt that the Avro 710 would no longer be necessary, as the final 698 airframe shape was now largely established, and work on the 710 would probably delay work on the 698 rather than contribute towards it. Avro therefore decided to abandon the 710 in favour of a high-speed 707, two low-speed 707s, and a full-scale 698, stripped of all but the most basic equipment, which could be used to gather full-scale flight data. However, the stripped 698 was also later abandoned, as it was felt that the 707s would provide sufficient data, and the full-scale machine would simply divert resources away from completion of the true

698 prototype. News of Convair's XF-92A delta served to eliminate further doubts about the flying characteristics of the delta design, and Avro's attention turned towards the production of the 707s.

The Avro 707 was a relatively inexpensive aircraft with great emphasis placed on simplicity. Specification E.15/48 (written specifically for the 707) reflected the need to save Avro's time and resources, and called for a fairly modest performance of 400 knots maximum speed. Plans were made to construct the 707's wing from wood, but a later decision was made to use a very basic pressed sheet metal construction, with two supporting spars. The fuselage was also very simple in terms of construction, and was used to house both the fuel and test monitoring equipment. The cockpit canopy and nose gear were taken directly from a Gloster Meteor and the main gear from an Avro Athena. The engine intake was placed on top of the fuselage, and conventional non-powered flying controls were fitted. Completed in August 1949, the first Avro 707 (VX784) undertook a series of post-completion engine runs and taxi-ing trials at Avro's airfield at Woodford, before being dismantled and transported to Boscombe Down on 26 August. The first flight was scheduled for 3 September, but a 20-knot crosswind over Boscombe's main runway prevented the aircraft from flying that day. On 4 September, however, Flight Lieutenant Eric Esler, Chief Test Pilot of the Aeroplane & Armament Experimental Establishment, taxied the diminutive 707 onto Boscombe's huge runway and then took to the air at 19:30, to complete a very satisfactory first flight. Two more flights (totalling 2½ hours) were made over the next couple of days, after which Esler flew the 707 to Farnborough, where the aircraft was placed on static display at the SBAC show. After returning to the A & AEE, various items of test data recording equipment were fitted before the flight test programme resumed. The 707 continued to handle remarkably well, and the handling characteristics were reported as being very similar to most conventional aircraft, apart from a fairly lengthy take-off run before unstick speed could be reached.

Sadly, the continuing success of the test programme came to an abrupt halt on 30 September when VX784 crashed near Blackbushe, killing Esler. The precise cause of the accident was never fully established, but there appeared to have been a loss of control at low speed. It was suspected that a control circuit had failed and this would have locked the airbrakes in the extended position, resulting in a low-speed stall from which recovery would have been impossible. However, despite the widespread gloom at the loss of both Esler and the 707, there was some relief when it was established that the delta wing design had in no way been responsible for the crash. As the second 707 was nearing completion, the test programme continued without any major changes, although plans were made to redesign the airbrakes and modify the elevators. It was also decided that an ejection seat should be fitted - which would have been impossible in the

__Below:__ Avro 707 prototype VX784 shortly after its 20-minute first flight on 4 September 1949. (British Aerospace)

707's confined nose - but as the high-speed 707A (produced to Spec. E.10/49) was nearing completion, production of its nose section was accelerated. This was later fitted to the second 707 (VX790), enabling both the ejection seat and new data measuring equipment to be successfully accommodated. As with the first 707, the newly designated 707B also utilized the Athena's main undercarriage, but the nose gear was taken from the Hawker P.1052. The wing air brakes were revised and the fuselage brakes deleted. The pilot for the first flight (at Woodford) was to be Wing Commander R. J. 'Roly' Falk, Avro's recently appointed Chief Test Pilot. Falk had previously worked as a test pilot for Vickers-Armstrongs and had been Chief Test Pilot at RAE Farnborough. VX790's maiden flight was scheduled for 5 September, but after a lengthy series of pre-flight tests, darkness had already begun to fall over the airfield, and Falk opted to make a series of taxi trials, culminating with a short 'hop' along the runway. The next day the aircraft made a successful maiden flight lasting 15 minutes.

After completion of the flight, Falk telephoned Avro's Managing Director, Roy Dobson, and Air Marshal J. N. Boothman, the Controller of Supplies (Air), to obtain immediate permission for the aircraft to appear at the 1950 SBAC show. The 707B duly appeared at Farnborough the same day, arriving towards the end of the day's flying display, to take its place in the static exhibition. The test programme was resumed after the Farnborough show, and the 707B was flown up to a maximum speed of 350 knots. The air intake suffered from air starvation at high speed, caused by turbulence from the cockpit canopy, and modifications were made before the entire flight envelope could be explored. Minor oscillations in the pitching plane were also discovered, but the cause was determined to be the out-of-phase movement of the elevators. As the 698 would have powered flying controls, the problem was ignored. The nosewheel leg was extended by 9in to increase the angle of incidence between the aircraft and the ground during the take-off run. This enabled the elevators to become effective at a lower speed, thus reducing the take-off run. Otherwise the 707B proved itself as a very stable aircraft, capable of loops and vertical rolls, and a 30deg angle of attack without stalling. Bearing in mind that most conventional aircraft could not maintain even 15deg AOA, this was quite a feat. The aircraft completed approximately 100 hours' test flying for Avro before being transferred to the A & AEE for use in other research programmes. Much of the information gleaned from the 707B was of no use to the 698 programme, as by May 1950 the first detail drawings of the prototype had already been finalized. However, some information was of direct value, not least the discovery that the 698's fin could be reduced in area, thanks to an increase in longitudinal stability created by angling the engine jet pipes outwards. It also became evident that the aircraft could achieve higher speeds if the engine intake was redesigned, and following tests in Rolls-

Below: *Avro 707B VX790 touching down at Boscombe, complete with prototype marking on the nose. (British Aerospace)*

Above: *An unusual and rare view of VX790 showing to advantage the elevators, ailerons and rudder surfaces, and the original intake configuration. (British Aerospace)*

Royce's wind tunnel at Hucknall, the 707B was suitably modified in February 1951.

With a revised air intake, and a nose section taken from the 'high-speed' 707A, there was some doubt as to whether the 707A was needed, but various changes to the original 698 design had yet to be tested in flight, not least the rectangular air intakes. The redesign of the 707A's wing and intakes would require a diversion of time and expenditure from the 698 prototype, and by the time the aircraft could begin test flying it would, in any case, be too late to influence the 698's design. But it was eventually agreed that the revised 707A design could contribute data which would guide the planning of the 698's flight test programme, so WD280 was constructed. This aircraft incorporated the new intakes, elevators and ailerons which were true-to-scale, and servo tabs and balances to assist the manual flying controls. The first flight was made from Woodford on 14 July 1951, by which time metal was already being cut for the 698 prototype. As predicted, although the 707A provided 92 hours of flight test data for Avro, the aircraft had no influence on the final design of the 698; indeed a great deal of time was devoted to test-flying the 707A

itself, almost defeating the object of the exercise. For example, time was spent investigating the pitching oscillations caused by the manual elevators, something that would obviously have no relevance to the 698, which would have powered flying controls. It was not until May 1952 that the 707A was fitted with powered controls, which eliminated the problem.

The 707 concept was an excellent idea but it was compromised by a lack of synchronization with the 698 programme,

Above: *Avro 707B VX790, breaking away from the camera, shows off its delta wing configuration, with slightly swept-back ailerons. (British Aerospace)*

Below: *The Avro 707B's maximum speed was limited by the air intake design. Following wind-tests by Rolls-Royce at Hucknall, the intake area was redesigned to give VX790 a higher top speed. The intake modification was made in February 1951. The nosewheel leg was lengthened at the same time to increase ground incidence and shorten the take-off run. (British Aerospace)*

Avro 707A WD280 was much closer to the Vulcan in terms of aerodynamic design than the previous 707s (VX784 and VX790). The aircraft (produced to contract 6/Air 3395/CB.6(a), dated 19.5.49) flew for the first time from Woodford on 14 June 1951. (British Aerospace)

often causing the designers to revise the 707 in order to keep up with the changing shape of the 698. Obviously things should have been the other way round. During 1952 it was discovered that the 707 airframe 'buzzed' (high-frequency vibration) at high speed and high altitude. To rectify the problem, wing fences were fitted, but they proved to be a disappointment and eventually the wing leading edge was redesigned, reducing the angle of wing sweep inboard before increasing it towards the tip, producing a 'kinked' effect. Unfortunately, by the time a solution to the problem had been found, the 698 was already in production, and the first sixteen leading edges had to be scrapped, an expensive modification which could have been avoided if the 707 programme had been better co-ordinated.

Above: *Avro 707A WZ736 made its first flight on 20 February 1953 at Waddington, having been assembled at Bracebridge Heath from components manufactured at Chadderton. WZ736 is seen at Woodford with an Avro Ashton, Shackleton and Lancaster in the distance. (British Aerospace)*

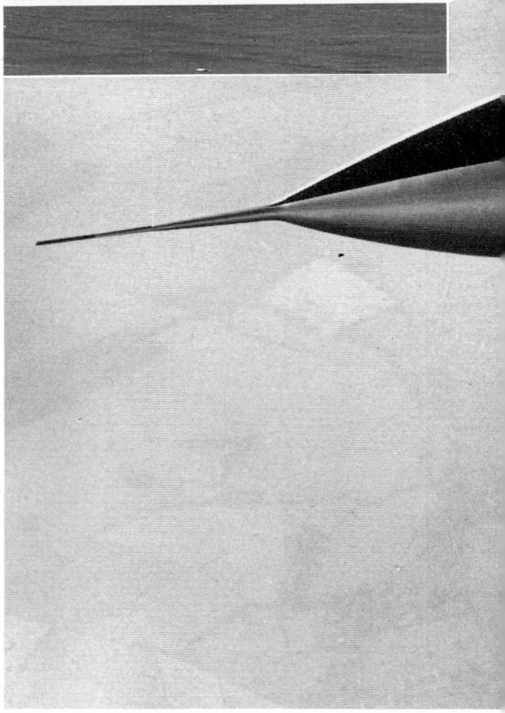

Right: *Avro 707C WZ744 (contract 6/Air/7470/CB.6(a), dated 31.1.52) flew for the first time on 1 July 1953 at Waddington, having been assembled at Bracebridge Heath. (British Aerospace)*

On the other hand, the 707A and 707B proved the delta design admirably, and served to reassure both Avro and, perhaps more importantly, the RAF, Farnborough and MoS that the radical design concept would work. Air Marshal Boothman flew the 707B himself during September 1951, and his delight in the handling qualities of the aircraft was reflected in his comment that 'twenty-five selected pilots must fly it at once'. It was clear therefore that, regardless of the amount of influence they might have had on the 698's design, the 707s convinced everyone that the delta-winged bomber was a practical proposition, and without them the 698 might have been cancelled as an unacceptable risk. A second 707A was ordered during 1952, flying for the first time on 20 February 1953. This aircraft (WZ736) was constructed specifically for the RAE which used it for a variety of trials, including automatic throttle development. Four side-by-side dual-control variants of the 707 were also ordered, in anticipation of a need for a conversion trainer for future delta-wing bomber pilots. As the docile flight characteristics of the 707 became more evident, the need for dual-control trainers became less important, and only one two-seat 707C (WZ744) was built. It was assembled at Avro's Bracebridge Heath factory and towed the short distance down the A15 road to RAF Waddington, from where the aircraft made its first flight on 1 July 1953 in the hands of Squadron Leader J. B. Wales. The 707C made no direct contribution to the 698's development but was used for various trials.

AVRO 707 IN AUSTRALIA
by Denis O'Brien

In early 1955, as a result of recommendations from the Commonwealth Aeronautical Advisory Research Council, the possibility of Australia obtaining an Avro 707 delta wing aircraft for research was investigated. Discussions between senior Government officials of Australia and the United Kingdom, including Wing Commander R. Falk, Squadron Leader J. Harrison and Squadron Leader J. A. Rowland, were held on 21 March, 1955 at A. V. Roe & Co's plant at Woodford. In November 1955, it was decided that the aircraft to be provided would be Avro 707A, WD280.

The third of the small Avro Deltas, WD280, was built under specification E.10/49. This specification called for a maximum level speed of not less than 500 knots T.A.S. at an altitude of 36,000 feet. WD 280 flew for the first time on 14 June, 1951.

WD280 on an early test flight after arriving in Australia, illustrating the revised wing leading edge as fitted to Vulcan B.1s. (Denis O'Brien)

The aircraft, a single seater experimental type of delta design, was powered by a Rolls-Royce Derwent 8 turbo-jet. The original Avro type 707 was built by A. V. Roe & Co Ltd under specification E.15/48. This specification called for the design and construction of a one-third scale model of the Avro Type 698, subsequently named the "Vulcan". This aircraft, VX784, flew for the first time at Boscombe Down on 4 September 1949. When it crashed near Blackbushe on 30 September, 1949, funding was promptly provided for a further two 707's: a 707B for low-speed work, and a 707A for high-speed work. The 707B was built under the original Specification E.15/48 with an amendment to include the provision of an ejector seat. The new specification documents for the A model required the air intakes to be relocated in the wing roots so that it would more closely resemble the Avro 698.

After more than a year of service and 92 hours flight time, the aircraft was withdrawn from testing to enable powered controls to be fitted. Emergency equipment fitted consisted of a jettisonable hood, a Martin-Baker pilot ejection seat, an emergency air system to enable the lowering of the landing gear, a Graviner fire-extinguisher system around the engine, a jettisonable anti-spin parachute and provision for reversion to manual control in the event of an hydraulic power failure. On delivery the aircraft was painted salmon pink but was later painted bright red. In this livery it flew in formation with the white Avro 698 and the blue Avro 707B at the 1952 Society of British Aircraft Constructors (SBAC) Airshow, thus giving a new meaning to 'flying the colours'. To overcome the uncomfortable buffetting at speeds and altitudes within the projected flight envelope of the Avro 698 it was decided to

redesign the leading edge of the wing. In January 1955, Avro 707A, WD280 was returned to the workshops for these wing modifications. The compound sweepback or 'cranked wing' was produced by extending the leading edge forward by 19.5% of the local chord from 80% semi-span going outboard to the wing tip rib. Going inboard, this forward extension washed out at 51% semi-span. Flight tests confirmed the theoretical advantage of the new wing and the Phase 2 Vulcan wing resulted.

A conference as held at the Woodford works of A. V. Roe & Co on 4 November 1955 with members of the firm, the Chief Test Pilot, representatives of the R.A.A.F., the R.A.N., the Department of Supply at Australia House and an officer of H.M.A.S. Melbourne. The main points discussed at this meeting related to the transportation to Australia, the provision of spares and arrangements for Squadron Leader F. Cousins to obtain flying experience on the Avro 707 type aircraft. With the R.A.N. due to take delivery of their new aircraft carrier, the H.M.A.S. Melbourne, the transportation problems were quickly solved. It was soon established that the aircraft would just fit on the aircraft lift to enable it to be safely stowed in one of the aircraft hangars below deck. The question of engine spares presented no problem as the Rolls-Royce Derwent Mk.8 was also fitted to the R.A.A.F.'s Gloster Meteors. It was during the course of this conference that a more important point arose concerning the bad handling and control characteristics that could make the aircraft dangerous to fly at mach numbers. This was due to the remote location of the jack that operated the system of rods that moved the control surfaces. This problem had been overcome in the only dual seat aircraft, Avro 707C

WZ744 and the other Avro 707A WZ736, by the use of double jacks that were closer to the control surfaces.

Avro 707A WD280 was transferred from the RAF on 3 March, 1956, having completed a total flight time of 283 hours 10 minutes. The aircraft was ferried from Manchester to Renfrew Aerodrome, from where it was transported by road to King George V Docks, Glasgow. The aircraft was loaded onboard the H.M.A.S. Melbourne on 9 March, 1956 along with 21 Fairey Gannets, 39 de Havilland Sea Venom FAW53, 2 Bristol Sycamore Hr51 Helicopters and 1 Gloster Meteor fighter. The Avro 707A was hoisted aboard the carrier and was taken below deck and stored in "C" Hangar. The H.M.A.S. Melbourne, Australia's new aircraft carrier, was built by Vickers-Armstrong at Barrow-in-Furness. It was launched in February, 1945, as the H.M.S. Majestic. The incomplete carrier was purchased from the Royal Navy in 1949. H.M.A.S. Melbourne sailed from Glasgow on 12 March for Australia via Gibraltar, Naples, Malta, the Suez Canal, Aden and Colombo, arriving in Fremantle on 23 April, 1956. Crossing the Bight, it arrived in Melbourne on 2 May, 1956. Departing Melbourne on 5 May, 1956, the carrier proceeded to Jervis Bay where it off-loaded some aircraft, air stores and equipment to the Royal Australian Naval Air Station at Nowra before sailing to Sydney. Before the aircraft's arrival, the Commanding Officer of the Aircraft Research and Development Unit was advised by thePrime Minister's Department of the limitations that were to be imposed on photography of the Avro 707A. Photography was not to be permitted of the cockpit or the exterior of the aircraft when the access panels were opened or the engine uncowled. Air-to-air and air-to-ground photography was permitted provided the interior was not visible. With much ceremony the carrier entered Sydney Harbour on 11 May 1956, escorted by the British submarine Thorough, the Australian aircraft carrier H.M.A.S. Sydney, the destroyer Arunta and the frigates Queenborough and Quickmatch.

The Avro was unloaded from the H.M.A.S. Melbourne at Garden Island and immediately transferred to the H.M.A.S. Sydney for the voyage back to Melbourne. After an uneventful voyage from the United Kingdom, disaster almost struck when the aircraft was unloaded at Princes Pier in Port Melbourne on Tuesday 29 May, 1956. This near mishap was widely reported and questions were asked in Parliament. It appeared that as the aircraft was unloaded on to a low loader, a metal support on the vehicle collapsed under the weight of the Avro. The aircraft was loaded on to another vehicle and remained on the pier until Sunday 3 June, 1956, when it commenced the road journey to R.A.A.F. Laverton.

As a research aircraft, WD280 had several important structural features not required by flight line aircraft. In the starboard wing were 5 chordwise rows of static pressure holes flush with the skin. These were designated chord A to E from the wing root to the tip. These pressure points, on both the upper and lower surfaces of the wing, were connected by a union on the inside of the skin to a tube leading to a pressure gauge. Whilst there were some 178 pressure points, most recordings were performed using 33 points from each of the chords. The chordwise position of the pressure points was such that the spanwise rows formed a certain percentage of the local chord measuring from the leading edge.

Situated in the aft part of the nose wheel bay was a large auto-observer. The main auto-observer consisted of an instrument panel, two cameras and a mirror in an open tubular box structure. The cameras, under the control of the pilot, were mounted on the rear side of the instrument panel. The mirror, mounted opposite the front of the instrument panel, enabled the cameras to photograph the reflected image of the instruments mounted in the same panel as the cameras. The cameras, running in sequence, could be operated continuously or in short bursts as required. For pressure plotting a pressure plotting auto-observer was fitted in place of the large handling observer and a small handling observer was fitted in the roof of the nose wheel bay. An S.F.I.M. A20 recorder was installed to record accelerations and aircraft attitude. This instrument recorded aileron, elevator and elevator trim tab positions.

The Centre of Gravity (C.G.) datum was 50 inches forward of the datum face of the front spar former and 4 inches below the aircraft datum. To enable varying C.G. positions to be obtained, or to allow for weight and balance changes resulting from varying test instrument configurations, ballast storage areas were provided in the nose and in the rear engine panel. In addition, provision was also made for the two aircraft accumulators to be fitted in either the nose or in the wing. The maximum ballast permitted was normally 418 lb. in the nose and 350 lb. in the rear. A short mast attached to the fuselage nose cap carried an Avimo high speed pitot-static head to provide pitot and static pressure direct to instruments in the auto-observer. Provision was also made by mounting a yaw vane on a horizontal mast situated on the starboard wing tip extremity.

The first flight in Australia was on 13 July, 1956. The first public display flight was made on 24 July, 1956, with Squadron Leader F.A. Cousins at the controls. The five weeks prior to this were spent servicing the aircraft and preparing it for the experimental programme. The auto-observer was removed and rewired so that it could be used for pressure plotting. The main auto-observer carried spaces for 38 dial instruments. After essential instruments such as A.S.I. and altimeters had been installed there were 33 places for pressure plotting instruments. To enable the aircraft weight to be accurately assessed, a 'Kent' type fuel flow meter was installed in the main auto-observer to record "gallons gone". The serviceable pressure points in the starboard wing were connected to a pressure switch designed and built in the Flight Group's workshop. It was not possible to connect up the mid-chord pressure holes at chord A. A swivelling pitot-static was mounted ahead of the starboard wing tip to minimise pressure errors. This was necessary as the wing angle of incidence approached 16 degrees with the aircraft in level flight at its highest Coefficient of Lift (CL).

During 1956/57, after initial flight tests and pilot familiarisation, flights were conducted to obtain pressure error calibrations and to establish lift and trim curves. Flights were conducted to perform pressure plotting and to establish high speed buffet boundaries. In the period 13 July, 1956 to 3 April, 1957, some 51 flights totalling 30 hours of flying time were conducted.

During the pressure-error calibrations it was established that pressure errors over the entire speed range were less at the wing tip than at the nose boom. The pressure error in the mid speed range between 140 and 250 knots was determined by the tower aneroid method. The error in the low speed range from 99 to 140 knots was determined by the formation technique using a specially calibrated Winjeel aircraft. During the course of this low speed flying to establish lift curves, it was found to be extremely difficult to accurately determine a lift curve for the higher values of lift coefficient. Subsequent flying confirmed the existence of two different flight conditions when flying in the high lift coefficient region. It was found that varying amounts of engine power were necessary to maintain altitude at the same indicated airspeed. It was concluded that two distrinct drag conditions existed between indicated airspeeds of 87 and 97 knots. The different drag states were associated with very definite alterations in the aircraft handling characteristics. The 'high' drag state was accompanied by considerable wing dropping, pitch changes and to a lesser degree some yawing. Studies aimed at determining the buffet boundary were undertaken during this period. Ten flights were made employing the spiral dive technique to determine the buffet boundary. In the following year, owing to fatigue limitations on the aircraft structures, the high speed buffet work was brought to a conclusion.

Simultaneously, with the flight tests of Avro 707, wind tunnel investigations were being conducted to supplement the flight tests. The low speed wind tunnel tests were conducted using the 9' by 7' wind tunnel and complete 1/8th scale model of the aircraft that had been supplied by A. V. Roe & Co. This model was fitted with adjustable elevators and trim flaps. Surface pressures were measured at low speed on both the Avro 707 in flight, and on the scale model in the 9' by 7' wind tunnel. The first phase of the research programme utilising WD280 consisted of making a detailed evaluation of the development of flow separation and comparing this with the model. The experiments showed that tip separation commenced and spread inboard at lift coefficients of 0.29 (approximately 5 degree incidence). This condition was associated with large increases of drag and deterioration of both lateral and longitudinal control due to poor aileron and elevator control.

Following on from the flow separation studies, the two different drag states that were discovered during the establishment of the lift curves were more fully investigated. Hysteresis was shown to exist between the two types of flow. That is it was possible to enter the high drag state from low drag at the same value of CL although the reverse was not true. These investigations called for a high degree of skilled flying on the part of Flight Lieutenant R. R. Green of the Aircraft Research and Development Unit. The "high" and "low" drag conditions were defined by the engine R.P.M. required to maintain height and airspeed. Qualitative assessment was provided by the pilot and his recognition of handling changes in the aircraft. The flying technique involved the careful deceleration from 180 knots with the dive recovery flaps (elevator trim flaps) fully extended to achieve the test airspeed and maintain height. Flying was conducted with the powered controls in operation and no attempt was made to trim out stick forces during a run. Precise flying was necessary to ensure that no excessive incidence was applied during the speed reduction as this would immediately produce the high drag condition. In the speed range 87 – 97 knots I.A.S. the pilot could change from low to high drag maintaining the same speed and altitude by co-ordinating the increase of incidence with the engine power.

A series of flight tests were undertaken by Flight Lieutenant R. R. Green to evaluate low speed handling. Carborundum dust was applied to the undersurface of the leading edge using an acetate adhesive. Varying sizes of grit and varying spanwise extent of the application gave rise to four different test conditions. Detailed measurements were only made when the pilot considered that a particular test condition had produced a significant alteration in the aircraft's handling characteristics or its performance. Generally, it was found that with leading edge roughness the aircraft was much better and easier to control at low speeds than with the clean aircraft and there was more aileron and elevator effectiveness. The improvement in aircraft handling with the application of carborundum dust prompted the series of tests employing turbulators. These testswere performed by the placement of small vane type protuberances (turbulators) on the wing. Four test conditions were produced by varying the height and spanwise extent. With the first turbulator test condition a greatly improved aileron and elevator effectiveness was apparent. In fact 10 degree banked turns executed at 107 knots were made comfortably – a manoeuvre not to be recommended with the clean aircraft. The first wing drops became apparent at 92 knots I.A.S. but were unassociated with any yaw and thus no wallowing. This latter effect was one of the most undesirable characteristics of the clean aircraft. The minimum level speed obtainable for 14,000 r.p.m. was 91.5 knots as compared with 89 knots for the clean aircraft.

In the period July, 1959, to February, 1960, extra instrumentation was fitted to Avro 707A in preparation for more extensive investigation of the aerodynamic hysteresis. The discovery of differences in total drag as great as 40% at high values of CL prompted this further investigation. The additional instrumentation was installed to permit a more accurate and detailed appreciation of the handling characteristics in the two different drag states. The auto observer panel was photographed every 4 seconds by a Robot recorder camera with a 2000 shot magazine. The results were processed by an IBM 650 computer. To visualise the very large scale vortices, a technique was developed by Mr. A. A. Keeler to trace the path of the boundary layer on the wing in flight. The pattern developed, by flowing kerosene over the specially prepared port wing, was photographed from a formating aircraft. This wing was meticulously prepared for these experiments by filling all the areas of uneveness with a filler and carefully rubbing down to ensure as smooth a surface as possible. This wing was painted with a coat of black shellac as an undercoat for a china clay surface. The upper surface of the port wing was sprayed with a fine layer of white china clay (i.e a mixture of kaolin, aircraft clear dope and dope thinners). The clay being highly porous, became translucent when wetted by the kerosene. The flow pattern within the boundary layer was thus visualised as the underlying black shellac wing was revealed beneath the now translucent china clay. The starboard wing was spray painted with a grey undercoat and whilst no attempt was made to polish this surface, it was still not as rough as the china clay treated port wing. A 5 gallon tank was fitted in the fuselage aft of the pilot's cockpit for the kerosene. This was pressurised from the compressed air bottle via a reducing valve. A remotely controlled pressure cock enabled the pilot to control the flow of kerosene. The kerosene was fed to a nozzle situated on the under surface of the wing, some 8 inches from the leading edge at 50% semispan. The delivery pressure was adjusted on the ground so that the spray from the nozzle extended five feet ahead of the leading edge. It was found that this pressure was sufficient to carry the kerosene around the leading edge and flow on to the upper surface at airspeeds between 80 – 120 knots. During these series of tests the Avro 707A was flown by Squadron Leader Blake, R.A.F., and Flight Lieutenant Cameron, R.A.A.F., both from the Aircraft Research and Development Unit, R.A.A.F., Laverton.

Following these tests the aircraft was used to determine dynamic stability characteristics at very low speeds. Initially, longitudinal motion was investigated by recording the decay of a short period of oscillation resulting from a single rapid fore and aft stick movement. The need for great precision in measuring the overall drag of the Avro 707 lead to the development of a most successful thrust-calibration technique.

This enabled the relationship between the installed thrust and the jet pipe temperature to be established.

The last flight was in 1963. During its seven years of research flying for the Aeronautical Research Laboratories, Avro 707A, WD280 flew 203 hours 30 minutes, with the flights mostly of 20–30 minutes duration. It was perhaps ironic that an aircraft designed for high speed flight research should spend so much of its operational life involved in low speed research. Whilst virtually all the flying involved aerodynamic research, some demonstration flights were conducted and the aircraft participated in the flying display for Air Force Week on 21 September, 1958. Upon cessation of flying duties the aircraft, with 486 hours 40 minutes "on the clock", was stored at Avalon until 1967.

In 1967 the aircraft was sold at auction by the Department of Supply on behalf of the British Air Ministry to Mr. Geoffrey Mallet for $A1000. Arrangements were made with Walter Wright, a transportation company, to deliver the aircraft to Mr. Mallet's home in Williamtown. On Friday, 12 June 1967 the aircraft was loaded on to a semi trailer in preparation for its journey to Williamtown. To take advantage of the quieter period on the road, it was planned to leave Avalon at 7.30am Sunday 14 June, 1967. A delay in the arrival of the police escort saw the actual departure an hour behind schedule. Whilst the transport company had allowed 4 hours for the trip, perfect weather conditions enabled it to be completed in just under one hour. On some stretches of the Geelong Highway speeds of 45 mph were attained. Delivery was accomplished with only a minor skirmish with a light pole. The port wing tip scraped against the pole when negotiating a median strip at North Williamtown. A 70 foot crane lifted the aircraft into the Williamtown back garden, the 42 foot 9 inch long aircraft only just fitting in the 44 foot long garden. Since that time the Avro 707A has been maintained in a near pristine condition by Mr. Mallet.

AIRCRAFT SPECIFICATIONS

Main Dimensions	
Span	34ft 2in
Overall length (level flight)	42ft 4in
Height to top of fin	11ft 7in
Track	15ft 3in
Wheelbase	13ft 7in
Wing Data	
Sweepback, leading edge	
Root to semispan	49.9 deg.
51% to 80%	45.8 deg.
80% to tip	54.6 deg.
Sweepback, trailing edge	
Root to 29.8% semispan	0 deg.
Outboard of 29.8%	3.9 deg.
Aspect Ratio	2.78
Aerofoil section	N.A.C.A. 0010 modified and with special drooped outer leading edge
Chord fuselage centre line	21ft 9.915in
Incidence	2.5 deg.
Dihedral	nil
Areas (in sq. ft.)	
Wings	420
Ailerons each	9.257
Elevators each	17.980
Trim flaps	each 6.05
Rudder and Fin Data	
Fin sweepback (leading edge)	49 deg. 24 min.
Areas (in sq. ft.)	
Fin	27.76
Rudder	9.264
Power Unit	
Name	Rolls-Royce Derwent 8
Type	Jet-turbine
Number	One
Direction of Rotation	Anti-clockwise viewed from the rear
Weight of engine dry	1,280lb + 2.5%
Compressor	Double entry single stage centrifugal
Combustion system	Nine straight flow combustion chambers
Numbering	Anti-clockwise viewed from the rear No. 1 top centre
Turbine	Single stage axial flow
Nominal thrust (sea-level static)	3,600lb

Left: *Avro 707A WD280, illustrating the port wing coated with china clay. Kerosene released from just below the leading edge is rendering the clay translucent, revealing the black paint underneath. (Denis O'Brien)*

***Above:** The Valiant was the first of the three V-Bomber types to enter RAF service and proved a successful design. Sadly, the type was withdrawn from service prematurely when metal fatigue was found in the fleet's wing spars. This rare photograph illustrates how trials were conducted to investigate the practicality of fitting V-Bomber rear crew positions with ejector seats. Although Martin Baker produced a workable escape system, the huge costs and associated delay in aircraft production prompted the RAF to abandon the idea.*

***Below:** The third of the V-Bomber types to enter service was the Handley Page Victor. Although marginally superior to the Vulcan in terms of performance, the Victor was ill-suited to low-level operations, and carriage of the Blue Steel stand-off bomb was particularly troublesome, due to the Victor's low-slung fuselage. XA930, a trials aircraft, was the only Victor Mk.1 to carry external fuel tanks.*

3. Testing the Delta

While the 707 programme continued, construction of the 698 had begun in 1951 after a three-month delay during which the design was altered quite significantly. Avro had virtually finalized the 698's layout when they were notified by RAE Farnborough of some fairly disturbing results that had emerged from RAE's wind-tunnel research into the proposed bomber's aerodynamic qualities. Tests had shown that the shape of the 698's fuselage was changing air pressure distribution over the wing surfaces and engine intakes, in ways which Avro had not predicted. The results suggested (but did not provide conclusive proof) that the onset of compressibility drag rise (which would effectively be the 698's maximum speed limit) would take place at a lower speed and altitude than had been envisaged. Clearly the design had to be revised. From December 1949 until May 1950 the Avro designers worked long and hard to produce new design drawings for a completely revised wing, with the thickest section now close to the leading edge, instead of the more conventional position near the root chord centre. The result was a wing root which was almost as deep as the fuselage to which it was attached (the fuselage diameter being 9ft), with additional benefits in terms of improved intake efficiency and extra space to accommodate later and larger engines. Indeed, it was the projected need for larger engines that finally persuaded Avro to change the wing design, rather than RAE's advice. Some 190 draughtsmen worked on the 698, together with thousands of engineers both with Avro and throughout Britain. Companies such as Dowty (who produced the huge landing gear assemblies) and Boulton Paul (who designed the powered flight controls) produced components for the 698 in response to Avro's fairly non-specific

Below: *A unique photograph of what appears to be VX770's roll-out at Woodford. The tail markings have yet to be applied. (British Aerospace)*

AVRO
VX770

requirement, long before a contract was issued by the MoS.

Finally construction of the 698 began, with the massive delta wings gradually taking shape at Woodford while the rest of the airframe was manufactured at Chadderton. In June 1952 notification was received that a contract would be placed two months later for 25 production aircraft. While this was welcome news, Avro's delight was tempered by the additional news that 25 Handley Page H.P.80s would also be ordered. Worse still for Avro, it was revealed that the H.P.80 had already been delivered to Boscombe Down, and was being assembled, ready to make its first flight. Everyone throughout the industry expected that just one of the B.35/46 contenders would be selected and it came as something of a surprise that both the Handley Page and Avro designs had been given a tentative go-ahead, even before they had flown. It was later learned that the original plan had been to order 50 examples of just one type, with 25 being built by Avro and Handley Page respectively, but nobody really knew which aircraft was going to prove to be the superior design. Some commentators suggested that another reason why both aircraft were ordered was because no one relished the task of informing the loser!

Left: *The Avro 698 (VX770) taking off on its maiden flight at Woodford on 30 August 1952. (British Aerospace)*

Below: *In-flight study of VX770, the Avro 698 prototype. (British Aerospace)*

Spurred on by the news of Handley Page's progress, Avro's team worked around the clock in order to speed the progress of the prototype's completion, in the hope that it would be ready to fly in time for the 1952 SBAC show. The huge centre section was carefully transported through the streets of Greater Manchester – where some street light posts were hinged sideways to make way for the massive component – on a slow seventeen-mile ride to Woodford, covered by a tarpaulin. Final assembly was completed during August and engine running trials began. On 30 August Roly Falk taxied the prototype 698 (VX770) onto Woodford's runway and made just one fast taxi-ing run, in order to establish the speed at which the nosewheel would lift. Falk decided that further runs would be unnecessary (possibly causing the wheel brakes to overheat), and the 698 was positioned for take-off. After clearing a flock of seagulls from the runway area, the four Rolls-Royce Avon RA.3s were opened up to full power (26,000lb), and with a mighty roar, the gloss-white bomber lurched forward, lifting smoothly into the air after a surprisingly short run. At last the gigantic delta-winged bomber was airborne.

As soon as the aircraft was comfortably clear of the ground, its undercarriage was raised and a steady climb to 10,000 feet was made. Falk then made a series of gentle manoeuvres, to establish the 'feel' of the controls, and once satisfied a gentle descent was made back to Woodford. Almost thirty minutes later, VX770 was back in the airfield circuit, and the undercarriage was lowered. At this stage observers in Woodford's control tower noticed something falling from the 698. Falk was notified of the occurrence. As everything appeared to be normal, with the undercarriage safely locked in the 'down' position, Falk circled over the airfield while observers were 'scrambled' in a Vampire and Avro 707 to take a closer look. Their investigations revealed that both rear undercarriage fairings had been torn off, but otherwise everything seemed to be satisfactory, so Falk descended towards Woodford's runway, making a gentle touchdown, after which the huge brake parachute was streamed. The first flight was hailed as a great success, and Falk later commented that the 698 was easier to handle than the Avro Anson! Two more test flights were made before the 698 was flown to Boscombe Down, where three hours' flying was completed, after which the aircraft made daily appearances over Farnborough at the SBAC show; for security reasons it was decided that the aircraft should not land at Farnborough. Five displays were made, with Falk piloting the all-white VX770 accompanied by the all-blue 707B (flown by Jimmy Orrell) and the all-red 707A (flown by Jimmy Nelson), enabling the new bomber to make a dramatic, and rather patriotic, public debut. The missing undercarriage doors were not replaced in time for the Farnborough show, and after each day's flying, strengthening work was carried out on the exposed micro switches and other components, in response to Falk's display, which got a little faster each day.

Following the SBAC show, media interest in the 698 led to speculation as to what name should be chosen for the aircraft. Bearing in mind the newly named Vickers Valiant, a variety of alliterative names was suggested, including 'Albion' and (perhaps most appropriately) 'Avenger'. However, the matter was finally settled in October 1952 when the Chief of the Air Staff, Sir John Slessor, ruled that both the H.P.80 and Avro 698 should also adopt names beginning with 'V'. The Handley Page bomber was consequently named 'Victor' and Avro's mighty delta became the 'Vulcan'.

After the SBAC show, the undercarriage fairings were strengthened, instrument positioning was partially revised, and the second pilot's seat was installed in the cockpit. Roly Falk had been primarily responsible for the cockpit configuration, and it was he who suggested the adoption of a fighter-style control stick, rather than a more conventional spectacle column. Although in retrospect there may have been a case for fitting the latter, Falk was keen to emphasize the Vulcan's light handling qualities, rather than perpetuating the notion that the Vulcan would be just another 'heavy bomber'; the small joystick certainly underlined the fact that the new bomber posessed a performance that outclassed many contemporary fighters. There was some media speculation that when the second pilot's seat was fitted, it was literally crammed into what was supposed to be a single-seat cockpit. That was not the case, as the design had always specified seats for both pilot and co-pilot, it being acknowledged that a 'high-tech' expensive bomber such as the Vulcan could not be entrusted to just one man. By the end of January 1953, VX770 had completed 32 hours' flying. Further modifications were made, including the installation of fuel cells in the wings; up until then a temporary fuel system had been incorporated in the bomb bay. The cockpit pressurization system was made fully operative, and the Avon engines were replaced by Armstrong Siddeley Sapphire ASSa.6s, each rated at 7,500lb. This gave the Vulcan the same thrust as the prototype Victor and allowed higher speeds and altitudes to be reached. It had been the Avro team's intention to fit Bristol BE.10 engines (which would be rated at 11,000lb) right from the start, but their development lagged behind that of the Vulcan; the Sapphires therefore acted as a suitable interim powerplant. Fying was resumed in July 1953.

By now the second prototype (VX777) was nearing completion, and although ground trials were conducted with Bristol Olympus Mk.99s the aircraft made its first flight, on 3 September 1953, powered by four 9,750lb-thrust Olympus 100 engines. VX770's nose gear leg was extended during construction, in response to 707 data which indicated that a shorter take-off run could be achieved if the 698 was positioned at a 3.5deg positive incidence; to accommodate the longer leg in the nose gear bay it was designed to telescope during retraction. VX777, on the other hand, had a fixed (longer) nose gear leg and a correspondingly larger bay into which it retracted. As a result the aircraft's nose section was slightly longer. VX777 also featured a visual bomb-aiming blister under the nose, being much more representative of a production Vulcan. Less

Left: *A famous and impressive view of the two Avro 698 prototypes, escorted by four Avro 707s, at the 1953 SBAC show. (British Aerospace)*

Above: *The second Vulcan prototype, VX777, displaying the classic delta wing shape, before the Phase 2 wing design was introduced. The port main gear door is still completing the retraction sequence. (via British Aerospace)*

than a week after its first flight, VX777 appeared over Farnborough at the 1953 SBAC show. The breathtaking spectacle of two Avro 698s flanked by four Avro 707s was, if anything, even more impressive than VX770's first appearance the previous year. Immediately after Farnborough, VX777 was delivered to Boscombe Down, to begin a series of high-speed and high-altitude trials. Before flying could begin, however, modifications were made to the Olympus engines, together with their control and fuel systems, and almost six months were to pass before full-scale trials work could be undertaken. Unfortunately, on 27 July 1954, VX777 suffered a heavy landing while flying on trials work at Farnborough, which resulted in major damage to the airframe. The accident was a major setback to Avro's development programme, not least in terms of powerplant progress, and the aircraft remained grounded for a further six months. During this time VX777 was fitted with Olympus 101 engines, each rated at 10,000lb, and the airframe was structurally reworked, utilizing data from a static test specimen. While VX777 was being rebuilt, the first prototype continued to fly a variety of test profiles, within its rather more limited flight envelope.

When VX777 resumed flying duties in 1955, the exploration of the high-speed and high-altitude characteristics of the 698 quickly confirmed the mild buffeting that would occur when pulling 'g' at speeds of Mach 0.8; this had been predicted, albeit at a fairly late stage, by the 707 programme. With the early 9,000lb engines, this phenomenon was of little importance, but when the projected improvements in engine thrust were taken into account, it became clear that this high-altitude buffet threshold would probably be reached with only the smallest application of power. There would be problems with flying accuracy during bombing runs, and a risk that the structure of the outer wings could fail. The result was the Phase Two wing, with a revised 'kinked' leading edge. However, the first production Vulcan B.1

Above: *The tragic end to VX770's career was captured on film at Syerston as the structure of the starboard wing failed during a display on 20 September 1958. Flying the aircraft beyond its speed/'g' limits caused the failure. (RAF Waddington)*

(XA889) was virtually complete, and although VX777 was fitted with the Phase Two wing (flying in this form on 5 October), the new design was not adopted by XA889, which was rolled out at Woodford in January 1955. Painted silver overall, and with a huge glass-fibre/Hycar sandwich radome, the aircraft made its first flight on 4 February, twelve months ahead of Handley Page's Victor. XA889 was eventually retrofitted with the revised leading edge and vortex-generators (designed to speed up boundary layer airflow over the wing) a year after its first flight. The second production Vulcan (XA890) joined the test programme during 1955, and although it was not fitted with a Phase Two wing, it was employed on a series of radio and radar trials. Roly Falk took XA890 to the 1955 SBAC show, and proceeded to execute a perfect upward barrel roll on the first day of the show, astonishing the many thousands of spectators. Unfortunately the SBAC President, Sir Arnold Hall, was also suitably astonished, and he forbade Falk to fly the manoeuvre on subsequent days, despite evidence from Avro's flight test personnel that the steady 1g manoeuvre was completely safe. The only reason Hall could offer for this decision was that it would set a bad example for future RAF Vulcan pilots. Of course, it had demonstrated quite vividly that the aircraft was immensely strong and very manoeuvrable. On 7 September the Prime Minister, Anthony Eden, arrived at Farnborough in a CFS Dragonfly helicopter and, after watching Roly Falk's display, climbed aboard XA890 to make a short flight. Eden occupied the co-pilot's seat and took the controls for a while, after which the Vulcan landed at Blackbushe. Falk later received a hand-written letter from Eden, thanking him for the flight.

In March 1956 the first production Vulcan (XA889) was delivered to Boscombe Down, to begin acceptance trials with the RAF. The initial CA (Controller of Aircraft) release was made on 29 May:

Aeroplane and Armament
Experimental Establishment
Boscombe Down
VULCAN B.Mk.1
(4 x Olympus 101)
Trials for initial C. A. Release
A & AEE Ref: AAEE/5701, n/1.
Trials Period: 26th March-17th April
1956

Tests have been made on the first production Vulcan B.Mk.1 to assess the type for use by the Royal Air Force, in the medium bomber role. The trials programme was completed

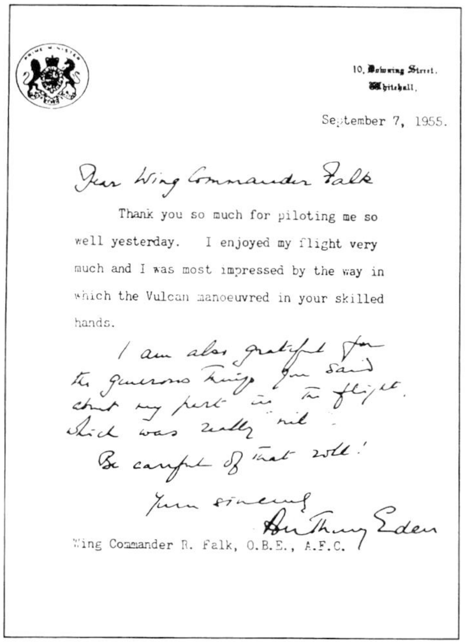

10, Downing Street,
Whitehall.

September 7, 1955.

Dear Wing Commander Falk

Thank you so much for piloting me so well yesterday. I enjoyed my flight very much and I was most impressed by the way in which the Vulcan manoeuvred in your skilled hands.

I am also grateful for the generous things you said about my part in the flight which was really nil.

Be careful of that roll!

Yours sincerely
Anthony Eden

Wing Commander R. Falk, O.B.E., A.F.C.

Below: *The Vulcan wing leading edge was manufactured in a novel 'reversed' jig, which acted as a mould and into which the sheet metal was formed. (British Aerospace)*

in 26 sorties, totalling 48 hrs 15 mins flying time.

During these tests the aircraft was flown over the full centre of gravity range, and at take-off weights up to a maximum of 165,220lb.

The first production Vulcan, XA889, was representative of service aircraft in all respects save those of operational equipment, automatic pilot, the rear crew stations and certain items of cockpitlayout. The aircraft incorporated the drooped leading edge outer wing with vortex generators, the longitudinal auto-Mach trimmer, the pitch damper and revised airbrake configuration. These modifications have successfully overcome the unacceptable flying characteristics exhibited by the second prototype in the preliminary assessment carried out by this Establishment, and when all stability aids are functioning, the Vulcan has safe and adequate flying qualities for its primary role as a medium bomber.

The CA Release reflected early concerns over the Vulcan's flying characteristics, following A & AEE trials with the second prototype VX777, after which the following comments were made:

'A preliminary flight assessment has been made on the second prototype Vulcan in 17 sorties totalling 27 flying hours. During these tests the aircraft was flown at a mid centre of gravity position and take-off weights of 119,000lb and 130,000lb. The expected operational take-off weight of production aircraft is about 165,000lb.

'The expected cruising Mach number is 0.87M (500 knots) and the design Mach number is 0.95M. Above 0.86M a nose-down change of trim occurred, which became pronounced with increase of Mach number towards the limit, making the aircraft difficult to fly accurately and requiring great care on the part of the pilot to avoid exceeding the maximum permitted

MAIN PLANE KEY DIAGRAM

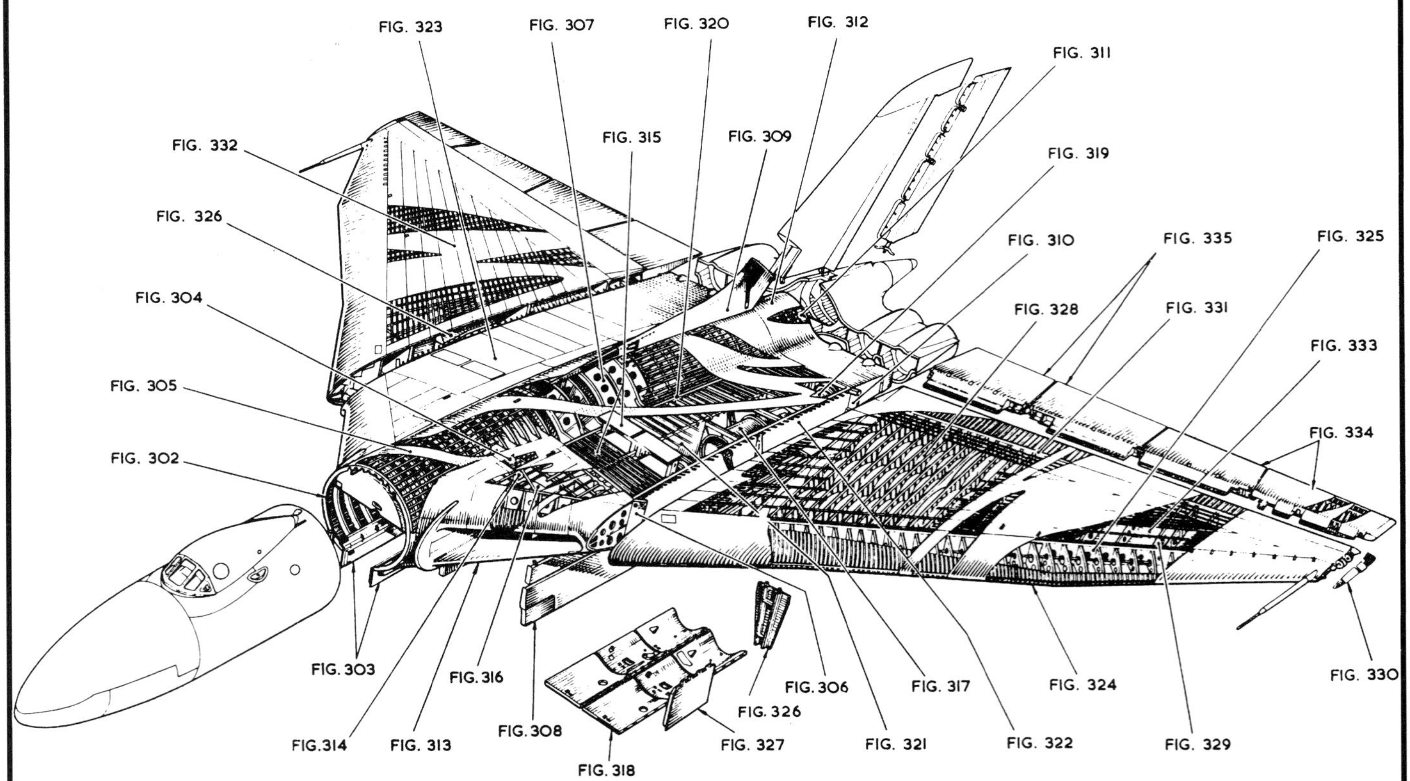

FIG. 302 NOSE WHEEL AND NUMBER ONE TANK BAYS
FIG. 303 NOSE WHEEL DOORS
FIG. 304 NUMBER TWO TANK BAY
FIG. 305 SKINNING NUMBER ONE AND TWO TANK BAYS
FIG. 306 FRONT SPAR – CENTRE SECTION
FIG. 307 BOMB BAY
FIG. 308 BOMB BAY DOORS
FIG. 309 DORSAL FIN
FIG. 310 REAR SPAR – CENTRE SECTION
FIG. 311 STRUCTURE AFT OF REAR SPAR
FIG. 312 SKINNING AFT OF REAR SPAR
FIG. 313 LEADING EDGE AIR INTAKE AND SKINS
FIG. 314 INTAKE FORWARD OF FRONT SPAR
FIG. 315 INTAKE AFT OF FRONT SPAR
FIG. 316 AIR INTAKE TUNNELS
FIG. 317 ENGINE BAY AND REAR STRUCTURE
FIG. 318 ENGINE ACCESS DOORS — PORT OUTER
FIG. 319 JET PIPE TUNNELS
FIG. 320 INBOARD ENGINE RIB
FIG. 321 CENTRE ENGINE RIB
FIG. 322 OUTBOARD ENGINE RIB
FIG. 323 CENTRE SECTION SKINNING
FIG. 324 OUTER WING LEADING EDGE
FIG. 325 OUTER WING FRONT SPAR
FIG. 326 UNDERCARRIAGE BAY AND AFT STRUCTURE
FIG. 327 UNDERCARRIAGE BAY DOOR
FIG. 328 TANK BAYS
FIG. 329 OUTBOARD WING STRUCTURE
FIG. 330 OUTBOARD WING TIP
FIG. 331 OUTER WING REAR SPAR AND TRAILING EDGE
FIG. 332 TOP SKINS – OUTER WING
FIG. 333 BOTTOM SKINS – OUTER WING
FIG. 334 AILERON PORT I/B.- O/B.
FIG. 335 ELEVATOR I/B.- O/B.

Mach number. This characteristic is unacceptable; the Firm propose to eliminate it in production aircraft by the introduction of an artificial stability device (a Mach trimmer).

'With increase of Mach number above 0.89 the damping in pitch decreased to an unacceptably low level, particularly near the maximum permitted Mach number, and the aircraft was difficult to fly steadily. The Firm propose installing a pitch damper in production aircraft.

'As tested the Mach number/buffet characteristics were unacceptable for a high-altitude bomber, but considerable improvement is hoped for with the drooped leading edge and vortex generators. Associated with the buffet were oscillating aileron hinge movements which in these tests imposed severe manoeuvre limitations from considerations of structural safety.

'Making due allowances for the differences in engine thrust and aircraft weight between the aircraft as tested and the production version, the performance, in terms of attainable altitude, was not outstanding. The likely target height with a 10,000lb bomb will only be about 43,000ft with 11,000lb thrust engines, and the high altitude turning performance will be poor. The level of performance is considered to be inadequate for an unarmed subsonic bomber, even under cover of darkness.

'In summary, although the aircraft has certain outstanding features, serious deficiencies are present, particularly in and above the cruising Mach number range, and until these are rectified the Vulcan cannot be considered satisfactory for Service use.'

Evidently, despite the Vulcan's radical design and performance capabilities, the A & AEE test pilots maintained a particularly sober view towards the Vulcan's operational condition, and it is remarkable to read the contrast between this early report and the final CA Release. As previously described, the incorporation of the various modifications as outlined in the A & AEE report, especially the Phase Two wing, completely eliminated the various handling difficulties, turning a less than ideal bomber design into a truly outstanding aircraft.

The first delivery to the RAF was made on 20 July 1956 when XA897, the ninth production aircraft, flew to RAF Waddington, joining the newly formed No. 230 Operational Conversion Unit. The arrival was essentially symbolic, however,

Above: *XA891, the third production Vulcan B.1, crashed in July 1959. (British Aerospace)*

as XA897 soon returned to Woodford to undergo a series of minor modifications in preparation for a long-range flight to New Zealand. XA895 was delivered to No. 230 OCU on 16 August as a substitute, although this aircraft was also a temporary resident, spending time with the A & AEE on Operational Reliability Trials. XA897's flight to New Zealand was primarily a diplomatic 'flag-waving' exercise, although it also presented an opportunity to test the Vulcan's long-range capabilities. The aircraft captain was Squadron Leader Donald Howard, with a very distinguished VIP taking the co-pilot's seat – the Commander-in-Chief of Bomber Command, Air Marshal Sir Harry Broadhurst. The rear crew comprised Squadron Leaders Albert Gamble, Edward Eames, AFC, and James Stroud, who was also a qualified Vulcan pilot, taking turns on the flight deck with Broadhurst; they were joined by Fredrick Bassett, a technical representative from Avro. Although the Vulcan had only just entered RAF service, the outbound flight went remarkably smoothly, via Aden and Singapore and then on to Melbourne, with a flying time of 47hr 26 min including stopovers. After visiting Sydney and Adelaide, the crew flew to Christchurch on 18 September. For the return trip, the aircraft was flown via Brisbane, Darwin, Singapore, Ceylon and Aden, finally departing for the UK at 02:50 on the morning of 1 October 1956.

The seven-hour flight back to England was scheduled to culminate with a VIP reception at London's Heathrow Airport, where representatives of the RAF, Ministry of Aviation and Avro were joined by the crew's families and the media. Unfortunately the weather conditions were very poor, and from inside the Queen's Building the airfield was completely invisible, shrouded in cloud and heavy rain. As XA897 approached the English Channel, Howard called Bomber Command Operations at High Wycombe and received the bad news that Heathrow's current weather status was eight-eighths cloud at 700 feet, with two-eighths cover at 300 feet. The airfield was in rain and visibility was just over 3,000 feet. Although the VIP spectators were somewhat disappointed by the prevailing

XA896

XA898

Left: *A 1957 photograph of XA986 rolling to a standstill at Waddington with its brake chute streamed, after completing another No. 230 OCU training sortie. The early silver colour scheme was swiftly replaced by anti-flash white. (MoD)*

Left: *Vulcan B.1 XA898 on the ramp at Pinecastle Air Force Base in Florida., September 1957. One of two Vulcans from No. 230 OCU which participated in the 1957 Strategic Air Command Bombing Competition, the aircraft wears the early overall silver colour scheme, with a grey/black radome. (Harry Holmes)*

conditions, there was no reason why XA897 could not land at Heathrow, as normal airliner operations were continuing without difficulty. However, Howard did have the option of diverting to Waddington, where the weather was much better, but the decision was his, and in view of his experience he saw no reason to divert; Broadhurst agreed. The aircraft entered an instrument approach at 5nm from touchdown, at 1,500 feet, and the hardy souls on top of the Queen's Building braved the elements to watch for the Vulcan's arrival. The GCA talk-down began as normal, with glidepath and centre-line corrections being given until the aircraft was three-quarters of a mile from the runway, when the ground controller instructed the captain that he was 80 feet above the glidepath. This was the last elevation advice received from the controller, and a few seconds later the Vulcan hit the ground. The first indication the assembled spectators had of the Vulcan's proximity was a roar of engine noise as all four engines wound up to full power. XA897 came into view, climbing steeply from the runway, with its landing gear extended. The noise subsided, and at around 800 feet the canopy was jettisoned and both pilots ejected, leaving the Vulcan to turn to starboard before making a 30deg descent back to the runway, where it instantly exploded on impact, killing all four rear crew members.

The VIP's inside the Queen's Building were informed that the aircraft had crashed. As the crash rescue crews battled to extinguish the burning wreckage (which continued to burn for almost an hour), it quickly became clear that the aircraft's main wheels were missing. Beyond the 300-yard scattering of wreckage, there was still no sign of the missing undercarriage, and Avro's Chief Aerodynamicist, Roy Ewans, who had been waiting for the Vulcan's arrival, drove along the runway to the airport boundary, where still nothing could be seen. He drove out from the airport and proceeded to search the fields surrounding the runway approach. He soon found two deep holes, which were rapidly filling with rain water. The holes had obviously been created by the Vulcan's main gear as it had briefly hit the ground, short of the runway by 1,988 feet (displaced to the north by 250 feet). Ahead of the holes were two swathes of Brussels sprouts which had been flattened by XA897's exhausts as the aircraft began to climb away. The main wheels were scattered about the field. Few aircraft have landing gear which is designed for landing on soft ground, but the loss of the Vulcan's lower leg assembly would not in itself have been too serious. However, the excessive backwards force created by hitting the ground had caused the drag struts to fail, allowing the legs to swing back on their main hinges to hit the lower surface of the wing, ahead of the trailing edge control surfaces. The gear assembly had penetrated the wing at a point where the aileron control rods were located, damaging them to such an extent that all lateral control was lost.

On the following day an RAF Court of Inquiry was opened, headed by Air Chief Marshal Sir Donald Hardman. On 26 October the Minister of Transport and Civil Aviation requested that Dr. A. G. Touch, Director of Electronics Research and Development at the Ministry of Supply, should carry out an independent investigation into the accident, particularly the GCA (Ground Controlled Approach) arrangements at Heathrow. The conclusions reached by Dr. Touch's report were as follows:

'The GCA equipment was correctly set up and calibrated: There is no evidence of malfunctioning or failure. The Controller failed to warn the pilot of his closeness to the ground. During the last ten seconds of the approach, the aircraft made a steep descent to the ground. The cause for this descent was probably due to the build-up of oscillations about the glide path. Poor talk-down by the Controller contributed to this, but as the approach was subject to the overriding judgment of the pilot, the Controller was not to blame for events arising from the control.

'The critical phase was the first four seconds after the descent steepened, during which no height guidance was given to the pilot. It is very difficult to pass judgment on this matter, but in view of all the circumstances, I do not think the Controller should be blamed. No warning was given during the final five or six seconds. It should have been, although it would have been too late. Although it cannot definitely be proved, the most likely theory is that the Controller made an error of judgment, concentrating too much on azimuthal corrections, and paying insufficient attention to the elevation error meter. Human errors are more likely to occur under stress or unusual circumstances. In my opinion, evidence exists to show that all the elements in the GCA "servo-chain" were strained.'

Dr. Touch later explained that the term 'servo-chain' referred to the way in which the GCA information was acted upon by the pilot, in a kind of 'servo-loop' between the pilot and the ground controller.

The post-accident technical investigation – part of the RAF Court of Inquiry – confirmed that the aircraft had not suffered any technical failures. The Inquiry did conclude that the captain of the Vulcan had made an error of judgment in selecting a break-off height of 300 feet, and also in going below that height. The ground controller had advised the captain that he was 80 feet above the glidepath, just seven seconds before hitting the ground, but no subsequent warning was given when the aircraft rapidly went below the glidepath; indeed the talk-down continued after the Vulcan had hit the ground, as if the approach was still continuing normally. Consequently, the RAF Inquiry concluded that this failure to warn the pilot that he was below the glidepath was the principal cause of the accident. This was a slightly different conclusion from that made by Dr. Touch, but as it is RAF policy not to make Court of Inquiry evidence public, Dr. Touch remained unaware of the RAF's views.

At the inquest into the deaths of the rear crew members, another contributory cause became evident – altimeter error. In his summing up, the Coroner, Dr. H. G. Broadbridge, stated that there was nothing in the evidence to show criminal negligence on the part of anyone in the aircraft or on the ground: everyone seemed to be doing their duty as they thought right at the time. Squadron Leader Howard said that before leaving Aden he had received a signal from Bomber Command saying that he was to land at Heathrow. 'I was going to make an attempt to land, in view of the weather. If I could not, I was going to overshoot and go to Waddington, where it was promised that the weather would be very good. I decided to come down to 300 feet on my altimeter, which represented to me a minimum approach altitude for London Airport of 150 feet over the ground.' Howard continued, saying that the talk-down from the ground controller was normal, and he acted on the information as soon as he received it. Before the talk-down was completed he hit the ground. Although he did not know it at the time, he now knew that he had been ahead of the runway when he hit the ground, and the last instruction he remembered hearing was that he was three-quarters of a mile from touchdown, at 80 feet above the glidepath. He increased the rate of descent. Continuing his account, Howard said:

'I asked the co-pilot to look for the high-intensity lighting which I was going to use for the landing. He told me he could see the lights over to starboard, and all this time I was looking at instruments, not looking out. I looked at the lights as he told me, and I did not recognise the pattern. They were not what I expected to see. Immediately I had looked I went back on instruments and he then told me I was very low and to pull up, so I did. At that precise time the aeroplane touched the ground and I decided to overshoot. This I tried to do, but as the aircraft accelerated it became obvious that I could not control it any more. It wanted to roll over to the right. I used all the control I had but I could not stop it and I realised I could do no more. My altimeter was showing slightly below 300 feet. I shouted to the crew to get out and when it was apparent that the aircraft was going to roll into the ground, I decided to eject.'

Right: *Vulcan B.1 XH497 breaks away to starboard, revealing the oil-streaked engine fairings which were a familiar sight on almost every Vulcan. The anti-flash white paint scheme was particularly prone to staining, and Finningley's OCU aircraft tended to attract dirt blown northwards from the Sheffield industrial area. (Air Ministry)*

Squadron Leader Howard was asked if the Vulcan's altimeter was gravely misleading him. He believed that it was, but he did not know how this could be accounted for. He stated that he held a Master Green instrument rating, the highest that an RAF pilot could have. Continuing, he said that his altimeter had a known error of 70 feet, and he set 80 feet as the height of London Airport above sea-level. He agreed that if he had been on the glidepath at three-quarters of a mile from touchdown, he should have been at about 260 feet, and if the altimeter had been functioning correctly he would have aborted his attempt to land at that stage.

Air Marshal Sir Henry Broadhurst was also questioned by the Coroner, and he commented that the talk-down was normal: 'There was nothing in it to alarm you. It seemed perfectly safe.' After hitting the

Above and below: The Woodford production line. Vulcan B1As nearing completion

Opposite page, top: Chadderton production line, Bay1, 1958.
Opposite page, bottom: Chadderton production line, Bay 2, 1958.

ground with a glancing blow, he was convinced that no damage had been done, and had even said, 'If we turn slightly left we can still make it.' However, the captain had answered, 'No. I'm going to overshoot' but quickly added 'I think we've had it.' Broadhurst tried the controls as Howard ejected, but failed to get any response, and so he also ejected. Returning to the altimeters, Broadhurst said that there was an error of between 50 and 80 feet between his and the captain's.

The ground control 'tracker', Miss A. C. Maley, said that as she watched and advised on height and range, she could not recollect any rapid descent. When the Vulcan was about two miles from touchdown it appeared to drop roughly 100 feet below the glidepath, but she agreed that it must have recovered height, as later in the approach it was above the glidepath. Squadron Leader Howard was asked if it would be an abnormal rate of descent to drop 300 feet in 500 yards. Howard said this would be 'fantastic, about 4,000 feet per minute' and that he would certainly have known if they had been going down at that rate. Finally, as if to confirm the underlying cause of the accident, Wing Commander C. K. Saxelby from the A &

AEE said that it had been discovered that the 70 feet altimeter error could become as much as 130 feet when close to the ground; added to which there was the 80 feet for Heathrow's height above sea-level. In addition, there could have been a further error of 70 feet because of friction phenomena.

Despite numerous investigations and a variety of theories, no single factor was ever identified as the principal cause of XA897's tragic accident. Clearly the crew were not to blame, and as Dr. Touch's report indicated, neither was the ground controller. The crash seemed to be the result of a culmination of errors. Sir Harry Broadhurst commented on the accident: 'The whole thing is a puzzle to me. It seemed to me an absolutely normal glide approach until the ground appeared in the wrong place. If we had been coming down at an unprecedented rate, we would have hit the ground, and the undercarriage would have been forced up into the wings. As it was, we touched so lightly we merely thought the aircraft had burst a tyre or something. We had no idea that the undercarriage had been ripped off. Until then the captain, obviously very experienced, imagined he was being talked-down normally. The fact is, they were still talking him down normally after he had gone up again. Obviously something went wrong. We cannot supply the missing link.'

Although the rear crew lost their lives, it was something of a miracle that the two pilots escaped. When XA897 returned to Woodford for modification, prior to embarking on the New Zealand trip, Avro had just designed a new system to interconnect the canopy release with the operation of the seat pull-down blinds which actuated the ejection sequence. Instead of requiring the pilot to make two separate actions – one to release the canopy, and the second to pull the seat handle – the single operation of either seat blind handle would now blow off the canopy and fire the seat in automatic sequence. Although the aircraft was scheduled to be delivered without this modification, the change was made prior to the overseas tour, and without it there is some doubt as to whether the pilots would have had time to eject safely from the Vulcan. It is also interesting to note that Sir Harry Broadhurst later went on to become Managing Director of A. V. Roe, after retiring from the RAF.

Left: *The ill-fated XA897 at Darwin, 31 October 1956. (Denis O'Brien)*

Below: *The second prototype Vulcan, VX777, with phase 2C wing at Farnborough in September 1962, shortly before the aircraft was broken up for scrap. (R. L. Ward)*

4. Into Service

It was not until January 1957 that No. 230 OCU finally received two Vulcans (XA895 and XA898) on a permanent basis, and following a period of intensive flying trials the task of training Vulcan crews began on 21 February. During March, April and May three more aircraft were delivered (XA900, XA901 and XA902) and it was on these machines that the first OCU course qualified, graduating on 21 May 1957. No. 1 Course then re-formed as 'A' Flight of No. 83 Squadron, the first RAF Vulcan squadron, and after a brief spell during which the unit borrowed aircraft from the OCU, No. 83 Squadron's first aircraft, XA905, was handed over on 11 July, the day on which the squadron was commissioned. Although the OCU Vulcan B.1s had been fitted with Olympus 101s, the five aircraft delivered to No. 83 Squadron were powered by 12,000lb-thrust Olympus 102s; the B.1 fleet eventually standardized on 13,500lb Olympus 104s.

The second OCU course also became a Flight of No. 83 Squadron, and subsequent courses, on graduation, transferred to Finningley where No. 101 Squadron was formed on 15 October 1957. By the end of the year four aircraft had been delivered to Finningley and the last aircraft from the 1952 order (XA913) had been handed over to the RAF. At the start of the new year, the first of a new batch of B.1s was completed, as part of a 37-aircraft order which had been placed in September 1954. Initial OCU and squadron flying proceeded surprisingly smoothly and no major problems were encountered during the Vulcan's introduction into RAF service. In fact, comments made in later years suggest that the Vulcan enjoyed one of the most trouble-free entries ever into RAF service. The Vulcans were operated far and wide across the globe, participating in exercises and goodwill tours to exotic locations such as the United States, New Zealand, Libya, Kenya, Rhodesia, Brazil and Argentina. Sadly, one tragic accident marred the success of the Vulcan's early years, this being the loss of XA908 on 24 October 1958. The aircraft was flying on a 'Lone Ranger' exercise from Goose Bay in Labrador to Lincoln AFB in Nebraska. When approximately 60 miles north-east of Detroit, the Vulcan's main power supply failed, and although the engines continued to feed the electrical generators, a short circuit in the main busbar blocked the power supply. This should, in theory, have presented few problems for the crew, as the aircraft had battery standby power for some 20 minutes' flying, so the captain requested an emergency descent to Kellogg Field, in Michigan. Unfortunately the batteries supplied power for only three minutes, after which the powered flying controls ceased to operate. The captain immediately requested directions to the nearest landing field, but without any power the Vulcan's control surfaces were useless, and the aircraft flew into the ground at a 60deg angle, killing all but one of the crew. The co-pilot managed to eject but tragically he landed in Lake St. Clair, and as the only member of No. 83 Squadron who could not swim (and without a lifejacket) he drowned.

Following this accident, the Vulcan B.1 fleet was quickly modified – the main busbar being divided in two – to prevent any such disaster happening again. Unfortunately it did happen again when XA891 suffered an electrical failure on 24 July 1959. This Vulcan had yet to receive the electrical system modification, and shortly after take-off from Woodford (where the aircraft was flying trials with Olympus 200 engines) the same problem arose. This time, however, the batteries provided a greater reserve of power and the entire crew was able to parachute to safety. Despite such tragic instances, the Vulcan proved to be a very reliable aircraft, enjoying an excellent safety record, probably as a direct result of Avro's adherence to design simplicity and reliability. Some doubt was cast over the Vulcan's safety when the prototype 698 (VX770) was destroyed at Syerston near Nottingham on 20 September 1958. The airframe broke up during a fast pass over the airfield during a Battle of Britain display. Investigation revealed that structural failure of the wing had been the cause of the accident, but more detailed analysis confirmed that the aircraft had been flying outside the safe speed 'g' flight

Hawker Siddeley (Avro) Vulcan B Mk 2

Power Plant: Four 20,000 lb st (9 072 kgp) Rolls-Royce (Bristol) Olympus 301 or 17,000 lb st (7 710 kg) Olympus 201 turbojets.

Performance: Max speed, 645 mph (1 038 km/h) at 40,000 ft (12 192 m) equivalent to Mach 0.98; max cruising speed, 627 mph (1 010 km/h) at 55,00 ft (16 750 m), equivalent to Mach 0.95; service ceiling, 65,000 ft (19 812 m); high-level tactical radius, 2,300 mls (3 700 km); tactical radius with low-level attack on target, 1,725 mls (2 780 km); combat radius with one flight-refuelling, 2,875 mls (4 630 km).

Weights: Maximum take-off, 204,000 lb (92 534 kg).

Dimensions: Span, 111 ft 0 in (33,83 m); length, 99 ft 11 in (30,45 m); height, 27 ft 2 in (8,28 m); wing area, 3,965 sq ft (368,3 m^2).

Accommodation: Flight crew of five comprising two pilots side-by-side and (facing aft behind pilots) navigator, air electronics officer and radar operator.

Armament: Internal bomb-bay can accommodate tactical or nuclear weapons, up to 21 1,000-lb (454-kg) HE bombs or similar loads.

VULCAN B. Mk. 2 (BRITISH AEROSPACE)

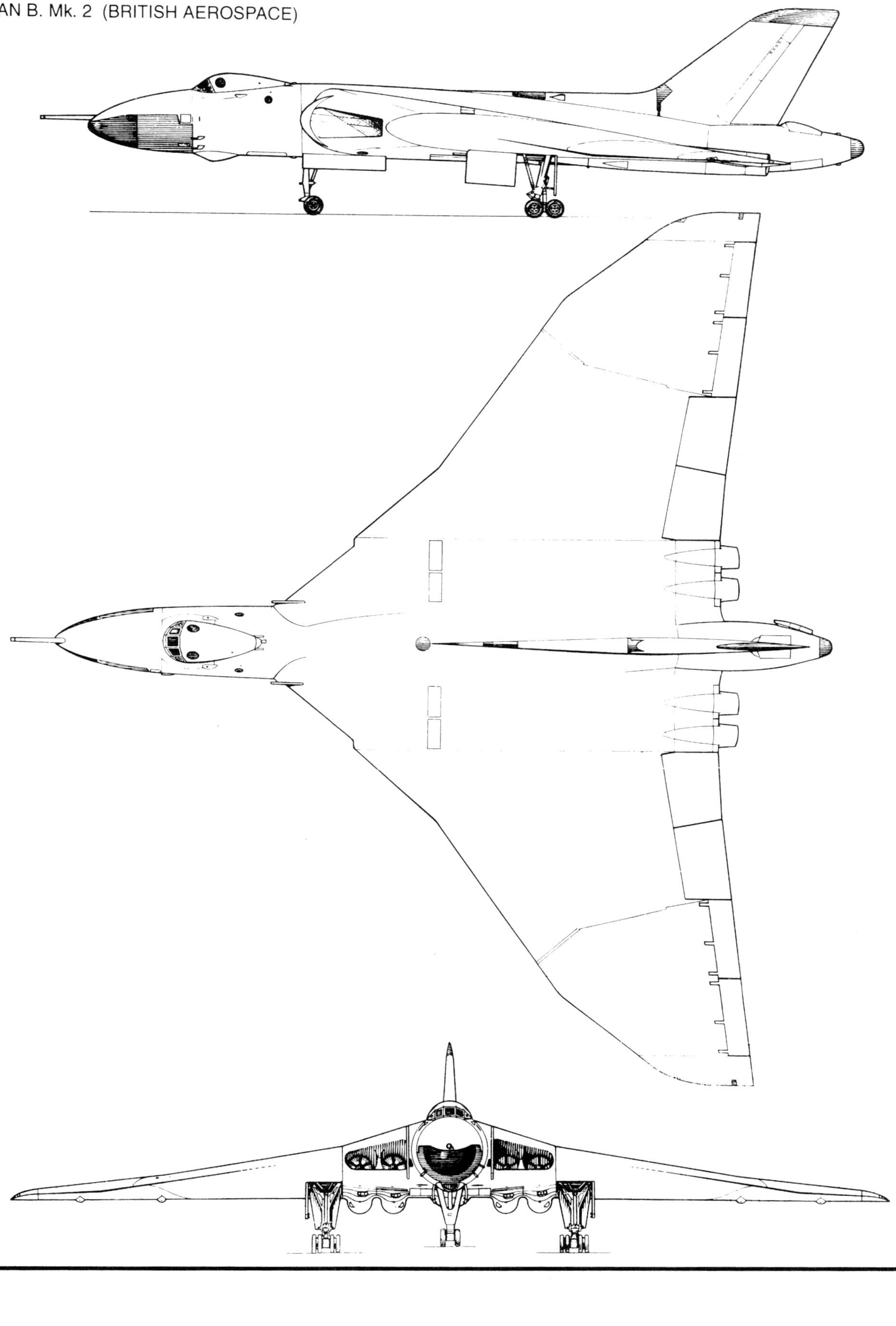

Above: *Vulcan B.1 XA896 wearing the markings of No. 230 OCU at Finningley, 15 September 1962. (J. A. Todd)*

envelope; so the aircraft's design was clearly not at fault. Although the Vulcan was an astonishingly manoeuvrable machine, it is worth emphasizing that it was a four-engined bomber, not a fighter, and like any other aircraft it could only be operated safely within clearly defined limits.

While deliveries of the Vulcan B.1 were still being made, Avro were already looking towards a second-generation Vulcan design, based on the promise of even greater thrust output from Bristol's Olympus engine series. During the first half of 1955 sufficient data were available to suggest that the Bristol B.01.6 engine would be capable of delivering 16,000lb thrust, with the prospect of even more powerful versions at a later stage. Design analysis indicated that, without suitable modifications, a Vulcan fitted with the more powerful engines would suffer from the high-speed/high-altitude buffet problems for which the Phase 2 wing had been developed. Clearly the wing would have to be redesigned again, and in September 1955 Avro submitted a brochure to the Ministry of Supply, describing what would become the Vulcan B.2. Avro had been discussing the possibility of a Vulcan Mark 2 with the MoS for some time, and having gained a great deal of encouragement from the Ministry, funds had been made available within the company to initiate development of the new design.

Although the revised wing layout was the most obvious external difference between the B.1 and B.2, many other changes were made to the Vulcan's design. Later the Vulcan was switched from high-altitude to low-level operations, and it was these less-noticeable modifications that did much to improve what was already an outstanding aircraft. The airframe was re-stressed to a gross weight of over 200,000lb, which was more than double the figure originally set by Spec. B.35/46. The landing gear was redesigned and strengthened to withstand much greater take-off and landing weights. The electrical system was changed to 200V AC, and instead of direct-drive 112V generators, each engine had constant-speed drive and alternators. A gas turbine auxiliary power unit was installed, driven by a Rover 2S/150 engine, and the flying controls were changed, the ailerons and elevators being replaced by inner and outer elevons (combined ailerons and elevators), each with independent power control units.

The new Phase 2C wing design extended the span by 12ft (to 111ft), the thickness/chord ratio changing from 7.92 per cent to 4.25, and the wing area being increased from 3,446sq ft to 3,965sq ft. The compound taper of the leading edge was increased further, and the trailing edge was also now swept. A contract for one B.2 prototype was received in March 1956. A further contract issued in April converted the order for the final seventeen B.1s into B.2s and added eight more machines. The second B.1 prototype (VX777) was selected for conversion into the B.2 prototype, and on 31 August 1957 it made its first flight in the revised configuration.

As the B.2 development programme continued, Avro received instructions to equip the Vulcan with new ECM (electronic counter-measures) gear. This required a fairly radical re-design of the rear fuselage, to accommodate the bulky equipment. Until this stage in the Vulcan's career there had been little need for an advanced ECM fit, thanks largely to the Soviet Air Force's rigid system of fighter control, which was well monitored by the West. Only a limited number of VHF channels were used to control Soviet fighters and just a single piece of equipment (code-named 'Green Palm') was capable of jamming all of them with a high-pitched wail. However, post-1960 developments suggested that something rather more sophisticated was now required, and a tail warning radar ('Red Steer') was to be fitted into the Vulcan, together with other ECM equipment, including a flat-plate aerial installation ('Red Shrimp') which was accommodated between the starboard jetpipes (and between both sets of jetpipes on later B.2s). Although the new ECM fit was intended primarily for the B.2, a contract was also received to convert part of the B.1 fleet to B.1A standard by installing the new tailcone and plate aerials. Consideration was given to the idea of converting the B.1 fleet to the full B.2 standard, but as the cost

of each aircraft's conversion was estimated at roughly two-thirds of the cost of a new-build B.2, the idea was never adopted. However, twenty B.1s from the 1954 contract were converted to B.1A standard, together with nine machines (those in the best condition) from the original 1952 contract.

With VX777 back in the air, the new Phase 2C wing was displayed at the 1957 Farnborough show where the prototype B.2 performed, powered by 12,000lb Olympus 102 engines. After the show the aircraft was put through a series of aerodynamic trials, while another seven B.1s were brought into the B.2 development programme, ensuring that every aspect of the redesigned Vulcan could be properly explored. Early in 1958 XA891 was fitted with the first Olympus 200-series engines, rated at 16,000lb. XA890 was employed on avionics work and XA892 on weapons research; XA893 was fitted with the B.2's electrical system, XA894 was used for development of the B.2/B.1A ECM fit, XA899 was also used for avionics research and XA903 was later employed as a Blue Steel trials aircraft. Flight trials with the B.2 prototype revealed a 25-30 per cent increase inrange over the B.1, effectively extending Bomber Command's target range by a similar amount. Certainly the high-speed/high-altitude buffet problem had been cured, and on 4 March 1959 the first production Vulcan B.2 (XH533) reached 61,500 feet during a test flight. XH533 made its first flight on 19 August 1958 powered by 16,000lb Olympus 200s and fitted with the original B.1-style tailcone. It is interesting to note that the aircraft first flew before production of Vulcan B.1s had been completed, the last B.1 making its first flight in February 1959. Likewise, the second production B.2 (XH534) took to the air ahead of the last B.1, in January 1959, and was the first aircraft to fly with production-standard Olympus 201s rated at 17,000lb, together with a full ECM fit; however, the next three aircraft from the production line first flew with non-ECM tailcones.

As production of the Vulcan B.2 got under way, the first seven aircraft (including the prototype) were all used for trials work, XH534 being flown on CA release trials at Boscombe Down. The CA release was given in May 1960, and on 1 July 1960 XH558 was delivered to No. 230 OCU at Waddington, becoming the first Vulcan B.2 to enter RAF service; many years later this particular aircraft was to become the last Vulcan B.2 to leave RAF service. XH559 was delivered in August, with XH560, XH561 and XH562 arriving before the end of the year. XH557 was loaned to Bristol Siddeley for further engine trials, and was fitted with what was to be the ultimate Vulcan powerplant, the Olympus 301 engine rated at 20,000lb thrust. Two engines were fitted, one in each of the outer nacelles, flying for the first time on 19 May 1961. Although these immensely powerful engines required a

Below: *XM574 and XM594 at Elvington during Exercise 'Mickey Finn', a no-notice dispersal exercise held in 1964. (D. Haller)*

Above: *The in-flight refuelling system was first tested on Vulcan B.1 XH478, supported by Valiant tankers. The dark-coloured tail cone suggests that some form of early tail warning radar may have been fitted, possibly for trials. (British Aerospace)*

Right: *Martin-Baker's ejection seat rig as designed for the Vulcan. The system was proved to be practicable but the MoD never approved the modification, probably because the Vulcan was almost always just 'a few years away from retirement'. Had the RAF known for sure that the Vulcan would be in business until 1984, ejection seats for the rear crew might well have been fitted. (Martin-Baker)*

greatly increased amount of intake airflow, compared with the early Vulcan B.1 powerplants, the first production Vulcan B.2s retained the same air intakes as the B.1. At this stage the lower lip of the intake was deepened on XH557 and all subsequent B.2s to accommodate the increased airflow mass. XH557 was later fitted with four Olympus 301s before entering RAF service, and approximately half the Vulcan B.2 fleet was completed to this standard, the remainder having 17,000lb Olympus 201s. Contrary to popular belief, the Olympus 301-series-engined aircraft were designated Vulcan B.2s, like their 201-series-engined counterparts. The much-quoted 'B.2A' designation never existed.

Although continued Vulcan production enabled the RAF to form more squadrons, policy dictated that the B.2s should first be delivered to an established unit, which would pass on its B.1s to newly converted squadrons. Consequently the first crews to leave 'B' Flight of No. 230 OCU went to No. 83 Squadron at Scampton, where transition to the B.2 began in November 1960. On 1 April 1961 No. 27 Squadron formed at Scampton on the B.2, and the Scampton Wing was completed in September 1961 when No. 617 Squadron started converting from B.1s onto B.2s. Waddington standardized on the B.1A, with No. 44 Squadron forming on 10 August 1960 with aircraft that had been operated by No. 83 Squadron (the first B.1A being delivered to No. 44 in January 1961), No. 101 Squadron re-locating from Finningley in June, and No. 50 Squadron forming on 1 August (using former No. 617 Squadron aircraft). The Vulcan OCU re-located to Finningley, where it was divided into 'A' Flight with Vulcan B.1/B.1As, and 'B' Flight with Vulcan B.2s. Finningley also provided a base for the Bomber Command Development Unit, which operated a mixed fleet of Vulcans, Valiants and Victors for various trials operations.

The second Vulcan B.2 Wing was established at Coningsby, where No. 9 Squadron formed on 1 March 1962, followed by No. 12 Squadron on 1 July and No. 35 Squadron on 1 December. The Wing later moved to Cottesmore in November 1964, and the last production Vulcan B.2 (XM657) was delivered there on 15 January 1965, joining No. 35 Squadron. Following the initial order for 25 B.2s, a further contract was issued for an additional 24 aircraft, followed by a final order for another 40 machines. The final Vulcan B.1A conversion was XH503, which was delivered to Waddington in March 1963, after which the remaining B.1s were either withdrawn from use or transferred to the OCU and the BCDU at Finningley. Starting in 1966, the Waddington Wing also began converting to Vulcan B.2s, completing the transition at the end of 1967. The OCU then relinquished its B.1s and the RAF standardized on the Vulcan B.2 from 1968 onwards.

Meanwhile Britain's nuclear technology had continued to develop, long after the production of 'Blue Danube' for which the

Vulcan was effectively designed. On 15 May 1957 a Valiant dropped the first British hydrogen bomb over Christmas Island, bringing Britain into the thermonuclear age with a very big bang. Code-named 'Red Beard', the bomb was 5ft in diameter, a little over 15ft long and weighed 10,000lb. The warhead which was developed for the Christmas Island tests later became part of a whole range of free-fall atomic and thermonuclear bombs carried by the Vulcan force, giving the RAF an awesome destructive capability. However, as more and more defensive missile systems appeared around Moscow and other high-priority targets, it became clear that delivering free-fall bombs would be a difficult business. In fact, as early as September 1954 a requirement had been issued for a 'propelled controlled missile'. In March 1956 Avro's Weapons Research Division was awarded a development contract for 'Blue Steel', a rocket-powered stand-off missile which would be carried by both the Vulcan and Victor. However, until Blue Steel could be delivered to RAF squadrons, the Vulcan force became increasingly vunerable to the growing capabilities of Soviet defences, such as the SA-2 missile, which had a 25-mile range and a ceiling of 60,000 feet. It would be wrong to suggest that the V-Force was ever anything less than a terrifying deterrent, but the Air Staff recognized the need continually to reappraise the V-Force's effectiveness.

To protect the Vulcans and Victors from an enemy attack, the RAF decided that, during an emergency, the bombers would be dispersed in groups of four to 36 airfields scattered around the United Kingdom. In addition to ten established bases capable of supporting V-bombers, a further 24 airfields were suitably modified to accommodate four Vulcans (or Victors) and their crews, ranging from Lossiemouth in Scotland, to St. Mawgan in Cornwall. With the exception of just six airfields, each dispersal site was equipped with an ORP (Operational Readiness Platform), allowing four bombers to be positioned adjacent to the runway threshold, ready to roll forward for a speedy take-off. A compressed air starting system was also produced for both the Olympus 301 and 201 (which became the 202 when modified), enabling each engine to be started with air bled from any other engine; alternatively, all four engines could be started simultaneously. By using this system, the Vulcan could be started and lifted into the air in less than two minutes, well within the predicted 'four-minute warning' anticipated in the event of an attack. The fact that the Vulcan was never called upon to drop a nuclear bomb would suggest that the deterrent concept worked. The closest the Vulcan force ever came to going to war 'for real' was in 1962, when, at the height of the Cuban missile crisis, the entire V-Force was put on an emergency standby basis.

During October 1962 the USAF placed 1,500 bombers on full alert, and for a few tense days it looked as if a nuclear war was imminent. Despite the USAF's readiness, Prime Minister Macmillan refused to allow the RAF's V-Force to disperse to its wartime bases. Whether Macmillan was upset at the USA's lack of consultation over Cuba, or whether he wanted to avoid increasing tension still further, remains unclear, but there is no doubt that had the USA or the Soviet Union initiated a nuclear exchange, the Vulcans would have been used. Indeed, had the Cuban situation deteriorated further, the entire V-Force would have flown to the 36 dispersal airfields, where each group of four aircraft would have been placed on a fifteen-minute readiness, connected by tele-

***Left:** Four Vulcan B.2s on the Operational Readiness Platform at Finningley. As this view illustrates, the Vulcans were positioned at the very edge of the runway, ready to roll forward for immediate take-off. (MoD)*

***Right:** XH533 before receiving an ECM tail modification. The Avro emblem can be seen on the tail and a Hawker Siddeley Group marking on the nose. Less visible is the title 'Bristol Olympus Engines', painted on the intake wall. (British Aerospace)*

***Right:** On 3 July 1958 Vulcan XH497 made an emergency landing at Scampton, following the loss of the entire nosewheel section. The rear crew baled out, although one man was killed when his parachute failed to open. Flight Lieutenant Smeaton landed the aircraft safely, minus wheel unit and canopy. (via Robert Jackson)*

***Right:** Following retirement from RAF service, XA900 was transferred to the Aerospace Museum at Cosford. Although it was the sole remaining Vulcan B.1, the museum decided to scrap the aircraft because of structural safety problems and the cost of renovation . One wonders what the museum is for, if not to preserve unique aircraft? (British Aerospace)*

scramble link to Bomber Command's Operations Centre at High Wycombe. Had the situation become more serious, the crews would have been ordered to 'Cockpit Readiness', and had the command been given from the War Room in London, the V-bombers would have been airborne in just a couple of minutes, climbing eastwards, leaving behind perhaps a minute or so of silence, before inbound nuclear weapons arrived over the United Kingdom. The Vulcans would have proceeded to their assigned targets in radio silence, anti-flash blinds down, entering Soviet airspace under a barrage of ECM jamming noise.

The Vulcans which escaped interception would have continued to their targets and released their weapons, before hauling round in tight evasive turns to head for safety. Outbound routes were carefully planned, although the prospect of routeing through hundreds of inbound USAF bombers must have been daunting. Of course, there is also the question of whether there would have been any airfields to return to, but it was generally accepted that the Vulcans could be expected safely to reach British Mediterranean bases such as Akrotiri in Cyprus or Luqa in Malta. By October 1962 only No. 617 Squadron had an emergency operational capability with Blue Steel; therefore the remainder of the V-Force would presumably have carried free-fall thermonuclear weapons. It has also been suggested that some aircraft might have been employed on conventional bombing missions because, although the Vulcan was primarily employed as a nuclear deterrent, it was recognized that should the deterrent fail, the realities of warfare might necessitate the use of conventional bombing in some circumstances. Consequently every Vulcan crew regularly practised conventional HE bombing missions alongside nuclear profiles. Indeed, since the end of the Cold War information obtained from East Germany suggests that, in the event of an East-West confrontation, the Soviet Union was firmly committed to all-out nuclear war, and even held the belief that the Soviet Union could prevail.

Having received a MoS contract, Blue Steel was developed by Avro at Woodford, with the first airborne trials beginning in 1957 when two-fifths-scale models were dropped from a Valiant (WP204) over the Aberporth range off the Welsh coast. During 1959 a Vulcan B.1 (XA903) was allocated to Blue Steel trials and carried a variety of full-scale missile bodies. A series of Blue Steel test missiles was constructed, powered by de Havilland Double Spectre engines; the production missile was fitted with an Armstrong Siddeley Stentor. Although test flights continued on the Aberporth range, much of the later trials work was conducted over the Woomera range, in Australia, where a pair of Vulcan B.2s (XH538 and XH539) joined the Blue Steel test programme. To accommodate the missile in a semi-recessed position under the Vulcan's fuselage, the bomb doors had to be redesigned, and the internal structure of the fuselage was revised. The Blue Steel modification was standard for all B.2s from the 26th production aircraft onwards, ending with the 61st machine (XM597). Although the airframe modifications were incorporated during the construction stage, the Blue Steel systems modification was made at station level.

No. 617 Squadron became fully operational with Blue Steel in February 1963, followed by Nos. 27 and 83 Squadrons. The missile was acknowledged as being an excellent design and in many ways was an early example of 'cruise

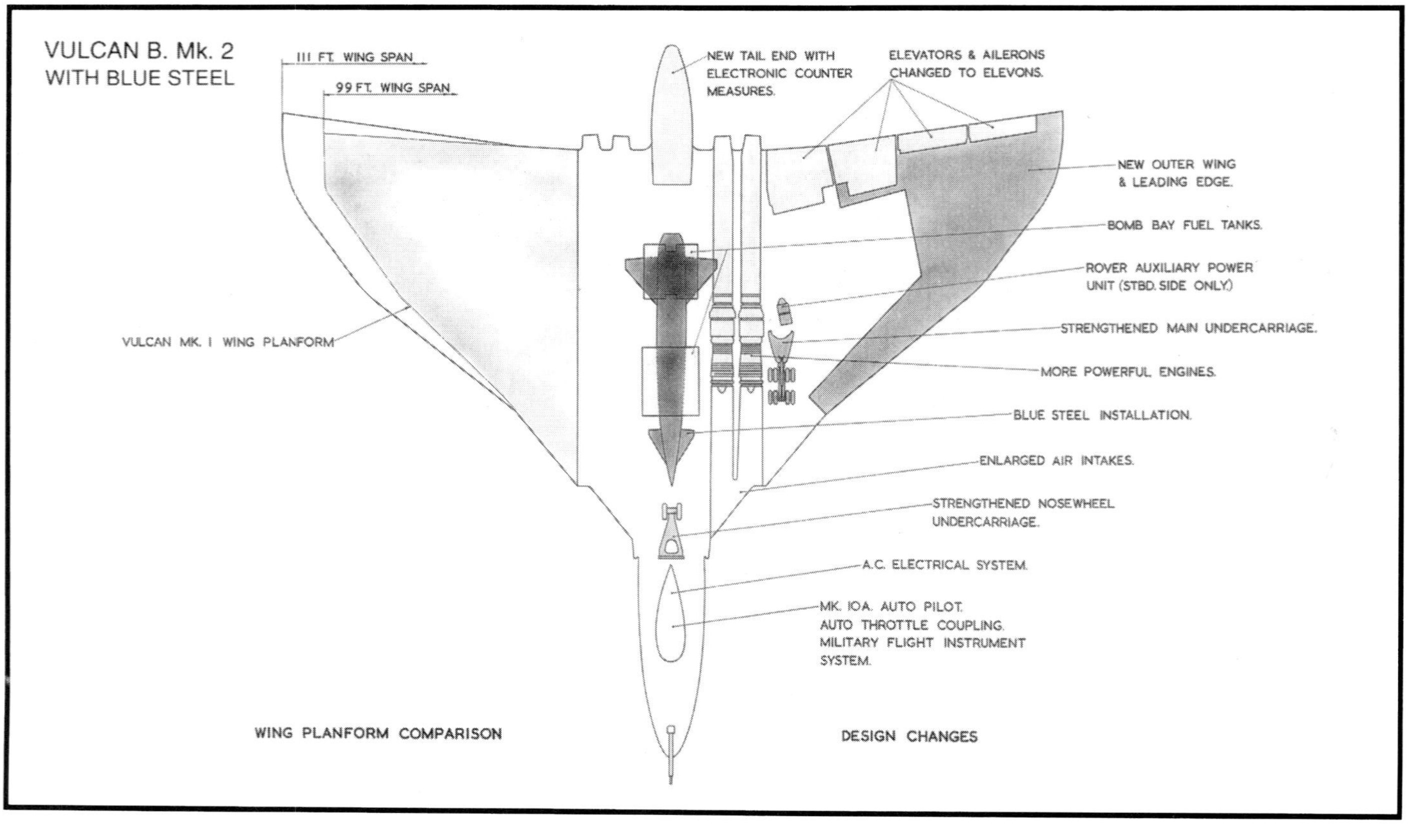

Above: *An Avro Blue Steel missile being attached to a suitably modified Valiant trials aircraft (WP204). Two Valiants were used for Blue Steel trials although the missile was developed only for carriage under the Vulcan and Victor. (British Aerospace)*

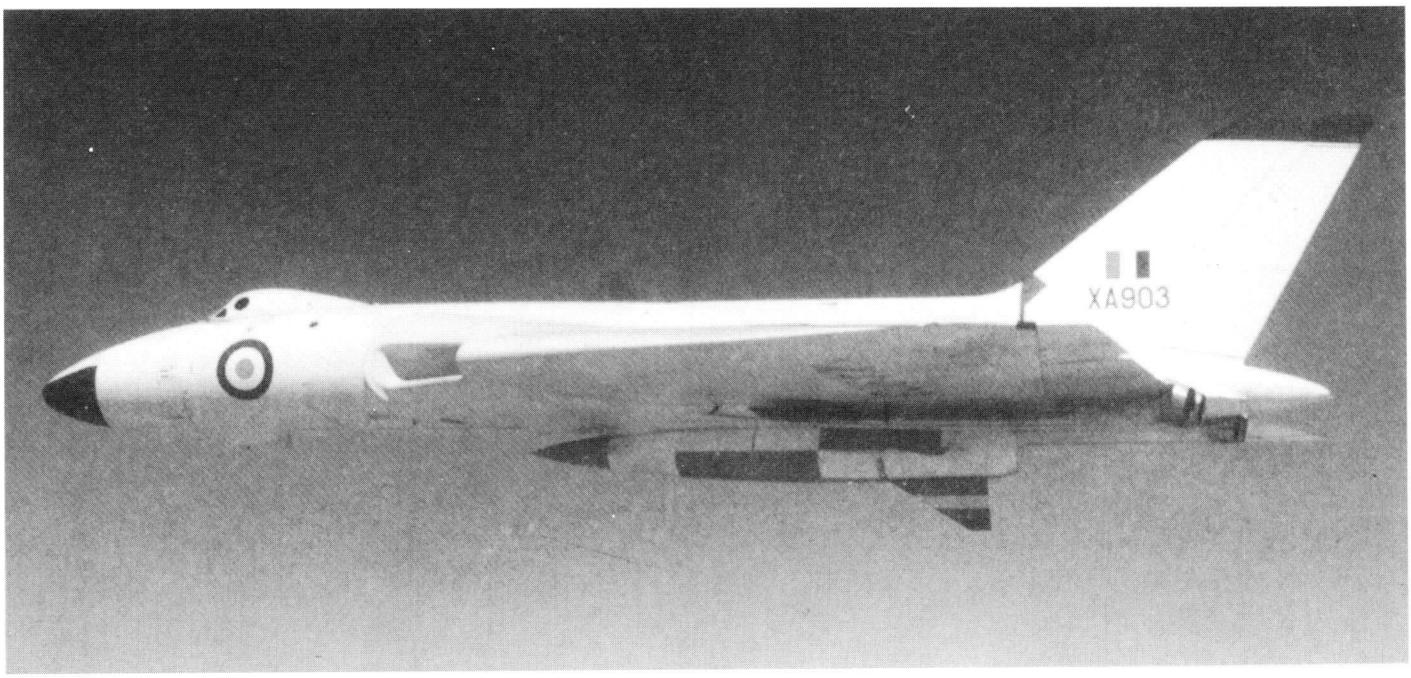

Below: *Seen over the Woomera test range in Australia, XA903 is carrying a Blue Steel aerodynamic test vehicle, painted in an unusual bright red/white scheme for photographic tracking purposes. (British Aerospace)*

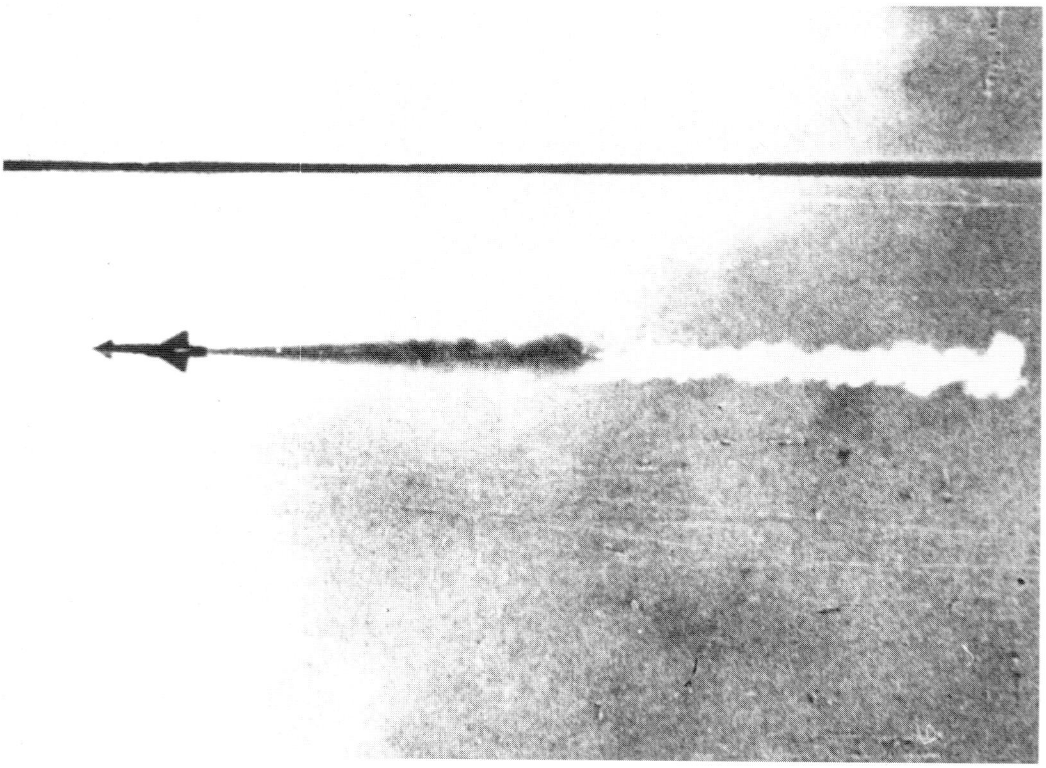

Above: *Blue Steel (No. 408680) undergoing maintenance at Scampton. (via J. Marshall)*

Left: *Unusual photograph of a Blue Steel test vehicle, seen from the Vulcan carrier, as the Stentor engine ignites over the Woomera range in Australia. (British Aerospace)*

Right: *An early Blue Steel test vehicle at Woodford, finished in an unusual semi-matt black colour scheme. Note the folded ventral fin. (British Aerospace)*

missile' technology. The 16,000lb Stentor powerplant was perhaps the most temperamental part of the Blue Steel system. Its fuel was HTP (High Test Peroxide) and kerosene. Handling HTP was dangerous because, unless it was treated with almost surgical standards of care and cleanliness, it would decompose, giving off oxygen in a violent and explosive fashion. This capacity to produce oxygen enabled the kerosene fuel to burn efficiently at any altitude, but of course the opportunity for accidents during ground handling meant that the fuel system was treated with as much care as the nuclear warhead. On hand alongside every Blue Steel was a supply of water, ready to saturate anyone who might come into contact with HTP, and running the risk of instantly bursting into flames.

Once released from the carrier aircraft, the Blue Steel would drop approximately 300 feet, at which stage the main motor ignited, accompanied by a smaller 4,000lb booster chamber, pushing the missile to an altitude of around 70,000 feet, with a speed of Mach 2.5. With an inertial navigation system totally independent of the carrier aircraft, the autopilot was constantly fed with information, guiding the bomb to its target with extreme accuracy (estimated to be within 100 yards) over a distance of up to 100 nautical miles. The Blue Steel missile's navigation system was continually updated by the carrier aircraft's navigator up to the point of release. The consequent requirement for accurate navigational charts necessitated a large-scale photographic mapping of potential Blue Steel 'routes', by No. 543 Squadron Valiant B(PR).1s. Avro anticipated a further contract to modify Vulcan B.1As into Blue Steel carriers, but the order never materialized and with the exception of XA903, the missile was only carried by the B.2 variant. Blue Steel became the spearhead of the RAF's QRA (Quick Reaction Alert) concept, and the primary British nuclear deterrent until 1969, when the Royal Navy took over the task with Polaris submarines.

Left: Blue Steel missile 753568 being fuelled with HTP (High Test Peroxide), an extremely volatile liquid, hence the protective suits. It was the HTP fuel, combined with the sensitive nuclear warhead, which made the missile extremely difficult to handle and maintain, particularly when called upon to operate from dispersal airfields. (Photo: via J. Marshall)

Above: Blue Steel missiles inside their servicing hangar at Scampton. (via J. Marshall)

Below: XA903 climbing above the clouds, carrying a Blue Steel test vehicle. (British Aerospace)

54AN45

Left: *Wethersfield 1969 – Vulcan XL443 is seen carrying a Blue Steel missile; just visible in the background is a Victor SR.2 with air sampling filters on its underwing fuel tanks. The air monitoring role was later assumed by Vulcan B.2(MRR)s belonging to No. 27 Squadron. (R. L. Ward)*

Below: *A Blue Steel in front of a Vulcan B.2 at Scampton. (MoD)*

XH535, completed in May 1960, crashed near Andover in May 1964. (British Aerospace)

XH535

Above: *Although XH478 was used for in-flight refuelling trials, the dayglo orange stripes were applied to the nose, tail and wings much later and their purpose remains unknown. (via John Morley)*

Right: *Vulcan B.2 XL385 suffered a fiery fate on 6 April 1967. Following the outbreak of an engine fire shortly before take-off, the aircraft was abandoned. (RAF)*

Below: *Three No. 83 Squadron Vulcan B.2s roll forward from their Operational Readiness Platform onto the eastern end of Scampton's runway, amid clouds of brown smoke, during a scramble demonstration in 1963. (D. Haller)*

Above: *Seen on what was obviously a hot day, XH555 is treated to a blast of cool air from an external cold air generator, keeping the cockpit interior temperature bearable for the aircrew. (R. L. Ward)*

AVRO VULCAN IN AUSTRALIA
by Denis W. O'Brien

On the 27th June 1956 it was announced by the Minister for Air, Mr. Townley that an RAF Vulcan B.Mk.1 aircraft would visit Australia for Air Force Week in September. This heralded the beginning of what would prove to be a long association between the RAF Vulcans and the RAAF. The ensuing years witnessed the involvement of Vulcan aircraft in weapons testing at Woomera, joint Air Defence Exercises (ADEX) in Darwin and at Butterworth and, of course, participation at numerous Air Shows in the Capital cities.

Vulcan B.Mk.1 XA897 departed Boscombe Down in Wiltshire on 9th September on the first leg of a journey to Australia and New Zealand. Staging via Aden and Singapore, XA897 arrived overhead RAAF Avalon about 1700 hours on the 11th September 1956, having logged a flying time of 22 hours 30 minutes. Onboard the Vulcan was the Commander-in-Chief of RAF Bomber Command, Air Marshal Sir Harry Broadhurst. Sir Harry was taking turns in the 'right hand seat' with regular Vulcan pilot, Squadron Leader James Stroud. The aircraft was under the command of Squadron Leader Donald Howard. The other crew comprised Squadron Leader Edward Eames, Navigator, Squadron Leader Albert Gamble, the Air Electronics Officer and a civilian, Avro's construction chief, Mr. Frederick Bassett. The aircraft flew the 3730 mile United Kingdom to Aden leg in 7 hours 20 minutes, the 4105 mile sector from Aden to Singapore in 8 hours 20 minutes and the final sector to Avalon in 6 hours 50 minutes. Soon after arriving overhead Avalon, the Vulcan circled the field and then flew on to Melbourne returning via Port Phillip Bay to Avalon, only to return again to Melbourne before finally landing at Avalon RAAF near Geelong. Among the VIP's waiting on the tarmac to greet Sir Harry, were Air Marshal Sir John McCauley, Chief of Air Staff, RAAF, and Air-Vice Marshal W. L. Heley.

The following day, Wednesday 12th September, Sir Harry Broadhurst attended the Parade of the Queen's Colour at Point Cook RAAF Base. As the order for the general salute was given, three De Havilland Vampire jets appeared overhead. The Vulcan remained at Avalon whilst Sir Harry flew to Canberra for talks with Air Force staff and politicians. On his arrival at RAAF Fairbairn, he was greeted by the Minister for Air Mr. Townley, the Commanding Officer of Fairbairn, Group Captain A. D. Garrisson and Mr. J. R. Fraser, the representative of the High Commissioner for the United Kingdom. The following morning, at 0930 hours, Sir Harry laid a Wreath at the War Memorial before attending a sitting of the House of Representatives and the Senate. He was a guest at a Cabinet luncheon before returning to Melbourne to rejoin the Vulcan for the trip to Sydney. Flying low over Canberra, en route, the Vulcan arrived at Sydney's Kingsford-Smith Airport where it taxied to a heavily guarded enclosure near the old A.N.A. terminal. The aircraft was on public display the following day, albeit, from a secure distance.

Whilst in Melbourne, Sir Harry Broadhurst created quite a controversy over statements he had made concerning the Avon Sabre. He was quoted in the press as saying, "the Sabre was well suited to its task when first built, but has been completely outdated by recent developments". This statement produced a quick response from the Minister of Defence, Sir Philip McBride. The Sydney press were quick to revive the issue when they interviewed Sir Harry. In an attempt to quell the debate, Sir Harry denied saying the Avon Sabre could not stop an atomic attack by a bomber like the Vulcan. "What I said was, the Vulcan flies at night, and there was not a night fighter in the world today which could stop her." "By day, however, the Vulcan is vulnerable and can be caught by a fighter like the Avon Sabre."

On Saturday, 15th September, the Avro Vulcan had to share the limelight when a B.O.A.C. Bristol Britannia, on her inaugural visit to Australia, landed at Mascot. The Britannia was, at the time, the world's largest turbo-prop commercial transport. Whilst a 24 hour guard was maintained on the Vulcan, which was, of course, one of Britain's top secret aircraft, Sir Harry attended a Battle of Britain Commemorative Service at the Cenotaph. During this service there was a flypast by six Gloster Meteors, followed by a second run of Sabres. Air Force Week concluded on the Sunday with an open day at RAAF Richmond. Having completed the ceremonial duties, Sir Harry boarded a RAAF Douglas Dakota at Richmond to fly to Mascot to rejoin the Vulcan. After take-off from Mascot, XA897 flew to Richmond where it gave a 5 minute display before flying to Adelaide where it would undergo a routine service before the flight to New Zealand.

The crowds that had flocked to RAAF Mallala for the Air Force Week air display were not disappointed when, as expected, the Vulcan arrived to give a display before landing at Edinburgh. Servicing complete, the Vulcan departed Edinburgh on the 18th for the trip to Christchurch, New Zealand. The route to New Zealand was via Launceston and Hobart. Landing at Christchurch's Harewood airport saw the trip successfully completed with an elapsed time of 4 hours 35 minutes. Avro claimed a point-to-point record for the 1,200 mile sector, Hobart to Christchurch, of 635m.p.h.

An Avro Shackleton aircraft landed at Amberley, Queensland, on the 19th September, in preparation for the return of the Vulcan to Australia. This was one of three accompanying the Vulcan and carrying spares and maintenance personnel. Anticipation was running high in Brisbane as the time for the Vulcan's visit approached. This enthusiasm having been generated by the local press coverage of the aircraft's visit to the Southern Capitals. Variously described as the 'flying triangle' and a 'giant bat' by the newspaper journalists, XA897 arrived over Brisbane from Ohakea Air Base in New Zealand, on the morning of 22nd September. A traffic jam was created as an estimated 20,000 people motored to Amberley Air Force Base to inspect the Vulcan. The following day, after a farewell circuit of Brisbane, the aircraft set course for Darwin, the last Australian port of call on the homeward journey.

The departure of XA897 from Darwin completed a celebrated and notable visit to Australia and New Zealand. It is ironic that tragedy would strike at the very zenith of its distinguished voyage. In poor weather conditions Vulcan B.Mk 1 XA897 crashed at London Heathrow. The aircraft was totally destroyed and the crew, except for the pilot, Squadron Leader Donald Howard and Air Marshal Sir Harry Broadhurst, who successfully ejected, were killed. In poor visibility and misty rain whilst on a Ground Controlled Approach to Runway 10L, the aircraft landed 2000 feet short of the threshold. In the attempted overshoot the aircraft uncontrollably banked slowly to starboard then dived into the ground at an angle of 20 to 30 degrees.

On the 13th October, 1959, four Vulcans of 617 Squadron departed Scampton for R.N.Z.A.F. Base at Ohakea, New Zealand. These aircraft staged via Darwin arriving at that destination on the 18th October. They departed the following day with their support aircraft, a Bristol Brittania. The visit to New Zealand was marred by a near disaster involving XH498. On the third attempt to land at Wellington's relatively short runway after two previous 'go rounds' the aircraft's main undercarriage struck the undershoot area. The undercarriage damaged the wing and pierced a fuel tank. The Vulcan pilot managed to retain control of the aircraft and climb away. Returning to Ohakea the aircraft landed safely. XH498 was destined to remain in New Zealand for a further eight months before repairs were completed. In June 1960 the aircraft returned to the United Kingdom via Edinburgh RAAF Base. Departing Edinburgh XH498 overflew Sydney on the 24th June en route to Darwin.

The Royal Aircraft Establishment and A. V. Roe began studies on a 'stand off' bomb in 1954. In November 1960, Vulcan B.Mk.1 XA903 ferried to Australia one of the first full scale Blue Steel missiles. This aircraft piloted by A. V. Roe's chief test pilot in Australia, Mr. J. D. Baker, arrived at Edinburgh on 17th November. The aircraft had been delayed in Darwin due to a minor technical problem. All trials connected with weapons research were conducted under a joint U.K./Australian Project agreement. Two other Vulcans, both early production B.Mk.2's, XH538 and XH539, were also sent to Australia for deployment in the Blue Steel trials at the Woomera Range. The Woomera range, red desert country consisting of sandhills, mulga scrub, claypans, and clumps of spinifex, was ideally suited to the tests because of the sparsity of popu-lation and the long hours of sunshine and clear skies. The first test firing took place from XH539 in early 1961. The programme continued until October, 1964. The history of Woomera, the aboriginal name for a spear throwing device, is currently in preparation under the auspices of the Defence

XA897 in Australia shortly before the long trip back to Heathrow Airport, which ended in disaster. (via British Aerospace)

Research Centre. XH539 now lies on her belly on Waddington's fire dump.

The non-stop flight to Australia by a Vulcan B.Mk.1A of No. 101 Squadron was indeed an historic occasion. Whilst it did not eclipse the round-the-world non-stop flight by three USAF Boeing B-52 bombers in 1957 or the supersonic flight from New York to Paris by USAF Convair B-58 Hustler that averaged 960 kts in May 1961, it was certainly significant in terms of RAF long range deployment. The England to Australia flight was the longest non-stop flight undertaken by the RAF and demonstrated the speed and long range strike capability of the aircraft. This flight still stands as a record for the Vulcan although the "Black Buck" operations flown against the Argentinian forces in the Falkland Islands in 1982 were not much shorter. The Ascension to Ascension round trip in the "Black Buck" missions was some 3000 nautical miles shorter than the 10,000 nautical miles England to Australia trip. Vulcan XH481 departed its U.K. base at 11.36 a.m. on 20th June 1961 arriving overhead the control tower at RAAF Richmond at 4.39 p.m. on the 21st June. The elapsed time of 20 hours 3 minutes and 17 seconds for the flight gave an average speed of 500 kts. Favourable winds on one sector east of Alice Springs gave a ground speed of 600 kts. En route refuelling from Vickers Valiant tankers occurred over Nicosia, Cyprus, near Karachi, near Singapore and a final 'top up' about 500 miles out of Singapore. Each refuelling took about 12 minutes, the Vulcan taking on about 5000 gallons (23,000 litres) during that period. To effect the transfer the Vulcan reduced speed to 350 kts.

The aircraft went on display at Richmond on 22nd June. The crew of the Vulcan, Sqd. Ldr. M. Beavis (Captain), Flt. Lts. D. Bromley, R. Taylor and G. Jukes, F/O J. Knight, and Chief Technician W. Alpine were guests of the De Havilland Aircraft Company on a harbour cruise whilst in Sydney. The following day the aircraft departed for RAAF Edinburgh although not before a spectacular flying display at 15000 feet down Sydney Harbour to Vaucluse and Watsons Bay returning to the Harbour Bridge thence to Bankstown. Whilst stationed at Edinburgh XH481 in company with one of the Victors overflew Hobart, Launceston and Melbourne on 27th June. Departing Edinburgh on 30th June theaircraft flew to RAAF Pearce were it went on display to the people of Perth on 2nd July before returning to the United Kingdom on the 3rd July.

The British Commonwealth and Empire Games held in Perth in November and December 1962 afforded RAF Bomber Command another opportunity to display their Vulcans. The three Vulcan Squadrons sharing RAF Scampton in Lincolnshire participated in the opening and closing ceremonies of the Games along with nine CAC Sabres of No. 75 Squadron RAAF, Williamtown. The Vulcan B.Mk.2s, XH556 of No. 27 Squadron, XL319 of No. 617 Squadron (now in North East Air Museum) and XL392 of No. 83 Squadron (now on RAF Valley fire dump) arrived at RAAF Pearce on 19th November 1962. Servicing crew for the Vulcans arrived in a Bristol Britannia of RAF Transport Command. The following day a fourth Vulcan arrived carrying Air Vice-Marshal P. Dunn, O.C. of No. 1 Bomber Group, RAF.

It was anticipated that one of the Vulcans would go on public display at Perth Airport. After hurried consultations with the Department of Civil Aviation it was considered that the Vulcan's tyre pressures of 190lbs/sq.in. were too high and the proposed landing at Perth was banned. Whilst the all up weight of the Vulcan B.Mk.2 was less than the Boeing 707 aircraft using the airport, the Vulcan's tyre pressures were 50lb/sq.in higher than the former aircraft.

In the interval between the flypasts for the Opening and Closing Ceremonies on the 23rd November and 1st December the aircraft flew to the Eastern States departing Pearce on 26th November and returning on 28th. Vulcan XL392 was involved in a spectacular flying exhibition at the Games on 29th November. Resuming their round-the-world flight the Vulcans departed Pearce on 2nd December for RAAF Edinburgh and thence on to New Zealand.

A major air-to-air refuelling exercise involving three Vulcans from the 'Waddington Wing' once again saw the Vulcans 'Down-under'. In July 1963 the three Vulcans, XH481 of No. 101 Squadron, XH482 of No. 50 Squadron, and XH 503 of No. 44 Squadron arrived in Perth having completed a non-stop flight from RAF Waddington. The first two aircraft arrived on the 9th July, the third aircraft arriving the following day. The first Vulcan to arrive completed the 8600 nautical mile trip in 18 hours 10 minutes. The commander of this aircraft, Wing Commander A. Griffiths, commented that they were not trying to establish any speed records. Unfavourable 'jet streams' were encountered on the leg to Aden producing headwinds of 100 kts. On the 3500 nautical mile final sector from Gan, Maldive Islands, more favourable 'jet streams' produced ground speeds of 625 kts. The co-pilot, David Bromley, was the co-pilot of the 1961 non-stop U.K. to Sydney mission in XH481.

Refuelled by Vickers Valiant tankers over Libya, Aden, and the Maldive Islands, they flew at 40,000 feet for most of the journey. Flight Lieutenant J. R. Ward, the captain of the second Vulcan to land, said the only problem encountered was the need to descend from their cruising altitude to 25,000 feet to enable the fuel transfer, overhead the Gan position, to proceed clear of cloud. Before returning to the United Kingdom the aircraft visited RAAF Richmond and RAAF Edinburgh. The aircraft arrived at Richmond after a 2 hour 50 minute dash from Perth, 2000 nautical miles away, ground speeds of 670 kts being recorded en route.

The confrontation between Indonesia and Malaysia in the early 1960's focused Government attention on the northern approaches to Australia. Not only was the efficacy of the defence complex in question but the lack of a modern strike aircraft capable of swift retaliation meant a serious lack of a credible deterrent. The now obsolete Canberra was, indeed, no match for Indonesian's Russian-built Tupolev Tu-16 "Badger" with its range of 4000 miles and a 6000 lb weapon load. Britain's treaty obligations to Malaysia had resulted in the maintenance of a detachment of the V-force in Tengah, Singapore, or Butterworth, Malaysia, during the period of the confrontation, in addition to their existing airforce detachments. These "Sunflower" detachments consisted of eight aircraft travelling in two waves, either by the Westabout Route, via Canada, U.S.A., Wake Island and Guam, or the Middle East Route.

Against this background the decision was taken to test our northern defences by simulated attacks by elements of the V-force. The Vulcans operated, initially, out of RAF Tengah, Singapore, flying a series of war training exercises in and around Malaysia and later flying onto Darwin flying day and night sorties to test the Australian defences. These visits to Darwin became a highlight of the 'Sunflower' exercises, providing realistic war training in tropical conditions and uncrowded skies. From the British Ministry of Defence's point of view these exercises and overseas flights had the following broad objectives:-

a) To demonstrate that the V-bomber could be deployed quickly around the world, and to practise such deployments.
b) To maintain the deterrent and its credibility.
c) To allow Allied and friendly nations to manoeuvre their own air forces, with and against large jet bombers.
d) To give crews practice in long distance flying.

On 17th December, 1965, Vulcans under the command of Sq. Ldr. D. S. Harris and Canberra bombers deployed from "enemy bases" at Alice Springs, Townsville and Amberley raided Darwin. The ADEX "High Rigel" had moved into its major phase. The RAAF Sabres and Mirages equipped with Matra and Sidewinder missiles opposed the attacking bombers. The defending fighters were directed to their targets by the No. 2 Control and Reporting unit, the RAAF's most modern radar unit which first became operaional in 1961. This major exercise involved, not only the RAAF and a Vulcan detachment but also some 40 National Servicemen of the 121st Anti-Aircraft Battery, Civil Defence and Emergency Services, the Fire Brigade and the St. John's Brigade. It was generally conceded in Air Force circles that this exercise would herald the end of the Bloodhound missiles as an effective weapon. Indeed, it was considered that the Vulcans were unlikely to be threatened by the Sabres, SAM's or the Bofors of the A.A. Battery. It was not until 1968 that the Bloodhound SAM Squadron was ultimately phased out of service.

The realism of the exercise was significantly enhanced by the weather pattern around Darwin. Tropical storms with massive cumulonimbus development extending up to 50,000 ft. ensured that the attacking Vulcans did not have a clear run to their targets. Darwin itself was subjected to intense cumulonimbus activity and heavy tropical rain showers. Following the exercise, the O.I.C., Air Vice-Marshal C. T. Hannah, commented that the capability of the Mirage as a day and night fighter had been fully tested. The aircraft involved had flown over 800 sorties and some 700 personnel had been deployed. During the exercise a fault was discovered with the Mirage starting system. The problem involved the Noelle starter engine for the SNECMA Atar jet engine. With the wind blowing into the jet pipe of the big Atar engine its turbine would start to rotate in the contra-direction to normal operation. The torque produced in the Atar could not be overcome when the Noelle's clutch engaged and the normal start sequence was aborted.

The Vulcans visited Darwin again in March 1966, this time to participate in ADEX "Short Spica". Four Vulcans combined with Canberras from No. 1 Squadron, Amberley, to test the defences of Darwin and its protective mantle of Mirage and Sabre fighters. Attacking bombers were deployed from bases at Amberley, Townsville and the civilian airport at Mt. Isa. "Hostilities" commenced at 0900 Z on the 17th March, the exercise continuing under the direction of Group Captain W. N. Lampe, until 1000 hrs. Zulu time on 23rd March. The all-weather capabilities of the RAAF Mirage of No. 75 Squadron were fully tested by the Darwin "wet". RAAF Lockheed Hercules aircraft from their bases at Richmond, N.S.W., were involved in the deployment of personnel and equipment to and from the exercise.

Following one of the missions, Flying Officer David Lee in his Vulcan experienced a hydraulic failure necessitating the use of an emergency system to lower the landing gear. Several lower passes over the control tower enabled engineers to visually inspect the gear and to conclude that it appeared locked. Finally, after flying several extended circuits to use up fuel the Vulcan came in for an uneventful landing with fire tender and rescue helicopter on standby.

ADEX "High Castor", held in August 1966 was the next major exercise in Darwin. Following along the lines of the previous exercises, all of the RAAF operational elements were involved including Lockheed Neptune maritime reconnaissance aircraft from No. 10 Squadron, Townsville, three RAF Vulcans and two RAF Canberras.

November 1967 was the date selected for a major joint exercise involving the Canberra bombers of No. 14 Squadron, RNZAF, based at Ohakea, in addition to four RAF Vulcans from No. 9 Squadron and a RAF photo-reconnaissance Canberra. The Canberras of No. 14 Squadron, RNZAF, were based together with Canberras of No. 3 Squadron, RAAF, Amberley, at the "enemy" base of Tindal. Tindal air base, situated some 200 miles south of Darwin and near Katherine, first became operational on 6th June 1967. Named after the first Australian officer killed on the Mainland in the Darwin air raids of 1942, Tindal cost $7 million to build. Built largely by personnel of the No. 5 Airfield Construction Squadron it consisted of a 9000 foot runway with two 1000 foot over-runs. The Tindal base was first used in the ADEX "High Venus", an exerciseheld in June 1967 involving Canberra bombers from Amberley and a RAF Canberra photo-reconnaissance aircraft.

The Minister of Air, Mr. Peter Howson, stated the principal objective of "High Mars" as a test of air defences and strike reconnaissance. Some 1000 personnel, including 80 men of the Royal Australian Army, participated.

"High Jupiter", conducted in June 1968, brought together in the north the largest peacetime deployment of men and equipment. Over 2000 personnel and 50 aircraft were involved in this exercise under the command of Air Vice-Marshal K. S. Hennock. The newly formed RAF Strike Command was represented by Air Officer Commanding Strike Command, Australian born, Sir Wallace Kyle, Sir Wallace assuming the role of an observer. This exercise also saw the Mirage in its new guise as a low level strike aircraft. Several Mirages were heavily camouflaged and specially equipped for the lower level attack role. The RAF contributed four Vulcans, under the command of Wing Commander D. J. Mountford, and two Canberra bombers from the Far East Air Force HQ in Singapore. The Royal Australian Army provided the 11th Light Anti-aircraft Battery from South Australia and an Airborne Platoon. The Army was responsible for refuelling facilities, temporary storage being provided by 8000 gallon capacity, transportable rubber fuel tanks and aluminium pipelines. Personnel in a mobile laboratory conducted purity checks on the fuel. Local defences were subjected to heavy pressure when paratroop landings, with the twofold objective of raiding both the radar installation at Point Lee and the Darwin airport complex, were launched.

At 0830Z on 20th June, Canberra bombers from Tindal attacked Darwin Airport. Intercepting Mirages, scrambled to meet the Canberras, soon found themselves engaging the ground attack "enemy" Mirages as well. Night raids on Friday, 21st June, saw a Mirage exceeding Mach 1 as it attempted to intercept an invader. The resulting "sonic boom" rumbling across the night sky, rattled Darwin and procduced a spate of complaints by local residents. The heaviest raid on Darwin occurred on 23rd June. Two Vulcans came in at high level and a third, evading the defence, flew in at low level.

The exercise in December, 1968, "Rum Keg" was more in the nature of a training exercise than an operational exercise. The OIC for the exercise, Group Captain Mick Mather, OIC RAAF Darwin, stated that there would be no 'open go' flying over the city as was the case in "High Jupiter". A detachment of four Vulcans of No. 44 Squadron arrived from Singapore on 5th December, 1968, returning to their Singapore base on the 11th December. This exercise would see the end of the Bristol Bloodhound SAM Squadron, a part of Darwin's defence since 1961. It had been announced in August by the Minister of Air, Mr. Gordon Freeth, in the House of Representatives that these missiles would be phased out of service, their role being taken initially by the Mirage but ultimately by the General Dynamics F-111.

The Vulcans of No. 50 Squadron were accompanied by RAF Lightnings of No. 74 Squadron when they visited Darwin in June 1969 to participate in "Town House". This exercise commenced officially at 1500 hours CST on 18th June 1969 and ended on the 25th June. The initial Vulcan raid occurred soon after 1000 hours on the 19th June. As the Vulcans tracked to Darwin they left a prominent 'foot print' in the form of contrails. Contrails, the cloud streamers formed in the wake of jet aircraft, were considerably important militarily, indicating not only the presence of the Vulcans but giving also their approximate heading and information of the winds aloft. Contrails were visible long before a visual contact could be established and

Above: *XH480 at RAAF Fairbairn, 12 September 1965. (Denis O'Brien)*

often before onboard radar could detect the intruder. In its European theatre of activity, the high level operations were conducted at altitudes that put the Vulcan above the tropopause. In this environment contrails are less likely to be produced because of the low ambient moisture above the troposphere. However, in the low altitudes of Darwin, the tropical tropopause is much higher extending up to 18 km. The raids on Darwin consisted of high level attacks by the Vulcans and low level attacks by the Canberras, the latter aircraft being based at Tindal. These raids were preceded by live bombing runs on the Quail Island and Leanyer Swamp ranges. Live bombs were not carried over the populated areas of Darwin and the Sidewinder and Matra missiles carried by the Mirages were unarmed.

Air Vice-Marshal Bill Townsend was the OIC of the next major ADEX, "Castor Oil", held in February 1970. Whilst many air-to-air exercises were conducted in the south-eastern states, Darwin, as the northern approach to Australia was favoured for the ground-to-air defensive exercise. The logistics of moving large numbers of men together with equipment was a vital part of these exercises, simulating a potential scenario. Thus the Darwin exercises involved all elements of Operational Command. Following the pattern of previous exercises, Darwin was to be subjected to attack by 'enemy' aircraft from Tindal. In this respect the exercise was rather one-sided as no counter offensive was planned against Tindal. Four Vulcans from RAF Strike Command arrived to support the 'enemy', which consisted of six Canberras, six ground attack Mirages and six Sabres. The defence of Darwin again rested with the Mirages of No. 76 Squadron. Paratroops, dropped from RAAF Caribou, in a pre-dawn raid, signalled the commencement of the exercise. At the conclusion of the exercise the defenders were claiming four Vulcans, four Canberras, three Mirages and two Sabres as 'kills'. This was not without heavy damage to the RAAF base, the City, fuel depots and the power station. The senior medical officer at the RAAF Base Hospital stated some 65 casualties were treated, three casualties being considered to have received fatal wounds.

In November 1970 four Vulcans of No. 27 Squadron departed their base at Scampton and flew to Singapore and Australia via the Westabout Route, staging through Gander, Offut AFB, San Francisco, Honolulu, Wake Island and Guam. Their arrival in Darwin was timed so they could participate in "Opal Digger", an ADEX consisting of high altitude exercises in conjunction with eight Mirages of No. 76 Squadron and the Darwin Base Radar Unit, 2CRU. The Mirages, half of the No. 76 Squadron complement from Williamtown, staged through Townsville, flying the Townsville-Darwin sector in 2 hours 15 minutes. Compared with "Castor Oil" this was a minor exercise. The OIC was Wing Commander Stewart Creswell with Air Commodore G. H. Steege from HQ Operational Command, Glenbrook, acting as an observer. As a salute to Darwin, one Vulcan and four Mirages overflew the city at the completion of the exercise. Two Vulcans returned to the U.K., the other two first visiting RAAF Williamtown.

Vulcans from No. 44 Squadron, Waddington Wing, visited Darwin in February, 1972 to participate in 'Whisky Sour'. Two Vulcans arrived on 4th February, the other two arriving two days later. Eight Mirages under the command of Squadron Leader 'Joe' Owens from No. 76 Squadron had already arrived on 1st February after having staged via Townsville. It was almost 30 years to the day that Kittyhawk aircraft of No. 76 Squadron were involved in the defence of Darwin against the Japanese. This ADEX involved day and night exercises with the Mirages defending Darwin from the attacking Vulcans. Vulcans would depart Darwin and later return from any direction at high or low level to attack the RAAF Base. A common spoof employed by the Vulcans was to send one aircraft in towards the target to ensure radar detection. When the Mirages were scrambled the Vulcan would hastily turn away. This ruse was designed to get all the Mirages into the air so they would be low on fuel when the real strike came. The Vulcans could carry 90,000 lb. of fuel and their fuel burn of some 10.000lb per hour gave them sufficient time in the air to permit some element of surprise in their attack. It was not too difficult for the Mirage pilots to establish visual contact with the Vulcans, they were large aircraft and even without contrails they left a telltale trail of black exhaust; establishing a "kill" was not so easy. At low level, coming in under radar they were often able to 'release' their weapons before being intercepted. At high altitudes they posed another series of problems, their ECM equipment and 'chaff' were effective in deflecting radar guided missiles and the heat seeking missiles required the Mirages to be at a similar altitude to their target. Success of the intercept and rocket launches was assessed by on-board equipment and ground radar assessment. A 'probability of kill' factor was established using statistical information that considered such extraneous factors as post-launch failure. During night exercises a safety parameter required aircraft to use their navigation lights. On a lighter note, the Mirage crews endeavoured to see that all the Vulcans were suitably decorated with red kangaroos before their departure.

The joint exercise "Top Limit" in May 1972 involved aircraft from the RNZAF as well as the RAF and RAAF. This exercise involved thirteen Phantoms from No. 1 Squadron, Amberley, led by Wing Commander Lyall Klakker. The RNZAF contributed eight Skyhawks, commanded by Wing Commander F. M. Kinvig, from their base at Ohakea in the North Island of New Zealand. The RAF was represented by four Vulcans from No. 9 Squadron and included XM600 and XM656. The exercise commenced on 9th May and ended on the 15th and was followed by a debriefing the next day. Tindal was brought out of 'moth balls' to serve as a base for the 'enemy'. RAAF Darwin was again defended by Mirages. FlightLieutenant R. J. Perry was back in action following an accident on the 24th April when his Mirage, A3-74, was destroyed following a bird strike soon after take-off. Two other Mirages were damaged during the exercise, one suffered a bird strike and the other struck a supply truck.

In accordance with established procedures, the Department of Civil Aviation instituted, by Notam, HO 12/1972, special procedures to be adopted during the course of the exercise. In addition to the activation of the Darwin restricted areas, at Tindal a temporary control zone and overlying temporary restricted area with lateral limits of 25 nautical mile radius of the aerodrome and vertical limits from ground level to 5000 feet and from 5000 feet to FL250 were established under Military control.

During the period of deployment of aircraft and pre-operational training from 26th April to 8th May, civil aircraft were advised to expect some delays when arriving at or departing from Darwin, Katherine or Tindal. The operational phase of the exercise from the 9th May to 15th May saw the implementation of the following special procedures. Within the period 2230 to 0230 GMT daily, no civil aircraft, other than regular public transport aircraft operating on schedule, were permitted to operate within 30 nautical miles radius of Darwin aerodrome between ground or water level to FL200. Pilots were to ensure that all operations within this airspace were completed prior to 2230 GMT daily. The period 0230 to 0330 GMT was reserved primarily for civil operations, and no military exercise aircraft would operate in the above mentioned zone. Urgent medical, mercy flights and aircraft subject to an emergency were given priority at all times. Throughout the exercise period all civil aircraft were required to obtain a start-up clearance. IFR holding patterns were established on the 141 and 293 radials of the Darwin VOR at 50 DME Darwin. These radials corresponding to the Airways, Amber 61-64 and Amber 64. All VFR aircraft were required to plan and approach Darwin via, and if necessary hold at Cape Gambier, Woolner HS or Manton Dam. NDB's were established at Woolner HS and Manton Dam. The Military authorities were responsible for providing radar separation between civil and defending military aircraft.

A third exercise in 1972 involving the Vulcans commenced on the 17th July when the Vulcans arrived to participate in "Dry Martini". This exercise was marred by the grounding of the 14 Mirages from No 76 Squadron. All the RAAF's Mirages were grounded following an engine failure of one of the aircraft at Butterworth in Malaysia. The Vulcans continued to fly bombing missions at the Quail Island range. Whilst engineers conducted checks on the Mirages, the pilots and other ground crew were kept busy with survival exercises, sport and recreational activities. The checks completed, the Mirages re-commenced flying operations on the 29th July. On the same day two of the Vulcans flew to RAAF Pearce, returning to Darwin on the 31st July. All four Vulcans departed Darwin for Britain on the 3rd of August.

The participation of the Vulcans in Australian Airshows always proved to be a great crowd pleaser. In the mid-1960's the Vulcans were often a feature at the various RAAF bases during Air Force Week celebrations, in 1971 a Vulcan participated in the Golden Jubilee celebrations of the RAAF and appeared in the skies accompanying aircraft of the RAAF. The final visit to Australia was by XM571, now on display at Gibraltar. This aircraft was in Adelaide for the 617 Squadron reunion in April 1980. The Vulcan was indeed a highly successful aircraft design. Fortunately many of the type have been preserved in the aircraft museums in the United Kingdom.

AIR DEFENCE EXERCISES (ADEX)

ADEX	DATE
High Rigel	December 1965
Short Spica	March 1966
High Castor	August 1966
High Mars	November 1967
High Jupiter	June 1968
Rum Keg	December 1968
Town House	June 1969
Castor Oil	February 1970
Opal Digger	November 1970
Whisky Sour	February 1972
Top Limit	May 1972
Dry Martini	July 1972

5. Arming the Vulcan

Although Blue Steel was a very successful design Avro continually looked to the future, and the missile was regarded as being the first in a series of stand-off weapons, eventually leading to an air-to-ground missile for the Avro 730. A futuristic bomber design, the Avro 730 was developed from a strategic reconnaissance project submitted to the MoS in 1955 and was in many respects a British equivalent of the Lockheed SR-71, albeit some years ahead of the US type. It was expected to be capable of speeds in excess of Mach 2.5, with a range of over 5,000 miles. The bomber derivative would have had a similar performance, and if it had been ordered into production the RAF would have possessed a strategic nuclear bomber with a performance better even than that of the Rockwell B-1 – more than ten years before the USAF's swing-wing bomber first flew! But British politicians had other ideas, and Defence Secretary Duncan Sandys decided that the Avro 730 was an aircraft that the RAF did not need and could not afford, so the project was abandoned.

However, Avro continued development of Blue Steel, which resulted in Blue Steel Mk.2, featuring the same forebody as the Mk.1, but with four Bristol Siddeley ramjets and two solid fuel booster rockets to provide the power. Performance was estimated at Mach 3, with a range of 800 miles at 70,000 feet. Sadly, like the bomber for which it was primarily intended, the

Below: *Line-up of No. 83 Squadron Vulcan B.2s at Scampton. When parked alongside other B.2s, the smaller (B.1-sized) intake fitted to XH554 is clearly evident. (MoD)*

Blue Steel Mk.2 programme was later cancelled, in December 1959. By then the British Government had decided that the Hawker Siddeley Blue Streak IRBM would eventually be adopted as the main British nuclear deterrent. To fill the gap while this missile was being developed, an agreement was reached with the US Government for the supply of sixty Douglas Thor missiles. Unfortunately the Thor was less than ideal for the task, not least because it was a liquid-fuelled rocket that required a considerable amount of pre-launch preparation. With an expected attack warning time of perhaps just four minutes, the Thor was obviously going to be vunerable to a pre-emptive strike. Likewise, Blue Streak was expected to use similar technology, and critics of the system (including both the Royal Navy and RAF) were keen to draw attention to this fact. By April 1960 the combination of projected vunerability, development problems and cost increases persuaded the Government to cancel Blue Streak too, leaving the Thor 'stop-gap', and a two-year wait until Blue Steel would be introduced. Interest now began to switch to another missile that would soon be available, a missile that could meet the requirement for a Blue Streak/Thor replacement and be likely to provide a credible deterrent even after Blue Steel had reached the end of its useful life.

The Douglas GAM-87A Skybolt was designed in response to a USAF requirement for an air-launched strategic nuclear missile to be carried by SAC Boeing B-52s and Convair B-58s. With a range in excess of 1,000 miles, the Skybolt represented a huge leap in capability over Blue Steel. In March 1960 Macmillan met President Eisenhower to discuss the possible purchase of the missile and it was agreed that Skybolt would be supplied to the RAF, following a projected introduction into USAF service at the end of 1963. Avro quickly became involved with the programme, not least because of their experience with Blue Steel, and because the Vulcan had been selected as the primary carrier aircraft. However, other manufacturers submitted alternative Skybolt carriage systems, with a proposal from Hawker Siddeley to produce a variant of the Trident airliner, a Vickers submission for a VC10 derivative, and even a Victor proposal, although Handley Page were working against the odds in attempting to mate two, four or even six 38ft-long missiles under the Victor's low wings and fuselage. The Vulcan was accepted as being the most compatible aircraft for the Skybolt system, and Vulcan B.2s on the production line were suitably strengthened and modified, beginning with the 61st aircraft (XM597).

During January 1961 Vulcan B.2 XH563 flew to Santa Monica in California for a series of electrical compatibility trials with Douglas; this was followed by a period with the Wright Air Development Division at Wright-Patterson AFB, Ohio. Meanwhile in Britain a British nuclear warhead was developed for attachment to the Skybolt missile. In November 1961 Vulcan XH537 made the first flight with a dummy Skybolt attached under each wing, and on 1 December it made the first dummy drop over the West Freugh range in Scotland, at 45,000 feet. XH538 later joined the trials programme and flew to Eglin AFB, Florida, to participate in trials there, as part of the British Joint Trials Forceestablished at the base. The Vulcan proved to be an excellent launch platform for Skybolt, but unfortunately the missile suffered from more than a few teething troubles. The first three live launches ended in failure because of powerplant and guidance problems, and the fourth launch was only partially successful as the second stage motor cut out after only fifteen seconds. These setbacks did little to encourage the US Defense Secretary, Robert McNamara, and although he gave his support to both the Polaris and Minuteman programmes, he became increasingly convinced that Skybolt was unnecessary. On 7 November 1962 McNamara recommended to President Kennedy that Skybolt be cancelled.

President John F. Kennedy was, at best, ambivalent towards the British. Furthermore, he preferred the concept of a

Below: *XH537 thundering along Woodford's runway while carrying two Skybolt aerodynamic test vehicles. The flight sheds, from where each Vulcan made its first appearance when completed, can be seen in the distance. (British Aerospace)*

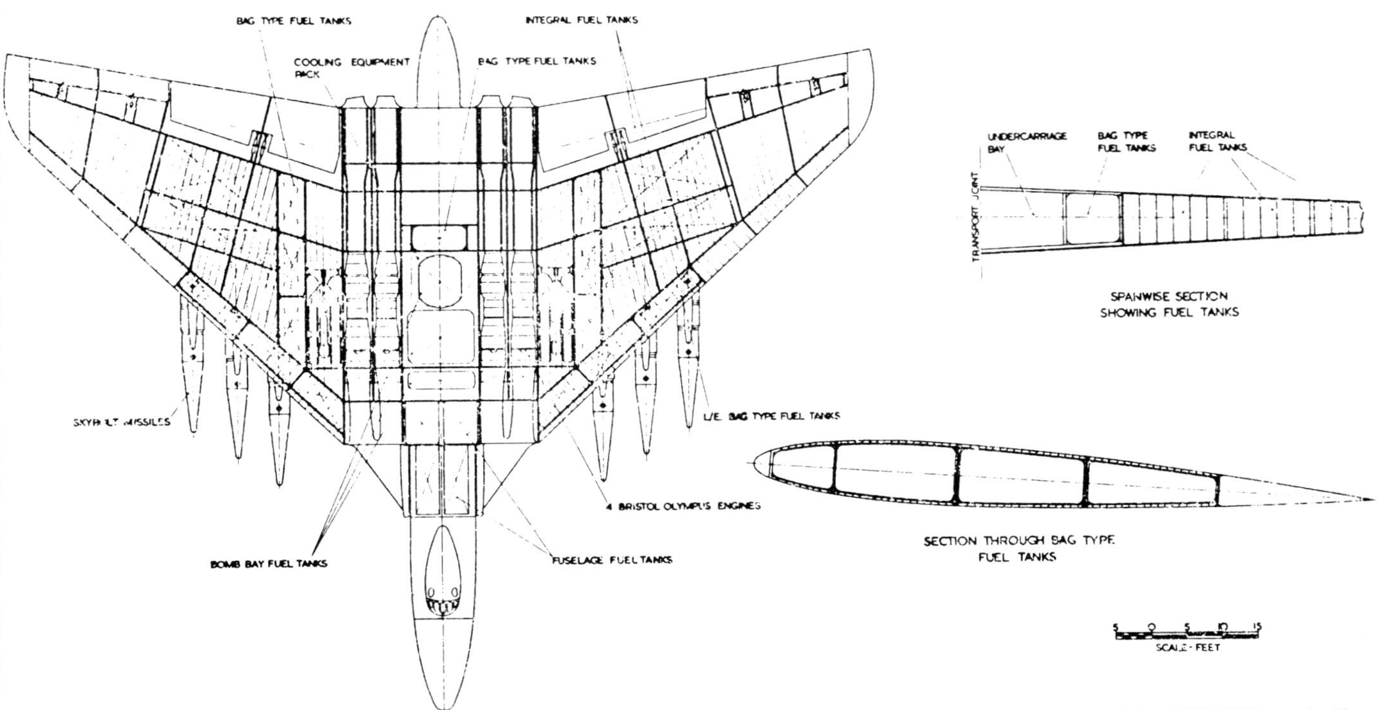

The Vulcan Phase Six design (which would have become the Vulcan B. Mk. 3), was to have been powered by four Olympus BS.01.23-2 engines, with a simplified reheat system and variable convergent nozzles. Two, four or six Skybolt missiles would have been carried, and with an all-up maximum weight of 358,000lb, and with a fuel reserve of one hour, the endurance would have been 12.2, 10 and 7.4 hours respectively. Ejection seats would have been provided for every crew member.

European multilateral nuclear force under NATO control, rather than independent British and French deterrents. The USAF had been warning the RAF for some time that Skybolt stood every chance of being cancelled; indeed, from the American point of view it is probably fair to say that the programme would have been terminated earlier had it not been for the British interest in the project. When Kennedy informed Macmillan in December 1962 that he had ordered the termination of Skybolt, he totally underestimated the British reaction. Macmillan, rightly or wrongly, believed that the cancellation was little more than a political move, intended to undermine the effectiveness of the British nuclear deterrent. Kennedy quickly tried to make amends. First he offered the entire Skybolt programme to the British; this was refused on cost grounds, although it would have been substantially cheaper than Polaris. He then offered to bear half the development costs, an act of extreme generosity since the programme was of absolutely no value to America. But even this was refused, as was a later offer of Hound Dog missiles. Macmillan opted for the submarine-launched Polaris missile system, effectively killing the concept of an airborne British nuclear deterrent. Ironically, on the day that Kennedy informed Macmillan of Skybolt's cancellation (19 December), the missile made a perfect test launch from a B-52, reaching a target 1,000 miles down range from Eglin.

If Skybolt had been delivered to the RAF, the Vulcan would probably have remained in production long after 1964, when the last B.2s were completed. The RAF concluded that Skybolt's deep strike capability would have made the Vulcan bases particularly high-priority targets in the event of a war. This led to the consideration of a Strategic Air Command-style Continuous Airborne Deterrent, with Skybolt-equipped Vulcans flying continuously around the clock, every day, ensuring that both the missile and its launch aircraft were invunerable to attack. However, this would have required an aircraft with greater endurance than the Vulcan B.2, which resulted in Avro's development of the Vulcan Phase 6 design, with increased wing span (reverting to a straight leading edge), a six-man crew (with rest bunks for off-duty personnel), more fuel, an extended nose, a larger tail fin, and uprated engines, together with a strengthened undercarriage. It was estimated that the Phase 6 design (which would have become the Vulcan B.3) would have had an endurance of approximately seven hours when carrying six Skybolts. With two Skybolts the endurance would be increased to twelve hours, and by using a combination of six-missile and two-missile Vulcan B.3s, together with two-missile B.2s, a total of 84 Skybolts could have been kept airborne at all times.

Avro also offered a conventional-bomb derivative of the design which would have carried 38 1,000lb HE bombs in the bomb bay and in wing pods attached to the

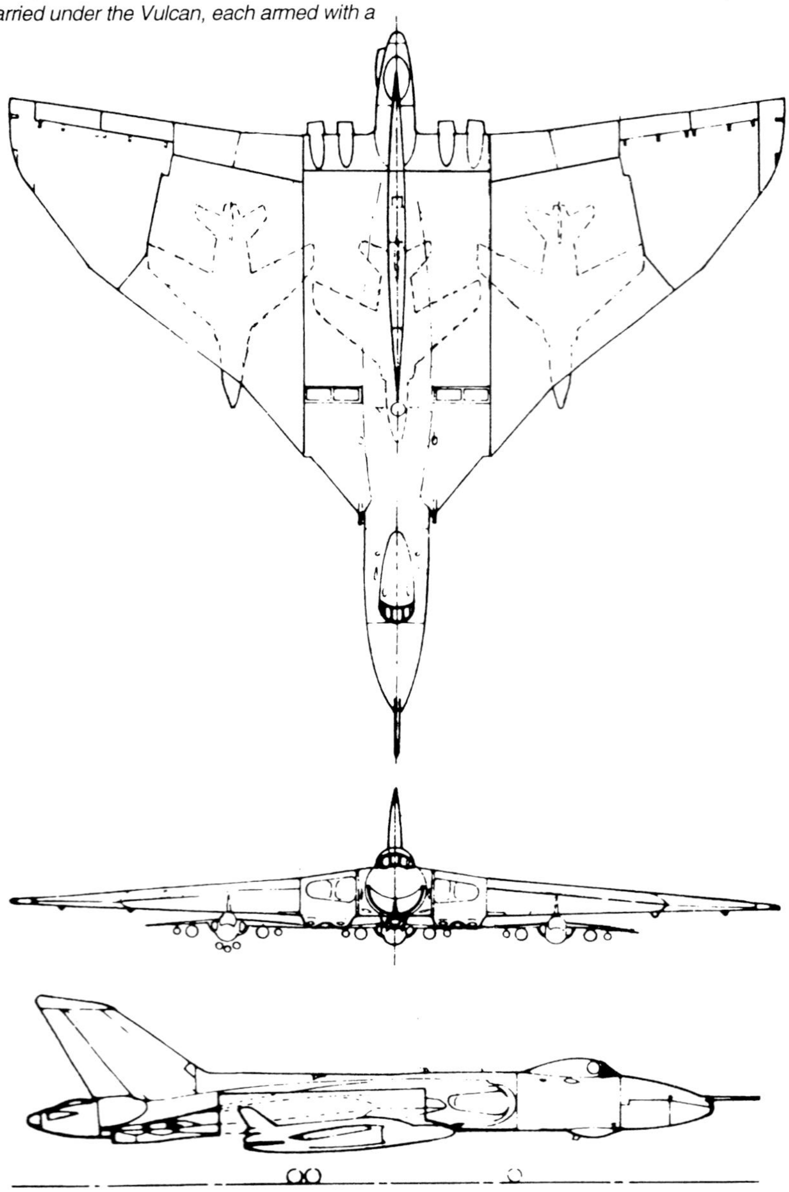

Following the cancellation of the Skybolt programme, various alternative stand-off bomb concepts were considered. One of the more unusual schemes was for three Folland Gnats to be carried under the Vulcan, each armed with a kiloton-range nuclear weapon. The scheme would suggest that the Gnat pilots would almost certainly have been obliged to fly a one-way mission. The idea was never developed.

Skybolt hardpoints. If Kennedy had not cancelled Skybolt, or if Macmillan had not so stubbornly refused to buy the programme from the USA, this awesome bomber might well have been built, and could still have been in RAF service today. But as so often throughout the history of British military aviation, politicians made the wrong decisions. The British nuclear deterrent was handed to the Royal Navy on 30 June 1969 and Blue Steel was withdrawn, most of the missiles being cut up for scrap. However, the Vulcan's RAF career was far from over, as it was decided to reassign the Vulcan force in the conventional bombing role, as part of an integrated NATO structure. The emphasis changed to the delivery of 1,000lb HE bombs (slick and retarded) at low level, at night. Although the Vulcan had been designed for high-altitude operations, it was well suited for low-level flight, thanks to the immense strength of the aircraft's structure. In recognition of the ever-improving Soviet air defences, the RAF abandoned the concept of high-altitude bombing in favour of low-level (500 feet or lower) delivery, in order to evade enemy radar detection until the last possible moment.

In fact, the Vulcan force had already switched to low-level, even for Blue Steel operations, because when Skybolt was cancelled it was acknowledged that Blue Steel would not be credible as a deterrent for much longer. The Russians had already proved that they could intercept even the highest-flying aircraft, when Francis Gary Powers was shot down in his U-2 by a Soviet SAM, while flying at approximately 70,000 feet on 1 May 1960. Following successful trials at Woomera, the Blue Steel squadrons went low-level in 1964. The revised delivery technique was to launch the missile at around 25 miles from the target, popping up from low level for release, after which the missile zoom-climbed to 17,000 feet. The delivery of free-fall nuclear weapons was also switched to low-level, although the final bomb release had still to be made at altitude; that is, until a specialized low-level 'laydown' thermonuclear weapon became available (which had originally been developed for the Buccaneer and TSR-2). In contrast to the anti-flash white paint scheme which the V-bombers had always carried, grey/green disruptive camouflage was applied to the Vulcans, Victors and the few Valiants which remained in service; the latter type was rapidly withdrawn from RAF service after severe wing spar metal fatigue problems were discovered in most of the Valiant fleet.

As usual, the British Government was incapable of establishing a clear and credible defence policy, and after one of the most outstanding combat aircraft designs ever developed was cancelled (the BAC TSR-2), the American General Dynamics F-111K was ordered, only to be cancelled itself at a later stage. The Vulcan, however, soldiered on and it was decided to retain the aircraft as a tactical bomber, replacing Canberras in this role. The initial plan was to retire the remaining Vulcans in 1975, but eventually it was the delivery of the first Tornado GR.1s to RAF squadrons that allowed the Vulcan to make a graceful, if not a little hasty, withdrawal from operational service. Thankfully, the Vulcan was well equipped to fly for many years – long after the original projected retirement date – as a conventional bomber and as a tactical free-fall nuclear bomber. The Victor was unsuitable for low-level operations, its flexible wing 'riding' the low-altitude turbulence, giving the crew a smooth ride, but rapidly destroying the structural integrity of the airframe. Avro however, with a tradition of simplicity in design, had effectively built the Vulcan around two mass-spar booms with mechanical joints, a technique perfected in both the Lincoln and Shackleton; and after the South African Air Force experienced fatigue problems with its Shackletons, Avro had gained plenty of experience in dealing with such matters by the time that the Vulcans switched to low-level operations. The Skybolt structural strengthening modifications also contributed to the robustness of the Vulcan, and with the addition of huge strengthening plates to various parts of the airframe, the Vulcan was equipped for service into the 1980s. The original specification called for a high-altitude airframe life of 3,900 hours, whereas Avro estimated that the Vulcan's life would be 5,900 hours. This was fixed as the 100 per cent fatigue life (100 Fatigue Indices), but with structural modification this figure was stretched to an incredible 320 FI – some 484 per cent of the original requirement.

The emphasis on low-level operations led to the installation of Ferranti terrain-following radar and most of the Vulcans were suitably modified. Likewise, the entire B.2 fleet was fitted with ARI.18228 passive ECM equipment, which was installed in a rectangular fairing on top of the fin. Provision for two long-range (8,000lb) fuel tanks in the bomb bay (for ferry flights) was made, and although the in-flight refuelling probes remained attached to the noses of every Vulcan B.2, the system had not been used since the aircraft swithed to tactical operations. All but the first fifteen production B.1s had been fitted with internal equipment for in-

Above: *How low can you get? Waddington VIPs about to get an intimate view of a Vulcan B.2. (via British Aerospace)*

Below: *XM597 performing a low-level turn with airbrakes extended. The aircraft has received TFR and RWR modifications but still wore full-colour roundels and a gloss-white underside when this photograph was taken. (British Aerospace)*

XL384 was the first of a batch of Vulcan B.2s with 300-Series Olympus engines and equipped for Blue Steel operations. The aircraft is seen on the apron at Goose Bay, Labrador, in typical snowy conditions. (D. Haller)

XL320

flight refuelling, but a suitable probe system was not adopted until 1963, following refuelling trials with XH478. Beginning with the Blue Steel squadrons, each Vulcan was temporarily withdrawn for modification by Flight Refuelling Ltd. Largely because the Victor was unsuitable for low-level bombing operations, most of the Victor bomber fleet was converted into tanker aircraft. In fact, owing to a curious twist of fate, the Victor K.2s were converted from bomber configuration by Hawker Siddeley at Woodford, occupying the same factory floor that the Vulcans had when they were being assembled by Avro. Some of the Victor K.2 conversions were made from former Victor SR.2 strategic reconnaissance aircraft which had been operated by No. 543 Squadron at Wyton until the unit disbanded in May 1974. The reconnaissance Victors were replaced by the Vulcans of a re-formed No. 27 Squadron at Scampton. This squadron's machines were somewhat different from the standard bomber variant, being designated B.2(MRR), the 'MRR' reflectingthe Vulcan's Maritime Radar Reconnaissance role. Terrain-following radar was removed, LORAN navigational equipment was installed and provision was made for the fitment of two underwing air sampling pods, together with a smaller locator pod under the port wing. Five aircraft had fixed fittings while another three had removable fittings. The B.2(MRR)s were all powered by Olympus 201 engines, and each aircraft was 'sealed' with gloss polyurethane to help protect the airframe from the corrosive maritime environment.

When plans for early deliveries of the Tornado GR.1 had been made, it was envisaged that the Vulcan squadrons would be stood down on a one-by-one basis, as each Vulcan unit was replaced by an equivalent Tornado squadron. However, with a growing climate of defence expenditure cut-backs, forcing cash savings wherever possible, it was decided that the entire Vulcan force would be withdrawn over a twelve-month period, rather than financing the refurbishment of even part of the Vulcan fleet. The first unit to disband was No. 230 OCU, which became redundant as the Vulcan training requirement suddenly disappeared. The first squadron to disband was No. 617, on the last day of 1981. No. 35 Squadron followed in February 1982 and No. 27 Squadron in March, although two Vulcan B.2(MRR)s were transferred to No. 44 Squadron to enable the RAF to retain this specialized Vulcan's capabilities for a few more months. Waddington then began the disbandment process in April, when No. 9 Squadron exchanged its Vulcans for Tornadoes, both aircraft types being present during the disbandment ceremony at Waddington, each wearing the unit's distinctive bat emblem. No. 101 Squadron followed in August, but by that time the Vulcan's RAF career had again been influenced by politics, and Avro's classic bomber had been afforded an extraordinary opportunity to go to war 'for real' at, literally, the eleventh hour.

Left: *No. 230 OCU Vulcan XL320 accompanied by a Hastings T.5. The Hastings was operated by the OCU ('1066 Flight') as a training aircraft for Vulcan rear crew members. (MoD)*

Below: *XM600 crashed near Spilsby, Lincolnshire, following an engine fire on 17 January 1977. The crew abandoned the aircraft safely. (Denis O'Brien)*

XM652

XA903
TURBO-UNION RB199

Top left: *Surrounded by breathtaking Nevada mountains, XM652 is seen at Nellis AFB during a 'Red Flag' exercise. The first Vulcan to carry 'wrap-around' camouflage, XM652 ended its days in a Sheffield scrapyard, although the cockpit section remains intact. (MoD)*

Left: *Rear view of XA903 illustrating the open (empty) brake chute housing and the unusual white-painted engine exhaust cowlings. (Rolls-Royce)*

Above: *An RB.199 engine attached to the under fuselage of Vulcan XA903. The engine housing is representative of a Tornado fuselage, complete with intake. (Rolls-Royce)*

Right: *Close-up of XA903's RB.199 engine with reheat selected. Note the pod under the port wing and the heat shield metal around the rear fuselage. (Rolls-Royce)*

TURBO-UNION RB199

The very last moments of the last flight by a Vulcan B.1, as XA903 approaches Farnborough's runway for the last time, 1 March 1979. (MoD)

6. Working on the Vulcan

Peter Rivers was one of many Avro employees during the years when the Vulcan was developed, but unlike most of his colleagues he had previously worked on Handley Page's competing design, the H.P.80 Victor. Here he recalls some of his experiences:

'Starting with my background, I graduated in 1943 from the University of London and joined the RAF as a junior engineering officer, passing through the Engineering School at Henlow during the summer of 1944. I later enjoyed an interesting service life, ending my war years on Sunderland flying-boats in Northern Ireland. I left the RAF in April 1945 on Special Release, in order to join Westland's, who were then developing the first cabin pressure control equipment for passenger aircraft, together with more established lines of pressure controllers and flow valves which had been used in the Welkin, Spitfire and Mosquito. After I had worked there for about a year, the pressure control and air-conditioning elements of Westland became Normalair, who have been the main suppliers of cabin control equipment since that time. I stayed with the company until 1948, working mostly in their high-altitude laboratory and pressure chamber. I then moved to Handley Page at Cricklewood.

'The design of the H.P.80, which later became the Victor, had been progressing for just over a year when I arrived, and the aircraft's shape had not yet settled into the final configuration, the tail in particular being much smaller, and with the tailplane "wandering" up and down the fin, as the design continually changed. The department that I joined was small but expanding, and was responsible for the theoretical design calculations for all mechanical systems such as hydraulics, cabin systems, de-icing, and anti-icing, fuel supply, etc. We shared a small area in the open-plan design office with the electrical engineers with whom we worked closely, but we had little contact with other technical departments or the general drawing office, which was in another part of the building. Maybe this was because we were not really involved with design detail at this stage, but there was a general practice at Handley Page of channelling our results to the Chief Designer, and the heads of the other departments, via the head of our own department. This was a system which contrasted dramatically with my experience at Avro.

'Compared to the stress and aerodynamic departments at Handley Page, our calculations did not involve any "higher mathematics". Even differential equations were very rare, but the range of environmental conditions which we had to investigate was vast, especially for the anti-icing systems. Endless computations of complex arithmetical relationships had to be carried out, and the discovery of a simple mistake could mean the scrapping of work which might have taken a month or two to complete. We didn't have the luxury of computers, as they didn't arrive in the industry until the late 'fifties, but the more favoured departments had electronic calculators, each one being about the size of a typewriter. We had hand-wound mechanical versions, rather like old-fashioned cash registers, and they always jammed if one tried to work too quickly. Thanks to Handley Page's "economical" ways, even pencils were rationed to one per month, so if one had a heavy spell of writing, one had to go begging to other people who hadn't used up their rations!

'Our main difficulty was that there was virtually no relevant input data to feed into our calculations, and whereas work was being done at the RAE and elsewhere into the radically new aerodynamic and structural aspects of the design, nothing was being fed into our side of things, or at least some work was being done, but tended to appear only after we had finished! This was especially true of icing work which depended crucially on the proportion of water droplets in an icing cloud which would be caught on the wing or deflected around it. That required detailed mapping of the streamlines around the nose of the aerofoil sections, and the only highly theoretical plots which had been made, in the USA, were for aerofoils that were most unlike the Victor's wing. All we could do was modify the results by factors which we hoped would be realistic. At least we knew that nobody else knew any better. The figures for the actual icing conditions were a little more reliable, but still subject to annual changes. They came from NACA (the predecessor to NASA), who had an ageing C-46 which spent each icing season plodding around, flying into freezing clouds, with a variety of weird instruments sticking out of the windows to measure things like the total water content in each cubic metre of air. When we had spent a year doing our complicated step-by-step "catch and heat" calculations, NACA would issue the next annual report, saying that last year's was wrong, so we had to start all over again!

'Another area which caused us headaches was the design of jet pumps to mix high-pressure air, bled from the engine compressors, which was too hot to pass directly through the light alloy wing structure, with cold ram air, in order to achieve the maximum usable air temperature while still delivering a high enough pressure to force the air through the heat exchange passages in the wing and tail leading edges. Although railway engine designers had been using the same principle for the better part of a century, there was no reliable theory for the mixing of air streams in the kind of proportions necessary to achieve the pressure performance that we needed. We adapted the few theoretical analyses that we could find, and pounced upon the odd wartime German paper that came through from the post-war translators, but the results, which had to be turned into some massive pieces of hardware, were based upon guesswork to an even greater extent than our usual work. Ironically, just after all this work was complete and the detailed design finalized, a classic paper on the subject was published, and although I was working for Avro by that time, I was able to check that our answers had been pretty accurate.

'I've described this work in some detail because the same things were going on at Avro at the same time, and when I joined them I found that very similar conclusions and guesses had been made there. It was interesting to have worked on the Victor during the "paper stage", and then the Vulcan, when the theory was being put into practice. One question did arise concerning the Victor, which didn't affect the Vulcan, and that was heat loss from the fuel during long flights at high altitude, which might cause the fuel to freeze or at least turn "waxy". The Vulcan's tanks were separate items within the deep wing structure, whereas the Victor's were integral, with the inner metal skin separated from the outer one only by stringers and heavy spar booms at the corners of each span-wise bay. The latter feature meant that as well as encountering heat flow directly from one skin to the other, some would flow along the inner skin to the conductive boom. A rather unusual adaptation of some standard school physics was needed to solve the problem, and a further surprising extension of my calculations was used years later, when we were trying to establish the fuel temperature variations through day and night, for the Avro 730 supersonic reconnaissance bomber, for which the skin temperature was expected to be around 225 degrees Celsius. In this design the fuel was to be the heat sink for all cooling purposes. The same system was later used in the Concorde.

'Towards the end of 1951 I was getting tired of Handley Page, and I needed some practical experience away from a desk, so I joined the test section of Fairey's missile division at Heston. They were developing the beam-riding Blue Sky missile at the time, and I quickly determined that missile work, especially trials, would not be much fun, so after a few months I was looking for a way out. In September of the same year I saw the Avro 698 prototype performing at Farnborough, never imagining that within three months I would be part of the Vulcan design team. I attended a lecture at the RAeS in London, presented by Dr. Still, the Technical Director of Teddington Controls, who were to supply much of the control equipment for the V-Bomber hot air systems. At the lecture I met a former colleague from Handley Page, who had joined Avro a couple of years previously. He was about to leave for Canada, and after introducing me to Avro's Chief Designer and the head of his own department, he virtually left me his job to step into.

'It's probably worth describing the design organization at Avro, as it was somewhat unusual for a British company. They had adopted a more American practice, with an individual Project Designer for each type of aircraft, all

Below: *The Vulcan engine test rig at Woodford. (British Aerospace)*

reporting to the Chief Designer, as did the heads of the separate technical departments, these being Stress, Aerodynamics, which in-cluded New Projects, Weight Control, and the Drawing Office itself. The job of each Project Designer was to push through his machine, regardless of the efforts of the other Project Designers, and this form of organization ensured that one man at least would be committed to the success of each project, ensuring that maximum effort was provided by every department that worked for him. Compared to Handley Page, the Drawing Office was enormous, as was the whole Avro organization, especially the production side. There was an old saying that when it was foggy outside, and it often was around Manchester, the far end of the Drawing Office was pretty hazy too! Each project was allocated a numberof Drawing Office sections to carry out all the detail design, and only the Project Designer could issue instructions to them, and he had six Project Engineers to do the necessary work.

'The group which I joined at Avro had grown up during the post-war period, and expanded with the Vulcan design requirements, but unlike my department at Handley Page, it had remained as a group of individual specialists, each reporting to the Chief Designer, in parallel with the Project Designers and heads of the major technical departments. We were called "specialists" but we were much less so than the people in the Stress and Aerodynamic offices. Our position was rather odd in that we had direct access to "the top", but we couldn't actually instruct any department to do anything without the authority of the Project Designers. Because the final assembly, test flying and work on the aircraft was done at Woodford, we travelled between there and the main offices at Chadderton, roughly fifteen miles away, several times each week. Because we were involved with the cabin and control system, we dealt directly with the test pilots and flight crews. The only person we didn't talk to was Sir Roy Dobson himself, although we did sit in on post-flight inquests which he chaired. With all of the other directors we were on first-name terms, with the people who had produced thousands of Lancasters.

'During 1954, the head of my department left for Woodford, to take charge of a new department that would produce our own control equipment, replacing the items previously supplied by companies such as Normalair and Teddington, as their supplies were often underdeveloped, and delivered late. I then took charge of the Systems group, essentially a bunch of individuals, as we didn't actually call ourselves a Department as such. Throughout the time I spent with Avro, from December 1952 to December 1960, the Vulcan was only one of several projects that we were working on simultaneously, and we were involved in every stage of development from initial project studies to sorting out problems in service, as nobody else within the company had a detailed knowledge of our systems. Before my arrival, the company had started a practice of writing simple descriptions of each system, describing the design and operation for the benefit of our Senior Designers, inspection staff, pilots, flight test crews, and anyone else who needed to understand. We called them "Children's Guides" but they also helped us to understand better what we were doing, and they were sufficiently well written to be used by the Technical Publications Department as the basis for Operating Manuals for the type.

'Apart from the very open form of organization, and the direct personal friendship at all levels, there were other noticeable differences between Avro and Handley Page. At the latter company, design had the upper hand over production, and no matter how complex or difficult the structural or detail design might be, the production side had to find a way of making it. At Avro, however, production was dominant, and if some feature was judged to be too difficult to produce easily or economically, it was simply redesigned. This resulted in more simple, and therefore generally more reliable and easily maintained, machines, and whenever we found ourselves thinking in too complicated a way, we'd say that it was becoming a "Handley Page design", and then reconsider the subject in an effort to simplify it. At the same time as trying to keep design simple and aiming to use established production methods, the Avro production "machine" was capable of thinking big, in a way that Handley Page never was. If a major alteration was found to be necessary, such as the Vulcan's extended and kinked leading edges, a modified production facility would be set up without delay, and massive jigs would often appear in the shops every few weeks.

'When I joined Avro, the Vulcan prototype VX770 had been flying for about three months. It was without most of the systems with which I was concerned. There was a hydraulics system for the undercarriage and bomb doors, electrical power for the airbrakes and the electro-hydraulic powered flying controls, but the cabin was unpressurized and had only a rudimentary ventilation system. The aircraft was a long way from being fitted with production-standard engines, but even then the engine bays were large enough to accommodate the ultimate Olympus variants. Handley Page of course had to redesign and enlarge the entire Victor centre section when they changed to Conway engines. Also when I joined, Avro was working on the 720 rocket-propelled fighter, early schemes for the Atlantic, an airliner derivative of the Vulcan, Shackleton developments leading to the Mark 3, and the clearing of the last of six Ashton high-altitude research machines for delivery. The main activities in 1953 were the testing of hot air systems on ground rigs, analyzing flight results on the first prototype's flying controls, and preparing for the fitting and operation of the fully equipped and pressurized second prototype which flew in time for the Farnborough show in September, but wasn't pressurized until the following year.

'The contracts for the V-Bombers called for all mechanical systems to be tested on realistic ground rigs before they were operated in flight. Before the first flight, the hydraulic system had to be tested with all components and pipework in their correct dimensional positions. A separate powerplant and engine intake rig was set up in a building behind the flight sheds. This had the wing root intake set at the correct height and angle above the ground.

Right: *A Vulcan B.1 at RAF Gaydon in 1958, illustrating the unpainted (silver) undercarriage units and the small air intake between the main intake splitter plate and the fuselage. In the background is an interesting mix of Canberras and a Valetta. (via R. Pocock)*

The rig simulating the hot air system which would feed the cabin and icing systems caused large problems. A source of air at a temperature and pressure corresponding to that of a jet engine compressor was not available, and a supply had been devised from standard ground-type compressors and storage vessels, with heat from combustion heaters. These were specified to burn with a clean flame so that their output, when mixed with the main airflow, would not contaminate the aircraft equipment. The ducting was supported on steel framework in the exact configuration of the aircraft system, with a used boiler of the correct volume, to represent the cabin. When the rig was started up, control of the flow and heat inputs seemed to be excessively tricky, and required the entire test department staff, standing at different valves and regulators around the system, frantically twiddling them in an attempt to get stable operation. After a few hours of this, without any useful results, the electro-pneumatic controllers started to misbehave, and they were found to be clogged with soot and corrosion from the supposedly clean burners. The whole concept of the rig was seen to be a disaster, but the difficulty was solved by the quick and forceful decision made by the Chief Designer, who ordered a complete ducting system to be removed from the powerplant test house. It

was laid beneath the engine intake, and connected to the engine compressor. With this realistic supply we began to get usable results for temperate conditions, although we were unable to simulate the maximum engine output temperatures. The engine test crew controlled the powerplant from inside their specially designed soundproof control room, but the mechanical test people had to stand in the open, below the engine bay, wearing what were obviously rather inadequate ear protectors to protect them from the terrific noise.

'The pressure cabins were built at Chadderton, and in their boiler-like form, with a blanking plate over the pilot's canopy, they were pressure tested to 1.5 times their maximum operating differential of 8psi, and leak tested to a schedule of pressure against time. Following the problems with the de Havilland Comet which occurred at the same time, structural testing to the point of failure was carried out in water tanks, in order to avoid the explosive effects of the rupture of an air-filled cabin, but obviously this could not be done with usable cabins, and in any case we hardly expected a failure at what was a normal proof pressure by industrial standards. All the same, the area at Chadderton where the tests were done, was roped off to keep bystanders away, and the inspector making the test had a heavy armoured screen to stand behind. The cabin of the first prototype had been completed and had flown before I arrived, and I doubt if it was ever pressure tested. The second prototype's cabin was tested, and the next one, for the first production aircraft, surprised us all by blowing up. This is how it happened: the front bulkhead of the cabin was domed, the usual way to carry pressure economically on the end of a cylinder. However, the rear bulkhead was flat because it could not take up space in the nosewheel bay, which was full of equipment. It was strengthened by massive vertical beams which carried the nosewheel leg and operating jacks. When the cabin was pressure tested the support was missing, as the cabin couldn't be tested once it was mated to the fuselage. So a dummy structural bay was bolted to the rear bulkhead to give it the necessary strength. When the prototype cabin was tested, the holes in the two pieces of structure didn't line up very well, and they were opened up and aligned to take the temporary connecting bolts. With the next cabin the holes were again out of line, the bolts were consequently a little slack, and the stiffening effect was inadequate, so the bulkhead blew out. The effect was like a sizable bomb going off, and impressed all concerned, especially the inspector who had only just retreated behind his screen after checking the manometers attached to the bulkhead, which were fundamentally more accurate than the gauges. So in total, one more cabin was completed than the actual number of airframes.

'With the first flights of the second prototype with full pressurization scheduled for early 1954, it was decided that I should go on all of the early flights to take charge of the pressure and air conditioning controls, which were on the panel of the port-side rear crew member. It was evidently thought that if the system misbehaved, I would understand, and know what to do. In case such a failure resulted in cabin pressure being lost at more than 40,000 feet, I had to wear a pressure suit. It was an American-designed, close-fitting, nylon partial pressure suit which pulled tight when required through laces and pneumatic tubes along the arms and legs. Unlike the original American version which had a helmet with opening visor, the British version had a cloth headpiece with a hard leather inner shield, and a fixed visor. Each one was custom-fitted, and all our test crews were provided with one, but the Chief Test Pilot, Roly Falk, refused to wear one, as he felt it would hamper his movements and create a potential danger. To take account of possible decompression, our Bomber Command liaison pilot, Wing Commander C. C. Calder, rode in the second pilot's seat, wearing a pressure suit, and really did little other than wait for an emergency. If a failure had occurred, his suit and my suit would have inflated, and we would have brought the aircraft down to a level where the other three crew would regain consciousness.

'Late in 1953, therefore, I was fitted with my suit at the appropriately named Frankenstein's works in Manchester, and had a trial inflation while seated on the edge of a table. It was shaped to a seated position, and when pressurized it took all the weight off one's arms and legs, and you felt like you were going to float up to the ceiling. I then went to the Institute of Aviation Medicine at Farnborough to experience a proper inflation of the suit in their decompression chamber, where pressure was explosively changed from 8,000 feet to 70,000 feet. I shared the chamber with a representative from an equipment company, who passed out and flopped over, but I couldn't do anything about it as I was held firmly on my chair by my suit.

'After all the preliminary testing, the actual flying seemed quite tame, but it was interesting to be amongst the first people in Britain to fly regularly at 50,000 feet, and near to Mach one. Most of the flights I participated in were around February-March 1954, and after five or six flights it was clear that the system was not going to fail or do anything untoward, so I stopped flying. The usual routine for each flight was to take off from Woodford, climb through what seemed to be a permanent overcast, heading south, and fly straight ahead for about thirty minutes. That would place us over the Isle of Wight. I could see the ground through the small porthole window above the rear crew's bench, when we were well banked over. We would then turn north, flying for an hour until we were over the central Highlands of Scotland, before turning south again, heading back to Lancashire, finally homing in on the voice transmissions from controllers at Woodford, and sometimes with the help of the radar controllers at Manchester Airport.

'The last flight I flew on included the Minister of Supply, the infamous Duncan Sandys, who was permitted to fly the Vulcan himself for a few minutes, making the customary flattering remarks afterwards. The flight was reported in many newspapers and I was listed as part of that crew. One particular feature of each flight was the buffeting which occurred when flying at altitudes in the high 40,000s, at high Mach numbers. It seemed quite gentle to me, just a low frequency shaking like driving along a bumpy road, but of course it led to the extended and drooped wing leading edges, retrofitted to early Vulcans.

'From early 1954 onwards, we were concerned with production machines, of which the first few were used for trials, and I remember XA894 and XA897 in particular, as they were used for cabin systems and anti-icing development. Perhaps it would be helpful if I described the arrangement of the hot-air systems on the Vulcan. These were fed by a tapping at the high-pressure end of each main engine compressor, and were designed for a maximum pressure of around 200psi, and a maximum temperature of 400 degrees Celsius, figures which were unprecedented at that time. The ducting was all stainless steel 0.28 inches thick, which led to some tricky welding problems. Simple things like joints, clamps, sealing rings, took on a great deal of our attention, and the long runs of ducting, typically four inches in diameter, had to be supported from the aircraft structure with flexible steel bellows at the anchor points, to allow for differential expansion of the ducts and structure, with the wide temperature ranges which went through. This is an area which troubles the designers of ground-based pipe systems even today, but we must have got things pretty well right, as I never heard of any major failures in RAF service.

'The ducts in each pair of engine bays ran forward, joined up into one from each side, and met on the rear wall of the nosewheel bay (in each wing root, a branch went off to supply the anti-icing jet pump, and as described for the Victor, each one was a hefty device, about eight inches diameter and six feet long). From the junction, a single duct ran forward along the port side of the nosewheel bay, to the air conditioning pack (consisting of a cold-air expansion turbine, usually called the CAU), heat exchangers (supplied with cooling air from that unobtrusive intake, inboard of the engine intake fence), and control valves. From the pack, the air entered the cabin through a non-return valve on the rear bulkhead (so that the cabin would hold pressure if the ducting or supply failed). Cabin pressure was controlled, as always, by an outlet valve on the front bulkhead (so that leakage from the cabin structure did not affect the control), ventilated the radar in the nose, and finally left through the small grilles low down on the nose. The flow of air to the cabin was far greater than necessary to keep the crew comfortable, because the requirement for cooling the radar and navigational sets was overpowering. These sets were in sealed drums about the same size as a typical dustbin, and what was inside was so secret that we were not allowed to discuss the cooling load, only supply what the Ministry specification called for. Years later, when we did find out what was inside, it confirmed our suspicions: the designers may have known plenty about electronics, but they hadn't a clue about heat, and all our efforts were being devoted to the cooling of a few hot spots, such as sensitive valves placed right above heat-generating components. This was the pre-transistor era, and the valves in this case were of the electronic kind, unlike those mentioned previously!

'The pressure control side of things, manufactured by Normalair, didn't give us any undue trouble, but the flow control side, made by Teddington, turned out to be a major headache, both on technical grounds and unreliability. At the time they were the only suppliers of high-temperature valves, with sliding carbon gates, which were used for shutting off airflows from the engines, and initially for regulating the flows to the different parts of the system. The valves were moved by electric motors, and it was therefore logical for Teddington to develop electrical flow sensing control units, to operate the valves. Unfortunately the controllers were underdeveloped when they were installed in production Vulcans, and I personally felt that they were designed to unrealistic specifications, typical of the time, especially in the case of equipment with which the Ministry was concerned. For example, a requirement for airflow to be controlled at 40lb/min with a tolerance of ±1lb/min led to complicated and unreliable gadgetry. To my way of thinking, it didn't matter if the flow was 40 or 45, as long as it was steady, and I later changed the systems to this standard.

'Our early tests, starting with the rig, showed that the flow controllers were not stable, and could not cope with various aspects of the special requirements that we considered unrealistic, but which the Ministry insisted upon. Teddington kept adding more fiddly units to back up the ones that were misbehaving, without doing much good. At one stage they turned up with yet another gadget, saying that it had got Handley Page out of trouble, and it would do the same for us. Of course, Handley Page was regarded as a major competitor, and during the war it was often said in Avro circles that the company had three enemies: Handley Page, the Ministry and the Germans, in that order! However, having previously worked for Handley Page, I telephoned my old colleagues to enquire how they were getting on with Teddington's new panacea. They said that Teddington had told them that the gadget had worked for Avro, so it would work for them too, just as they had told us. At one stage I visited Teddington's factory, and found that the inspection department, to save themselves undue effort, were leaving ready-signed clearance forms for items that had yet to be tested. That didn't improve my opinion of them, and when their deliveries turned out to be late and unreliable, Avro, in typical ruthless style, virtually took over their test and inspection department with our own people, ensuring that whatever happened to everyone else's orders, the Avro units would be completed on time, and work properly.

'In the end I solved our flow problems by throwing out all the Teddington equipment, except for the shut-off valves for which there were no alternatives, and putting in Normalair controllers of an extremely simple kind, based on the ones which had been used in smaller aircraft since World War Two. One thing which we could not do with the Vulcan was to keep the aircrew comfortable on the ground in hot conditions, although neither could any other military or civil aircraft design at the time. By the time we had reached the Vulcan Mk.2, the operational procedure had changed, making crews spend long periods on board the aircraft on standby, and the heat situation could not be tolerated. The RAF's answer was to put the crews in ventilatedsuits, which were a light nylon overall design, with fine tubes directing conditioned air to evaporate sweat from appropriate areas of the aircrew's bodies. The additional airflow, from idling engines or a ground supply, and the tight temperature control needed (too hot or too cold either cooked or chilled the unfortunate crewman) meant that we had to install a separate conditioning pack, which was somehow squeezed in next to the existing one. This was again a Normalair unit, with a fighter-sized air turbine running it at over 100,000rpm, and we did not have any particular troubles with it. I should add that there was no connection between the fact that I'd worked for Normalair and the way that they took over many of the Vulcan's systems; it was just that they were slightly less unreliable than the other suppliers!

'I cannot recall doing any useful testing of the icing system as installed. All we could check was that the surfaces were being evenly heated, as it would have been impossible to fly in real icing conditions, as the RAE's attempts to find such conditions with an instrumented Valetta had indicated how difficult it would have been, and we couldn't have measured the complicated icing factors anyway. As the extended and drooped leading edges were introduced on the Vulcan Mk.1 and extended further on the Mk.2, our heating passages were getting hacked about and restricted by the changes in internal structure, and there was nothing we could do about it. Airframe icing was becoming less of a concern, and I presented a paper at a Napier icing symposium to show that with the fast-climbing and descending flight profile which the V-Bombers were designed for, they would go through the icing layers in a matter of seconds, so that even with no heating system, the amount of ice picked up would be unimportant. Of course I did not anticipate that in a few years' time virtually all operations would be conducted at low level, but I never heard of any icing problems with the Vulcan.

'I made myself pretty unpopular at one stage by pointing out that years of calculating anti-icing performance, and agonising over the assumptions we had to make, simply resulted in our demanding more bleed air from the engines then we were allowed to take, so all we were able to do was to take as much air as we could and spread it around evenly. Nevertheless, the Ministry insisted that we certify that the system would meet their requirements on paper, as we were still calculating and refining our figures when Avro installed the first computer in the industry. It was about the same size as a bungalow, and we jumped at the chance to have many more points in the icing envelope calculated.

'Of course, the occasional accidents which the Vulcan suffered often affected us on the design side, and such events have only been briefly mentioned in other historical accounts. Aircraft accidents often have a funny side when nobody gets hurt, and the first one we had was like that. One of the prototypes, VX777 was being demonstrated to one of the RAE pilots at Farnborough in 1954, and at the time the early Vulcans were being thrown about in an almost carefree way, and on this

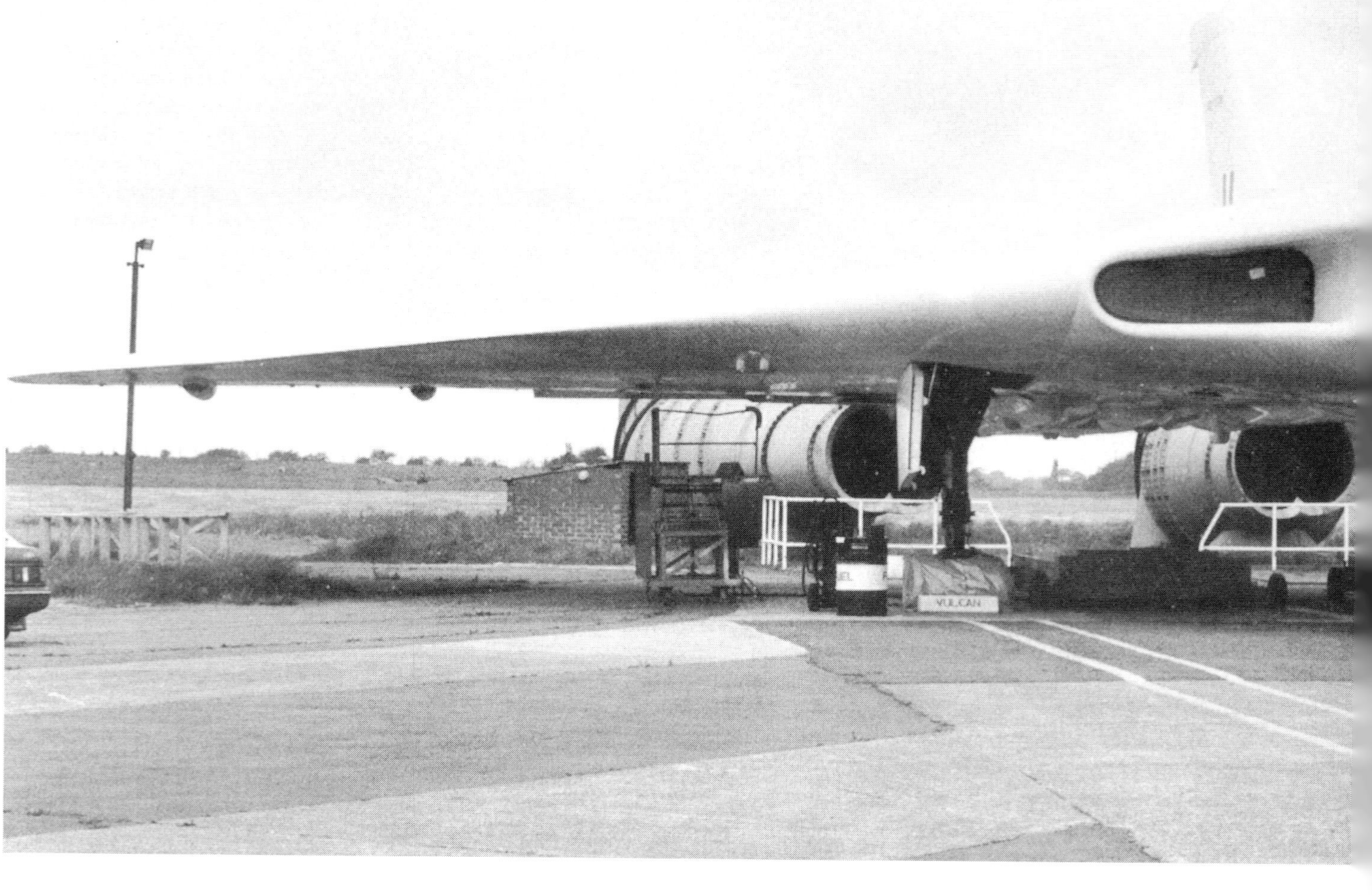

occasion the crew had made a rather snappy yawing manoeuvre, probably a sort of stall turn, as the rudder was locked hard over, but stayed there. At this stage the aircraft didn't have any periscopes, so the pilots could only see the wing leading edges as far as the wingtips, and no further aft. Periscopes were later fitted for navigation and were essential to enable the crew to see what was going on behind them, such as the undercarriage position, bomb doors position, or in this case, whether the fin was still attached. The crew flew VX777 past Farnborough's control tower, and received confirmation that the fin was still there. They then landed, using asymmetric power to counter the jammed rudder, but this meant that the brakes were unable to stop them before the aircraft rolled off the end of the runway onto soft ground, where the undercarriage collapsed. As there was no great danger of a fire, there wasn't any hurry to abandon the aircraft, but the question on the crew's minds was how to actually get out, with the entry door firmly wedged into the ground. Oddly enough the situation had been discussed in our design office a few weeks previously, and it had been concluded that the pilot would have to hold up the canopy while everyone else climbed over the side. The canopy could be jettisoned in flight, and sucked away by the airflow, but there was no way of getting rid of it on the ground, other than by unlocking it and tipping it over the side. The crew were unwilling to do this, feeling that they'd caused enough damage already, so Roly Falk, who was quite tall, held the canopy on his shoulders while everyone got out. After that, explosive jacks were fitted to the canopy for ground jettison. The next job was to raise the aircraft, by digging holes under the wings for lifting jacks, and it was then revealed that the ground had been used by cavalry regiments for a century or so of army occupation, and they were digging into feet-deep layers of manure! When the Vulcan was finally lifted, the undercarriage was fixed down with structural steel, and VX777 was flown back to Woodford.

'The cause of the rudder failure was a fine example of how deadly tiny details can be. The power controls were all Boulton Paul electro-hydraulic units, in which an electric motor drove a swashplate pump (one with an angled driving block which could be swung in either direction to give flow either way) to a jack which moved the surface. The pilot's control moved the swashplate of each unit, and for the rudder there was a standby unit, which idled while the normal unit did the work, with a spring strut arrangement to keep the standby out of action until the normal unit stopped. On the wing units, four of which operated elevators, and four on the ailerons (the Mk.2 changing to elevons), the philosophy was that if one stopped, there would still be three to keep going, and even two failures left half power available. In the case of the VX777 accident, the rudder had been kicked over so hard that the spring in the telescopic strut had expanded more than was intended, so that it jammed inside its tube. A simple problem really, and one which didn't take much of a modification to prevent it from happening again.

'The next accident which affected us was the infamous Heathrow tragedy, at the end of a very successful tour of Australia and New Zealand, with Air Marshal Harry

Left: *XM603 resplendent in its original anti-flash white colours at Woodford in 1992. The aircraft has been restored almost to flying condition, and with further work the aircraft could undoubtedly fly again. However, despite the fact that the aircraft belongs to BAE Systems and resides at the Vulcan's birthplace (where lots of local expertise still exists), there has been no effort to get the aircraft back into the air. It is sad to see how a major aerospace company can seemingly ignore its past achievements. (via British Aerospace)*

Broadhurst as second pilot. There was no technical failure of the aircraft this time, but the fact that the pilots were able to eject and the rear crew could not led to a media and political outcry about ejection seats for navigators and other crew, creating a great deal of design investigation for us. The basic cause of the crash was as old as flying itself: We must land at place A because the welcoming VIPs and brass bands are there, never mind the weather, even though our alternative place B is basking in sunshine. The inquiry into the affair was revealing; it was conducted by an electronics pundit, and the Vulcan's final flight path was a perfect example of divergent oscillation, due to the time lag between the GCA controller and the pilot. You could have reproduced it exactly on a cathode ray tube, with appropriate time resistances for the two participants. The controller hadn't handled a fast jet before, and Podge Howard, the pilot, had not used civilian GCA before. The delay in the pilot's response to the controller's instructions, and the delay in the controller following the radar plot, led to the flight path swinging further and further above and below the correct one, until the final low point caused the aircraft to hit the ground, pushing the undercarriage through the wing's flying controls. When we came to investigate the fitting of rear crew ejection seats, the problems became quickly apparent. Apart from having to remove virtually the complete top of the pressure cabin, which would have been a structural nightmare, there was no way that we could get the rear crews out safely. As they sat facing aft, the seats would come out on a forward trajectory, and probably hit the tail, which the pilots' seats would probably clear. To enable the rear seats to fire on a rearward trajectory meant a complicated drill of turning one round at a time, because of the cramped width, and the procedure would take so long, they would never get out in time at low level. At high altitude there was no problem in getting out by the normal crew entry door, as designed. Although Martin-Baker did later offer a suitable escape system, it was never adopted, probably because the huge expense was felt to be wasteful, for an aircraft that wouldn't be in service all that long, never realizing just how long the Vulcan's service career would be.

'Once the RAF got their hands on the Vulcan, they started touring all around the world, and one aircraft, XA908, suffered a major electrical failure while flying over Canada. The Vulcan Mk.1s had DC electrical systems with batteries to supply reserve power. The machine suffered a progressive generator failure in which the load cascaded in the main distribution system so that an initial failure of one generator led to all four cutting out. Following the accident, all Mk.1s were modified, including our test aircraft at Woodford, but before our last aircraft (XA891) was modified, it suffered the same fate, soon after taking off from Woodford. Fortunately our Chief Test Pilot, Jimmy Harrison, and his crew were able to aim for open countryside and bale out close to Hull. Jimmy later remarked that he hadn't previously realized what a beautiful machine the Vulcan was until he saw it from above, presumably after he had got rid of the ejection seat face blind, and disengaged from his seat.

'The last Vulcan accident for which we provided a design explanation, although there was no fault with the aircraft as such, was the crash of the 698 prototype, VX770, at Syerston in 1958. Our old friend had been passed to Rolls-Royce at Hucknall for engine test work, and it was being flown at a Battle of Britain display by a Rolls-Royce crew, when it broke up during a low flypast. The visual evidence was primarily drawn from an amateur 16mm cine film, from which the famous picture featured in many books and articles was taken. We took the film to Chadderton and ran it through many times, but major changes took place between frames, and the complete disintegration took place over no more than four or five frames. However, we had some solid technical evidence to work on. The accelerometer on the normal flight panel showed the maximum "g" which had been applied, and we were also able to read the airspeed at which electrical power was cut off from the artificial feel units, and we quickly concluded that the combination was outside the aircraft's safe flight envelope. Once power flying controls were introduced, pilots had to be given some sort of artificial feel, pushing against springs in effect, to stop them from breaking the aeroplanes. The Vulcan's feel units were "q" feel, in which the leverage against the spring increased in proportion to the pitot pressure, and was thus the square of the speed, which was the way manual control forces normally behaved. The actual mechanism was a lever and roller moving in a curved slot, known as the "banana lever", shifted by an electric motor responding to a signal from a pitot pressure capsule, as in an airspeed indicator. So the position at which the levers stopped, when the aircraft disintegrated, gave us the speed at which it happened.

'Power controls and the associated technology were taken out of my care early in 1956, but my group was still involved with cooling the controls and everything else too. On the Mk.1, the Boulton Paul units were inside the wing, which was relatively deep all the way along, and one unit was positioned in front of each section of control surface. Each had a small NACA-type intake in the lower wing surface ahead of it, and the outlet air spilled into the wing interior, escaping through gaps around the control surfaces. With the Mk.2, the two inboard units on each side were the same, but the new outer wing was too thin for the outboard units to fit inside, so they were mounted underneath the wing, in long blister fairings. There was no fundamental difference from our point of view, and as we were busy with other work, we let the drawing office get on with the new installation, without paying attention to what they were really doing. So on the Mk.2's first flight, these outboard control units overheated drastically, and the drawing office, backed up by the Project Designer's people, quickly descended upon us to find out what we had allowed them to do wrong! I had a look at the drawings and pointed out that the units were in sealed fairings with air intakes, which they had faithfully copied, but there was no outlet, because there had been no obvious one before, so how could they expect air to go in and around the power unit, if it could not get out? There was a great fuss about needing to fly the next day, so I said that they simply needed a backwards-facing hole, and the easiest way to get one would be to cut the back end of the fairing blisters. A quick guesstimation of how forward to cut, and off they went. The cooling was adequate thereafter, and that is why, if you look at the Mk.2's control blisters, you'll see that they are cut off a few inches short of the trailing edge, even though the riveted flanges continue all the way. Designing with a hacksaw was one of the things that the great Roy Chadwick was noted for, so I felt like I was following a great tradition.

'My last flight in a Vulcan was in the first Mk.2, as I claimed a flight every now and then, just to see how things were feeling inside the aircraft, while in flight. This flight was also the only one where I rode in the second pilot's seat, and was given a chance to handle the machine at altitude, not doing anything fancy, just gentle turns and speed variations. However, it was a notable flight, as Jimmy Harrison did a beat-up over Woodford, culminating in a climbing roll, so I was able to experience one of the famous Vulcan manoeuvres which had been a feature of almost every display up until that time. It was just as well that I did have a good forward view, as if I'd been in the back I wouldn't have known that we were doing anything more than a gentle turn. The trick of doing these rolls was to keep the manoeuvre barrelled just enough to keep a little over 1g all the way around. I called in at Woodford during 1984 in connection with some work I was doing at the time, and in the reception hall I met a member of the flight shed staff from late 'fifties, and without. introduction he immediately recognized me, and recalled the day when Jimmy Harrison had rolled me in the Mk.2. Eventually the RAF asked Avro to stop rolling the Vulcan, as some service pilots were trying it, but hadn't quite got the knack, so the airframes were in danger of being overstressed. One funny incident was when Jimmy visited Finningley for some reason, departed with the usual beat-up and roll, only to return to Woodford to find a letter from Bomber Command asking him not to do it anymore. But the letter had arrived after he'd left!

'Navigation on these test flights had some amusing moments too. Having described the typical flight plan of the early tests, I recall that the later flights tended to amble around the coastline, as even with extensive weather systems and low-level cloud, there was normally some recognizable part of the coastline visible. If we could only see a small area of the ground, the first thing we checked was the colour of the soil, which tended to establish the region we were flying over pretty well, with red soil in Devon, chalky soil in Sussex, black in the Fenlands, and so on. If an aerodrome was visible the type of aircraft on it gave us a second clue, the RAF having a huge variety of aircraft in those days. One day, though, the crew had been flying on a steady course for some time, while taking performance measurements that required steady conditions. We were below 40,000 feet when a flight of Meteors shot past, and one of the pilots commented that he'd never seen Meteors carrying red, yellow and black roundels before. It turned out that we were over Belgium! After that, the first visual check we made was to see which side of the road the cars were driving on!

'In the summer of 1958 I attended a meeting at White Waltham where we discussed the whole question of escape from the Vulcan's cabin. To start with, there was a move to co-ordinate the various connections that the crews, pilots in particular, had to make on getting into their seats, and therefore had to break on leaving to bale out, such as intercom, oxygen, suit air and so on. Each item had been developed by small departments in the Ministry, and a crew member had many separate pipes and plugs to undo every time he got out of the aircraft. Eventually two companies were given contracts to do what the Ministry apparently could not, to bring all the systems to a common point, and develop a multi-way connector, so the crew member had only one fitting to connect. M. L. Aviation did the job for bomber aircraft, and they also had a contract to improve escape systems generally, so they built a full-size mock-up of the cabin, with no skin so that one could see what was going on inside. In theory, every piece of equipment, or bracket on which one could get snagged, was in place. We gave them all the drawings and they gathered equipment from various sources, but I doubt if every item could have been fitted. However, a meeting was set up at White Waltham, with myself and a deputy from Avro, representatives from the Ministry, the Air Staff, Institute of Aviation Medicine, and so on, plus an RAF crew from Waddington to act as guinea pigs in the cabin. The mock-up cabin was in a large room, with everyone seated on benches either side. It was an incredibly hot day, and we sweated away until M. L. brought in an air-conditioning van they had built, and poked a large hose through the room's window to provide cooling air. It made so much noise that nobody could hear what was being said, so we opted to go back to the heat. The crew of, course, played up and pretended to be as clumsy and awkward as possible, so it was a lengthy performance. When it came to looking at belly landings, the pilots climbed over the side, having disposed of the canopy, but the rear crew pointed out that the narrow gap between the ejection seats would delay their escape. They sugggested that they should have a switch to blow the pilots' seats out, but the pilots were obviously not very enthusiastic about the rear crew having the power to shoot them out, if they had a disagreement, or, more seriously, trigger the switch by mistake. This was the tone of the meeting, and it continued throughout the day, finally ending at about seven, with no real conclusions having been reached.

'I left Avro at the end of 1960 to try my luck in general industry, and it was the only company that I was ever really sorry to leave. The last year or so had been darkened by the shadows of missiles. Avro set up their missile division at Woodford, and introduced a bunch of rather high-toned individuals from Farnborough and places like that. Their attitude was that their work was far beyond anything that we had being doing, and our old-fashioned ideas about sound engineering didn't really apply to missiles. However unprecedented the performance we were designing for, we always had been very careful to stick to sound principles of reliable engineering. The missile work was regarded as being so advanced and secret that the service requirements couldn't be discussed with us, and we just had to provide the airflows or whatever else was called for, and not ask any questions. It reminded me of the radar cans mentioned earlier, and we always thought of the Vulcan as "our" aeroplane. In my final year we were talking to Douglas people about the system needed for the Skybolt installation, and I found them to be perfectly reasonable people to deal with. Bet you never knew designing aircraft and their systems could be so much fun!'

7. Training and Flying

Flight Lieutenant Peter Thompson, DFC, RAF (ret'd), joined the RAF in August 1937 as an Aircraft Apprentice at Cranwell, training to be an instrument maker. With the outbreak of war, he was posted to No. 613 Squadron at Odiham in January 1940. Having joined the RAF to fly, he applied for aircrew training and during 1941 he was accepted, moving to Canada to fly Tiger Moths and Oxfords. Back to the UK in 1943, he flew Wellingtons, Halifaxes and Lancasters, moving to No. 12 Squadron at Wickenby. After the war he moved on to Lincolns, Meteor conversion and Canberras. By 1956 he had been flying for fourteen years, and was Flight Commander on No. 82 Squadron at Wyton, having been with them for five years. On learning that he was to be posted to a ground tour, he asked what other postings were available. There was a possibility of becoming a captain on a Valiant squadron, but Peter Thompson suggested that he would rather wait until the Vulcan came along. Consequently, as the Vulcan was not yet in regular service, he was posted to No. 230 OCU as an instructor on the Vulcan simulator, arriving at Waddington in July 1956. He continues his story:

'We had no Vulcans at the time, just an Anson and a couple of Canberras for continuation training; the Anson was mainly used for ferrying crews between Waddington and Boscombe Down, where two Vulcans (XA895 and XA897) were completing service acceptance and intensive flying trials. The simulator was basically an analogue computer, driven by

compressed air and electrical power. It used to take nearly two hours to set up the simulator each day. My first Vulcan flight was in XA895 on December 31st 1956 with the CO of 230 OCU, as on that day we had to return the aircraft to Boscombe Down, after it had been on loan to us. It was only a forty-minute flight, but for me it was well worth waiting for. By January 1957 we had two aircraft (XA895 and XA898) and the flying instructors were able to work out a flying sequence ready for the first conversion courses. I had my first night flight on January 23rd, a cross-country flight to Gibraltar and return, non-stop, in XA895, which took us seven hours and fifteen minutes.

'In those days there was an enormous amount of interest in the Vulcan, lots of visits by high ranking officers, and lots of displays to be given. In August 1957 I introduced Air Chief Marshal Sir Harry Broadhurst to the simulator, Major General Blanchard from the USAF, and Air Vice-Marshal Walker too, who had no problems, even with just one arm. We formed crews for the various displays, and in May 1957 I flew to Honington in XA895 for a static and flying display for the Philippine Air Force Chief. On the return flight, we were cruising at 40,000 feet, up in the sunshine, flying manually as we had no autopilots at that time. The captain, Flight Lieutenant Norris, suddenly said "how about a roll?" I was all for it, so he just pulled the nose up slightly, moved the stick to one side, a little rudder and round we went, maintaining the same "g" loading all the way around. Rolling back the other way, someone in the back commented that something odd was going on, as the sun was going round and round! With only two small portholes, the rear crew's visibility was virtually non-existent, and by maintaining the same "g" loading right through the roll, they didn't know we'd even done it. Visibility wasn't much better for the pilot, the view forward was fairly narrow, and one could see nothing of the wings or the rest of the aircraft, and one just hoped it was following along behind the front end!

'Approaching the aircraft on the ground could be a little overwhelming at first, with such a huge wing area, lots of wheels and so on. Once in the cockpit it was much like any other aircraft, but one had to remember how far back the wheels were when taxiing, and that the cockpit was about eighteen feet above the ground. 1957 and 1959 were very busy, building up the crews. The early Olympus engines only had a life of about twenty hours before they had to be checked or replaced. I remember one student on his first Vulcan solo, losing

***Below:** Vulcan B.2s at Richmond, Sydney, Australia, 27 November 1962. XH556 on the left and XL392 right. (via P. Thompson)*

one engine on take-off, followed by the adjacent engine, as some turbine blades had been shed, these going through to the other engine. However, he made a safe landing, and in the hangar afterwards the engineers opened the engine bay doors, and I remember the sound of all the turbine blades falling onto the floor.

'In 1959 I went through the flying course myself, and was posted to 617 Squadron at Scampton. One of my early tasks was to practice formation flying for the 1959 SBAC show. That was very interesting, and in October we went to New Zealand, to open the new airport at Wellington. I was a "spare" captain for the trip, and received instruction to get out to Butterworth, in Malaysia. The Vulcans arrived accompanied by a Britannia, and I was required to fly XH502 to Darwin, and then to New Zealand, and we made a number of flights out there during our stay. I was amazed at the interest shown in the aircraft by everyone. We flew at 500 feet over most of the cities, towns and schools, and all the schoolchildren were given time off to stand outside and wave. At many of the smaller airfields we were asked to make approaches. We received many letters thanking us for our displays. XH498 was the display Vulcan for the official airport opening day. The runway there was roughly twenty feet above the surrounding water at the approach end, and on the day of the airport opening, there was a gusty wind blowing over the airfield, and during the Vulcan's final approach, there was a great gust of wind which tipped the aircraft to port, causing the aircraft to tip over, the port undercarriage leg catching the rocks at the end of the runway, slamming back, and puncturing a wing fuel tank. The wing scraped along the runway, but the pilot was able to apply full power and get the aircraft away. It had all the makings of a major tragedy, but back at our temporary base at Ohakea, the Vulcan landed safely, holding the aircraft level until the wing dropped and the Vulcan stopped on the grass beside the runway. The canopy was jettisoned before landing, in case the other two

Left: Dramatic night shot of three Vulcan B.1s at Ohakea, New Zealand. (RNZAF)

landing gear legs collapsed on landing, causing the crew to climb out from above, although this didn't happen, and the Vulcan was later repaired.

'Back on 617 Squadron, our training continued, and we again returned to the SBAC show, this time to demonstrate operational stream take-offs. The best time achieved for this was one minute forty-seven seconds, for all four aircraft to get airborne. We took part in Quick Reaction Alert duties too, which required us to remain in full flying kit for twenty-four hours, sleeping in caravans on the airfield, with four aircraft on the ORP at the end of the runway. When the alert sounded we would race to the aircraft, the crew chief would have already pressed the buttons to start the engines, and as soon as the crews were inside and the door was closed, the throttles were opened for immediate take-off, all the pre-take-off checks having been done earlier in the day. Once the gear was retracted and we were climbing away, we had time to strap in! The idea was to get our aircraft airborne within four minutes, the time it would have taken for an enemy ICBM to reach the UK after being detected. The alert could always be cancelled at any time before we would enter enemy territory, and of course it always was. If the alert was cancelled after we got airborne, we still had to fly a cross-country exercise to reduce our fuel to landing weight.

'In September 1960 I heard of an in-flight refuelling exercise, and when the details were released my crew was to be the back-up crew in an attempt to fly non-stop to Australia. My first practice at in-flight refuelling was in a Valiant, and after flying the Vulcan, with its fighter-type handling, the Valiant seemed more like a ten-ton truck. Back on the Squadron we had received two Vulcan B.1As (XH500 and XH505) with in-flight refuelling gear. Our conversion to the B.1A consisted of a one hour and forty minute flight, which usually included the acceptance air test. We flew a huge number of "dry" refuelling contacts, and the Vulcan's refuelling probe had a weak point built in, so that if the drogue's clamps wouldn't release, the probe tip would shear off, enabling the Vulcan to pull away, without damaging the whole installation, a dangerous prospect with the Vulcan's intakes nearby. Sure enough, on breaking contact at one stage, the probe broke off and blew out both starboard engines. Most of these practice runs were flown over the North Sea, and by January 1961 we were fully solo, able to make day or night refuelling contacts. The first overseas "tankex" was to Nairobi, an eight and a half hour flight each way. Another "tankex" on April 12th saw us fly out from the UK to overhead Akrotiri, where we took on 44,000lb of fuel before flying back non-stop. We flew as far as Gan in the Indian Ocean, on May 6th, and we landed there, had a day to recover, and then made the return flight to Scampton.

'On June 20th 1961 the big day came, and the primary crew set off from London Airport, arriving in Sydney after the non-stop flight, twenty hours, three minutes and seventeen seconds later, a magnificent achievement by everyone concerned. We were disappointed that as the reserve crew we didn't make the trip, but we were pleased that it had been done. We converted to Vulcan B.2s not long afterwards, so we didn't do any more big exercises of that nature. September 1961 saw us convert to the Vulcan B.2, a magnificent machine, and from then until April 1962 we carried out training to maintain our classification status, which included "Western Ranger" flights to Offut AFB via Goose Bay, and "Lone Ranger" flights to Nairobi via Luqa in Malta. We then started on Blue Steel trials.

'Training was quite intensive, and almost every sortie was a Blue Steel profile. The missile was very accurate, regularly landing within 100 yards of the target during trials in Australia. Nine out of the first ten shots were completely successful. The only real snag was the HTP used with kerosene to fuel the Stentor engine. It was very dangerous stuff, and with one speck of dust it would explode. So when we carried a live weapon, the most frequently examined instrument in the aircraft was a gauge to measure the temperature of the HTP in the missile. The drill was that if the temperature started to rise within five minutes of the base, return immediately, and if you were further away, head to the sea, and abandon the aircraft. Luckily it never happened. When a weapon was being fuelled, a fire tender was always present. In June/July 1963 we were the only Blue Steel select star crew in Bomber Command, so we were chosen to ferry a Blue Steel missile out to Australia for firing. The idea was that if the missile could be kept clean and serviceable on the way out, it would save a great deal of time in preparation when it arrived. We carried our crew chief with us on the trip, and a second crew chief to look after the missile. The Blue Steel we ferried out there was fired over Woomera just five days after we handed it over.'

Below: *Vulcan XH498 at Ohakea, New Zealand, after making a successful landing in October 1959. The port main undercarriage had been severely damaged during an undershoot of the runway at Wellington Airport. (RNZAF)*

***Above:** Three Vulcans (XH556, XL319 and XL392) escorted by RAAF Sabres during a flypast at the opening ceremony of the 1962 British Empire and Commonwealth Games in Perth. (Denis O'Brien)*

Report on Blue Ranger 4902 28th June, 1963 – 17 July, 1963

Aircraft: XM570 of No 27 Squadron. Missile B.S.A.R. 065
Crew:
Captain Flt. Lt. P. F. Thompson D. F. C. No. 617 Squadron
Co-pilot Fg. Off. J. M. McCracken No. 617 Squadron
Nav. Plotter Flt. Lt. J. G. Talliss No. 617 Squadron
Nav. Radar Flt. Lt. P. F. Steele No. 617 Squadron
A.E.O. Flt. Lt. R. J. Swift No. 617 Squadron
Crew Chief (A/C) Chief Technician Gaukroger No. 27 Squadron
Crew Chief (Missile) Chief Technician D.I. Rosser No. 617 Squadron.

1. The object of the flight was to ferry Blue Steel missile No. 065 from Royal Air Force Scampton to No. 4 J.S.T.U. at Edinburgh Field, South Australia.
2. The route to be followed was Scampton – El Adem (N/S) – Khormaksar (N/S) – Gan (N/S) – Butterworth (2 N/S) – Darwin (N/S) – Edinburgh Field. The return flight would be over the same route in reverse with the two night stops at Khormaksar.
3. Timing. The flight was due to leave Scampton at 0900Z on 28th June, arrive Edinburgh Field on 4th July, leave Edinburgh Field at 0030Z on 11th July, 1963 and arrive back at Scampton on 17th July.
4. For the purpose of this report the flight has been split up into sorties, each sortie with its own report as follows:-
5. *Sortie No. 1 Scampton – El Adem*

Transport	0745 local	E.T.D. 280900Z
Met.	0755 "	A.T.D. 280917Z
Meals	0800 "	A.T.A. 281325Z
At Aircraft	0845 "	

Local time Z+1

Take-off from Scampton was made in drizzle and low cloud. On the climb out at 10000ft. the refrigeration pack stopped but was reset immediately and gave no further trouble throughout the flight. Soon after this the S.T.R. 18 began to stick on transmit, but it was decided to continue the sortie and rectify the fault, at the next stop. At approx. 1130Z the starboard centre windscreen started to crack on its inner surface, the crack eventually extending to two thirds of the distance across the windscreen. After an uneventful flight across France except for the usual difficulty in contacting and understanding the French radar services, Malta control was contacted at 1200Z, and then El Adem on U.H.F. at a distance of 220 miles. A let down was started at 100 n.m. range straight down into the circuit and a landing made at 1325Z. The temperature at El Adem was +33°C. After closing down a ladder was not immediately available for the crew chief to enter the bomb bay and close the freon lines to the missile, therefore the freon drained down into the missile and was lost to atmosphere on the next day's servicing. It was decided that on subsequent sorties the two inner engines would be kept running until a crew chief has located a ladder and was in position in the bomb bay.

On the post flight inspection most of the main wheel tyres were found to be scuffed and cut so that replacement was necessary. In consultation with the Air Traffic Control Officer it was assumed that I had touched down too short on the runway on a tarmacadam area that was covered in stones. Subsequently the co-pilot's A.S.I. was found to be over reading by 5 knots which accounted for the early touch down.

Signals were sent off to base re the cracked windscreen and replacement wheels, and an alteration in flight plan became necessary.

On the 29th June the replacement wheels arrived by Britannia, also two signals, one of which said that the crack in the windscreen was acceptable for flight as it was on the inner surface, and the other that diplomatic clearance to overfly Indonesia was only available on 4/5th July, which meant another day's delay at Butterworth.

The aircraft was finally made serviceable at 2100Z on 29th July.

Accommodation at El Adem was in the Transient Block, and meals were taken in the Transit Hotel adjacent to A.T.C. All calls, meals, transport etc were booked through the Movements Staff in the Transit Hotel.

6. *Sortie No. 2 El Adem – Khormaksar* E.T.D. 300600Z
A.T.D. 300558Z
A.T.A. 301020Z

Call	0530 local
Transport	0600 "
Meals	0600 "
Met. & Flt. Planning	0615 "
At A/C	0645 "

Local Time Z+2

Take-off from El Adem was normal with clear skies and a ground temperature of +23°C. V.H.F. contact was maintained to 150 miles distance. After a turn over the mountains of the S.W. corner of Egypt, Asmara was the first town sighted visually and contact made with Khormaksar at 150 miles range. A straight let-down started over Perim Island brought us down into the sand haze and humidity of Aden. The temperature was +34°C, and with a wind of 20 knots rising sand made it imperative to get the engine blanks in as soon as possible.

Met. briefing, transport and in-flight rations were ordered through Transport Operations on the airfield. Accommodation was arranged by Merifield House, the transit hotel about 200 yds from the Officers Mess. Early calls and meals requirements were made with the staff of the transit hotel and the air conditioned rooms made a good night's sleep certain.7. *Sortie No. 3 Khormaksar – Gan*

E.T.D. 010600Z
A.T.D. 010607Z
A.T.A. 011032Z

Call	0615 local
Meal	0645 "
Transport	0715 "
Met. & Flt. Planning	0730 "
At A/C	0745 "

Local Time Z+2

A Palouste was available for engine starting at Khormaksar, which was fortunate as the A.A.P.P did not seem to give full power according to the crew chiefs, although the volts and frequency were normal. It became evident too that an external cold air unit was a must in that temperature (+35°C) and humidity.

Take off was normal except for a slight delay due to the traffic density, and a straight climb-out to height available. During this leg the S.T.R. 18 finally failed completely, but luckily we maintained V.H.F. contact with a Valiant on the same route and our position reports were passed on by him.

Gan radio beacon was picked up aurally at 400 miles, U.H.F contact made at 170 miles, and a straight let-down started at 100 miles.

Visibility was excellent, the island sighted visually from 50 miles, and the circuit and landing presented no problems. The ground temperature was +27°C, W/V 150/12 kts.

No. 214 Valiant (Tanker) Squadron were maintaining a detachment at Gan and we received considerable help from them. It was here that the S.T.R. 18 was finally repaired, the trouble being a U/S power unit.

Met briefing, calls, meals etc. were booked through the Air Movements staff who met the aircraft on landing.

8. *Sortie No. 4 Gan-Butterworth*

E.T.D. 020300Z
A.T.D. 020300Z
A.T.A. 020712Z

Call	0515 local
Meal	0545 "
Transport	0615 "
Met. and Flt. Planning	0620 "

Local time Z+5

All arrangements worked perfectly at Gan, in addition a Palouste was available for starting. Take-off was made on time, runway 10 temperature +27°C. No problems en route, cu and cu. nimb, skirted with caution, and Butterworth Control were contacted at 170 miles range. A straight let down from 100 n. miles, visual from 40 miles and normal landing. Members of the R.A.F. element Butterworth met the aircraft in dispersal. Diplomatic clearance to overfly Indonesia was available only for 4/5th July, which meant a day's delay at Butterworth.

Met. briefing, transport and in-flight rations were booked through operations, early calls and meals through the respective messes.

9. *Sortie No. 5 – Butterworth-Darwin*

E.T.D. 040030Z
A.T.D. 040029Z
A.T.A. 040525Z

Call	0515 local
Meal	0545 "
Transport	0615 "
Met. and Flt. Planning	0620 "
At A/C	0645 "

Local Time Z+7 1/2

An external 200v supply was available at Butterworth but no Palouste, so No. 4 Engine was started using the A.A.P.P. The start was slow, with the outside air temperature at +25°C, but quite satisfactory. No. 4 Alternator frequency was high at 411 cycles and would not parallel with other alternators. It was therefore left isolated carrying its own loads.

Take off was normal, Singapore Airways contacted shortly afterwards and normal airways procedures followed. There were a few cu nimb clouds down the coast of Malaya and over the Indonesian islands but otherwise the weather was good.

Darwin were contacted on HF/RT 2 hours out and a request made that the health authorities at Darwin would allow a crew chief to leave the aircraft before the engines were closed down to carry out essential servicing on the missile. The request was acknowledged as having been passed to the requisite authorities.

On throttling back for the descent into Darwin 100 miles out, No. 3 Alternator came off line, but was successfully reset and gave no further trouble.

However on landing at Darwin a hiatus developed with the health authorities in that they would not clear a crew chief to leave the aircraft before the engines were stopped. And I would not stop the engines until the crew chief was in position to close the freon lines to the missile.

After some twenty minutes of argument I informed operations via A.T.C. that I could not guarantee the safety of the missile if the engines were closed down prior to servicing by the crew chief. This brought immediate results, the crew chief was cleared to leave the aircraft, and the engines closed down. A full report on this incident was made to Group Captain P.O.V. Green, A.F.C., Senior Royal Air Force Officer, H. Q. Edinburgh Field.

Due to an exercise being held at Darwin the Messes were full and we were accommodated at the Sea Breeze Hotel, paying our own bills. These amounted to £4-15s per night, so it is as well to have sufficient funds available.

The Mark 1B Nitrogen trolley, along with all other Blue Ranger stores, was still in its original wrappings in Main Stores, and therefore unusable.

This was typical all along the route and could cause considerable delay.

10. *Sortie No. 6 Darwin-Edinburgh*

E.T.D. 042230Z
A.T.D. 042255Z
A.T.A. 050205Z

Call	0515 local
Transport	0545 "
Meals	0600 "
Met. and Flt. Planning	0615 "
At A/C	0645 "

Local Time Z+9 1/2

First light at Darwin is at 0700 local time, and as take-off was planned for 0800 it meant working on the aircraft in the dark, with only one light available. As local time at Darwin and Edinburgh are the same, a change in E.T.D. Darwin to 2330Z, 0900 hours local time, is considered to be more reasonable.

Thick fog, the first at Darwin for a number of years, delayed take-off for 25 minutes.

Crews should ensure they are au fait with the clearance terminology at Darwin, as climb out is not always on track, but from the beacon via lanes 1, 2, or 3, which means 10°, 20°, or 30°, port or starboard of required track until clear of any civil traffic in the local area.

After take off the weather en route was clear until approaching Edinburgh. Adelaide Control were contacted about 160 miles out and a free let down authorised into Edinburgh circuit. The cloud base was 2000 feet in drizzle, similar to the original take-off.

11. At Edinburgh 4 J.S.T.U., commanded by Wing Commander S. T. Underwood O.B.E., received the missile and undertook the necessary day groups and servicing of the aircraft.

12. *Sortie No. 7 Edinburgh-Darwin*

E.T.D. 110030Z
A.T.D. 110105Z
Local Time Z+9 1/2 A.T.A. 110420Z

The late take off from Edinburgh was due to a sticking bleed valve on the A.A.P.P. When the engine start button was pressed the bleed valve only opened half way. The start was fiddled by having the air selector switch to normal and the A.A.P.P. cabin bleed switch open. The A.A.P.P. bleed valve then fully opened and No. 1 engine started off the A.A.P.P. This method was used for the whole of the return flight.

The flight from Edinburgh to Darwin was uneventful except for being intercepted by two R.A.A.F. Sabres on the let down into Darwin.

On arrival at Darwin a signal was handed to me re a mod 1760 to be incorporated before the next flight. The spares were being sent out via B.O.A.C. arriving on 13th July at 0445 (local time). When the B.O.A.C. Comet arrived although the spares were manifested, they could not be found on the aircraft, which carried on to Sydney and Melbourne. At Melbourne the aircraft was unloaded, the spares found and returned to Darwin by 1530 hours the same afternoon.

The modifications to the brake hydraulic lines were completed by 1930 hrs. and we were airborne for Butterworth at 2016 hours (local).

13. *Sortie No. 8 Darwin-Butterworth*

E.T.D. 112230Z
A.T.D. 131046Z
Local Time Z+7½ A.T.A. 131525Z

This was a complete night stage and presented no undue difficulties. Night flying facilities at both airfields are good, the only slight snag being the lack of glide path indicators at Butterworth. The aircraft was bedded down and refuelling etc. left until the morning.

14. *Sortie No. 9 Butterworth-Gan*

E.T.D. 130030Z
A.T.D. 140427Z
Local Time Z+5 A.T.A. 140807Z

Take off was arranged for mid day local time and in the event was accomplished with three minutes in hand. Climbing out via Alor Star a number of cu. nimb clouds were visible en route but a few heading alterations kept us in the clear. Once again a straight let down into the circuit at Gan was approved, visual from 40 miles, and a landing temperature of +30°C.

15. *Sortie No. 10 Gan-Khormaksar* E.T.D. 140300Z

A.T.D. 150255Z
Local Time Z+3 A.T.A. 150645Z

Arrangements at Gan worked well except for the usual delay in obtaining ground equipment which seems to be common to all staging posts. The flight was made at flight level 440, in and out of the tops of cirrus for much of the time, until Aden centre were contacted on126.7mcs at a range of 220 miles. A straight let down from 80 miles took us into the crowded circuit at Khormaksar, with visibility 4n. miles in dust haze. No ground crew help at all was available at Khormaksar due to the number of Transport movements.

The crew were accommodated in the Red Sea Hotel, a transit hotel 2½ miles from the airfield.

16. *Sortie No. 11 Khormaksar – El Adem* E.T.D. 160500Z

A.T.D. 170537Z
Local Time Z+2 A.T.A. 170932Z

Once again the servicing arrangements at Khormaksar were chaotic. No ground equipment was available until after take off time due to other Transport Command aircraft taking priority. The Palouste when it arrived was less batteries and when the batteries eventually arrived the electrical connection to the aircraft was U/S, so the engines were started using the A.A.P.P.

Take off was delayed 37 minutes solely due to lack of assistance with ground equipment.

17. *Sortie No. 12 El Adem – Scampton*

E.T.A. 170700Z
A.T.D. 171128Z
A.T.A. 171542Z

A turn-round at El Adem was accomplished in less than 2 hours, which enabled us to regain schedule and avoid any complications with a French Air Traffic strike due to start the next morning. The flight back to Scampton was normal and weather good at base.

18. The following notes may be of use to future Blue Ranger crews.

(a) With missile on need to be at aircraft 1 hour 15 mins. before take off time.

(b) Palouste makes starting easy in high temperatures.

(c) Never start P.F.C.s etc. until alternators on line, as 200v external supplies are unreliable.

(d) Keep Nos. 2 and 3 engines running after landing until the crew chief has a step ladder in position otherwise freon may be lost from the frig. pack.

(e) The external 28v supplies are normally unmodified sets, therefore trip off line when A.A.P.P. is started.

(f) Administrative arrangements work well in general, but servicing is largely "do it yourself".

(g) The Blue Ranger pack ups are held in main stores, even at Edinburgh Field, and outside working hours it is a matter of calling out the Orderly Officer, Duty Storekeeper etc before access to the stores can be obtained.

(h) Suggest take off on the Darwin-Edinburgh leg be one hour later to avoid working on the aircraft in the dark.

8. Displaying the Vulcan

Squadron Leader David Thomas, in addition to his regular RAF duties as a Central Flying School instructor, was also one of two pilots qualified to fly XH558, the RAF's last flying Vulcan. His account of display flying is a fascinating 'insider's look' at how the Vulcan was displayed to the public:

'Planning for each display season began during the month of April, when the Ministry of Defence Participation Committee issued a list of venues that XH558 would be released to appear at. The situation was slightly different in 1992, as this was acknowledged as being the "last year", and the Vulcan Display Flight was given some choice as to the show selections. Amazingly, although we obviously wanted to fit in as much as we could that year, we only managed to add

another two or three displays, as we just ran out of crews. People were just not available.

'So, a great deal of time was spent putting together a show programme for the season, making sure the aircraft was fully serviceable, and that the crews were available at the right times, and then we would liaise with each individual show venue, finding out exactly what they wanted, and what time they wanted us and so on. At Biggin Hill in 1992, for example, we flew out there on the Friday, and they used us as a static exhibit. Then on the Saturday we flew out to do a display at Locking, a flypast at Lyneham, and then back to Biggin to do a display and land.

***Left:** XH558, the first Vulcan B.2 to be delivered to the RAF, was also the last Vulcan to leave RAF service. Seen at Woodford before delivery, the aircraft wears full-colour RAF markings and is not equipped with a refuelling probe. (British Aerospace)*

That was quite a difficult one, as I had to fly the aircraft in a heavy configuration at Locking, and of course the aim is always to have the aircraft as light as possible during displays, not only because the aircraft is then more manoeuvrable and therefore more impressive, but because she also uses less fatigue ... it also causes less fatigue for the pilots!

'Ten thousand pounds [weight] makes an incredible performance difference, and we try to display with around 20,000 pounds of fuel, but at Locking I had 31,000 pounds of fuel. On the Sunday I launched early at thirteen-oh-six to do a short display and land, and then after a quick turnround we took off again to fly to Cosford for another display, and then on home to Waddington. In that way we fly two sorties which means more ground work, but the actual flying element is much easier. It sounds fairly easy, but sometimes it was very difficult to tie three different venues together on time. Some organizers are better than others at doing it. We always had freedom in deciding where we would stop and mount our displays from, but there would always be naturally imposed limitations such as flying hours and fatigue, which was always kept to a minimum.

'Once we got to the venue, we always tried to get maximum exposure, so whenever possible we tried to park close to the crowd, in order to let everyone see the aircraft. But both Paul Millikin and myself always preferred to be removed from any outside interference. People are very well-meaning and interested in the aircraft, asking lots of questions, but about an hour before take-off I liked to get myself under control, calming everything down, thinking about the wind, working out how I'm going to fly the manoeuvres. So we always aimed to keep the spectators away from the aircraft at least an hour before take-off. That allowed me to get into the right frame of mind, so that I could fly the aircraft to the limit of its performance, but still have spare capacity to see what's going on around me. Obviously the last thing I wanted was to climb into the aircraft all hot and bothered, irritated and angry at someone maybe. It didn't always work like that though, and it's amazing how things could disrupt the flow. One of the Vulcan's problems was that it didn't have air conditioning, and sometimes you could be operating in cockpit temperatures of up to 130 degrees, so you got pretty hot. You always took cans of drink along to keep replacing lost fluid, but it was a problem.

'The amount of information we received from the display venue tended to vary. For example, taking Biggin Hill again, they were always very good, providing the material well in advance, creating no hassle. Other show organizers won't come clean until the last minute. Obviously you need to know the time you're wanted on display, how long you've got to display, where the crowd and display lines are, and where the holding points are. Otherwise I expected them to know what the display would be like, but things were kept flexible and, for example, where we usually included a touch-and-go, we would convert this to a low flypast when the runway was either unsuitable or didn't exist. But organizers knew our display sequence pretty well.

'However, although we kept ourselves flexible, once we'd agreed a timing, I expected them to stick to it. If they cameto me and said that we'd be ten minutes late, that would then create a knock-on effect right down this list of displays for that day, making things very difficult. So we insisted they stuck to their word, although in all honesty we always included some timing flexibility, but we kept that as an emergency back-up, rather than allowing show organizers to go crazy. We would receive an instruction "package" from each venue, with things like a drawing of the airfield layout, support services that would be available, who else would be displaying, and a time schedule. We always flew to the clock, even on pre-show arrival days, and we planned to arrive at each venue within a couple of seconds of our scheduled time, purely as a matter of professionalism. We didn't include any diversions, touch-and-goes, anything like that in our transit flights; the aim was always to go straight to the venue, fly a circuit to look at the airfield traffic pattern, and then land. The only exceptions were things such as the

occasional flypast, not least at Cranwell during their graduation ceremonies, and we would time our departure to include things like that.

'For pilot continuation training we would fly specific dedicated sorties, often going over to Marham to run through a practice display. We had a fourteen-day currency requirement, and if we hadn't displayed within the preceding fourteen days we would have to fly a practice display before flying before a show crowd. We always flew our display practices over Marham, simply because XH558 was a part of No. 55 Squadron, and we had to fly there in order to be seen by our supervisors. It may seem rather odd that the aircraft was hangared at Waddington, but one should bear in mind that Waddington was an established Vulcan base, where lots of technical support remains, and where all the spares are kept. Hangar space was also available too.

'The aircraft was always flown clean, without any equipment, although our golden rule was to never separate ourselves from our personal baggage, so we carried that with us. Otherwise we transitted as we displayed, to the clock, and with a light fuel load, to minimize flying time and fatigue. We usually carried two members of the ground crew with us so that there would be someone with us, as soon as we arrived at a show site. We would often send a ground party ahead of us by road, but we carried people with us, just in case their transport broke down. We could then drop them off on a taxiway, and let them guide us into our parking position. Most

***Left:** The sad sight of Vulcans being scrapped on site at RAF Scampton in 1982. In the foreground are the crumpled remains of an ECM tail cone, while the cockpit section of XM595 is loaded on to a truck, possibly for resale. (Photo: via Haydn Hughes)*

people these days are not familiar with Vulcans, and it's not very manoeuvrable on the ground. One thing we had to watch was the organizer who stuck you in a slot that you couldn't taxi out of. If you didn't have a towing arm with you, then you had a problem. It happened maybe once a year, and if there was any doubt we would take a towing arm with us by road.

'I tended to become a little hardened to the whimpering of some show organizers who expected us to move Heaven and Earth to accommodate their wishes, but after so many years of display flying, we knew where the line was to be drawn, and we'd do so much and then no more, simply saying that if we were messed around anymore we'd go home. And that has a very sobering effect on people! There were some shows where we came very close to just going home, but in the end the organizers saw sense. It's not a case of us being bloody-minded, it's just that when you have two or three shows to do in one day, you figure that if the organizer can't give you a take-off time within five minutes of a desired time, there must be something wrong with their ability, and you can't disrupt maybe three displays because of a delayed take-off someplace.

'Over the years we tended to display at the same venues, so there wasn't much that surprised us. However, you did see some incredible contrasts. For example, when we flew at Mildenhall we had 9,000 feet of concrete and an enormous airfield. But after displaying there we went to Barton in Manchester, where there's about 3,000 feet of grass, and the visual perspective is completely different. Instead of performing well within the boundaries of the airfield, you get a great urge to fly a really tight display, in order to stay within the boundaries of a much smaller airfield, and of course it just doesn't work, and it's something you have to watch carefully. In a more conventional aircraft you could inadvertently stall the aircraft by trying to fly in a tightly confined space, whereas the Vulcan's very good as it just doesn't stall.

'All the military shows we flew at were provided free, although the organizer had to provide the cost of accommodation, food, bringing equipment and so on. The civil shows had a blanket charge of something less than two thousand pounds, a nominal fee which obviously didn't pay for much. It's interesting to note that towards the end of the Vulcan's display career, one show organizer simply stated that they would pay whatever the necessary asking price was, because they just had to have the Vulcan at their show. It's an incredible display aircraft, as it's a unique design, and XH558 is the only one of its kind. It flies very slowly, it's very manoeuvrable, it's big, it's noisy, quite unmistakable.

'A great deal of the pre-flight preparation was entrusted to the ground crew, but we still made a walk-round check, really just looking for the more obvious things. Personally I didn't regard the Vulcan as a lump of metal, but as something closer to an animate object, and each aircraft has its own characteristics. I tended to touch the aircraft, talk to her even, just to get myself together, to become "at one" with the aircraft. Sure you look at the tyres and hydraulic lines, but it's more to do with becoming part of the aeroplane. Sounds strange with a 120-ton aeroplane maybe, but that's how it was. Once inside the aircraft we ran through the whole pre-flight checks right from square one, in complete detail. You could rush things, but that's no way to go into a display, and we'd always allow plenty of time. If everything went smoothly you could expect to go from climbing-in to getting airborne in maybe thirty-five minutes, but you don't want to erode your margins, and we'd aim to work with about fifty minutes to spare, and then we could sit and hold at engine start, until the required time.

'It's an electrical jet, so if the aircraft had been standing out in the damp for any length of time, we'd get silly little electrical failures, especially in the navigation system, but luckily that wasn't really necessary for most displays. Since the Vulcan was dedicated purely to flying displays, we only lost just two displays, one because of engine intake cracks and one because the undercarriage failed to retract, and with only a minimal amount of fuel it would have been impossible to fly the display with the gear down, so I recovered back to Waddington. Problems were mainly of a minor nature. The vital things such as the flying controls and engines never caused us any problems. It's only when the weather is bad that things like the navigation kit and the bombing system become important. It's amazing that back in the days of regular squadron service, you'd have to drag the rear crew into the aircraft kicking and screaming, whereas now you couldn't keep 'em out! Certainly, if the rules allowed, you could have flown displays without the navigators,

but you had to have the Air Electronics Operator on board, as certain switch selections had to be made in the event of an electrical malfunction, in order to safeguard the integrity of the aircraft.

'Basically there are two systems to start the engines. One is to use a ground air supply, to pump air into the engine. The other is to use stored air in high-pressure bottles contained inside the aircraft. We generally insisted on having a Palouste air starter at each display site, so that we could use the internal rapid start system as a back-up, rather than our primary means of starting the engines, another instance of not eroding your margins. Additionally, you can use one engine to start the others by cross-bleeding air to turn the other three in turn, the normal procedure being to start each engine directly from the Palouste unit. The internal rapid start system has sufficient pressure to make six individual engine starts, so there was always a great deal of redundant capacity in terms of engine start capability. The starting procedure was indicative of 'sixties technology, and unusual by modern standards, in that you would deliver air to the engine, let it wind up, then manually control the fuel flow into the engine before igniting it. So you started with a small fire, helping the engine to accelerate, and then you'd add more and more fuel until it was self-sustaining. Of course you could start all four engines at the same time with the rapid start system, and you could prepare the aircraft so that just one button needed to be switched to fire up everything automatically, but that was obviously not something we needed for display flying.

'There was more than sufficient thrust to get a good taxi-ing speed with the engines at idle speed, but we would use a bit of thrust to gain a little inertia, and then throttle back and use the brakes to keep speed in check. You can use differential braking to steer, but the Vulcan also has a nosewheel steering system, using hydraulics in relation to the position of the rudder pedals. You can barely see the wingtips from the cockpit, and they're a long way behind the main wheels, so when you make a tight turn you get what is called "Swept wing growth", and the wings seem to swing out much wider than you expect, but we were aware of the situation. At display venues you had to be very conscious of the problem as there was often great pressure to put the aircraft into tight spots.

'For take-off we'd run up to 80 per cent power and hold on the brakes, check that the engines are functioning correctly, and go to full power as the brakes are released. You check that the engine acceleration stabilizes at a predeterminedrpm, which was dependent on air temperature. On a hot day we'd be looking for a minimum of 98.5 per cent rpm. Okay, the power isn't critical with so much in reserve, but if I didn't get that figure I'd obviously want to know why, as I might have an engine failure on my hands. In the take-off phase, if you lose an engine, you're likely to lose the adjacent one as well, which can be

Left: *XH560 was transferred to the Vulcan Display Flight at Waddington to replace XL426 (seen behind XH560). Investigations revealed that XH558 (on Marham's dump) had more flying hours remaining, and a last-minute transfer saw XH560 fly to Marham (where she was later scrapped), and XH558 fly back to Waddington for restoration. (Ray Ball)*

serious if you're flying slowly, or flying a display. Operationally we would practise three-engine take-off procedures, as the aircraft has more than adequate performance with just two engines, and it has a climb-away capability even at a heavy weight on only one engine, but for display flying we always required all four to be functioning perfectly. XH558 has the Olympus 200 Series engines, whereas many Vulcans had the more powerful Olympus 300 engines, and these aircraft featured a combat cruise selector restricting maximum power to the same figure as that attained by the less powerful aircraft like XH558. After some years in service, the aircraft with 300 Series engines had the cruise selector permanently wired in, in order to conserve engine life which was degraded at full power, due to resonance inside the engine.

'Normally we aimed to take off into a holding position, to give us time to settle down, but we often went straight into the display sequence. The rotation speed was usually 135 knots, and that remained the same until the aircraft weight rose quite significantly. With no wind, the take-off run was about 2,000 feet. The display datum speed was around 155 knots, and even the tight turns were entered at that slow speed. You were able to manoeuvre fully at slow speed, and it always appeared to be close to the crowd because of its size, so the display was always impressive. Because the aircraft was essentially built to fly long, straight lines, it has a very heavy feel when you're flying a display sequence, and we tend to use full control deflections. For example, in a steep turn we have full up elevator, and that gets very tiring. An eight-minute display is like twenty-four hours of normal work. It's physically demanding to fly a display in the Vulcan, and despite the Vulcan's fighter-type control stick, we tend to use both hands in a steep turn. Another point to consider is the need to balance the adverse aileron yaw that is created by the Vulcan. If you roll quickly, one set of ailerons goes up, the others go down, and you start to yaw. So before you move the ailerons you must move the rudder to counter the yaw. There's no finesse involved in Vulcan display flying. The only reason we used so much bank at the top of the turns was to bring the nose down more easily. The climb angle was very steep, and trying to bring the nose down with wings level would create a significant bunt, and the Vulcan isn't designed to fly a negative-"g" manoeuvre. So we rolled the Vulcan onto its side and allowed the nose to fall through.

'The Vulcan's negative-"g" limit was zero, the positive limit being just two, so the secret of how we made the display look

Below: *Inside XH558's huge bomb bay with the bomb doors closed. The rear portion of the bay is occupied by a fuel tank. (Tim Laming)*

so impressive was to fly slowly. Modern aircraft can't perform well when they're close to their stalling speed whereas it was no problem for the Vulcan. At the top of a tight turn the speed was even lower than the datum display speed. All the manoeuvring was done in a heavy buffet, which in a conventional aircraft would mean a deep stall, real trouble, but in the Vulcan we didn't have that problem. Basically, you cannot stall the Vulcan's wing. If you look at the stalling angle, the point where lift starts to decrease, it's 48½ degrees angle of attack, but by that time the aircraft would have so much drag that it would be difficult to recover. What you actually get is a great deal of airflow separation over the top of the wing, so when we're manoeuvring we're sitting in very heavy buffeting, but at a low speed, flying a big, flat plate through the air. The only stall warning as such would be a low speed indication and a very high angle of attack, but with a unique aircraft like the Vulcan, you could get out of that situation easily by just unloading the wing. There is so much thrust that you could quickly get into a situation where you could overstress the airframe, so it literally requires just a couple of seconds at most to just unload the wing, get the speed back, and then heave back into the deep buffet, because we control the aircraft speed by flying in the heavy drag area. That's why the aircraft display was so noisy, as were just sat there with the engines roaring away, maintaining a minimum radius turn, using drag to control speed.

'Our minimum manoeuvre height was 500 feet, the level flypast at 300, and for a touch-and-go, we'd hope it was zero feet! The top of the turns was around 1,600 feet, sometimes a little lower. As you can imagine, there was quite a level of interest from the guys in the back, and the AEO called out heights, while one of the navigators called out speeds, especially if it went significantly high or low. It was very much a team effort, as when things start to go wrong, they go wrong pretty quickly, so a nudge from the rear crew about our speed or height was always very useful. As for other things going wrong during the display, we had very few problems. Once at a display over Barton we had an aircraft call short finals with an engine failure while I was flying a display, but I was able to reposition, and continue the display without creating a hazard to either his safety or mine. It was always our policy of not having any other aircraft flying over the airfield while we were displaying. You'd think that was pretty sensible, but many display organizers like to maximize their earning potential by having pleasure flights taking place during displays. But despite this, you'd see them flying as you were running in, which is very dangerous.

'Touchdown speed was around 130 knots, and with the high nose angle you couldn't actually see the touchdown point; you were looking some way ahead of you down the runway, so you used your vision either side to judge your position. Close to the runway, the Vulcan sat on a cushion of air, so with the nose high, it was very difficult to have a bad landing. You allowed the aircraft to simply sink gently. If it was slightly fast it would balloon quite significantly. With the whole trailing edge acting as a flap, pulling the stick back would reverse the flap, causing the aircraft to smack onto the ground, so, to stop an impact you pushed the nose down, although that would provide only a very temporary respite, because the aircraft pitches quite rapidly. So the easy way out of a difficult landing is to hold a high nose attitude, put on power and go around again. Going down the runway with the nose held high, the aircraft remains quite responsive, but you reach a speed where you no longer have any control. It will sit there quite happily, but we tended to lower the nose at around 70 knots. With short runways where we used the brake parachute, the nosewheel had to be on the ground in order to steer the aircraft.

'The final retirement of XH558 really does mark the passing of an era. It's tremendously sad for me and the rest of the Vulcan's crew. In the military you have to get used to losing loved ones sometimes, and the Vulcan is yet another loved one which we're having to say goodbye to.'

The following is a Royal Air Force official document issued in 1979 to Vulcan display pilots. It provides some interesting background information on how the Vulcan was displayed to the public.

INTRODUCTION

1. The Vulcan has been taking part in Air Displays since 1955 and has impressed all by its sheer size and manoeuvrability. Roly Falk "barrel rolled" the prototype at Farnborough in '55 and later "rolls off the top" by Sqn Ldr Les Lunn at the Paris Air Show in the early '60s. However our imagination may be fired by these displays, reality controls the event, and aircraft fatigue and other considerations dictate that the limits set out in GASO1-1-1-8 are to supply. The aircraft is impressive anyway, and the best use of its qualities must be made within the limitations laid down whilst observing the most rigorous Flight Safety Parameters.

2. These notes are designed to give crews and their supervisors guidance on display techniques and pitfalls.

AIRCRAFT CHARACTERISTICS

3. The Vulcan being of Delta form will not stall in the accepted sense. If flown at the accepted display speed between pattern and then approach it may be banked to 45° and still remain buffet free. However, it is then on the edge of a huge increase in drag and, should the speed be allowed to decay, large increases in power will be necessary to prevent sink developing. At the same time, yaw may develop and, unless controlled by sensible use of rudder, full crossed controls may result. All displays should sensibly be flown at minimum practical weights and this will give a thrust weight ratio of 0.55:1 – this ration allows more than adequate thrust to give an impressive display and power the aircraft out of any sink situation.

GROUP AIR STAFF INSTRUCTIONS

4. Re-study the GASOs on display flying. Know them intimately. As you will see permissible manoeuvres are limited to:

a. Steep turns of up to 45° bank at 500 ft above height of

highest obstacle.

b. Teardrop turns not exceeding 90° bank, 1500 ft agl/asl, or 90% power in the climb.

c. Straight runs past the crowd at 500 ft (or 300 ft when followed by a wings-level climb to end the display).

d. No undercarriage manoeuvres.

e. Take-off, roller landings, land with stream.

These parameters are intentionally restrictive and some thought has to be given to the format of display to remain within the limitations while displaying the aircraft to its best advantage.

DISPLAY FORMAT

5. The aircraft is large, even at 500 ft it remains so, and noisy and if its safe manoeuvrability is explained it can be kept in constant view of the crowd. No display should exceed 8 minutes to avoid crew fatigue and excessive repetition of manoeuvres. A suggested routine, with all heights quoted meaning height above the highest obstacle in the display area, might include:

a. An entry not below 500 ft from behind the crowd line (but not overflying the crowd itself) at an angle of 45° to the display axis. This gives the pilot the chance to enter the display area at the correct speed unseen and the subsequent turn onto the display axis shows the top surface of the aircraft to advantage. A slow entry from either end would entail the aircraft being on view for an excessive length of time, while a faster entry would give the pilot the difficult problem of trying to slow down without either overstressing the aircraft or disappearing from view. Nevertheless, some display locations may rule out entry from behind the crowd line, so consider the slow entry.

b. Climbing teardrops.

c. Steep turns (+ bomb doors and airbrakes).

d. Simulated bomb run at 300 K, with pop-up manoeuvre to end display.

6. A satisfactory 1978 display, assuming a start AUW of 130,000 lb, involved:

a. 45° entry to display axis with 30° bank, at pattern speed and with high drag airbrakes. Airbrakes in at crowd centre.

b. 60° turn off display axis – teardrop.

c. Steep turn 360° clean.

d. 60° off display axis – second teardrop.

e. Steep turn 360° with bomb doors.

f. 60° off display axis – third teardrop.

g. Steep turns 360°.

h. Descent from approximately 2500 ft at 200 K through 180° with acceleration when on centre line to fast run past at 300 K, 300 ft. 1.5G pull up to 8000 ft+.

Target speed for most of the manoeuvres is pattern speed, with a minimum of pattern speed minus 10 K. A very good display can also be flown with the speed never exceeding 200 K.

INDIVIDUAL MANOEUVRES

7. *Steep Turns*. To enter steep turns use pattern speed for weight with a brisk co-ordinated rudder and aileron roll into 45° bank. Outside references should be used and attitude flying employed. A close watch must be kept on the speed and constant power adjustments made to maintain pattern speed. If a level turn of 500 ft is made it will seem to the viewer that the aircraft has descended at the far side of the turn. Aim to climb the aircraft to 700 ft at the far side and descend back to 500 ft opposite crowd centre and this will appear to be a level turn. If bomb doors are required the navigator should open them at the command of the pilot and they should be timed to open as bank is applied to start the turn and closed as the aircraft passes crowd centre after 360° turn.

8. *Teardrops*. A full 60° off crowd axis must be made at the start of this manoeuvre to give the aircraft adequate displacement from crowd axis. Rolling in can start from 500 ft, but until you are absolutely confident with this teardrop manoeuvre start at 700 ft. 45° bank should be used as a continuation of the steep turn. Wings should be levelled at the 60° point and 90% power applied. Before banking, the aircraft must be pitched nose up to maintain pattern speed and climb initiated. At 900 ft rudder and aileron should be applied in the desired direction and full airbrakes selected – 90% power to be maintained. (Alternatively, airbrakes should not be used as part of the normal technique but reserved to adjust the rate of descent, if required.) Bank will increase to 90° using the real horizon as reference, the nose will drop and when the nose has reached desired level bank is then reduced to about 40°. When speed has stabilized at pattern speed power may be reduced and a descending turn back onto crowd centre may be made. If the speed is lower than pattern speed minus 10 K, immediate efforts must be made to increase this by lowering the nose and increasing power. Highest point reached should be 1500 ft and rate of descent adjusted by use of power, with or without airbrakes. Should high drag airbrake not be employed then the speed may well increase to 180 K, overstressing can occur in the turn and great difficulty found in descending to 500 ft by crowd centre. Two final thoughts. Beware of over-banking as the rate of roll is still remarkably good at these speeds. Another hazard is that if the nose is allowed to drop too low – easily done if 90° bank is held a little too long or the horizon is not good – this can lead to risk of overstress or worse. The remedy is to level the wings, then to pull back on the control column to maintain 150–160 K and be prepared to use full power; this brings the nose up and checks the rate of descent without allowing "G" to build up.

9. *Simulated Bomb Run*. When aircraft is on extended crowd axis, airbrakes may be selected in and 93% power applied. Acceleration in descent to 300 ft is vivid and great care must be taken to trim forward smoothly. It is possible to induce PIO by out of phase application of trim. When 300 K has been reached a gentle rotation of 1.5G may be made: this will result in bumpy conditions increasing G meter readings to about 1.8G. Final pitch up angle should be about 60° and as speed reduces to 180 K, rudder and aileron should be used to put on bank to about 80°.

RESPONSIBILITIES OF CREW

10. The co-pilot must be fully aware of the display format and know the run in and timing. During the display use him to call angles off the crowd axis for teardrops. Tell him to select airbrakes out or in if the workload is high. His job is always to monitor height and airspeed.

11. The navigator must preplan the run in to the display with timing calculated on 1:50,000 maps. Accurate time on stage is very important in display work, therefore practise this during rehearsals: late or hurried arrivals on the day could detract from your performance or worse. A bomb steer in poor visibility is a wise precaution. During the display his job is to monitor timing, speeds and heights; opening and closing of bomb doors is his also.

12. The AEO is naturally in charge of communications and should monitor air brake position through periscope. Too many teardrops can be made with full airbrake without this precaution. (NB: A four-man crew which, preferably, should be constituted and certainly must have practised together as a display team may be used.)

VULCAN DISPLAY FLIGHT SEQUENCE, AS FLOWN BY XH558.

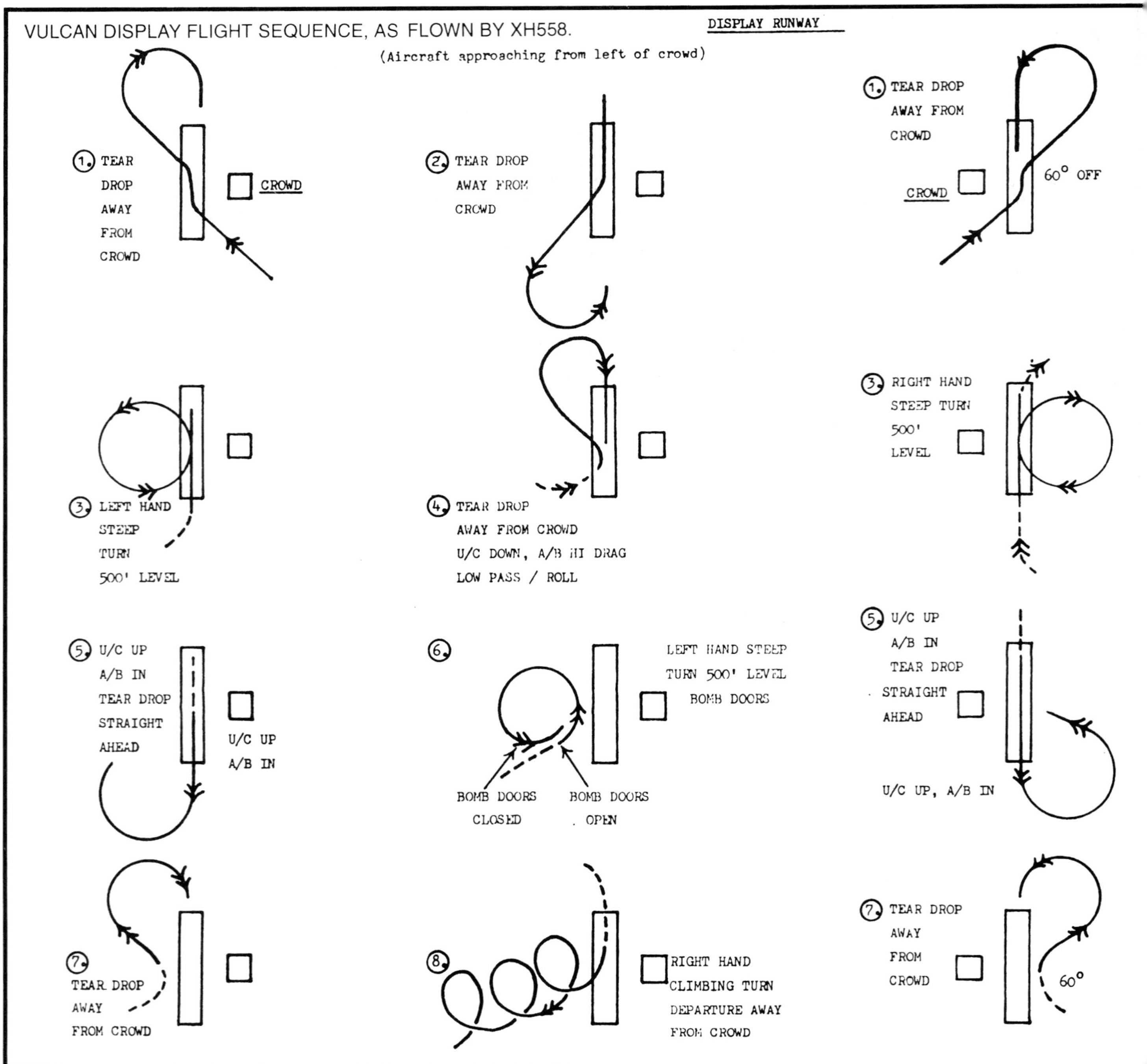

PITFALLS

13. *Wind.* The greatest difficulties are presented by strong surface winds. For example, a 360° steep turn takes 1 minute; a 20 knot wind will displace the aircraft in one turn 1800 ft in the direction of the wind. Should the wind be up or down the crowd axis due consideration must be made. It is very difficult to adjust the turn itself – the aircraft is already turning to its maximum. If bank is increased beyond 45° a large increase in power is required to maintain speed and height. Start of turns going downwind should be before crowd centre and a brisk "roll in" executed. Conversely, a turn started into wind should be past crowd centre and roll in made more slowly. Teardrops made into wind should be adjusted to an angle off of 50°, whilst those downwind made more briskly to prevent too great a displacement from crowd centre. A wind blowing on crowd presents great problems and much care must be exercised to prevent being blown over the crowd. Roll into turns must be gentle, with the last 90° of turn made at increased bank. Teardrops may be extended into wind by climbing at reduced power, while roll outs may be tightened by using increased

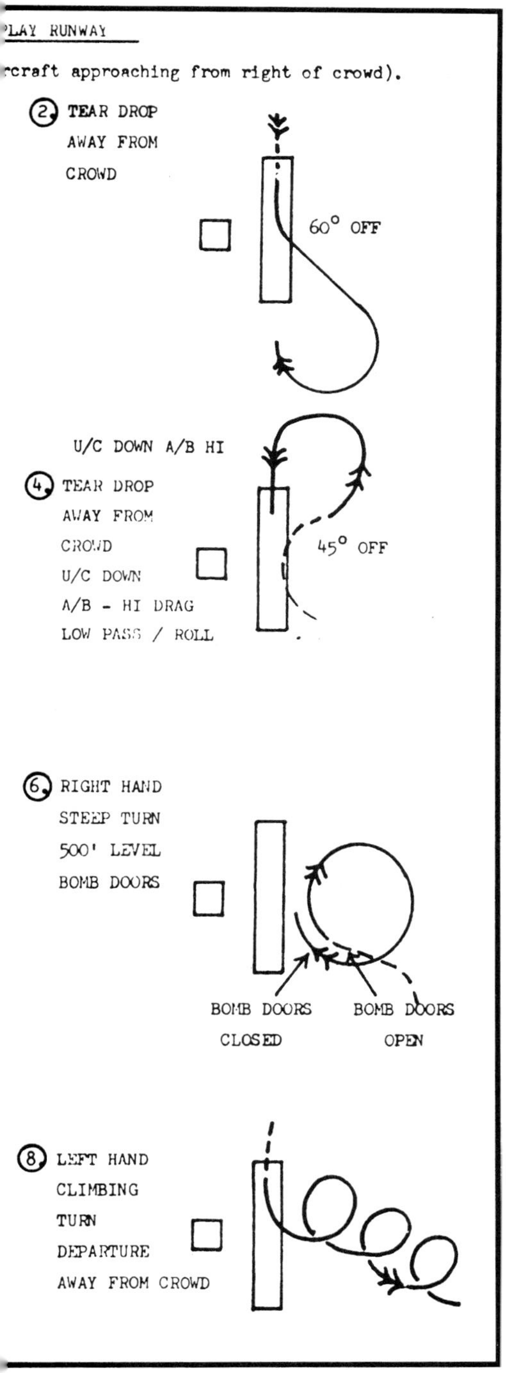

Informal notes made by a 44 Squadron display pilot. It is interesting to note how each aircraft possessed individual characteristics, ranging from the less-than-popular XM594 to the now-famous XM607 which was (perhaps not surprisingly based on these notes) used quite frequently for display performances in the 1970s, when the Vulcan was thrown around in startling fashion before an awestruck public. The fighter-style take-off involving a tight turn away from the runway, often with little more than ten feet separating the wing tip from the ground, was always a crowd-stopper!

AIRCRAFT

575 – Throttles stiff, handles well.

647 – At 130,000 lb AUW Below 155kts aircraft becomes directionally difficult and begins to run out of 'E' authority @ C of G + 2.

655 – Right turns good but in left turns below 150kts up to full outboard aileron is necessary to control bank. AUW 129,000 lb.

657 – Reported by Les Aghtl – good. Woodford display. Seems to like being slow. Lots of power needed to keep speed up. Not quite so responsive in 'E'

652 – Not too responsive in 'E' sense. Needs 130kts over top of wing over to give pitch for pull out. Yaws right decel through Vapp. – Needs 150kts min in turns. (130,000 lb)

445 – Flies well. No problems

594 – 'Orrible

512 – Good

607 – Good (Jez)

bank. Rate of descent must be monitored lest super sink develops – power and increased speed will reduce this sink increase.

14. *Altimeter Setting*. All practices at base are to be done using airfield QFE as datum. Most displays will be done away from base or overseas. Ensure that you have all altimeters with display QFE set. It is far too difficult to be certain of your real height at the top of a teardrop with QNH set and all recoveries are to be made with constant reference to altimeter. Displays made over water (Toronto and Chicago) present added difficulties of perspective and there is a need to obtain display QFE from Rad Alt 7 comparison with pressure altimeters. Use altimeters – not forgetting the Rad Alt – exclusively for recovery from teardrops for the visual cues from 1500 ft down to about 500 ft are not sufficient.

15. *Super Sink*. It is possible in a Vulcan to obtain high rates of descent for three reasons:

a. Low speed.
b. Low power.
c. Too much bank.

The remedy for all three is to level the wings, lower the nose if possible, and apply full power. The situation, once recognised, is very easy to rectify by using the above procedure.

16. *Roving Displays*. Many airfields are too small to allow the Vulcan to operate from them for their airshows. Pre-flight planning in depth is vital. Your *whole* crew must know the position of the airfield, your approach direction, timing and display format. If possible a practice diversion during the days preceding the display will allow you to check for local visual features and crowd line. Displays at other airfields may entail starting the manoeuvres at higher fuel weights than usual; ensure that you have practised at these weights, as a Vulcan at 150,000 lbs is more difficult to fly than a minimum fuel one and is more inclined to yaw and sink at the appropriate approach speed. Speeds and timings will need amending for these higher AUWs.

17. *Extemporization*. You will be asked at times, usually in the middle of a display, to extend or curtail your display. Never extemporize. Your display format is known to yourself and crew and any additions are repetitious at best and dangerous at worst. Curtailing of a display may be expeditious for flight safety reasons, but be aware of the reasons given for such curtailment (eg other aircraft approaching or taking off) and take appropriate precautions.

18. *Engine Failure*. Think about this aspect before it happens. It has never yet happened during a display but do have planned escape manoeuvres. Should power be lost during a climb, immediately initiate a roll in the direction of lost engine(s) to lower nose. Full directional control may be maintained with rudder down to MPFS with 93% applied on live engines. If available use height to gain speed. Should power be lost in a steep turn, immediately level wings, increase power on live engines to 93% and climb away.

19. *Unusual Circumstances*. A variety of circumstances can present unusual problems. Poor weather and visibility – unexpected changes in cloud base – distractions caused by display Air Traffic Control – unexpected aircraft in circuit pattern – strong wind causing concentration to be focused on positioning to the detriment of flying accuracy. Any number of such events can cause disorientation and a lack of concentration in the vital areas of height and speed. If at any time you recognise that all is not well, level the wings, apply power and climb away. It may seem an obvious answer and unlikely to happen – but it happened twice to a very experienced display captain, once for loss of horizon in poor visibility, and once when displaying to a fete where so much effort was being made to position the aircraft that height and speed control were degraded.

SUMMARY

20. Practise your displays with thought.
21. Do not extemporize.
22. Treat the Vulcan and your crew with the respect they deserve.
23. Never be too proud to throw away a display if you are not entirely happy.

Above: *A display of the Vulcan's armament options, minus a small collection of free-fall nuclear bombs which were also carried. Blue Steel in the centre dwarfs the Martel ASMs, LGBs and Shrikes. (RAF Waddington)*

Below: *XH558 earned the double distinction of being the first Vulcan B.Mk.2 to enter service and the last B.Mk.2 to leave service, ending her days as a dedicated air display demonstration aircraft prior to being sold to a civilian buyer.*

9. Into Battle – and Beyond

Early in April 1982 when the prospect of war with Argentina seemed likely, no one imagined that the Vulcan would play a key part in the recapture of the Falkland Islands. Only three Vulcan squadrons remained operational and the type's complete retirement from RAF service in June seemed to be certain. However, on 5 April ground crews at Waddington were instructed to begin restoration of air-to-air refuelling capability in ten Vulcans, to enable aircrew to begin training in refuelling procedures as soon as possible. Although the Vulcans had retained their bolt-on refuelling probes since they were first fitted during the early 1960s, the fuel system had not been used since the aircraft had switched from strategic strike to tactical bombing. The internal fuel transfer system had either been deactivated or, in the case of many aircraft, the seals and valves had deteriorated to such an extent that the system could no longer be used. To add to the mechanical engineering team's problems, most refuelling probes had recently been removed, for attachment to Nimrods and Hercules, and personnel had to search far and wide (including the USA and Canada) to locate and obtain sufficient numbers of usable items.

From the ten aircraft that had their refuelling systems restored, five machines were selected for conversion to full conventional bombing operational standard, these being XL391, XM597, XM598, XM607 and XM612. They were the only Vulcans remaining in service that had full forward and aft Skybolt attachments, and the associated refrigeration ducting that would be required for the carriage of external stores. Under the code-name Operation 'Black Buck', these Vulcans would be prepared for attack missions over the Falkland Islands, carrying 21 x 1,000lb HE bombs over the staggering distance of 3,900 miles from the nearest operating base – Ascension Island. Preparing the aircraft for a conventional bomb load was a fairly simple task as although the Vulcans had been operating primarily in the tactical nuclear role for over ten years, they retained a conventional capability, and only a change in bomb carriers and cockpit control panels was required. A Delco inertial navigation system was also installed. This was purchased off-the-shelf from British Airways, who use the same INS in their Boeing 747s, and also taken from former British Airways Super VC10s which were in storage at RAF Abingdon, awaiting conversion to tanker standard. The first trial INS fit was made at Marham, where the resident Victor fleet had already been equipped with Carousel and Omega, but although the idea of fitting Omega in the Vulcans was considered, the modification was not made.

Five crews were selected (although only four were eventually fully trained) for 'Black Buck' duties, two from No. 50 Squadron, one from No. 44 Squadron, one from No. 101 Squadron, and another crew from the recently disbanded No. 9 Squadron. Some of the crews had recent 'Red Flag' exercise experience, which it was felt would be of value when faced with a real combat situation. Aerial refuelling training sorties began on 14 April – 'catching up on thirteen years of inexperience in thirteen days'. It quickly became apparent that the Vulcan's refuelling probe was prone to fuel spillage and leakage, and various short-term 'fixes' were improvised to prevent fuel flowing back over the windscreen, almost totally obscuring the pilot's forward view. No perfect solution was found, and two rows of flat plates were attached to the nose behind the refuelling probe in an effort to direct the stream of fuel away from the canopy. On the evenings of 16 and 17 April the crews flew night refuelling sorties with Victor tankers, and even the Victor crews had to familiarize themselves with the skills necessary to refuel from other Victors at night, as until now there had been no requirement for such operations.

The Vulcans selected for 'Black Buck' were all equipped with Olympus 301 engines, and in an effort to extend their service life the throttle mechanisms had been fitted with a restriction device, which effectively gave the engines a maximum thrust of 18,000lb. This was removed and the engines were restored to their original full power status. Because the Argentine Air Force was known to be operating a Boeing 707 in the airborne early warning role over the South Atlantic, and because ground-to-air radar had been positioned in the Falklands, it was decided to equip the Vulcans with additional ECM protection; the only readily available equipment was the Westinghouse AN/ALQ-101 pod normally carried by Buccaneers. Fortunately Avro's Skybolt modifications now proved to be invaluable, as the wing hardpoints provided a suitable location from which to attach the ECM pod. Moregood fortune revealed the presence of some mild steel girders at Waddington, which had been mistakenly ordered some time previously, and when suitable sections were welded together, a near-perfect weapons pylon was produced. The electric cables necessary for operating the pod were run through the Skybolt's coolant pipes and connected to a control panel fitted in the Air Electronics Officer's crew position. XM645 had also originally been selected for 'Black Buck' modifications but because it was a late production machine, manufactured after Skybolt had been abandoned, it was consequently devoid of the appropriate hardpoints and ducting, so no further modifications were made to this aircraft. The 'Black Buck' Vulcans retained their normal service camouflage, although all squadron markings were

Above: *XM612 returns to the apron at Wideawake, Ascension Island, May 1982, with a pair of Harrier GR.3s in the distance and RAF personnel unloading supplies in the foreground. Just visible is the AN/ALQ-101 pod under the Vulcan's starboard wing. (Ministry of Defence)*

removed and the undersides were hastily painted Dark Sea Grey.

With no sign of a political solution to the Falklands crisis seeming likely, the crews continued intensive training, flying night missions down to 200 feet AGL – much lower than ever before. The first two Vulcans (XM607 and XM598) left Waddington for Ascension Island at 0900Z on 29 April, with XM597 taking off as a reserve but later returning base. Supported by Victor tankers, the two Vulcans made their 4,100-mile journey to Ascension, arriving at 1800Z. The first mission ('Black Buck One') was to be an attack on the airfield at Port Stanley, which the Argentine Air Force was expected to use as a forward base for Mirage, Skyhawk and Super Etendard fighters. Only one Vulcan would be used as the tanker support required to support just one Vulcan on such a lengthy mission was phenomenal; in any event, Wideawake airfield was not large enough for any larger 'packages' to be assembled.

Shortly before midnight on 30 April, the two Vulcans (XM598 with XM607 as a spare) taxied to the threshold of Widewake's runway, accompanied by four Victors (including one spare). At one-minute intervals, in radio silence and with all navigation lights switched off, the fearsome combine then thundered into the air. Each Vulcan carried a bomb load of 21 x 1,000lb bombs (with an overload take-off weight of 210,000lb, compared with the normal maximum of 204,000lb), while the Victors were heavily laden with transfer fuel. Shortly after their departure, a second wave of seven Victors (one a reserve) also rumbled skywards, and the thirteen-aircraft formation began to head south, climbing to 27,000 feet.

The crew of the primary Vulcan (XM598) encountered problems with the aircraft's port direct-vision window which refused to seal, thus preventing the crew cabin from pressurizing properly. Consequently XM607, captained by Flight Lieutenant Martin Withers, became the primary aircraft, and the reduced formation climbed at 260 knots to 33,000 feet, a compromise altitude between the optimum cruising height for each aircraft type. The plan was for the Vulcan to make five refuelling contacts ('prods'), but six were actually made as the Vulcan's unusually high operating weight, together with the additional drag of the ECM pod, required even more fuel than envisaged. The long haul south was maintained at heights varying between 27,000ft and 32,000 feet, severe thunderstorms and turbulence being encountered along the way. Most of the supporting Victors gradually peeled off and headed north, eventually leaving just two Victors and XM607. Although the Vulcan crew were obviously unaware of it at the time, the Victor tasked with the Vulcan's final pre-attack refuelling flew into turbulence while refuelling from the second Victor (XL189), causing contact to be broken. This caused the receiver to head back to base, leaving XL189 to refuel XM607.

Squadron Leader Bob Tuxford, captain of the Victor, was forced to wave off the Vulcan (using signal lights), before XM607's tanks were completely topped up; otherwise there would have been no way in which the Victor could have returned to Ascension safely. At 300 miles from the target, XM607 descended to approximately 250 feet for an under-the-radar approach to the target, the co-pilot re-taking his cockpit from an AARI (Air-to-Air Refuelling Instructor) who had sat there temporarily while refuellings were being made. At forty miles from the target, Flight Lieutenant Withers hauled the Vulcan back up to 10,000 feet and turned onto a heading of 235deg, for Port Stanley's airfield. Some initial difficulty was encountered in establishing a radar picture, as the H2S had been switched off for most of the flight (the nose probe fuel pipe runs through the radar bay), but a good picture of the Falklands was eventually secured. At least one Argentine AAA radar illuminated the Vulcan en route to the target, but it fell silent when the AN/ALQ-101 pod was activated, and the Vulcan crossed the airfield runway diagonally, ensuring that at least one bomb stood a good chance of hitting the tarmac runway. In five seconds (although the crew later said that it seemed like an eternity) the 21 bombs dropped from the bomb bay in a single stick, and a few seconds later the airfield erupted into a brief blaze of light. A few of the bombs were fitted with 30- and 60-minute delay fuses, adding to the confusion of the occupying Argentine forces, who had been enjoying a peaceful night until XM607 made her violent appearance. At 0746Z the codeword 'Superfuse' was relayed to base, signifying the success of the attack (a 1982 equivalent of the Dambuster's famous 'Nigger' codeword). This enabled Squadron Leader Tuxford in Victor XL189 to radio for another Victor to be scrambled from Ascension, so XL189 would not run out of fuel some 400 miles from Wideawake.

Turning back northwards, the plan had called for an initial outbound height of 300 feet, but to conserve fuel XM607 began to climb towards the first refuelling rendezvous which was eagerly awaited, the Vulcan being some 8,000lb short on fuel. As the time for the Victor rendezvous came and went, the Vulcan crew began to worry but thirty minutes later contact was made, thanks to the assistance of a Nimrod crew in the vicinity who directed the two aircraft to each other. With roughly one hour's-worth of fuel remaining, the refuelling was complicated by a considerable amount of leakage, making forward vision difficult. This prompted the Vulcan's Nav Radar officer to stand half-way up the pilot's access steps, to peer through a small portion of the lower windscreen which remained clear, in order to co-ordinate the 'prod'. The rest of the flight back to Ascension was largely uneventful and XM607 touched down at Wideawake at 1452Z to complete what was the longest bombing mission ever flown by any aircraft. The attack was successful, the oblique approach to the airfield ensuring

Below: *Stanley airfield after the first Vulcan bombing run.(Crown Copyright)*

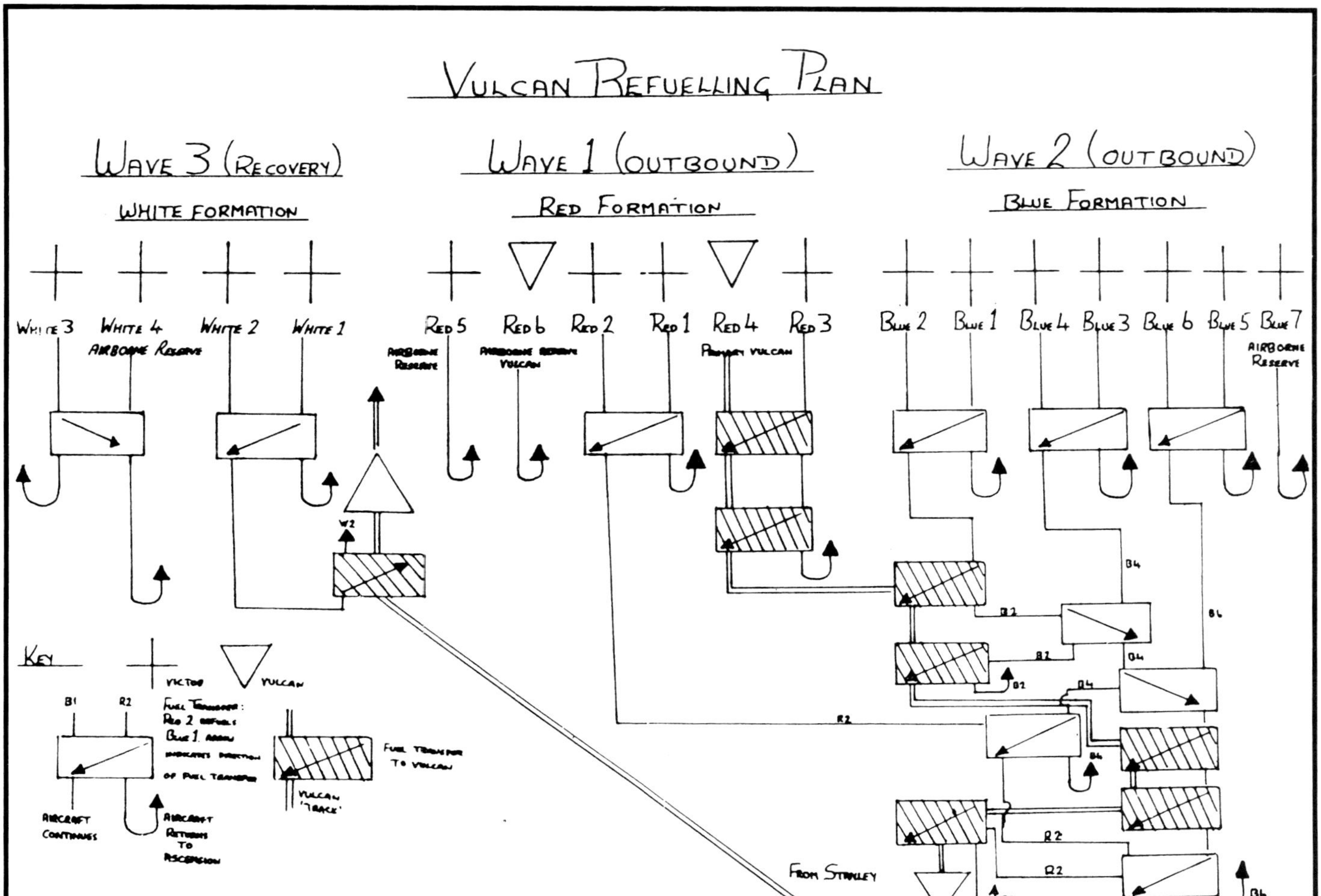

REFUELLING PLAN FOR BLACK BUCK 1

that one bomb would fall on the runway. One such bomb produced a crater in the centre of the runway's width, midway along its length. Additional damage was caused to other parts of the airfield, including the destruction of a hanger. The Agentinians were denied the unrestricted use of the airfield and the attack had also produced an obvious deterrent effect. It demonstrated to Argentina that even her mainland bases were not invulnerable and prompted the allocation of resources away from the Falklands, in defence of these airfields, even though the practicalities of attacking Argentina directly were never actively considered by the RAF.

A second mission ('Black Buck Two') was flown on 3 May, with the same aircraft, effectively making a repeat performance of the first sortie. However, the attack altitude was raised to 16,000 feet, and no bombs hit the runway, even though significant damage was caused to surrounding parts of the airfield. A third mission ('Black Buck Three') was scheduled for 16 May, but forecast winds would have reduced fuel reserves beyond an acceptable limit and the mission was cancelled before take-off. In the meantime, XM607 had returned briefly to Waddington where the port pylon was removed (the crews thought, erroneously, that it would cause excessive drag), and XM598 had been replaced by XM612. Perhaps the final word on these bombing missions should go to Flight Lieutenant Withers: 'Thanks to the massive team effort involving twenty aircraft and about 200,000 gallons of fuel, we managed to put a bomb on the runway, which was the aim of the exercise. We thus denied its use to high-performance aircraft and showed the Argentinians that we had the capability to attack their mainland – a threat which they certainly took seriously, because many of their Mirages which had been deployed south were recalled to defend their own bases. This must have considerably helped the Harriers to attain air superiority.'

Following the attacks on Port Stanley's airfield, attention now turned to Argentine radars, in particular a Westinghouse AN/TPS-43F and a Cardion TPS-44. Skyguard and Super Fledermaus were also in use, and back at Waddington plans were being made to equip the Vulcan for anti-radar attacks. The AS.37 Martel anti-radar ASM was selected as a suitable weapon, as the RAF already had these missiles in good supply for the Buccaneer squadrons. With roughly eight times as many wires to attach than needed for the ECM pod, the engineering crews at Waddington worked long and hard until, on 4 May, XM597 carried the missile into the air for the first time under the port wing hardpoint, with an ECM pod attached to the starboard pylon. A live firing was made over the Aberporth range the next day, after a cold-soak at

Above: *XM597, seen emerging from a hangar at Waddington, carries a Martel ASM and an AN/ALQ-101 pod. Note also the fuel dispersal vanes in front of the windscreen. (RAF Waddington)*

Below: *Martel ASM attached to XM597's port wing hardpoints, prior to a trial flight. (RAF Waddington)*

altitude. Although the test firing was successful, there was some concern over the reliability of the missile after a long flight south at high altitude. However, the US Government stepped in and offered to supply the AGM-45A Shrike, after the Secretary of State (Alexander Haig) had ended his famous 'even-handed' mediation between Britain and Argentina. The Vulcan's pylons were reconfigured to accommodate one Shrike under each wing and moretrial flights began; the pylons were subsequently adapted to carry twin-missile launchers on each pylon.

On 26 May XM596 flew to Ascension, followed a day later by XM597 which was fitted with missiles at Wideawake. The first operational mission ('Black Buck Five') was launched on the night of 28 May, but the attack was aborted five hours into the mission when one of the supporting Victor's HDU's (Hose Drum Units) failed. 'Black Buck Five' began the following evening and everything went well, with XM597 descending to 300 feet when approximately 200 miles from the Falklands. At 20 miles the aircraft climbed to 16,000 feet and quickly picked up signals from the primary target, the AN/TPS-43F radar, although the unit was quickly switched off. It was later learned that the Argentine operators were attempting to make the radar's signal strength weaker than normal in order to fool the Vulcan crew into thinking that the radar was further away than it really was, and thus lure the Vulcan within the range of anti-aircraft guns. However, 40 minutes later the radar was reacquired and two Shrikes were launched at 0845Z on 31 May. One of the missiles caused damage to the radar, but it was quickly repaired and a revetment was constructed to protect it from further damage. 'Black Buck Six' was launched on the evening of 2 June, this time with four Shrikes, and the same radar unit was again identified during the run-in to the Falklands. After spending 40 minutes in the area, waiting for that, or any other radar, to illuminate the Vulcan, a dummy run was made towards Port Stanley's airfield, and a Skyguard radar was quickly identified. Two Shrikes were launched and made a direct hit; four Argentine soldiers were killed. As the Vulcan's fuel state deteriorated, XM597 began the long journey north, making a rendezvous with a Victor with assistance from a Nimrod crew.

The Vulcan's refuelling was not without incident and during the 'prod' the aircraft's probe broke off at the tip, leaving XM597 without sufficient fuel to reach Ascension. The only alternative for XM597's crew was to divert to the nearest airfield, which was Rio de Janeiro in Brazil. Even so, there was little chance of reaching the Brazilian coast if the Vulcan remained at the refuelling height of 20,000 feet, so a climb to 40,000 was initiated to conserve the remaining fuel. The two remaining Shrikes were fired but one hung up; there was no other way to jettison the missile and it remained attached to its pylon. Various sensitive documents were collected and loaded into a hold-all bag, before being dumped through the crew entrance. In

Below: *Perhaps the most famous of all Vulcans, XM607 is seen at Waddington a few weeks after completing its historic bombing mission to the Falklands. A Shrike training round is attached to the port wing weapons pylon. XM607 is now on display at Waddington, although the aircraft is out-of-bounds to the public. Sadly, the one Vulcan which really should be inside a museum is parked outside, suffering from the extremes of the British climate. (Tim Laming)*

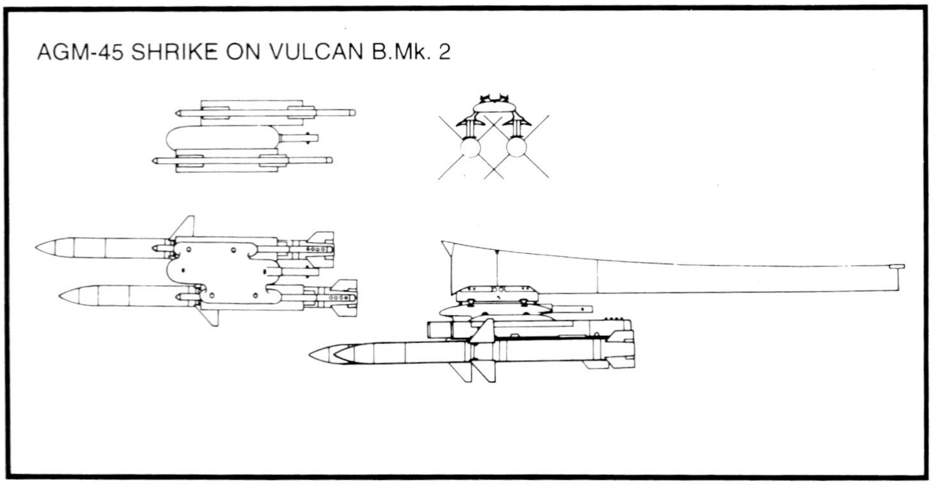

order to open the door at 40,000 feet, the cockpit was first de-pressurized, while the crew breathed oxygen. At a distance of around 200 miles, a 'Mayday' call was made to the airport at Rio. Contact with Brazilian ATC was difficult at first because XM597's crew attempted to keep their identity concealed for as long as possible, while diplomatic staff contacted Embassy officials in Rio. However, an initial descent to 20,000 feet was eventually cleared and, with the runway just six miles away, a straight-in approach was initiated, with a steep spiral descent, airbrakes out and throttles closed. Thanks to some careful flying by the captain, Squadron Leader Neil McDougall, XM597 straightened out at 800 feet, just one and a half miles from touchdown (at twice the normal speed), and then made a gentle touchdown with only 2,000lb of fuel remaining – less than that necessary for just one airfield circuit. After landing, the remaining Shrike was made safe, before it was impounded by Brazilian authorities. The Vulcan crew were well treated and although they were soon allowed to leave, they elected to stay with XM597 until she too was cleared to leave, minus the Shrike. On 10 June the aircraft returned to Ascension and on the 13th flew home to Waddington, complete with a new refuelling probe.

__Left:__ Two Shrikes fitted to XM597's port wing hardpoint. The 'Ascension 82-Go Brits' artwork was applied to the mainwheel door at Wideawake by enthusiastic USAF personnel. (Mike Jenvey)

__Below:__ XM597 wearing Dark Sea Grey undersides as applied for Operation 'Black Buck'. Visible on the nose are the two Shrike mission markings together with a Brazilian flag, the latter in recognition of XM597's unscheduled visit to Rio de Janeiro. Note the fully deflected wing control surfaces, as the nose is held high for aerodynamic braking. (British Aerospace)

'Black Buck Seven' took off from Ascension on the evening of 11 June, with Vulcan XM607 flying a bombing mission against airfield facilities at Port Stanley; as the British forces anticipated capturing the airfield, there was no desire to cause further damage to the runway. Apart from an engine flame-out which required three re-light attempts, the mission was completely successful, a full load of 1,000lb HE and anti-personnel air-burst bombs being delivered over the airfield. Four days later the Argentine forces on the Falkland Islands surrendered, and no further Vulcan missions were undertaken. While the 'Black Buck' sorties were being made, other weapons options for the Vulcan were considered, including the fitment of Sidewinder AAMs and laser-guided bombs; indeed, LGB trial flights were made. However, none of these options was used operationally. After the Vulcans had returned to Waddington, conventional bombing training flights continued, together with some anti-radar defence supression sorties; XM597 and XM607, among others, were noted carrying Shrike training rounds. No. 44 Squadron finally disbanded on 21 December 1982, marking the end of Vulcan bomber operations. But even this was not to be the end of the RAF's association with the Vulcan as No. 50 Squadron remained in business, operating Vulcan K.2 tankers.

As a direct result of the Falklands conflict, the RAF suddenly had a huge requirement for air-to-air refuelling tankers, to support the seemingly endless supply flights to and from the Falklands, while still maintaining day-to-day activities back in the UK. The Victors were heavily committed and although the conversion of VC10s into tankers was under way, there was still a short-term requirement for more tankers. While the USAF supported RAF operations in the UK with Boeing KC-135 tankers, it was decided to convert a number

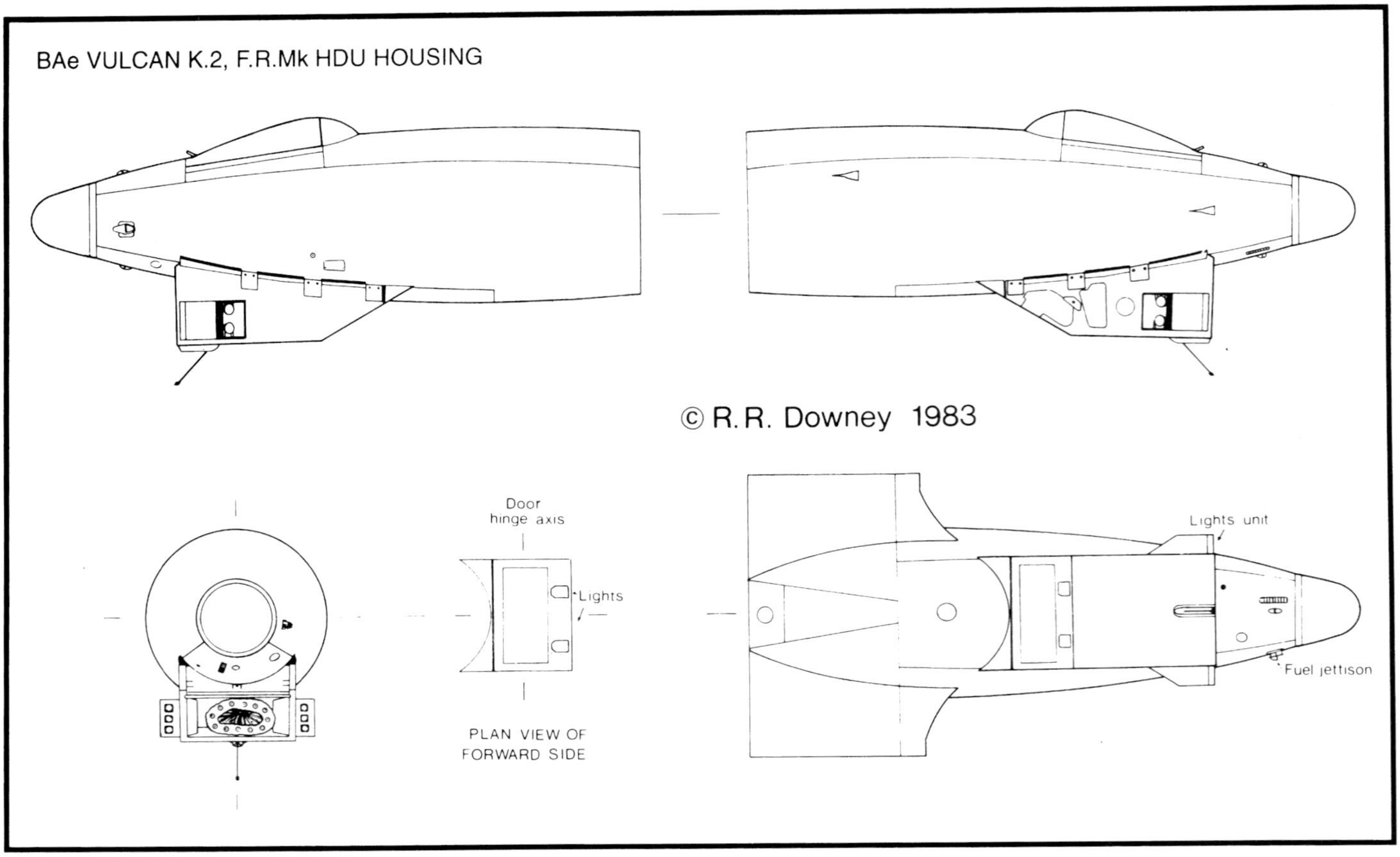
BAe VULCAN K.2, F.R.Mk HDU HOUSING
© R.R. Downey 1983
Door hinge axis
Lights
PLAN VIEW OF FORWARD SIDE
Lights unit
Fuel jettison

XH560

of Hercules and Vulcan aircraft into single-point refuelling tankers. The initial proposal, sent to British Aerospace at Woodford, was to install a hose drum unit (HDU) in the aft section of the Vulcan's bomb bay, the Vulcan then being designated B(K).2. But this idea was dropped, mainly because of the resulting proximity of the receiver to the tanker aircraft. It was felt that for safety the HDU should be placed as far aft as possible, to provide adequate separation between the tanker and receiver. The ECM bay was identified as being a suitable location, and this would also allow an additional fuel tank to be installed in the bomb bay. XM603, which had been delivered to Woodford after retirement, was used as a mock-up platform and, as J. J. Sherratt (BAe's Assistant Chief Designer for Victor tanker systems) explains, the task of fitting the HDU was far from simple:

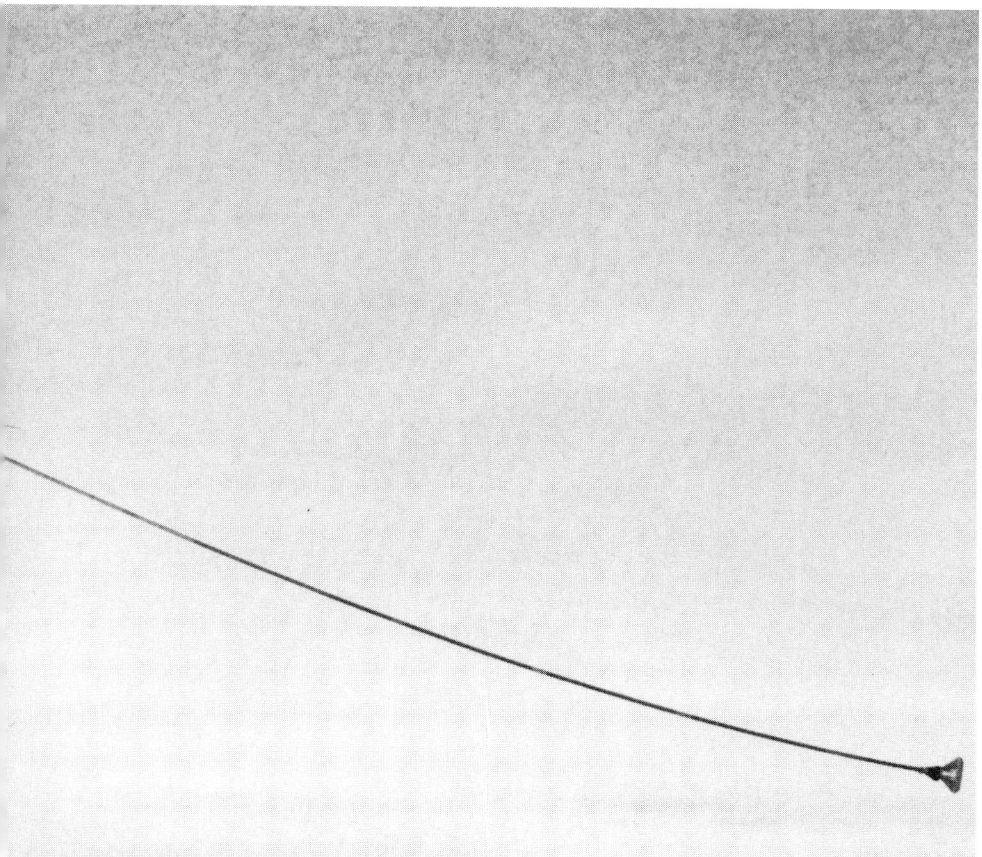

Below: *XH560 trailing a single refuelling hose and basket. Although the air sampling pods normally associated with the maritime radar reconnaissance role are not fitted, the smaller 'localizing' pod is attached under the port wing. (Mike Jenvey)*

'Sunday morning saw a group of us standing around a crated HDU, thinking that if it was anything like the size of the crate, we wouldn't stand much of a chance of fitting it. Even with the crate removed it looked big, but by this time we had resolved to get it into the Vulcan even if it meant restyling the back of the aircraft. There was no way of straight-lifting the five-and-a-half foot wide HDU through the existing ECM opening of four feet, but we noticed that the top part of the HDU could be separated from the bottom, and that we might be able to get the top half through the opening, leaving the bottom half to be straight-lifted in. A piece of wood the same size as the top section was called for to investigate the possibility. The verdict was that there was plenty of room if we had a good shoe-horn, and if necessary we could put the odd blister here and there to cover any awkward bits. After a design team meeting in the afternoon, we agreed to tell the MoD that we could do the job, and in the general euphoria, a target of three weeks to first flight was set. On Monday two representatives from Flight Refuelling arrived to advise us on splitting the HDU, and at around midday we received authority from MoD to proceed to the conversion of six aircraft. The first aircraft, XH561, arrived on Tuesday, by which time a whole army of workers had been mobilised to work all the hours it needed to do the job. Seven weeks to the day, on Friday 18th June, the first converted aircraft made its first flight at 12:32pm. An interim CA release was granted on June 23rd, and the first aircraft was delivered to the RAF on the same day.'

Sadly, the Vulcan K.2 did not enjoy a particularly long career with the RAF. Although the Vulcan proved to be an excellent tanker aircraft, the hose drum units had been out of production for some time, and the Mk.17 HDUs fitted to the Vulcans had already been allocated to the VC10s which were being converted to tankers. As the VC10s were completed, the HDUs were removed from the Vulcans, starting with XJ825 on 4 May 1983. On 31 March 1984, No. 50 Squadron, the last operational Vulcan unit, disbanded at Waddington, leaving just six K.2s and three B.2s to be delivered to museums and fire dumps.

XM597, which had been used for anti-radar strikes during the Falklands conflict, was flown to East Fortune, where it remains today with the Museum of Flight. XM652 was dismantled at Waddington and moved by road to Sheffield, where a private purchaser planned to house the aircraft in a leisure complex. Apparently the new owner had failed to establish the precise proportions of the Vulcan's airframe and decided that it was simply too big. The aircraft was therefore offered for re-sale and the nose section now resides in an unknown (private) location, while the rest of the airframe was scrapped – except for a few pieces which now reside in the author's attic! A happier fate was in store for XL426, as the MoD decided to retain the aircraft on a temporary basis for air display purposes.

Of the Vulcan tankers, XM571 was flown to Gibraltar where it was placed on display next to the runway and became a popular attraction for thousands of passing tourists. Astonishingly, the aircraft was scrapped during 1989. XL445 was flown to Lyneham where it was used for crash rescue training until 1991 when it too was scrapped. XJ825 remained atWaddington,

Vulcan K.2 XH560 transfers fuel to Vulcan B.2 XL426 over the North Sea in 1983. XL426 wears dayglo orange markings on the wing leading and trailing edges (top and bottom), presumably connected with Vulcan tanker trials. (Mike Jenvey)

XH560

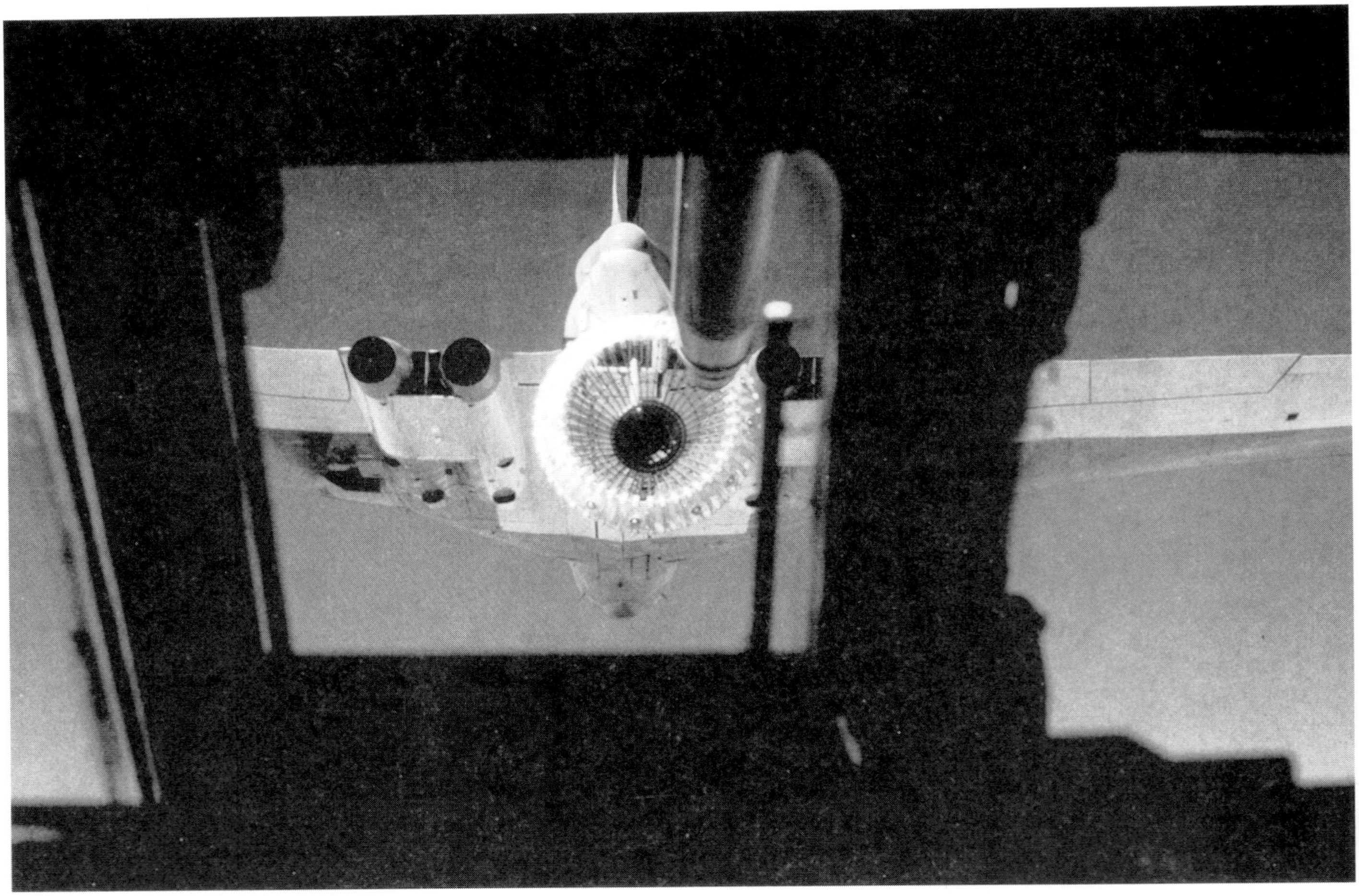

in use as a crash rescue and battle damage repair airframe until 1992 when, again, the scrap merchant arrived. Likewise, XH561 was destroyed at Catterick after serving for a few years as a crash rescue trainer.

XH558 was flown to RAF Marham on 17 September 1984 on what was to have been the aircraft's last flight, before suffering the same fate as the other Vulcan tankers. XH560 managed to survive for a time, being designated as a replacement for XL426 (which was running out of hours) on the air display circuit. But once again fate intervened; as a crew from Waddington began to remove all usable items from XH558, a study of XH560's paperwork revealed that only 160 flying hours were left before a major service was due. After examining the logs of the other recently retired aircraft, it was discovered that XH558 had 600 hours left until its next major service was due. Consequently XH560 was flown to Marham (where it was eventually scrapped during 1992), and XH558, looking rather battle-worn, was restored to a basic flying condition and ferried back to Waddington on 30 November.

The next major task was to convert XH558 back to standard bomber configuration. A draft SEM (Service Embodied Modification) was compiled by Chief Technicians Brian Webb, Al Hutchinson and Bob Leese. This was submitted to both the MoD and British Aerospace at Woodford for approval and in February 1985 the conversion began. The HDU housing, associated fuel pipes, air pipes and huge quantities of wiring were removed and the original electrical system was restored. After two months (and roughly 1,200 man-hours) XH558 was once again a B.2, albeit slightly modified as the ECM equipment was not replaced in the tail fairing because of structural modifications made by BAe during tanker conversion. The associated cooling duct on the starboard side of the tail cone was not replaced either, and is the only external difference between XH558 and a standard B.2. Internally, however, some tanker systems were retained, and one of the three bomb bay fuel tanks was also left in place to counterbalance the missing ECM equipment.

Following minor servicing, the aircraft departed for RAF Kinloss where it was stripped and resprayed in a 'wrap-around' camouflage, representative of the tactical scheme worn by many Vulcans towards the end of their careers (although XH558 never carried the scheme). Another non-standard 'mod' was a high-gloss polyurethane finish, helping to protect the airframe from the harsh British climate. Emerging from the paint shop at Kinloss in November,

Above: *Receiver's eye-view of Vulcan K.2 XH561 as the Nimrod's probe (which had been taken from a Vulcan) moves towards the refuelling basket for a 'prod'. (British Aerospace)*

Right: *Although never used operationally, laser-guided 1,000lb HE bombs were dropped by a Vulcan (XM597) during trials carried out in 1982. This unique photograph illustrates the mounting positions for three LGBs. (RAF Waddington)*

XH558 made its public debut the following year. XL426 was finally sold and ferried to Southend in December 1986, leaving the illustrious XH558 as the sole remaining airworthy Vulcan.

The future was not exactly secure however as the continuation of the Vulcan Display Flight at Waddington (XH558 actually belonged to No. 55 Squadron at Marham for administrative purposes) was regularly reviewed by MoD. While XH558's countless fans watched with delight as Squadron Leader David Thomas and Flight Lieutenant Paul Millikin put her through her paces, there was continual doubt as to how long the aircraft could remain in RAF service. Sufficient airframe hours remained to allow XH558 to fly a full 1992 display season, and a more restricted number of venues during 1993, but no official word was given until a few months ago, when the aircraft was offered for sale.

It was this final act by the MoD that prompted an endless number of campaigns and petitions to keep XH558 flying. The 'Vulcan Association' was formed in 1987, dedicated to publicizing the uncertain future of XH558 in the hope that continual public support would encourage the MoD to keep the Vulcan flying. Sadly, internal problems befell the group and, despite its many thousands of members, the VA effectively disappeared long before the aircraft it was supporting. But even this severe blow did not silence the Vulcan fans. The Vulcan Display Flight continued to receive huge quantities of fan mail, all of which said basically the same thing: 'What can I do to help keep XH558 flying?' Unfortunately the answer seemed to be not much, unless you happened to have around a million pounds to spare.

The future for XH558 continued to be just as uncertain as it ever was. There was no official statement from the Secretary of State for Defence, and a number of varying statements from MoD departments. The cost of maintaining XH558 was doubtless a major factor in the decision to ground the Vulcan, but the biggest factor appears to have been the cost of refurbishing the aircraft for another five to ten years of display flying. Cost estimates from the MoD varied wildly from a quarter of a million pounds to around £2½ million, depending upon who was asked. Whatever the true figure, it was clearly a ridiculously small amount when compared with the annual operating costs of the 'Red Arrows', for example. But who could claim that the Vulcan was any less effective as an RAF publicity/recruiting medium? The petitions continued to be signed (estimated at over 100,000 signatures already); MPs continued to be questioned; but the final disposal of XH558 remained in the balance. In November 1992 the MoD announced that XH558 was, at least for the time being, no longer for sale. In addition, the RAF confirmed that the aircrew had been instructed to remain current, and that the Vulcan's groundcrew had not received postings to new units.

Consequently, there was great optimism within the many enthusiast communities, that XH558 would be retained for further display flying, and the possibility of civilian sponsorship began to look like a workable proposal. Most notably, the 'Save the Vulcan 558 Campaign' made great efforts to convince the MoD that XH558 could be operated by the RAF on a 'no cost' basis, with civilian finance, and the future began to look a little brighter. But sadly, the Ministry of Defence had evidently decided to dispose of the Vulcan almost regardless of any sponsorship proposals which could have been

organised, given sufficient time. The 'final blow' was the announcement that the RAF would not be able to provide suitably qualified manpower to service the Vulcan beyond the end of 1993. The Mod based this statement upon the fact that the remaining Victor tankers would be retired at that time, and consequently the RAF would no longer retain any technicians with 'V-Bomber' experience. Whether this really was a valid point is open to question, as the RAF will continue to train crews to service 'heavies' such as the VC10 and Nimrod, and the predictable reaction of the Vulcan's supporters was that the MoD was simply 'washing its hands' of the whole affair, and was looking for a suitable excuse.

Above: *Shortly before retirement, four of the No. 44 Squadron Black Buck Vulcans made a four-ship formation tour of locations associated with the Vulcan. Thankfully, all four aircraft escaped destruction and were delivered to museums. XM597 went to East Fortune, XL391 to Sunderland, and XM612 to Norwich, while XM607 – possibly the most famous Vulcan of all, remained at Waddington where the aircraft was placed on public display in a small park, in company with a Victor which was also used during the Black Buck missions. Subsequent changes resulted in the Victor being scrapped (for no reason other than bureaucracy), and Waddington later extended the base's public access well beyond sight of the Vulcan, so that only a favoured few are now able to see this historic aircraft.*

But whatever the reason, the MoD stood by its view that XH558 was a public expense which simply could not be afforded any longer, and early in 1993 it was announced that XH558 was once again 'for sale'. The announcement was perhaps inevitable, but the debate as to whether it was the right decision, will doubtless continue for many, many years. It was estimated by some commentators that the Vulcan had become the RAF's most popular air show attraction, and yet, the MoD had decided to end XH558's career, authorising monthly continuation flights to keep her crew 'current', until a final delivery flight could be made to her permanent resting place.

For some time, the final fate of XH558 was unclear, and while the aircraft continued to make occasional crew continuation sorties from Waddington, there appeared to be some hope that the aircraft might be kept airworthy once the RAF had finally disposed of her. However, romantic notions of seeing a Vulcan operate under civilian ownership did seem to be a little unrealistic, when the Civil Aviation Authority had made their position quite clear – the Vulcan was a complex aircraft which could not be permitted to fly as a civil 'warbird', at least not without the direct support of its manufacturer (British Aerospace, which was equally unenthusiastic). There were various bids made to the Ministry of Defence for the aircraft, including one bizarre plan to turn the aircraft into a restaurant, but among the interested parties was David Walton, head of a profitable family business based at Bruntingthorpe in Leicestershire.

Among Walton's business interests was a huge airfield facility at Bruntingthorpe, once used by the USAF as a B-66 base, and now utilised primarily as a car storage and test facility. A number of preserved aircraft had already arrived on the site, and Walton was persuaded to put in a bid for XH558. His offer was accepted, and on 23 March 1993 the aircraft was prepared to make the relatively short ferry flight to Bruntingthorpe from Waddington. Not surprisingly, the event had reached the attention of countless aviation enthusiasts, and a large number of spectators assembled around Waddington's perimeter to see the Vulcan's very last flight. Although there was plenty of optimism surrounding the aircraft's future, almost everyone believed that this would indeed be the last time that a Vulcan would fly.

Shortly after 11a.m., XH558's four engines were started, and the assembled crowds (which by now resembled a small air show audience) prepared to witness the historic event. Although there was a great deal of excitement, there was a also a tangible feeling of sadness, and more than a few tears were wiped away as XH558 made her way to the runway threshold for the very last time. Finally, the Vulcan's Olympus engines gave out their ear-splitting roar, and XH558 thundered skywards, heading west to begin a short tour of some familiar Vulcan sites, including Finningley, Coningsby and, of course, Woodford. Returning via Scampton, the Vulcan was directed above Lincoln Cathedral for the last time before heading directly over Waddington, bomb doors open (with the legend 'farewell' painted inside) for a final salute, a gentle wing rock signifying the very end of the Vulcan's long and illustrious career. Just a few minutes later, XH558 arrived overhead Bruntingthorpe before making her final touchdown on the airfield's 10,000-foot runway.

This would have been the end of the story, but David Walton persevered, and continually maintained contact with both the CAA and British Aerospace, carefully exploring the many and varied concerns which the authorities expressed as being good reason to keep the Vulcan grounded. Months of inactivity began to run into years, and although XH558 was occasionally treated to a full-power take-off run, her wheels remained on the runway, seemingly doomed to remain flightless forever. But Walton's dedication was rewarded, and finally the CAA agreed in principle that a Permit-to-Fly could be given to the Vulcan (now registered as a civilian aircraft G-VLCN) if a whole series of very detailed but vital steps were taken. First, a feasibility study was undertaken, revealing that the project was indeed a viable one, and this led to a technical survey, specifying the actual maintenance and restoration that would be required to make the aircraft fit to fly again. Both British Aerospace (now BAE Systems) and Marshall Aerospace were heavily involved in this task, and following a very thorough investigation, it was concluded that XH558 was in remarkably good condition, and that restoration could begin.

And so XH558 disappeared into her hangar at Bruntingthorpe, before being slowly disassembled into her main component parts. Many of these items were transferred to companies which were appointed to undertake specific restoration tasks, before reassembly at Bruntingthorpe, ready to begin flight testing if and when permission is granted. Of course, even if the restoration process is completed to the CAA's satisfaction, there is still the task of finding sufficient funds with which to pay for the restoration and subsequent operation of this huge aircraft. Cost estimates for the restoration are around £1.7 million, plus a further annual expenditure of £1.6 million (one RAF observer commented that the Battle of Britain Flight's complete display fuel bill would be consumed in just getting the Vulcan to the end of the runway!)

Sadly, the protracted nature of the project has led to a great deal of reluctance from potential sponsors. While many companies have expressed interest in the scheme, very few, apparently, are willing to commit funds to it, either because they are unsure of its likely outcome or (as one member of the restoration team commented) because they believe (wrongly) that other people will be only too eager to finance the aircraft, and so their own support won't be needed. Consequently, although XH558 has earned a great deal of corporate goodwill, it hasn't attracted nearly enough money to allow the project to proceed with complete confidence.

The Vulcan's story continues, with a mix of hope and uncertainty. The year 2002 marks the fiftieth anniversary of the Vulcan's first flight. Furthermore, it is the fiftieth anniversary of the type's famous first appearance at Farnborough, and it is also the year in which HM The Queen celebrates her Golden Jubilee. Interestingly, the 2002 Commonwealth Games will be held in Manchester, the city where the Vulcan was designed and built. Not surprisingly, many people have remarked that it would be quite a spectacle to see XH558 appear at the opening ceremony, in the skies above Manchester where she was created precisely fifty years previously. Whether this tremendous event actually happens depends on a mixture of goodwill and good fortune, plus a great deal of very hard work. But whatever happens, it is certainly clear that the magnificent Vulcan hasn't yet been forgotten.

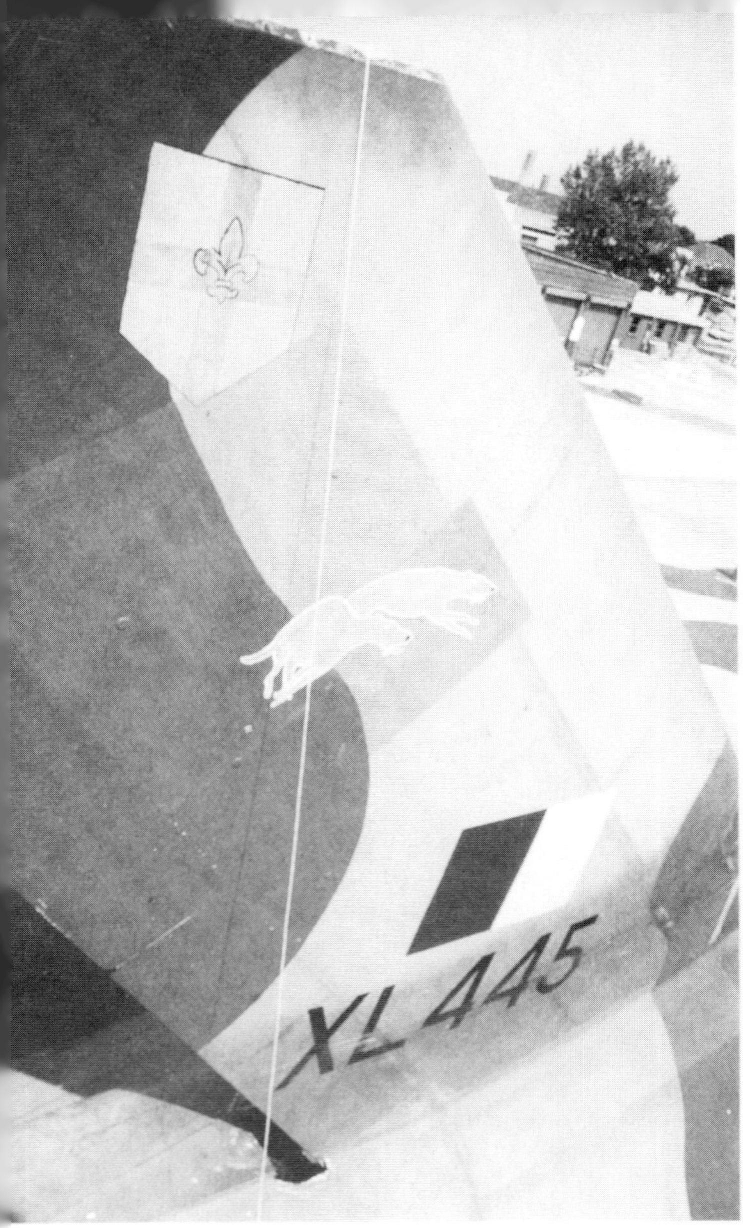

General views of a No 50 Squadron tanker undergoing line maintenance, illustrating the 200-Series engine jet pipe and the tail-mounted parachute housing. The tail-mounted RWR housing is missing on this aircraft, having become detached while returning to Waddington from a refuelling mission – hence the appearance of a small cover and attachment cable.

Above: *Prior to becoming the RAF's dedicated display aircraft, XH558 ended her 'proper' RAF service career as a refuelling tanker aircraft with No 50 Squadron. Unusually, both XH558 and XH560 were also occasionally equipped with air-sampling pods to continue the monitoring duties previously undertaken by No 27 Squadron.*

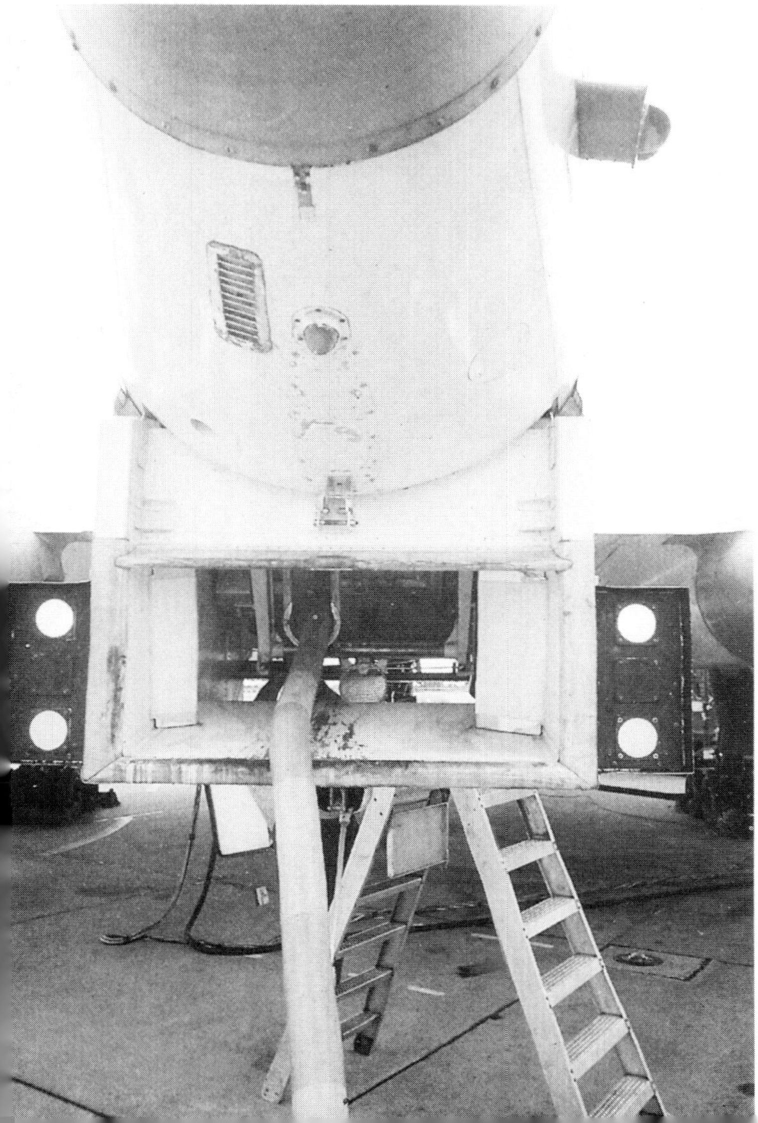

Left and above: *The rather rudimentary design of the hastily conceived hose drum unit (HDU) housing is clearly evident in these two photographs.*

Top: *An underside view of XH558, bomb doors open to reveal the standard tanker fit of three bay-mounted fuel tanks. Note also the ECM plate under the starboard jet pipes.*

Left: *Close-up view of the Vulcan's HDU mounting, with the external fairing removed.*

Inset: *The Vulcan tanker's HDU refuelling basket.*

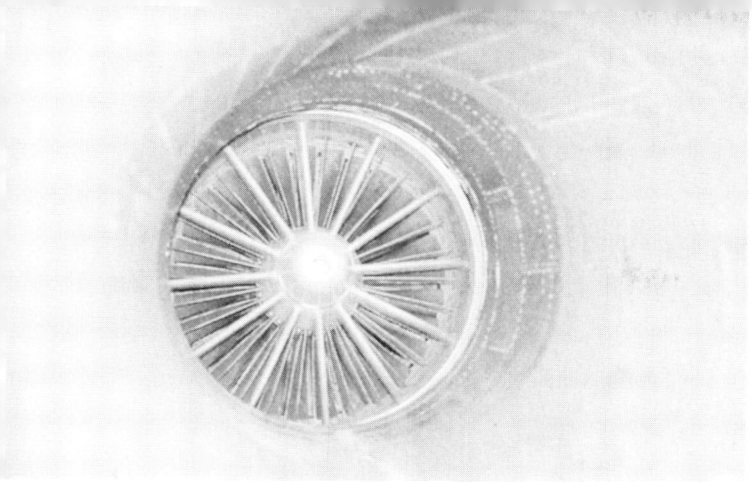

Top left: *A glimpse into the Vulcan's port outer engine intake, illustrating the deeply recessed engine intake blades.*

Top right: *Although the Vulcan's flight deck canopy could be completely removed, this was only done during servicing. Crew access to the flight deck was always made via the lower fuselage entrance.*

Above: *With the huge nose fairing removed, the Vulcan's substantial radar antenna is clearly evident.*

Left: *Looking up into the Vulcan's port wing engine bay, illustrating the position of the two Olympus engines in relation to the main undercarriage bay.*

This is the flight deck of XH558, illustrating the relatively cramped accommodation for the captain and his co-pilot. Of particular note are the fighter-style joysticks, unusual for an aircraft of the Vulcan's weight and size. The small glazed sections afforded a fairly restricted view of the outside world, but could easily be blacked out for a nuclear strike.

Above: *This shows the upper surface of the Vulcan's port wing, with the airbrakes extended.*

Left and below left: *Starboard wing missile rails on XM597 with two AGM45 Shrike missiles fitted. Once again there are evident signs of hasty design in the pylon construction.*

Below: *Live 1,000lb high explosive bombs loaded into the Vulcan's bomb bay.*

The Aircrew Manual

The Vulcan B.Mk.2 Aircrew Manual was prepared by the Ministry of Defence Procurement Executive, based on information provided by A & AEE test crews at Boscombe Down. The following (edited) pages are taken directly from the publication, and provide precise details of the Vulcan's systems and operating procedures.

INTRODUCTION

General The Vulcan B Mk 2 delta-wing, all-metal aircraft may be powered by four Olympus 200 series engines, each developing 17,000 lb static thrust at sea level in ISA conditions, or by Olympus 301 engines, developing 18,000 lb static thrust. Provision is made for air-to-air refuelling. A ram air turbine and an airborne auxiliary power plant provide for emergency electrical supplies. Equipment bays outside the pressure cabin contain power distribution and fuse panels in addition to various components of the main services:

a. Nose section.
b. Nosewheel bay.
c. Main undercarriage bays.
d. Bomb bay.
e. Power compartment (aft of bomb bay).

Crew The aircraft is operated by a crew of five: 1st pilot, co-pilot, navigator/radar, navigator/plotter and air electronics officer (AEO). The pilots sit side-by-side in ejection seats on a raised platform at the front of the cabin normally referred to as the cockpit. Behind the pilots, facing aft, the rear crew members sit on bucket-type seats (the outer two swivelling) facing one long table, behind which is a crate carrying their equipment. A prone bombing position is in a blister below the pilots' floor.

Instrument Layout The pilots' instruments and controls are on the front panel (divided into four sections), the port and starboard consoles, the centre (retractable) console and the throttle quadrant.

Magnetic indicators and warning lights for the vital systems are grouped across the top of the pilots' front panel and consist of:

a. Two amber MAIN WARNING lights, one at either side, which indicate failure of the PFC units, feel units or autostabilisers (except the yaw dampers).
b. One red alternator failure (ALT FAIL) light which illuminates following a single alternator failure and flashes when two or more alternators fail.
c. Eight magnetic indicators (four each side of the alternator light) for PFC units, artificial feel, auto-stabilisers, airbrakes, bomb doors, canopy, entrance door and pressure-head heaters.

On the coaming above the pilots' front panel are four engine fire warning lights which also serve as fire extinguisher pushbuttons.

In addition, two red fire warning lights for the wing fuselage and bomb bay fuel tanks are at the top of the co-pilot's instrument panel. Post-SEM 012, only the bomb bay fire warning light is fitted.

AAPP	Airborne auxiliary power plant
ADD	Airstream direction detector
ADF	Automatic direction finding
ADP	Azimuth director pointer
AEO	Air electronics officer
ARI	Air radio installation
AVS	Air ventilated suit
BCF	Bromochlorodifluoromethane
BRSL	Bomb release safety lock
CSDU	Constant speed drive unit
DG	Directional gyro
DV	Direct vision
ECM	Electronic countermeasures
EHPP	Emergency hydraulic power pack
FRC	Flight reference cards
GPI	Ground position indicator
HF/SSB	High frequency, single side-band
HFRT	High frequency radio telephony
HRS	Heading reference system
IFF/SSR	Identification friend or foe, secondary surveillance radar
ILS	Instrument landing system
MFS	Military flight system
NBC	Navigation & bombing computer
NBS	Navigation & bombing system
NHU	Navigator's heading unit
NMBS	Normal maximum braking speed
NRV	Non-return valve
O/H	Overheat
PDI	Pilot direction indicator
PEC	Personal equipment connector
PESJ	Pilots emergency stores jettison
PFC	Powered flying controls
PFCU	Powered flying control unit
PSP	Personal survival pack
RAT	Ram air turbine
TASU	True airspeed unit
TBC	Tail brake parachute
TFR	Terrain following radar
TFRU	Terrain following radar unit
TRU	Transformer/rectifier unit
VSI	Vertical speed indicator

Leading Particulars

Principal Dimensions

Overall length	105ft	6in
Wing span	111ft	0in
Height to top of fin	27ft	1in
Wheel track	31ft	1in
Wheel base	30ft	1.5in

FuelSystem

Type of fuel:	*NATO Code*	*Designation*	*UK Spec*	*US Spec and Type*
Normal use	F34	Avtur	DERD 2453	MIL T-83133 (JP8)
	F40	Avtag	DERD 2454	MIL T-5624 (JP4)
Operational necessity	F35	Avtur	DERD 2494	—
	F44	Avcat	DERD 2452	MIL T-5624 (JP5)

Fuel Capacities

MAIN TANKS

Tank Group	*Tank No*	*Avtur (8 lb/gall): Gallons*	*Pounds*	*Avtag (7.7 lb/gall): Gallons*	*Pounds*
1 and 4	1	2 x 610	2 x 4880	2 x 620	2 x 4774
(outboard, port	4	2 x 630	2 x 5040	2 x 640	2 x 4928
and starboard)	5	2 x 515	2 x 4120	2 x 525	2 x 4042.5
	7	2 x 565	2 x 4520	2 x 575	2 x 4427.5
	Total each group	2 x 2320	2 x 18,560	2 x 2360	2 x 18,172
	Total both groups	4640	37,120	4720	36,344
2 and 3	2	2 x 935	2 x 7480	2 x 945	2 x 7276.5
(inboard, port	3	2 x 630	2 x 5040	2 x 640	2 x 4928
and starboard)	6	2 x 745	2 x 5960	2 x 755	2 x 5813.5
	Total each group	2 x 2310	2 x 18,480	2 x 2340	2 x 18,018
	Total both groups	4620	36,960	4680	36,036
	Total fuel	9260	74,080	9400	72,380

BOMB BAY TANKS

Tank	*Gallons*	*Pounds: Avtur*	*Avtag*
A (fwd saddle)	718	5744	5529
E (aft saddle)	721	5768	5552
Cylindrical (each usable) ...	995	7960	7662

Nitrogen Pressurisation

Cylinders	3 (6D/1825)
Charging pressures	2 at 3000 PSI
	1 at 1800 PSI

Power Units

Name	Olympus 200 series or Mk 301
Type	Turbo-jet
NumberFour	
Static thrust (200 series)	17,000 lb, sea level, ISA
Static thrust (Mk 301)	18,000 lb, sea level, ISA
External starting air	0.8 lb/sec at 40 PSI

Engine Oil System

Type	Integral with engine
Oil	OX-38 (34A/9100591, NATO O-149, D Eng RD2487)
Tank capacity (200 series)	$4\frac{1}{2}$ galls oil, $1\frac{1}{2}$ galls air space System capacity $2\frac{1}{4}$ galls
Tank capacity (Mk 301)	$3\frac{7}{8}$ galls oil, $1\frac{1}{8}$ galls air space System capacity $2\frac{1}{4}$ galls

Constant-Speed Drive Oil System

Type	Attached to engine
Oil	OX-38 (34A/9100591, NATO O-149, D Eng RD2487)
Tank capacity	11 pints oil, $3\frac{1}{2}$ pints air space, system capacity $12\frac{3}{4}$ pints

Starting System

Low-pressure air starter motor	Rotax CT0806/1 (one per engine)
Rapid start	CT1303

Engine Driven Auxiliaries

Hydraulic pumps	Three (Nos 1, 2 and 3 engines)
Constant-speed drives and alternators	Four, 40 kVA, one per engine

Airborne Auxiliary Power Plant

Type	Gas turbine (Mk 10301)
Number	One
Oil System	Sump type
Oil	OX-38 (34A/9100591, NATO O-149, D Eng RD2487)
Sump capacity	$4\frac{1}{2}$ pints (total oil in system 5 pints)
Starting	Cartridge or electric

Ram Air Turbine

Type	Plessey TRA 170/26
Output	17 kW, 200 volts, 3-phase, 400 Hz

Hydraulic System

Pumps	Three (engines Nos 1, 2 and 3)
Working pressure	3600-4250 PSI
Reservoir capacity	$2\frac{1}{4}$ galls
System capacity	12 galls
Fluid	OM-15 (34B/9100572, NATO H-515)

Hydraulic Power Pack

Type	E8908Y
Operating pressure	3500 to 3900 PSI
Motor	AC, 3-phase
Capacity	11 pints
Fluid	OM-15

Undercarriage Emergency Lowering System

Cylinders	Two Mk 5
Charging pressure	3000 PSI

Pneumatic System (Nitrogen)

Entrance Door System	
Cylinders	Three Mk 5F
Charging pressure	2000 PSI
H2S Scanner	
Cylinder	One (6D/9429885)
Charging pressure	1800 PSI
NBS	
Cylinder	One (6D/9429885)
Charging pressure	1800 PSI

Air Conditioning System

Turbine unit	Type BT15, Mk 2A
Oil	OX-38 (34A/9100591, NATO O-149)
Capacity	210 CC

Flying Controls

Power Units	
Outer elevons (four)	P135
Inner elevons (four)	P132
Rudder (two)	P138
Oil	OM-15 (34B/9100572, NATO H-515)
Motor gearbox oil	EEL3
Capacity (each)	
Outer elevons	4 pints
Inner elevons	4 pints
Rudder	8 pints
Airbrakes	
Oil (gearboxes)	OX-14 (34B/9100589, NATO O-147)

Bomb Aimer's Windscreen De-icing

Tank capacity	12 galls + 1/2 gall air space
Fluid	AL-8 (34B/9100475, NATO S-738)

Aerofoil and Engine Anti-Icing

Thermal system, using engine air

Fire Extinguishers

Engines	
Type	Mk 13A, methyl-bromide
Number	Four
Wing Tanks	
Type	Mk 14A, methyl-bromide
Number	Twelve
Fuselage Tanks	
Type	Mk 13A, methyl-bromide
Number	Four
Leading Edge	
Type	Mk 13A, methyl-bromide
Number	Six
Crew's Cabin	
Type	34H, BCF
Number	Five
AAPP	
Type	Mk 4AX, methyl-bromide (27N/152)
Number	One
External Compartment	
Type	34H, BCF
Number	One
Bomb Bay	
Type	Mk 13A, methyl-bromide
Number	Eight

Oxygen System

Regulator	Mk 21A, 21B or 17F demand system
Cylinders	Mk 10A (6D/9429900) (2250 litres)
Number	Twelve
Charge pressure	1800 PSI

Safety Equipment

Ejection Seats	
1st pilot	Type 3KS1 Mk 4
Co-pilot	Type 3KS2 Mk 4
Life raft	MS5

Electrical System

Type	AC
Alternators	
Number	Four
Type	Type 175, 40 kVA
Voltage	200 volt, 3-phase, 400 Hz, neutral earth
RAT alternator	22 kVA
AAPP alternator	40 kVA
Transformer rectifier units	Two, 7.5 kW, 28 volt, earth return One, 0.75 kW One, 112 volt
Battery	One, type K, 24 volt, 40 AH
Transformers	Two, 3 KVA, 115 volt, 400 Hz, 3-phase One, 1 kVA, 115 volt, 400 Hz, 3-phase One 40 VA, 115 volt, 400 Hz
Frequency changers	Two, 3 kVA, 115 volt, 1600 Hz, single phase

PART 1: AIR CONDITIONING

CABIN AIR SYSTEM

Cabin Air, General The cabin air conditioning and pressurisation system maintains comfortable temperatures and pressures within the crew compartment. Hot pressurised air tapped from the engine compressors, cooled by cold ram air and a cooling turbine, is distributed throughout the cabin via ducting. The temperature of the conditioned air is controlled by varying the proportion of hot air which flows through or bypasses the air cooler or the cooling turbine. The controlled air flow out of the cabin is used to cool equipment in the radome. Provision is made for conditioning the cabin air both on the ground and in unpressurised flight.

The cabin pressure is determined by the amount of air allowed to flow out of the crew compartment and is maintained by two pressure controllers. Pressurisation can be set for either cruise or combat conditions. Provision is made for emergency depressurisation.

The main controls for cabin heating and pressurisation are grouped together on the starboard console.

Cabin Air Conditioning Unit The air conditioning unit in the nosewheel bay consists of an air-to-air cooler, a temperature control valve (TCV), a cooling brake turbine unit and a water separator.
The cooler is supplied with cold air from a ram air intake between the cabin and the port engine air intake. The cold air passes through a rearward-facing duct below the unit.

The brake turbine unit is an inward flow turbine coupled to a centrifugal braking compressor. The turbine passes air from the TCV to a water separator and thence to the cabin. The compressor passes filtered air from the nosewheel bay through the exhaust duct. The speed of the turbine is monitored by a pressure ratio switch which, if the turbine overspeeds, automatically selects a warmer setting on the TCV thereby reducing the amount of air passed to the turbine. The COLD AIR UNIT OVERSPEED WARNING MI on the starboard console shows white, reverting to black when the overspeed has ceased.

The temperature control valve is electrically-operated, either automatically or manually. When maximum heat is selected, engine air passes directly from the flow valves, through the TCV, to the cabin. As the temperature setting is reduced, air is progressively allowed to pass through the cooler en route to the TCV. At the colder settings, the air passes to the cabin through the cooler, TCV and turbine.

An underheat sensing element opens a bypass valve when the air from the turbine falls below 2°C value, thus allowing warm air to mix with the cold air before it reaches the water separator.

An overheat switch operates to move the control valve towards the cool position when the output temperature rises to 175°C.

Cabin Pressurisation Cabin pressurisation is achieved by controlling the rate at which the air fed into the cabin is allowed to escape. Each of two pressure controllers, in the nose below the pilots' floor, supplies counterpressure to one of the bellows of the combined valve unit in the front pressure bulkhead. One controller is motorised allowing a CRUISE or COMBAT setting to be selected. The other is unmotorised and acts as a standby in the CRUISE setting. The ground test levers on the controllers must always be fully down in flight.

Pressurisation begins at 8000 ft and a cabin altitude of 8000 ft is maintained until the maximum differential pressure is reached. In CRUISE the maximum differential pressure is 9 PSI, attained at approximately 47,000 feet. In COMBAT, the maximum differential of 4 PSI is reached at approximately 19,500 feet. Above these altitudes, cabin altitude increases. The change from CRUISE to COMBAT setting takes place at 12 PSI per minute and from COMBAT to CRUISE at 1 PSI per minute.

SAFETY DEVICES. If cabin pressure falls ½ PSI below selected pressure, a contact in the motorised controller operates a warning horn and illuminates three red warning lights, one at each rear crew member's position. The warning horn may be isolated by a switch at the rear of panel 4P. To prevent the build-up of negative differential pressure, an inward relief valve on the front pressure bulkhead operates at ½ PSI. An outward relief valve, also on the front pressure bulkhead, operates at 9½ PSI to limit over-pressurisation. To safeguard against the cabin extractor ducting collapsing during rapid outflows of air, the combined valve unit is fitted with a duct relief valve. A decompression flap, visible from the cockpit on the upper port side of the nose fairing, allows excess air to escape from the nose radome.

FLOOD FLOW. Provision is made for flood flow but the system is inoperative.

DECOMPRESSION. To allow decompression of the cabin in an emergency, air release valves (in the lines between the pressure controllers and the bellows of the combined valve unit) can be operated to remove the counter-pressure from the bellows. Operation of the valves is controlled electrically by either pilot and electrically and mechanically by the rear crew. While the combined effect of the operation of the air release valves, duct relief and decompression flaps ensures a rapid release of cabin pressure, it may take up to 30 seconds for the pressure to fall sufficiently to allow the door to open.

Cabin Ventilation During unpressurised flight, the cabin can be ventilated via the ram air valve on the port side of the cabin. This allows air from the cabin conditioning ram air intake to enter the cabin but, unless the cabin switches are shut, the effect is negligible. The ram air valve should be closed before pressurising the cabin. The cabin may be ventilated on the ground with air supplies from the cooling air unit, via the normal control valves.

Individual face blowers (punkah louvres) for the rear crew are powered by a 200V AC blower unit under the navigator's table, controlled by a FACE BLOWING ON/OFF switch on the edge of the AEO's table.

Cabin Air Conditioning, Controls and Indicators GENERAL. The main cabin conditioning controls and indicators are grouped on panel 7P.

ENGINE AIR SWITCHES. The four ENGINE AIR OPEN/SHUT switches on the outboard side of the panel control the supply of engine air to the flow control valves, airframe anti-icing systems and to certain other services.

CABIN AIR SWITCHES. The two CABIN AIR OPEN/SHUT switches, beside the engine air switches, open the shut-off valves, allowing the engine air to pass to the air conditioning unit. One switch controls the starboard supply and one the port. When a switch is at OPEN, the auto-flow valve automatically regulates the volume of air passing to the system.

CABIN TEMPERATURE CONTROLS. Cabin temperature can be controlled automatically or manually. When the CABIN TEMP CONTROL switch is moved outboard to AUTO, the temperature is automatically controlled according to the setting of the AUTO TEMP SELECTOR rotary control beneath the TEMP CONTROL VALVE indicator. For MANUAL control, the switch is moved inboard and either forward or aft to the COLD or HOT position until the desired setting is obtained. The switch is spring-loaded from both these positions to the central (neutral) position.

RAM AIR VALVE. The ram air valve is controlled by a guarded SHUT/OPEN switch, spring-loaded to the central (neutral) position, as shown on the adjacent RAM AIR VALVE indicator.

CABIN PRESSURE CONTROLS. Cabin pressurisation is controlled by a 3-position CRUISE/COMBAT/NO PRESSURE (gated) PRESSURE SELECTOR. Cabin decompression (or lack of pressurisation) can be achieved by selecting the PRESSURE SELECTOR to NO PRESSURE, or by operating either pilot's ABANDON AIRCRAFT switch, the EMERGENCY DECOMPRESSION switch on the port console or the CABIN PRESSURE RELEASE lever above the Nav/plotter's position. There is also a switch in the nosewheel bay. The ABANDON AIRCRAFT and EMERGENCY DECOMPRESSION switches are lock-toggle types which must be pulled up before selection.

Operation of the Pressurisation System Before starting the engines, set the controls as given in the Flight Reference Cards.

After starting engines, set all ENGINE AIR switches OPEN and instruct the ASC to carry out a ducting leak check, after which all ENGINE AIR switches are to be SHUT. Except when airframe anti-icing is required or if flight safety considerations dictate otherwise, switches are normally to be as follows:

a. During taxying, all ENGINE AIR switches SHUT.

b. For take-off, climb and descent 1 and 2 ENGINE AIR switches with the PORT CABIN AIR switch, or 3 and 4 *ENGINE AIR* switches with the *STARBOARD CABIN AIR* switch *OPEN*. The port system is to be used on odd-numbered dates, the starboard on even-numbered ones.

c. At cruising altitude, all *ENGINE AIR* and *CABIN AIR* switches *OPEN*.

d. For roller landings, all *ENGINE AIR* switches *SHUT*.

If ram air flow is required, set the *PRESSURE SELECTOR* to *NO PRESSURE*, the *CABIN AIR* switches *OFF* and the ram air switch to *OPEN*.

Air conditioning is marginal when the *OAT* is near +29°C. Before descent to low level use the cold air turbine to pre-cool the cabin.

Cold Air Turbine Overspeed If the *COLD AIR UNIT OVERSPEED WARNING* indicator shows white, the pressure ratio switch has operated to stop overspeeding; the indication should be only temporary. If the system is being operated in *AUTO*, a warmer setting should be selected to prevent the recurrence of overspeeding; in *MANUAL* no action should be necessary as the temperature control valve will back off and remain at a warmer setting. If overspeeding persists on the climb, close an *ENGINE AIR* switch and check that the indicator goes black; re-open the *ENGINE AIR* switch at altitude. If a colder setting is needed and cannot be obtained because of turbine overspeed, reduce the air supply to the turbine at cruising altitude by closing a *CABIN AIR* switch. When non-essentials are tripped, the overspeed magnetic indicator still functions although the temperature control valve cannot be moved. The overspeed can be terminated by selectively closing *ENGINE AIR* switches.

Loss of Cabin Pressure If there is a serious leak in cabin pressure, or if, during the climb, the aircraft rate of climb exceeds the rate of pressurisation, the warning horn sounds.

Emergency Decompression In an emergency, cabin pressure can be released by any of the following:

a. Rearward movement of the *EMERGENCY DECOMPRESSION* switch (1st pilot).

b. Rearward movement of either *ABANDON AIRCRAFT* switch.

c. Selection of *NO PRESSURE* on the *PRESSURE SELECTOR* (co-pilot).

d. Operation of the *CABIN PRESSURE RELEASE* lever (nav/plotter).

Methods a. to c. are electrical and operate via a common fuse (3P 636). Method d. operates mechanically and electrically via a separate fuse (4P 562).

To increase the rate of depressurisation, switch off the *CABIN AIR* switches at the same time as decompression action is taken. When re-pressurising the cabin, select *COMBAT* initially.

AIR-VENTILATED SUITS SYSTEM

Normal Air-Ventilated Suits (AVS) System The air-ventilated suits are supplied from an air conditioning unit, similar to the cabin conditioning unit. The AVS unit uses hot air from the engines or AAPP, and cold air from the cabin system ram air intake. A ground-conditioning connection is provided, so that an external supply may be plugged into the suits.

AVS Air Conditioning Unit The AVS air conditioning unit, in the nosewheel bay just aft of the cabin conditioning unit, comprises an air-to-air cooler, a turbine and fan, a flow augmenter, a water extractor, a heat exchanger, and a filter. Hot air from the flood flow supply line passes, via an electrically-operated on-off cock, to the air-to-air cooler and then to the turbine and the water extractor. A branch line of the hot air bypasses the cooler and turbine and feeds into the water extractor via a temperature control valve, while a further line passes through another temperature control valve to the heat exchanger.

The temperature control valve in the hot-air line to the water extractor is controlled by a sensing element in the line between the water extractor and the heat exchanger. The temperature control valve in the hot-air line to the heat exchanger is controlled by a sensing element, set at 15°C, in the manifold inlet.

A tapping from the air from the cooler passes through a flow augmenter to the forward side of the water extractor, to provide additional pressure at altitude. This air, mixed with the air from the turbine, passes through the filter to the manifold in the cabin via a non-return valve.

AVS Components in Cabin The temperature and pressure of the air in the manifold are regulated by a sensing element, which operates to regulate the cock supplying hot air to the conditioning unit, and a pressure relief valve and pressure controller. From the manifold, individual lines (each with an electric heater and a manual flow control valve) pass to the crew positions. The AVS hoses for the 6th and 7th seats are fed from the nav/radar's and AEO's AVS lines respectively.

Auxiliary AVS System The auxiliary AVS system, for cooling, operates by drawing cabin air through the crew's AVS. A 200V AC exhauster unit under the navigator's table is controlled by an AVS *ON/OFF* switch on the edge of the AEO's table. The pilots select auxiliary AVS by means of individual AVS *CHANGEOVER COCK* switches which operate changeover cocks under the navigator's table. Rear crew members have a separate line and flow cock. To prevent overheating, the exhauster motor is not to be switched on unless at least one flow cock is open.

AVS Controls

a. The normal AVS system is controlled by an *OPEN/CLOSE* switch at the rear inboard edge of panel 7P, which controls the main cock in the hot air supply and makes power available to the individual suit heaters.

b. Temperature and flow controls are provided for each individual suit, as follows:

(1) 1ST PILOT AND CO-PILOT. Rear end of port and starboard consoles.

(2) BOMB-AIMER. On starboard side adjacent to oxygen regulator.

(3) RADAR AND AEO. On forward edge of the navigator's table (also control heating to 6th and 7th seat positions).

(4) PLOTTER. Temperature control on port side and flow control on starboard side of seat.

c. Temperature is adjusted by a rotary control, consisting of two concentric knobs. The outer allows the systems to be operated automatically or manually and the inner selects the desired temperature, which is held automatically if AUTO is selected and the temperature selected is below 21°C. This switch is also used as an *INCREASE/DECREASE* control if *MANUAL* is selected. The system is designed to maintain the temperature of the air supply between +15°C and +46°C but, because of the length of ducting within the pressure cabin, the temperature at the suit inlet is affected by the cabin temperature and, if the cabin temperature is high, the minimum suit inlet temperature of +15°C is not achieved.

d. The flow is controlled by an ON/OFF starwheel beside the temperature control. The control is turned anti-clockwise from the OFF position to open the flow valves, flow increasing with increased movement of the control.

e. Overheat protection is provided for both the main air supply and the individual heaters. If the manifold temperature rises above 70°C, an overheat switch operates to shut down the air supply to the suits and to shut off the AVS heaters. Select the switch to *CLOSE* and allow the manifold to cool (60°C). Attempt to regain the system by selecting *OPEN*. If the system overheats again, select *CLOSE* and leave it off. A further thermostat control in each heater unit operates if the temperature in the heater duct becomes excessive.

BOMB BAY CONDITIONING

Bomb Bay Conditioning System Twin dorsal intakes provide cold air through ducts via a cold air valve. An outlet louvre in the port bomb door exhausts the air to atmosphere. Controls at the nav/radar's position consist of an *OFF* (centre)/*COLD* (down) switch which controls the cold air valve, a temperature selector and a manual heat control (both inoperative) and a temperature gauge.

WINDSCREEN THERMAL DEMISTING

Windscreen Demisting Supplies To demist the inside of the windscreen, hot air is supplied from a slotted duct on each side of the centre panel. Cabin air is supplied to a blower motor, below the pilots' floor on the starboard side. From the blower motor, the air passes to a 1 kW heater unit and thence to the windscreens. An overheat switch in the system cuts off electrical supplies to the heater if the temperature of the air in the ducting rises above 70°C and switches supplies on again when the temperature falls to 60°C.

Windscreen Demisting Controls and Operation Windscreen demisting is controlled by an ON/OFF switch on the co-pilot's instrument panel. When switched ON current is supplied to the blower and the heater. The system should be tested before flight by switching on and physically checking the airflow from the ducts.

ELECTRICAL SUPPLIES

200V AC. The windscreen demisting heater and motor are supplied from No 1 busbar and the AVS heaters from No 3 busbar.

115V AC. The cabin conditioning magnetic amplifier uses 115V AC from the starboard main transformer.

28V DC. The cabin conditioning, cabin pressurisation, bomb bay conditioning and windscreen demisting system use 28V DC for switching. The cabin conditioning and pressurisation warning systems also use 28V DC.

LOAD SHEDDING. If non-essential loads are shed, the following services are lost:

a. Cabin conditioning control.

b. Cold air turbine overspeed control; indicator still operative.

c. The bomb bay cold air valve remains in the last selected position; control is lost. Temperature indication goes to maximum deflection.

d. All AVS heaters.

e. Auxiliary AVS and face blowers.

PART 2: AIRCREW EQUIPMENT ASSEMBLIES AND OXYGEN SYSTEM

Warning: The aircraft is safe for parking when safety pins are inserted in both ejection seats and in the canopy as follows:

a. Canopy jettison firing unit sear.

b. Guillotine sear.

c. Canopy jettison and time delay trip lever.

d. Ejection gun sear.

e. Seat pan firing handle.

It is emphasised that pins should *not* be inserted in the fabric straps above the pilots' heads.

General The aircrew equipment assemblies comprise the seats, the flying and safety clothing and associated connectors. The pilots are provided with ejection seats while rear crew members have sliding, bucket-type seats, the outer two of which swivel. There are two positions for extra crew members, forward of the nav/radar and AEO seats. There are oxygen and intercom connections at all seven crew stations and static line connections at the five rear crew stations.

EJECTION SEATS

Ejection Seats, General The ejection seats, type 3KS1 for the 1st pilot and type 3KS2 for the co-pilot, are similar but partially handed. Each has a horseshoe-shaped parachute pack, a back pad with adjustable kidney pad and a personal survival pack (PSP) type ZC. The seats have a nominal ground-level capability, provided that the speed is at least 90 knots. Any deviation from straight and level flight at the instant of ejection reduces the seat performance.

The seat pan is adjustable for height by means of a lever on the outboard side of the seat. The trigger in the end of the lever is pressed in to adjust the height and, when released, locks the seat in the selected position.

The adjustable armrests are controlled by either of two levers on each rest, one at the forward end and one at the rear, on the side of the rest.

A lean-forward lever, forward on the port side of each seat, allows the occupant to lean forward, by unlocking the attachment between the shoulders and the back of the seat. The straps wind in and out, following the pilot's motion and are locked on application of negative g and/or rapid acceleration.

A negative-g restraint strap is attached to the seat pan and is adjusted by a downward pull.

The seats have pressure-demand emergency oxygen, a Mk 42 parachute and a static-line operated guillotine.

Ejection Gun and Firing Handles Each seat is fitted with an 80 ft/sec telescopic ejection gun fired by either the face-screen B-shaped firing handle above the occupant's head or the seat pan firing handle in the front of the seat pan. Either handle must be pulled to its full extent to fire the gun. Safety pins for each firing handle are stowed, when not in use, in a combined stowage for all safety pins one on each side of the cockpit.

Canopy/Seat Connection An interconnection between the seat-firing mechanism and the cockpit canopy enables the canopy to be jettisoned automatically when any firing handle is pulled. Because of this interconnection, there is always a 1-second delay between pulling an ejection seat handle and the seat ejection gun firing, even if the canopy has already gone.

Leg Restraint Leg restraint lines ensure that the legs are drawn back and held close to the seat pan during and after ejection. The lines pass through snubbing units below the front of the seat pan and are then fastened to the cockpit floor with rivets which shear at a pull of 400 lb. The snubbing units allow the lines to pass freely *down* through the unit but prevent them passing *upwards*, except when released by the spring-loaded toggle at the front of each snubbing unit. The leg restraint lines are unfastened when the man portion or cover of the PEC is removed from the seat portion.

NOTE: Before ejecting, place the feet on the rudder pedals.

Drogue Gun The drogue gun has a time-delay mechanism and fires half a second after the ejection gun has fired, withdrawing the duplex drogues to stabilise the seat. The time-delay mechanism is operated by a static trip rod, which withdraws a sear from the gun as the seat rises on the rails.

Barostat/g-Switch Time Delay Automatic separation is controlled by a time delay switch, which is inhibited by a barostat and a g-switch. The time delay runs for 1¼ seconds and is started by a static line as the seat moves up the rails, provided that:

a. The height is not greater than 10,000 feet.

b. The acceleration is not greater than about 4g.

If either condition is exceeded, the barostat and/or g-switch interrupt the running of the time switch until the conditions are satisfactory (seat below 10,000 feet, speed below 300 knots). When the time switch operates, the harness, leg restraint lines, personal equipment connector, face blind and parachute pack are all released from the seat. Simultaneously, the drogues are detached from the seat but remain attached to the apex of the parachute canopy, withdrawing it upwards. The parachute subsequently develops and pulls the pilot out of the seat.

NOTE 1: When the seat pan handle is used to initiate ejection, the handle remains attached to the seat and cannot be retained during separation. Conversely, the face-screen handle, if used, remains in the pilot's hands after separation and should be discarded as soon as convenient.

NOTE 2: For flights over mountainous territory, a 5000 metre capsule can be substituted for the normal 10,000 foot capsule.

Manual Separation To allow the occupant to release himself from the seat, if the automatic devices fail to operate, means of manual separation are embodied.

A static-line operated guillotine is provided on the port side of the drogue box. A safety pin is provided for the gun sear and, when not in use, is stowed with the other safety pins on the cockpit coaming.

Separation is achieved by pulling out and up the manual separation lever to the rear of

THE TYPE 3KS2, Mk 4 SEAT EQUIPPED (STARBOARD VIEW)

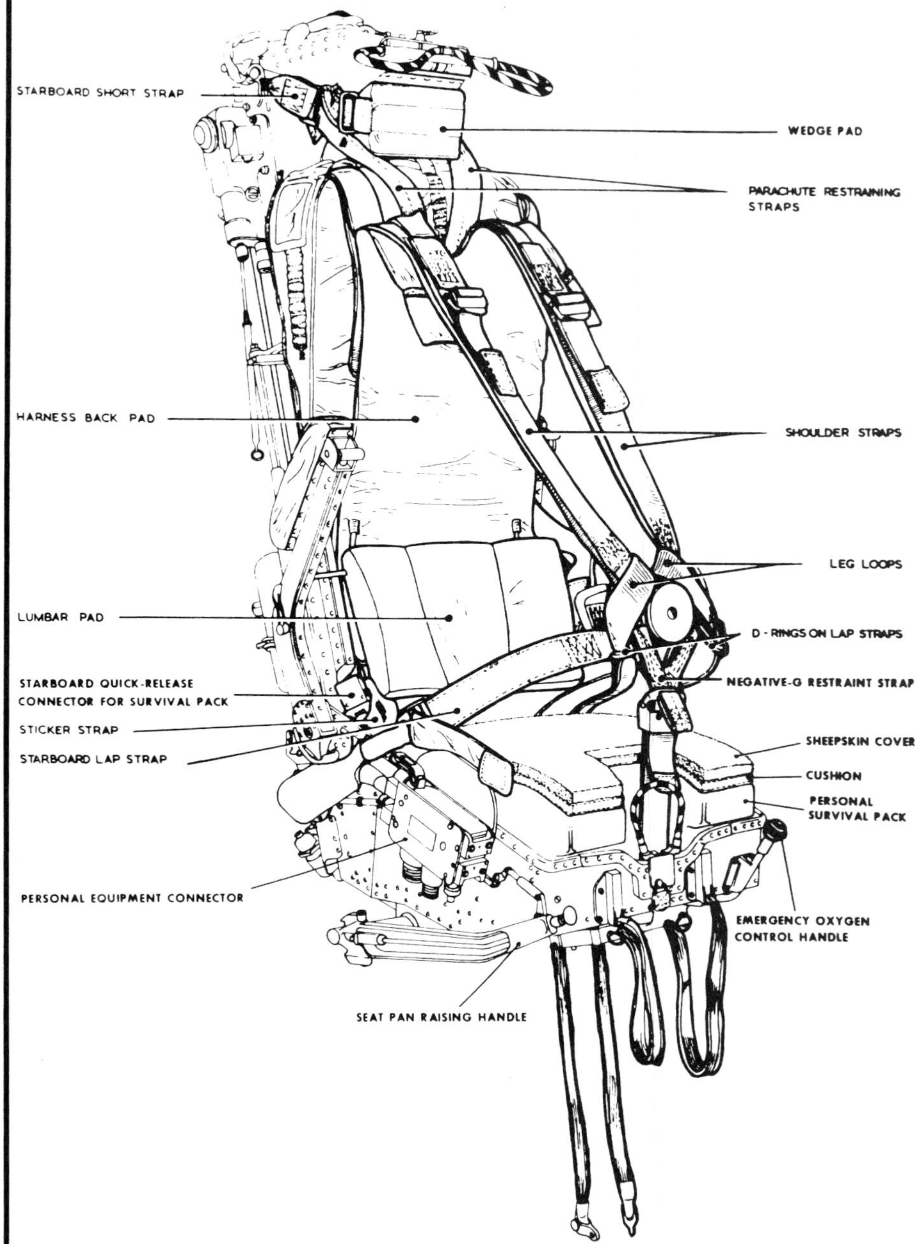

the seat pan on the left side. This releases the harness locks, the parachute retaining straps, the leg restraint lines and the man portion of the PEC and, as the seat occupant falls clear of the seat, a static line attached to the rear of the parachute pack withdraws the sear from the guillotine and severs the drogue link line. After leaving the seat, the parachute is opened by pulling the D-handle on the waistbelt.

Rear Crew Seats

Crew Seats, General

a. The navigator/radar and the AEO have seats which are capable of swivelling inwards, to face almost forward (aircraft sense). The navigator plotter's seat does not swivel.

b. Each seat has an assistor cushion to help the occupant rise from the seat in emergency. The backrests embody spring clips to help retain the top of the parachute pack against the seat back; they also embody clips for stowage of the shoulder straps. A Mk 46 or Mk 49 parachute, including a demand and inflation emergency oxygen set, is used. All three seats can be slid fore-and-aft on rails.

Swivel seats for navigator/radar and AEO

a. These seats have a lever to the *left* of the seat pan to control seat movement. In its spring-loaded central position, the seat is locked. When moved forward, the seat is unlocked for the rake of the seat back and swivelling. The rake is spring-loaded to the forward position to clear obstacles when swivelling; in normal use, the rear position is adopted. The control lever may be released once either motion has begun and automatically relocks when the full travel has been reached.

b. When the seat is locked in the fore-and-aft direction to face the table, the same lever may be pulled aft against its spring, to free the seat for sliding. There are several finite positions in which the seat may be locked when the lever is released.

c. For use by persons not occupying the seat, a handle at the top of the back rest, when moved to the right, duplicates the forward motion of the lever for swivelling and raking. Similarly, a toe-operated lever behind the base of the seat, when moved to the right, releases the seat for fore-and-aft travel (but, unlike the lever, is effective even if the seat is swivelled).

d. In order to clear the table, the seat must be at the forward (aircraft sense) end of its rails before swivelling.

e. Thigh supports at the front of these seats can be adjusted up or down as desired, by a central star wheel beneath them.

f. An S-type Mk 2 personal survival pack in the seat pan is attached to the outside of the parachute harness. It is provided with a lowering line and should be lowered from the harness during the parachute descent.

Sliding seat for navigator/plotter

a. The lever permitting the seat to slide fore-and-aft is on the *right* of the seat pan in this seat.

b. An S-type Mk 2 personal survival pack is provided.

c. To prevent trapping the knees under the table, the seat must be at the forward (aircraft sense) end of its rails before operating the assistor cushion.

Assistor Cushions To assist the occupant to his feet, under conditions of positive g, each seat has an assistor cushion fitted in the seat pan which can be inflated by air at a pressure of 1200 PSI. A pressure gauge is fitted on the bottle. The air bottle is stowed on the back of the navigator/radar's and AEO's seats and in the back of the seat pan of the navigator/plotter's seat. Pins are provided for the assistor cushion bottles. To make the bottles operative, the navigator/plotter's pin must be removed and the other two must be inserted.

A knob on the right of the seat pan of the navigator/radar's and AEO's seats and a lever on the left of the navigator/plotter's seat pan, when pulled upwards to the full extent of their travel, release the air to inflate the cushion. The initial inflation, in turn, releases the safety harness lap strap anchorages, freeing the occupant from the seat.

Clothing and Personal Equipment Connectors

Personal Equipment Connectors (PEC)

Pilots

a. The pilots' PEC are in three portions, the aircraft portion, the seat portion and the man portion. The aircraft portion is attached to the underside of the seat portion, on the right-hand side of each seat. The man portion, an integral part of the clothing, is attached (during strapping-in) to the top of the seat portion. When not in use, the seat portion is protected by a dust cover, for which a stowage is provided on the back of the co-pilot's seat.

b. The PEC connects all the personal services to the man. The aircraft supplies (main system oxygen, ventilation air, mic/tel) are fed into the aircraft portion. As the seat ascends the guide rails on ejection, a static rod causes the seat portion to break away.

c. To prevent loss of emergency oxygen, the lower orifices of the seat portion are closed by valves when the aircraft portion is removed.

d. The man and seat portions are mated by sliding the nose of the man portion into the hooks at the front of the seat portion and then pressing the handle at the rear downwards.

e. To release, press down on the thumb button in the handle and lift the handle. (This also releases the leg restraint lines).

Rear Crew

a. The rear crew and spare seat positions are each provided with an aircraft hose assembly consisting of an oxygen hose, mic/tel lead and a static line, all taped together in a protective sleeve. A switch and associated electrical wiring, connected to the static line, are also incorporated in each assembly to operate the 'crew gone' lights in front of the 1st pilot.

b. The assemblies are of sufficient length to enable the crew members to move about the cabin and to pass through the door in order to abandon the aircraft.

c. Separate AVS hoses are provided for the crew members, the spare seats and the sextant positions. Quick-release connectors are fitted.

Air Ventilated Suits (AVS) AVS Mk 2A (nylon) or Mk 2C (cotton) may be worn; the hose from the suit is passed through the clothing to connect with the aircraft supply. The pilots' supply is through their PEC while the rear crew have separate connectors.

Pressure Jerkins and Anti-G Suits (High Altitude) Pressure jerkins (Mk 4 for pilots and Mk 3 for rear crew) are worn in conjunction with anti-g suits Mk 7B when flying at high altitudes. These two items form a pressure suit to protect the crew member if cabin pressure fails; they inflate automatically if the cabin altitude reaches 40,000 feet. They are inflated from the oxygen system, both being connected to the pressure jerkin hose assembly. The jerkin connection is permanently made but the hose from the anti-g suit has to be threaded through the outer clothing and then attached. The pressure jerkin embodies a life jacket. The attached hose assemblies terminate in the man portion of the PEC for the pilots and a bayonet connector for the rear crew.

Masks and Helmets Either a G-type helmet with a Mk 1 protective helmet, or a Mk 2 or Mk 3 protective helmet, may be worn; in all cases either a P2C or Q2C oxygen mask is worn. These masks are of the chain-toggle, pressure-breathing type with a bayonet hose connection; they are identical apart from size. A toggle on the front of the harness is normally in the up position. The mask should be tested before flight and the knurled screws adjusted so that there is no leakage during operation of the press-to-test facility with the mask toggle in the down position. If cabin pressurisation failure occurs, the toggle is put to the down position, to clamp the mask more tightly on the face for pressure breathing. When pressure clothing is worn, the mask is plugged into the top end of the jerkin hose assembly.

Low-Altitude Clothing Assemblies For flights below 45,000 feet (cabin pressure), it is not essential to wear pressure clothing with the Mk 21 regulator. In such cases and when using a Mk 17 regulator, normal flying clothing is worn, with a separate life jacket. To enable the aircraft connections to be made, a special mask hose assembly is required, Mk 2 for pilots; Mk 7 for rear crew (Mk 2 post-Mod 2393).

Rear Crew Safety Equipment The rear crew members wear back-type Mk 46 or Mk 49 parachutes with type S Mk 2 personal survival packs (PSP). When the static line is used, a barostat control delays deployment of the parachute until below 13,000 feet. This can be overriden by a handle on a strap between the legs.

A demand and inflation emergency oxygen set is provided. The cylinder and opening head are in the top of the parachute pack and the regulator is on the right-hand waist-belt. The operating handle is on the strap between the legs.

Oxygen System

Description of Oxygen System Oxygen is carried in 12 x 2250 litre bottles. On early aircraft, all the oxygen bottles are housed in the power compartment, aft of the bomb bay. In later aircraft, four bottles are housed in the power compartment and the remainder in the bomb bay. The bottles are all charged through a connection in the power compartment; the correct charging pressure is 1800 PSI. Two pressure gauges at the AEO's position show the pressure in each half of the system.

From the oxygen bottles, the high pressure supply lines pass along the sides of the bomb bay and into the pressure cabin. Master valves, one for each side of the system, are below the crew's flooring; these valves are normally wire-locked to the open position. From the master valves, the supply lines pass along the cabin and are interconnected by transverse lines at four points.

The transverse connections are protected by non-return valves so that, if there is a leak on one side of the system, oxygen is not lost from the other side. From the transverse lines, the supply is fed to pressure-reducing valves, one for each regulator, which reduce the pressure to 400 PSI. The medium pressure lines pass from each pressure-reducing valve to the regulators. From the regulators, oxygen at breathing pressure is fed to the PEC on demand.

Oxygen Regulators, General

a. The oxygen regulators may be Mk 21A, 21B or 17F, one being supplied for each crew member. The 1st pilot's and co-pilot's regulators are at the forward end of the port and starboard consoles, while the rear crew regulators are at their respective stations.

b. The Mk 17F and 21 series regulators have the same characteristics up to 39,000 feet cabin altitude. Above this altitude, the Mk 21 series automatically delivers a higher pressure than the Mk 17F. The Mk 2 emergency regulators have the same characteristics as the Mk 21 series.

c. In all cases of cabin pressure failure, an immediate descent is to be made until cabin altitude is below 40,000 feet. When flight safety and fuel considerations allow, the descent should be continued, at normal rate, to below 25,000 feet.

Regulator Characteristics

The regulators provide:

a. A mixture of oxygen and air, or 100% oxygen; the flow and volume delivered is in direct relation to the breathing demands of the user.

b. The correct ratio of air and oxygen according to cabin altitude. Above 33,700 feet, 100% oxygen is provided automatically. 100% oxygen may be selected at any height.

c. A safety pressure; the mask cavity pressure is slightly higher than cabin pressure when cabin altitude reaches 11,000 to 14,000 feet and pressure breathing when the cabin altitude exceeds 39,000 feet. Additionally, the Mk 21 series regulators inflate pressure clothing at the same altitude as they give pressure breathing.

d. Positive oxygen pressure by manual selection:
(1) Emergency use (100% and *EMERGENCY*), ie, for toxic fumes.
(2) Mask and regulator testing (Mk 17F).
(3) Mask, regulator and pressure clothing testing (Mk 21 Series).

Oxygen Regulators, Controls and Indicators

MK 21 REGULATOR CONTROLS

a. *OXYGEN SUPPLY, ON/OFF Lever (wire-locked at ON).* This lever controls the supply of oxygen to the regulator and must be ON at all times in flight.

b. *NORMAL OXYGEN/100% OXYGEN Lever.* When in the normal position, this lever allows air to mix with the oxygen in suitable proportions, up to an altitude of 33,700 feet. Above this altitude, the air inlet is closed and 100% oxygen is delivered to the mask. With the lever at 100% OXYGEN, the air inlet is closed regardless of the altitude; this position should always be used if toxic fumes are present.

c. *JERKIN TEST / MASK TEST/ EMERGENCY/NORMAL Lever.* When this lever is set to *NORMAL*, oxygen or a mixture of oxygen and air as selected by b. is fed to the mask at the required pressure when the user breathes in. When the lever is set to *EMERGENCY*, the pressure of the oxygen to the mask is slightly increased above the delivery pressure appropriate to the altitude. This increase is constant at all altitudes. The *EMERGENCY* position should be used if toxic fumes are present in the cockpit. To reach the *MASK TEST* position, the knob in the end of the lever must be pulled out; in the *MASK TEST* position, the mask can be tested under pressure for leaks. The *JERKIN TEST* position is similar in operation to the *MASK TEST* position but gives a higher pressure and is used to test mask, jerkin, and a g-suit simultaneously for leaks.

MK 21 SERIES REGULATOR INDICATORS

a. A gauge on the regulator shows the pressure of oxygen being delivered to the regulator, while two gauges at the AEO's station show the main pressures.

b. A magnetic indicator on each regulator shows white when the user is breathing in. The pilots' and three rear crew members' indicators are duplicated on their respective panels, and the bomb aimer's is also duplicated, on a rear central support for the pilots' floor, where it can be monitored by other crew members.

MK 17F REGULATOR CONTROLS AND INDICATORS

The Mk 17F regulator carries a pressure gauge, a magnetic flow indicator, a *NORMAL*/100% selector, an *ON/OFF* control and an *EMERGENCY* lever. This last control is pressed in to test the mask for leaks and deflected to either side to obtain oxygen at higher pressure in an emergency.

Emergency Oxygen

PILOTS' EMERGENCY OXYGEN

a. Pilots can obtain emergency oxygen automatically on ejection or by pulling up a yellow and black knob inboard of the ejection seat on the forward corner of the seat pan.

b. As the bottle is attached to the seat, emergency oxygen is not available after separation from the seat.

c. A pressure-demand emergency oxygen set is fitted to each ejection seat, the cylinder and operating head on the back and the regulator Mk 2 or 3 behind the PEC. The operating head initiates the action and delivers medium pressure oxygen to the regulator, which then delivers it to the user on demand. Mk 2 and Mk 3 regulators have similar characteristics to the Mk 21 and Mk 17 series regulators respectively, except that safety pressure is delivered from ground level upwards. The cylinder contents are indicated on a pressure gauge. The endurance of the set is approximately 10 minutes provided that the mask is fitted correctly and that there are no leaks in the hose assembly.

REAR CREW EMERGENCY OXYGEN

a. The rear crew are provided with Mk 2A and 3A regulators which are identical in performance to the pilots', only the fitting and method of operation being different. An emergency oxygen bottle in the top of each rear crew parachute pack is turned on automatically when the parachute static line is operated. It can also be operated manually by a control on a strap between the user's legs.

b. The pressure demand regulator is on the right-hand waist-belt and a contents gauge is on the bottle in the pack. The bottle is filled to capacity when the gauge needle is on the white line between the sectors marked FULL and REFILL.

USE OF AIRCREW EQUIPMENT ASSEMBLIES

Clothing Assembly

When wearing pressure clothing, the air ventilated suit and anti-g suit are put on beneath the shirt and trousers and the jerkin is put on top of the flying overalls. The hoses from the anti-g suit and AVS are fed through the outer clothing; the AVS hose is connected to the PEC for the pilots and to an individual connector for the rear crew, the anti-g hose is connected to the main oxygen hose. The oxygen hose from the mask is subsequently attached to the bayonet socket at the top of the main oxygen hose. When pressure clothing is not worn, the mask hose assembly is used.

PART 3: ARMAMENT AND OPERATIONAL EQUIPMENT

General There are two methods of bomb aiming in the aircraft, the NBS and the co-pilot's visual sight.

Bomb Release and Jettison

RELEASE. BOMBS are released automatically by the NBS release pulse or manually by a bomb release button. The first pilot has a bomb release button to the left rear of the throttle quadrant. The co-pilot's bomb release button, stowed in a clip below the coaming, operates through a time delay unit at the navigator/plotter's position. The navigator/radar's bomb release button is stowed in a clip adjacent to panel 9P. There is a further bomb release button at the prone bomb aimer's position.
WARNING 1: If one or more 1000 lb bombs have fallen on to or against the bomb doors, the doors must be closed (if open) and must not be opened again in flight, except in emergency. If they are opened, a bomb may be trapped against the bomb bay wall, damaging the flying controls and/or the hydraulic lines.
WARNING 2: Failure to switch on the time delay unit at the navigator's/plotter's station when the co-pilot's release button is to be used results in a failure to release.

JETTISON

a. The bombs may be jettisoned live by selection of the *LIVE JETTISON* switches on the navigator/radar's side panel and on the visual bomb aimer's oxygen panel.

b. An *EMERGENCY BOMB JETTISON* switch on the 1st pilot's console panel enables the bombs to be jettisoned safe through a wiring system separate from the normal bomb release system. The switch is a guarded, double-pole switch labelled *JETTISON/OVERRIDE*, spring-loaded to the off position. When the switch is held momentarily to the *JETTISON* (rear) position, the bomb doors open, the bombs fall and the doors close. Movement to *OVERRIDE* cancels jettison, provided that the bomb doors have not reached the fully open position. The selection can also be used to close the bomb doors before the time sequence unit does so. The bomb doors close when the time delay unit on the cabin wall at the AEO's position completes the manually preset 24-second cycle.

c. If hydraulic power has failed, the bomb doors must first be opened by the emergency system before attempting to jettison.

d. When nuclear stores and practice bombs are carried, the jettison circuits are rendered inoperative.

BOMB RELEASE SAFETY LOCK. A bomb release safety lock (BRSL), to prevent inadvertent weapon release, is controlled by a guarded wire-locked switch on the port console marked *LOCK/UNLOCK*. An amber light comes on if the safety lock is released; a green light shows the lock is engaged. Press-to-test facilities on both lights are used to check a duplicate electrical circuit.

A SFOM bombsight is fitted. The sight is a collimated fixed-angle sighting head, on the coaming in front of the co-pilot. A lighting control is adjacent to the other cockpit lighting controls. The sight line is fixed relative to the aircraft in azimuth but the depression angle can be adjusted to allow for speed, AUW, height and relative air density. There are two scales on the sighting head, one calibrated in degrees and the other in milliradians. In flight, the milliradian setting knob should be used for adjustments to the sighting head. One complete revolution of the milliradian scale adjusts the sighting head by 10°. The optical glass is stowed in a container on the starboard console and must be inserted in the sighting head prior to bombing. Care must be taken to avoid scratching the glass while handling.

Window Launchers The gravity/cartridge window installations are operated by the AEO. Three gravity window containers (two port, one starboard) and one cartridge discharger are fitted.

Camera Installation An F95 Mk 9 camera on a frame above the bomb aimer's window is controlled from the navigator/radar's position. The film can be marked to show bomb release automatically by the NBS release pulse or manually by the event marker button. (Command modification 0291/Mod 2505 transfers the event marker supply to fuse 569 from fuse 970 in the weapons release circuit to eliminate the possibility of the latter fuse rupturing due to a defective camera.) The event marker facility is not incorporated in the F95 Mk 4 camera fitted to MRR aircraft pose-SEM 045 (Mod 2502).

PART 4: ENGINES AND AAPP

OLYMPUS ENGINES

General The aircraft may be powered by Olympus Mk 200 series or Mk 301 engines which, due to differences in mechanical details, thrust and limitations, are never installed together on the same aircraft. In the *TAKE OFF* setting, Mk 201 series and Mk 301 engines produce approximately 17,000 lb and 18,000 lb of thrust respectively; in the *CRUISE* setting they produce approximately 16,000 lb and 17,000 lb of thrust respectively. A rapid starting system is embodied.

The basic engine consists of eight main sub-assemblies. The intermediate casing houses the drives from both compressors for the mechanically driven auxiliaries:

a. LP COMPRESSOR COMPONENTS
(1) LP driven fuel pump
(2) Tacho generator (RPM)

b. HP COMPRESSOR COMPONENTS
(1) HP driven fuel pump
(2) Main oil pump
(3) Main oil scavenge and four auxiliary scavenge pumps
(4) Constant speed drive unit (CSDU)
(5) Hydraulic pump
(6) Tacho generator (not used)
(7) Rotax air starter drive

Engine air is automatically supplied on start-up for the following systems:

a. Turbine cooling.

b. Pressurisation of bulkhead seals, oil bearing seals and CSDU oil tank.

c. Induced cooling of alternators, CSDU oil and Zone 2B.
Air is also available for engine anti-icing when selected.

Engine control is provided by a combined throttle/HP cock. Automatic control is effected by components in the fuel chassis which allow an optimum supply of fuel to the engine, dependent on ambient conditions, airspeed and acceleration stage in the engine. Limitation on engine output is controlled by the position of a Take-off/Cruise switch which determines both the RPM governing datums and the corresponding JPT limiting datums for all four engines. Also, a jet-pipe temperature limiter is installed which controls the engine speed below the selected governing speed, if necessary, so that the corresponding jet-pipe temperature limit is not exceeded. When JPT limiting is overridden, manual control of the throttles may be necessary to maintain the engines within JPT limitations.

The Mk 200 series jet pipes are fitted with convergent/divergent nozzles for improved cruise performance; the Mk 301 jet pipes are fitted with convergent nozzles.

To minimise damage to the outer wing and the bomb bay following structural failure of an engine, containment shields are fitted outboard of the outer engines and inboard of the inner engines.

Throttle and HP Cock Controls The four throttle levers, which also control the HP cocks, are forward of the retractable centre console, in a quadrant marked *OPEN/IDLING*. The quadrant is gated at the *IDLING* position and the part of the quadrant below this, which controls the *HP* cock position, is marked *OPEN/HP COCKS/SHUT* and has a further gate at the *SHUT* position.

To move the throttle levers forward from the *HP* cocks *SHUT* gate and to move them aft from the *IDLING* gate, the sleeves on the levers must be raised.

The throttle friction lever is on the starboard side of the throttle quadrant; forward movement of the lever increases the friction.

Engine Fuel System The engine fuel system controls the correct amount of fuel the engine requires in the varying conditions of flight. The factors which affect this are:

a. Throttle setting.

b. Engine air intake pressure (P1).

c. Compressor delivery air pressure (P3).

d. JPT limiter isolate switch position.

e. JPT/RPM (datum limits selected by the *TAKE-OFF/CRUISE* switch).

Fuel from the tank booster pumps flows through the LP cock and fuel filter into the engine fuel system in the following order:

a. LP AND HP DRIVEN FUEL PUMP. Two engine driven pumps are inter-connected and driven by the LP and HP compressors respectively.
(1) The LP pump incorporates a double datum hydro mechanical RPM governor, allowing it to control RPM to take-off or cruise limits with the throttle at *OPEN*. The two RPM datums are controlled by the *TAKE-OFF/CRUISE* switch to the left of the throttle levers. In addition to selecting the required RPM datum, operation of the switch also selects the corresponding temperature datum for the engine JPT limiter. Therefore, actual RPM on the engines may be less than the limit selected in order to keep the JPT within limitations. The hydro-mechanical governor maintains the selected RPM datum regardless of changes in temperature and density of fuel; RPM may vary very slightly with increase in altitude.
(2) The HP pump incorporates an overspeed governor set at 3% above maximum HP compressor revolutions should the governor on the LP driven pump fail.

b. FULL RANGE FLOW CONTROL (FRFC). Fuel is passed from the fuel pumps to the FRFC which meters fuel to the engine depending upon:
(1) Throttle–HP cock position.
(2) Engine air intake pressure (P1).
(3) JPT DATUM LIMITS. Control is accomplished by the Electro Pressure Control (EPC) which is activated by the JPT amplifier when the JPT approaches the limit selected by the *TAKE-OFF/CRUISE* switch. In the *TAKE-OFF* setting a depressed datum is brought into operation which prevents turbine temperature overswing during rapid throttle opening by slowing down the rate of temperature rise during the last 5°C. Above about 20,000 ft, the *TAKE-OFF* and *CRUISE* datums may exceed their respective limits by up to 5°C, therefore in the *TAKE-OFF* setting at

altitude the JPT may have to be kept within limits by use of the throttles. The output from the JPT amplifier may be isolated by means of a JPT limiter *ON/OFF* switch aft of the *TAKE-OFF/CRUISE* switch. The switch must always be ON before *TAKE-OFF* is selected, so that the depressed datum will prevent turbine overswing during rapid throttle opening. The *OFF* position of the switch is for use when ground testing the RPM governors, or for use if a limiter runs away or fails in flight. In these circumstances, the throttles must be handled carefully to prevent JPT rising to the limits. The limiters may be tested on the ground by isolating the governors; two RPM *GOVERNOR ISOLATION* switches are provided at the top of the port fuse panel behind the AEO's seat. When held *ON* they permit take-off RPM to be selected when the pilot's switch is at *CRUISE*, without altering the cruise setting of the JPT limiter. Nos 1 and 4 and Nos 2 and 3 engine JPT amplifiers are supplied by the port and starboard main transformers respectively. If automatic load-shedding occurs, the system is de-energised and JPT control must be maintained by use of the throttles.

c. AIR FUEL RATIO CONTROL (AFRC). The AFRC is the engine acceleration control. During acceleration it senses compressor delivery pressure (P3) and thus determines how much fuel may be passed to the burners.
(1) In Mk 200 series engines the AFRC overfuels the engine in the early stages of acceleration. As fuel delivery is proportioned to P3 pressure, it is merely necessary to restrict the P3 pressure fed to the AFRC. This is done by incorporating P1 P3 switch which measures the compression ratio of the compressors, and decides how much P3 pressure may be fed to the AFRC. Above 82/83% RPM the overfuelling condition ceases and the P1 P3 switch allows full P3 pressure to the AFRC.
(2) In Mk 301 engines overfuelling is not a problem, so a P1 P3 switch is not required. The internal bellows of the P1 P3 switch are removed, thus it becomes an air potentiometer an full P3 pressure is fed to the AFRC. The AFRC is now working at its designed limit, but engine acceleration is still too slow. To enhance acceleration, a Speed Term Switch is fitted. It senses LP fuel pump pressure, and after 65% progressively allows more fuel to bypass the AFRC to the burners, until max RPM is reached.

d. FLOW DISTRIBUTION AND DUMP VALVE. During start up, a fine fuel spray is required and fuel is initially only fed to the primary orifices of the duplex burners. Above about 15% RPM fuel is also allowed to the main orifices of the burners. The dump valve ensures that when the HP cock is shut, all fuel from the burner pipes is drained into a collector box on the engine doors. The box is drained by the ground crew. It will only partially drain in flight.

e. DIPPING VALVE. It is only used during a rapid start of the engine and ensures that excess fuel returns to the suction side of the pumps. It is automatically de-energised at the end of the start cycle. However, it can be held open by fuel pressure. To ensure that it has closed, the throttle must be briefly returned to the idling gate at the end of the start cycle.

Engine Starting Systems

Each engine embodies its own air starter motor. Air can be supplied from a ground air starter unit, feeding through a connection on the underside of the starboard wing, or from the rapid start system. The ground air supply feeds into the main lines of the engine air system and thence to the starter motors, through electrically-actuated valves. Compressed air from a running engine can be used to start the others, singly or simultaneously, provided that the appropriate *ENGINE AIR* switches on the starboard console are at *OPEN*.

The rapid starting system is so arranged that the powered flying controls and artificial feel are switched on automatically when the simultaneous *RAPID START* button is pressed; because of the peak loads involved, electrical power during starting must be supplied by a 60 kVA ground power unit and not from the AAPP.

A gyro hold-off system is embodied, whereby the MFS, JPT limiters, refuelling relays, contents gauges, fire warning, autostabilisers and artificial horizons are de-energised until the engine start master switch is selected ON. The power to the gyros is initially boosted to 200V for approximately 20 seconds, to obtain fast run up.

CONTROLS

a. The starting control panel on the 1st pilot's port console carries the following controls:
Four buttons for individual engine starting, each embodying a light.
A *GYRO HOLD OFF* button.
A *RAPID START* button, for starting all engines simultaneously.
A *NORMAL/RAPID* lock-toggle switch, for selecting Palouste or high pressure air.
An *IGNITION ON/OFF* switch.
An *AIR CROSSFEED* three-position magnetic indicator.
An *ON/OFF* lock-toggle start master switch.

b. An *AIR CROSSFEED* indicator shows *OPEN* whenever the start master switch is ON. When the air selector is at *NORMAL*, engines can only be started by the individual buttons, using an external air supply or crossfeed. When the air selector is at *RAPID* and the master switch *ON*, all engines can be started simultaneously using the *RAPID START* button or separately, using the individual buttons. If, for any reason, an engine fails to start on this system, there is sufficient air for one further start on each side; the individual start button must be used for this attempt. With the air selector switch at *RAPID* and the master switch *OFF*, the gyro hold-off system is effective when the *GYRO HOLD OFF* button is pressed.

c. RELIGHTING CONTROLS. A relight button in the head of each throttle/HP cock provides a means of relighting the engines in flight. When one of the buttons is pressed, 28V vital busbar power energises the igniter plugs regardless of throttle position or switch selections on the engine start panel. The igniter plugs remain energised until the relight button is released.

OPERATION (*NORMAL*). With the *IGNITION* switch *ON*, *MASTER* switch *ON* and air selector switch to *NORMAL*, pressing a start button energises three circuits:

a. Solenoid to open position on starter air control valve.

b. Engine igniter plugs.

c. Palouste air bleed valve.

The increase in Palouste air opens the air control valve and a pressure switch lights the start button. The air now rotates the starter turbine which drives the HP compressor. Fuel from the HP pump is directed to the primary burners where the igniters initiate combustion. The engine accelerates to self-sustaining speed and disengages from the starter turbine. An overspeed switch on the starter turbine operates the start relay which now de-energises the engine igniter plugs and the Palouste air bleed valve and operates the solenoid on the air control valve to the closed position. When the air control valve closes, the pressure switch breaks, cancelling the light in the starter button.

OPERATION (*RAPID*). The rapid start facility uses a mixture of bottled air and fuel from the booster pumps. When this mixture is ignited, the resulting hot gases turn the starter turbine.

a. Air at 3300 PSI is stored in four bottles in each of the two engine bays. A charging point is on each wing between the jet-pipe tunnels. Sufficient air is available for three engine starts per side. Air passes from the bottles to the manifold and thence to air bottle solenoid valves on each engine.

b. A solenoid-operated valve opens when the starter button is pressed and allows high pressure air from the storage cylinder to pass to the reducing valve, which reduces the pressure to 300 PSI for delivery to the combustor. A safety disc, which bursts at 550 PSI, protects the combuster from excessive pressures if the valve fails. If the disc bursts, air exhausts into the same ducting as the normal exhausts from the starter.

c. Air from the bottles, reduced to 300 PSI, flows to the combuster unit and mixes with pressurised fuel in the chamber. The remaining air passes between the two walls of the combustion unit for cooling purposes and also to a non-return valve to prevent air escaping through to the air control valve. The fuel is then atomised, mixed with the air, ignited and ejected on to the starter turbine. A pressure switch then operates the light in the starter button and maintains the electrical circuit to the start components, while a 2-second timer switches off the combuster igniter. The combuster continues to operate until, after a successful start, the cycle is terminated by the starter overspeed switch or the 12-second delay in the time delay unit. The light in the starter button goes out, the air bottle solenoid is de-energised and the time delay units are reset.

d. If the igniter plug fails to ignite the mixture, the pressure switch does not operate. This breaks the electric supply to the time delay units after 2 seconds and the air bottle solenoid and the time delay units are reset.

e. If the combuster ignites but the engine fails to light up, the rapid start sequence is terminated by the 12-second delay and the time delay unit is reset.

Oil Systems
Each engine has its own integral oil system. In 200 series engines, the tank is in the nose-bullet, a float-operated contents gauge is on the port side of the air-intake casing and the tank filling point is on the lower port side of the engine front bulkhead. In 301 engines, the tank is on the port side of the LP compressor casing and has a contents sight glass, the filling point being below the tank. The oil capacities are as follows:

Engines	*Tank oil capacity*	*Airspace*	*Total oil (tank and engine)*
200 series	4½ galls	1½galls	6¾ galls
301	3⅞ galls	1⅛ galls	6⅛ galls

Each engine also has an independent oil system for the alternator constant speed drive unit. The 14½ pint tank (3½ pints air space) is attached to the starboard side of the intermediate casing. A tank sight glass shows tank contents. The tank filling point is on the underside of the constant speed drive unit, at the lower starboard side of the engine. The tank must be replenished within 15 minutes of shutting-down the engine. Great care must be taken not to overfill the tank or oil will find its way into the cabin conditioning system.

Magnetic chip detectors (five) are in all oil recovery lines, as follows:

1. No 1 bearing

2. Nos 2 and 3 bearings and auxiliary drives

3. Nos 4 and 5 bearings

4. No 7 bearing

5. No 8 bearing

Engine Instruments The following engine instruments are grouped together in the pilot's centre panel:

a. Four JPT gauges which are DC operated.

b. Four fuel pressure magnetic indicators, which show white when there is insufficient pressure.

c. Four RPM indicators, of the percentage type. The main scale is calibrated in tens from 0 to 100%, while a small scale gives readings from 0 to 10%.

d. Four oil pressure gauges.

e. One *ENGINE CONTROL* magnetic indicator (inoperative).

Throttle Detents

a. To reduce the possibility of compressor instability leading to engine flame-out, a detent is provided on the inboard throttle of 301 engines to increase flight idling above 15,000 feet. It gives an increase of about 5% RPM over the outboard engines at 50,000 feet. The detent can be manually overridden in emergency, eg rapid descent or relighting.

b. A detent isolation switch at the forward end of the starboard console permits withdrawal of the detent under air-to-air refuelling conditions, ie at airspeeds not exceeding 250 knots at medium altitude.

c. For use on the ground, a detent test switch is provided on Panel 4P.

Airborne Auxiliary Power Plant

AAPP Description The AAPP is a gas turbine engine, outboard of No 4 engine. It provides an emergency 200 volt supply below 30,000 feet. On the ground, the AAPP supplies electrical power and air for the ventilated suits.

The engine has a single-side centrifugal compressor, driven by a single-stage axial turbine on a common shaft. The air intake is on the underside of the engine and air passes through a single, reverse-flow combustion chamber. The jet efflux is directed downwards from the wing. The air intake is held in the closed position by hydraulic pressure, electrically operated. If hydraulic or electrical failure occurs, the intake opens.

No throttle control is provided, as the engine is designed to run at a constant speed. The air-intake shutter is controlled automatically by operation of the master switch which, with all the other controls, is at the AEO's station. Chapter 4, Electrical System, describes the use of the AAPP as a standby electrical supply.

For starting at higher altitudes, oxygen enrichment is provided. The unit carries its own supply in two bottles at the rear of the engine.

AAPP Oil System Engine lubrication is provided by a gear-type pressure pump, which draws its supply from an oil sump formed by the lower part of the compressor casing. The sump capacity is 4½ pints. The sump must always be filled to capacity.

The oil pressure varies very rapidly with temperature; the minimum pressure is 4 PSI.

PART 5: FLYING CONTROLS

Cockpit Controls and Indicators
The flying controls in the cockpit are conventional in operation. Dual interconnected control columns and pendulum-type rudder pedals are provided; these operate powered controls through a series of linkages.

The rudder pedals can be adjusted for reach by a starwheel at the lower inboard edge of each pilot's instrument panel. Toe-buttons are provided on the pedals for brake operation.

The controls for the powered flying controls, artificial feel, artificial feel lock, auto-stabilisers and mach trimmer are grouped together on a panel on the port console. The elevator and aileron trim and feel relief switches are duplicated on the two control columns, while those for the rudder are on the fuel contents panel. The emergency trim control is on the forward end of the retractable console.

At the top of the pilots' centre panel is a bank of warning lights and magnetic indicators. The three left-hand magnetic indicators are for the PFC units, the artificial feel and the auto-stabilisers respectively. The amber *MAIN WARNING* lights at either end of the group come on if a fault develops in any of the systems (except the yaw damper); this warning is cancelled by pushing in the button of the channel concerned. The appropriate magnetic indicator shows white, as a reminder that a channel is unserviceable. The main warning lights are then available for any subsequent failure.

Below this group is the control surfaces position indicator, representing a view of the aircraft from the rear. There is a separate indicator for each of the control surfaces, with datum lines to show the surface position relative to the take-off position.

All button warning lights can be dimmed by rotating the bezel. With the exception of the mach trim reset buttons, which are blue, all lights are amber.

Powered Flying Controls

Elevons Control of the aircraft about the longitudinal and lateral axes is achieved by eight elevons hinged into the wing trailing edge, four on each side. Each group of four is divided into two outboard and two inboard elevons. For identification purposes they are numbered 1 to 8 from port to starboard. Each surface is operated by a separate electro-hydraulically powered flying control unit (PFCU). Therefore, if a single unit fails, only one of the eight elevons is affected. After failure of a unit, the pilot is unable to move its elevon which will slowly assume the trail position.

The dual interconnected control columns

are operated in the conventional sense to control the aircraft in pitch and roll, any movement of the control column causing all eight elevons to move. To simplify subsequent references, the term 'aileron' is used when referring to lateral control and 'elevator' when referring to longitudinal control.

Control column movement is transmitted to a mixer unit which, in turn, transmits the appropriate signals to the elevons. Full elevator and full aileron travel cannot be obtained at the same time. In all cases, the movement of the outboard elevons to the inboard elevons is in the ratio of 5:4.

Rudder The single rudder is controlled by two powered flying control units, one main and one auxiliary. Normal control is by the main unit with the auxiliary unit idling; changeover occurs automatically if the main unit fails. During ground checks, when the main PFCU is stopped a delay of up to 15 seconds occurs before the auxiliary unit takes over. Since the control inputs to both rudder PFCU's are mechanically interconnected, a restriction of the input to one unit would prevent the pilot's demand being felt at the other. To prevent this, a trip mechanism is incorporated which, when activated, disconnects the faulty unit from the input linkage, gives failure warnings and, if the main unit is at fault operates the changeover mechanism.

Powered Flying Control Units (PFCU) Each PFCU consists, basically, of an electric motor driving main and servo hydraulic pumps and a hydraulic jack to move the control surface. Movement of the cockpit control operates the assembly to supply fluid to the appropriate side of the jack, thus moving the control surface. When the control surface position coincides with the new position of the cockpit control, jack movement ceases and the control surface remains in the selected position until further control movements are made. A stroke limiter prevents excessively harsh movements of the control surfaces.

Incorporated in the assembly is a surface lock valve. As long as servo pressure is available, the valve is held open to allow fluid to pass to either side of the jack. If, for any reason, this pressure is not available, the valve closes under a spring load and no further fluid can pass to or from either side of the jack. This prevents the surface from flapping in flight and acts as a ground lock. A bleed in each valve allows pressure on both sides of the jack to equalise slowly, thus allowing the surface to trail to the no-load position. When the valve closes it operates a micro-switch and a warning light on the pilot's panel comes on. There is only one control surface lock valve for the rudder assembly and it is housed in the auxiliary unit. An interconnection between the main and auxiliary units holds the lock valve open until no servo pressure is available from either unit. Indications of an individual rudder PFCU failure is given by a pressure switch in each unit.

Electrical Supplies

a. A 200-volt, 400 Hz AC supply is required to operate the PFC motors. This is supplied from the main busbars, the distribution of loads being as follows:

(1) Elevons:	Nos. 1 and 8, No. 1 busbar
	Nos. 3 and 6, No. 2 busbar
	Nos. 4 and 5, No. 3 busbar
	Nos. 2 and 7, No. 4 busbar
(2) Rudder:	Main, No. 3 busbar
	Auxiliary, No. 2 busbar

b. PFC failure warning is operated by 28-volt DC.

Controls The 10 push (off) spring-loaded stop buttons for the individual PFC units are arranged along the inboard edge of a panel on the port console, those for the elevons being grouped in pairs of elevons. The inboard button of the rudder pair controls the main unit. Each button incorporates a warning light which comes on if the unit malfunctions. Three PFC *START* pushbuttons, which also engage the feel systems, are at the rear of the panel and are marked A, R and E; A signifies the outboard elevons and aileron feel, R the rudder and rudder feel and E the inboard elevons and elevator feel.

The PFC MI shows white if any PFC button is pressed when the servo pressure has fallen below 10 to 15% of normal and a 28 volt supply is available. If the system pressure is normal, the PFC MI shows white only while any PFC button is being pressed.

Artificial Feel

Artificial Feel Units As the flying control system is irreversible, aerodynamic loads are not transmitted to the pilots' controls. To compensate for this lack of feel, artificial feel units are provided in the elevator, aileron and rudder control runs. Each unit is designed to give a suitable degree of feel for its particular control, the load on the pilots' controls varying with airspeed and/or control surface displacement. The feel units are positioned alongside the three control runs in the bomb bay and are basically electric actuators which move under the influence of speed change. The starboard pitot/static system provides the feel actuators with the airspeed signal. Movement of the actuator moves a follow-up potentiometer which is compared with a warning potentiometer supplied with port pitot/static information. If the guard system senses a discrepancy equivalent to 30 knots of airspeed, the pilot is warned of a failure in that feel channel.

Rudder and Elevator Feel The feel for each of these circuits is operated by a combination of spring-loading, related to control surface displacement, and electrical actuation, governed by airspeed, which varies the pilots' mechanical advantage over the feel spring. For the elevator circuit, the airspeed factor varies as the square of the airspeed, starting at 90 knots, with a maximum value of 460 knots. The rudder circuit varies as the cube of the airspeed, starting at 130 knots with a maximum value of 460 knots. In addition, a pre-loaded centring spring is fitted in the elevator and rudder circuits, to overcome the effects of friction in the control runs and the feel spring. The centring spring is on the input side of the feel unit and therefore provides a loading which is constant at all airspeeds but varies with the amount of control movement made by the pilot.

Aileron Feel Aileron feel is not airspeed controlled, although the range of control travel is reduced with increased airspeed. Stick loading is produced by resistance from torsion bars and, therefore, increases with increase of control displacement, the load being constant for any given angle. To prevent the pilot applying too great a control angle, variable stops in the feel unit decrease the range of movement as the airspeed increases above 150 knots with a maximum value of 365 knots. This circuit is also pre-loaded to overcome the effects of friction.

Feel Relief

a. Elevator and rudder feel can be reduced to the minimum speed position by use of feel relief buttons. The aileron variable stops can also be withdrawn, thus allowing the full range of control movement.

b. If any part of the artificial feel system malfunctions or if, in an emergency, it is desired to regain low speed feel conditions, the artificial feel may be relieved using the appropriate button. The button on the control column relieves both the aileron and the elevator systems. The system in which relief is not required may be restarted by pressing the A start button for aileron feel or the E start button for elevator feel. Feel relief on the rudder is achieved by pressing the button on the fuel contents panel. To regain normal feel, the appropriate start button should be pressed. Relieving the feel also removes power from the system and gives failure warning. When any part of the artificial feel system is relieved, care in handling the aircraft must be exercised if over-stressing is to be avoided.

c. Initial application of 28V to the aircraft causes feel relief in all three senses.

d. The flap covering the feel relief button on the stick is spring-loaded to closed.

Electrical Supplies The actuators for the artificial feel are operated by 28 volt DC.

Controls The three push (off) pull (on) buttons for the artificial feel warning systems are at the forward end of the panel and are marked *FEEL A, R, E*. In this case the letters are for aileron, rudder and elevator feel. Each button embodies a warning light; when the button is pushed in, the main warning on the pilots' centre panel is cancelled or inhibited for that channel but feel system operation is not affected.

The artificial feel indicator is either a 3-position indicator which shows black, white or ILS, or a 2-position indicator which shows black or white. It shows black during normal flight conditions and white if any artificial feel channel fails or is relieved.

Feel Locking To prevent possible feel unit runaway after a feel unit failure a locking facility is provided for all three channels. It is controlled by a single guarded switch. When LOCK is selected, a green light comes on to show that no further movement of normal or relief actuators can take place until NORMAL has been selected, although failure warning is given if the speed is altered by 30 knots from that at which LOCK was selected.

If the speed is changed by more than approximately 30 knots from the locking speed the main warning lights and the lights in the feel indicator buttons come on and the magnetic indicator goes white. If speed has been reduced, out-of-trim and manoeuvring forces are higher than usual. To prevent the main warnings coming on, push in the feel indicator buttons. The lights in the indicator buttons come on and the magnetic indicator shows white.

Before the feel is unlocked, reduce speed to below 250 knots, trim out the control forces and then raise the feel indicator buttons. The main warning lights come on.

After unlocking the feel, ensure that all failure warnings disappear, the green light goes out and the feel forces are at their appropriate level before making large control movements.

Trimmers

Description Control forces felt by the pilot in flight are produced by compression or extension of the feel mechanism, in response to control movement or change of airspeed. Trim adjustment is made by varying the length of the control run between the pilots' controls and the feel unit using an electrically operated actuator which removes the load from the feel spring. Double-pole wiring and switching is used to prevent runaways.

The trimming systems are duplicated as a precaution against failure and no warning indicator is provided. If the main systems become inoperative, however, the emergency system can be used. Trimming in the elevators sense is not permitted above 0.90M.

Controls

a. Each pilot's control column carries a double-pole 4-way aileron and elevator trim button. The button-cover covers the two switches controlling the paired trim systems. A catch on the forward edge of the button, when operated, opens the cover and allows each switch to be operated independently, to test the systems. If the 1st pilot and co-pilot attempt to trim in opposite directions, the circuit first selected operates and the other is ineffective.

b. Twin rudder trim switches are on the fuel contents panel, spring-loaded to the centre (off) position. They are marked RUDDER TRIM, PORT/STBD; both switches must be moved for the system to operate.

The emergency trimmer control on the retractable console is moved fore-and-aft for longitudinal trim, sideways for lateral trim and rotated for rudder trim; the button in the top of the control must be depressed during trim selections.

Electrical Supplies Electrical supplies for the system are 28V DC.

Autostabilisers

General Pitch and yaw dampers in the elevon and rudder circuits improve the natural damping of aircraft oscillations. A mach trimmer counteracts the nose-down trim change at high mach numbers.

Controls At the outboard side of the port console panel are controls for the autostabilisers and automach trimmer.

a. A YAW DAMPERS NO 1/OFF/NO 2 switch.

b. A RESET COMPARATOR spring-loaded button (for the pitch dampers and auto mach trim).

c. Four PITCH DAMPERS push (off)/pull (on) buttons, each embodying a warning light (amber).

d. Two AUTOTRIM RESET spring-loaded buttons, each embodying an extension indicator light (blue).

e. An AUTOTRIM ON/OFF pull/push button, embodying a warning light (amber).

The autostabiliser magnetic indicator shows white if any system is switched off or fails.

Electrical Supplies The gyros and amplifiers in the system are operated by 115V, 3-phase, 400 Hz AC, while the servos, motors and relays are operated by 28V DC.

Yaw Dampers The yaw damper system is duplicated, the YAW DAMPERS No 1/No 2 switch being selected as required. From each detector rate gyro, signals are passed to the actuator between the feel unit and the rudder PFCU. Yaw damping is in operation at all heights when either channel is selected but is airspeed monitored; rudder displacement is constant up to 200 knots and then decreases as airspeed increases. The monitoring supplies are from both the port and starboard pitot/static systems.

If a system malfunctions, no warning indication is given. The magnetic indicator, however, shows white when the switch is off or following certain power failures. The switch must be put to the off (centre) position after flight.

Pitch Dampers

a. Pitch dampers improve longitudinal stability at high altitudes and high mach numbers (above 0.90M).

b. There are four channels in the system, each one feeding to one of the inboard elevon PFC. A comparator links the four channels and if any one channel differs in operation from the other three, the warning system operates.

c. The system is height-monitored and is inop-

Below: *Close-up of the Vulcan B.2's extended port wing airbrake. (John Hale)*

erative below 20,000 feet. Above this altitude, the amplitude of control movement increases with increase of altitude.

d. The pitch damper servos are electrically heated whenever the undercarriage is retracted, the heating current being connected by a microswitch in the port undercarriage.

The pitch dampers are energised by pulling out the selector buttons on the port console. The buttons may be pulled out at any stage in flight but the dampers are inoperative until the height switch permits their operation. The buttons must be pushed in after flight.

It may be necessary to use the RESET COMPARATOR button before all or some of the channel lights can be extinguished before take-off.

Auto Mach Trimmer

a. The tandem mach trimmer system operates on the elevator control run, thus controlling all eight elevons. Signals are passed from two transmitting machmeters, separately fed by each pitot-static system, through a follow-up system and an amplifier to the servos. The system is brought into operation by a height switch at 20,000 feet.

b. The mach trimmer applies up-elevon as the mach number increases above 0.88 ± 0.01 (200 series engines) or 0.87 ± 0.01 (301 engines). The amount of up-elevon applied is always the sum of the movement of the two actuators. They should be extended by the same amount. Full extension of both actuators represents three-quarters of the total up-elevator movement available but this is only achieved at a mach number of approximately 0.96M, which is outside aircraft limits. A malfunction could result in full travel of the actuators at lower mach numbers.

c. An accelerometer control in each half of the system is set to limits of 1.5 and 0.7g. When g values exceed 1.5 the servos are prevented from extending but are still able to retract; when g values are below 0.7 the servos cannot retract further but are able to extend. The servos return to their normal function when g is between the limits, provided that there is no misalignment.

d. A comparator monitors the system and indicates to the pilot if there is any misalignment of the two servos. Independently wired switches are provided to reset the servos to the minimum position.

Both mach trim channels are energised by pulling out the single ON/OFF button on the port console. The blue lights in the RESET buttons are on whenever the servos are extended.

AIRBRAKES

General The slat-type airbrakes in the mainplane, above and below the engine air intakes, are electrically operated by two motors, using 200V, 3-phase AC; the emergency motor is supplied by No 2 busbar, and the normal motor by No 3 busbar. The supplies to the airbrakes are disconnected if load shedding occurs.

The airbrakes have three extended positions:

a. Medium drag 35°.

b. High drag (UC up) 55°.

c. High drag (UC down) 80° (STI/410 77° ± 3°. The transition from 55° to 80° (77° ± 3°) is automatic when the undercarriage is lowered but raising the undercarriage does not retract the airbrakes to 55°.

Control and Operation The airbrakes are controlled by a ganged switch on the rear face of the throttle quadrant. The switch has three positions: IN, MEDIUM DRAG AND HIGH DRAG; the button in the centre of the switch must be pressed in before the switch can be moved to the HIGH DRAG position.

a. The airbrakes are operated by either of two electric motors, connected to torque tubes through differential gearing.

b. The normal motor is isolated when the NORMAL/EMERGENCY switch on the throttle quadrant is selected to EMERGENCY; the emergency motor only is then used for all selections. The emergency motor is isolated when the AIRBRAKE ISOLATE EMERGENCY switch on top of panel 3P is selected to ISOLATE; the normal motor only is then used for all selections.

c. Without isolation, both motors drive any selection from IN, only the normal motor being used for subsequent selections. However, current operating practice is to use one motor only, usually the normal motor for all selections.

d. Pre-flight, the airbrakes are to be checked initially using the emergency motor. After retraction, providing the airbrake slats are flush or slightly proud of the aircraft skin, a further check is to be carried out using the normal motor.

WARNING. If, using the emergency motor, the airbrakes retract further than the flush position, remain in EMERGENCY. A NORMAL selection may result in damage to the wing or airbrake mechanism.

The 3-position magnetic indicator for the airbrakes at the top of the pilots' centre panel shows black when power is on and the airbrakes are in; white when no power is available, when airbrakes are selected out or if the airbrakes extend without selection or fail to retract completely. It shows cross-hatched when the airbrakes are in, selected in, and a main contactor has welded (a momentary cross-hatched indication is given when the airbrakes are selected from IN to MEDIUM DRAG with the emergency motor isolated; as soon as the airbrakes start to move the indication reverts to white).

The airbrkaes must not be operated on the ground when the bomb door access panels and the bomb doors are open.

The airbrakes must *not* be selected from HIGH to MEDIUM DRAG, or MEDIUM DRAG to IN, if iced up as this may cause damage to the drive mechanism or airframe.

Sustained flight with airbrakes extended against engine power is not recommended.

BRAKE PARACHUTE

A brake parachute in the tail cone aft of the rudder provides additional braking during the landing run. Operation is electrically controlled (28V DC) by a split, 2-pole, JETTISON/STREAM switch on the centre instrument panel. Both halves should normally be used but either half of the switch can stream and jettison the parachute (at a slower rate). If both are used for streaming, both must be used for jettisoning.

A magnetic indicator, beside the external intercom point, is visible when a small access panel on the starboard side of the rear fuselage is raised. The indicator shows black when the parachute door is locked and all switches and relays in the circuit are at their correct setting for streaming.

If unselected streaming occurs, the action of the door opening without electrical selection causes a supply to be fed to the jettison unit and the parachute is jettisoned automatically.

PART 6: FUEL SYSTEM

General Fuel is carried in 14 pressurised tanks, five in each wing and four in the fuselage, above and to the rear of the nosewheel bay. The tanks are of the flexible bag type and each tank is enclosed by a metal casing which is part of the aircraft structure. The tanks are not self-sealing but are crash-proof.

The tanks are divided into four groups, each group normally feeding its own engine. A crossfeed system enables the various groups to be interconnected. Automatic fuel proportioning is normally used to maintain the fuel CG position.

Provision is made for carrying two fuel tanks in the bomb bay, either saddle-shaped or cylindrical. Fuel from these tanks passes into the main system through two delivery lines, one each side of the fuselage, to each side of the centre crossfeed cock.

An air-to-air refuelling probe is in the nose and pipes from it join the normal refuelling lines.

A pressure refuelling system is provided for ground use.

The majority of the controls and indicators for the fuel system are grouped in the form of a mimic diagram on the retractable console. The air-to-air refuelling controls are on the starboard console.

ELECTRICAL SUPPLIES. All fuel system components operated from the aircraft electrical supplies are listed in Tables 1, 2 and 4 of Chapter 4. All fuel pumps utilise 200V AC but the fuse-

MAIN FUEL SYSTEM

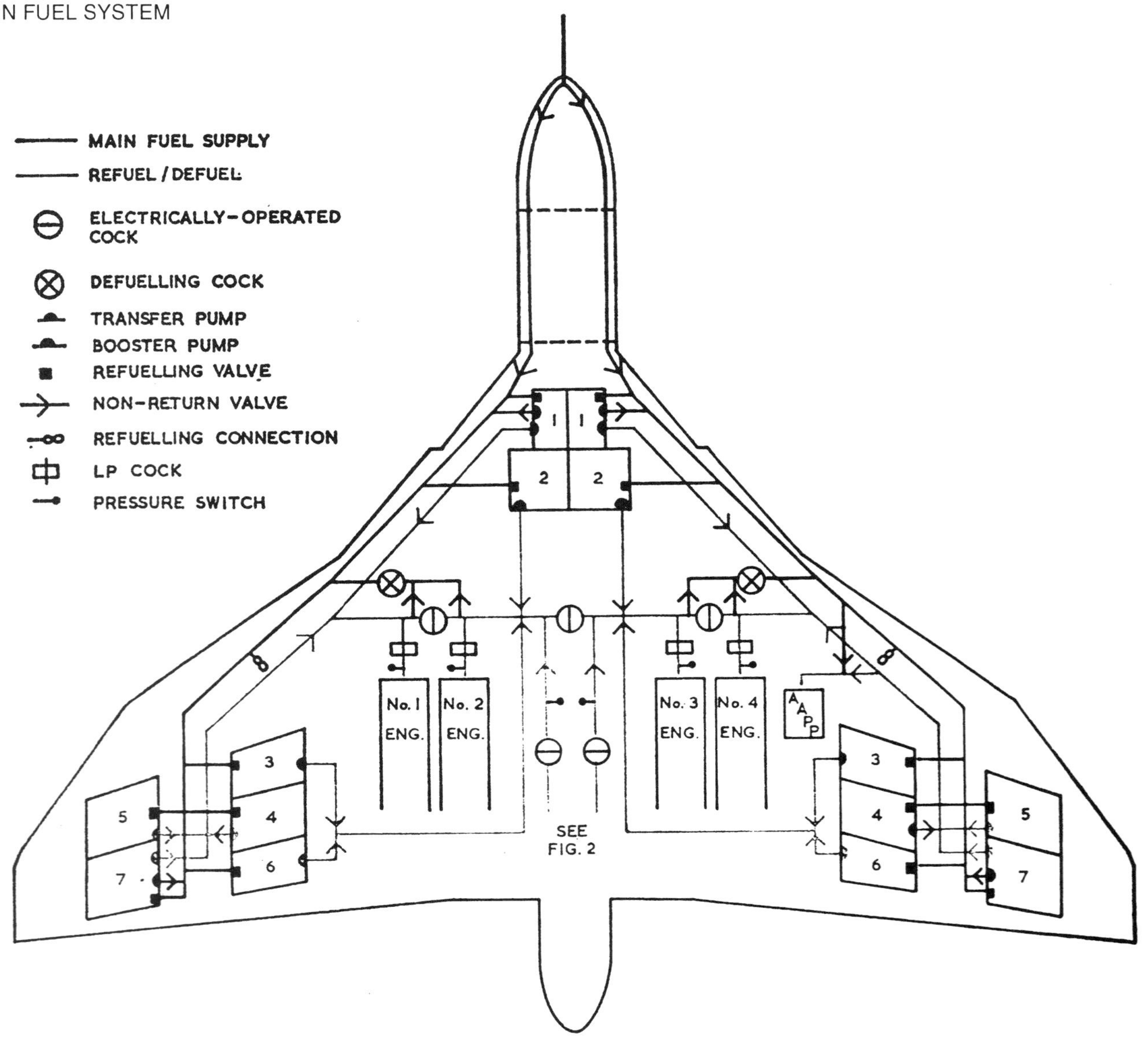

lage tank pumps are controlled by 28V essential DC while the bomb bay and wing tanks pumps are controlled by 28V DC non-essential supply.

Fuel Tanks and Recuperators

Main Tanks The tanks on each side of the aircraft are numbered from 1 to 7, No 1 and 2 being the fuselage tanks and the remainder the wing tanks. The tank numbers correspond to the CG position of each tank, No 1 having the furthest forward CG and No 7 the furthest aft. No 1, 4, 5 and 7 tanks comprise the outboard tank group (No 1 group port, No 4 group starboard). Similarly, No 2, 3 and 6 tanks comprise the inner tank groups (No 2 port and No 3 starboard). Each group normally feeds its associated engine.

The total contents, in gallons, varies between different fuels because the point at which the refuelling valves close is affected by the permittivity, specific gravity and temperature of the fuel used.

Each wing tank contains a reservoir, with clack valves at its base. These valves are normally open but close when the head of fuel in the reservoir is built up by the auxiliary pumps.

Bomb Bay Tanks Two fuel tanks may be carried in the bomb bay, one at the forward and one at the rear end. The tanks can be of the saddle or cylindrical type; the former being referred to as the 'A' when fitted forward or the 'E' when fitted aft. If only one bomb bay tank is carried it must be fitted in the forward position.

Saddle tanks. Each saddle tank has four pumps, two on each side; each pair of pumps feeds into the delivery line on that side.

Cylindrical tanks. Each cylindrical tank has three pumps, feeding into a common line, which feeds both delivery lines. The tanks are referred to as the forward and aft tanks.

Tank capacities The approximate tank capacities are as follows:

Tank	*Gallons*	*Avtur*	*Avtag*
A	718	5744 lb	5529 lb
E	721	5768 lb	5552 lb
Cylindrical (each, usable)	995	7960 lb	7662 lb

AAPP Tank The fuel tank for the airborne auxiliary power plant, in the starboard wing to the rear of the AAPP, has a capacity of 10 gallons.

The tank is filled from the main fuel system via a pipe line from the wing tanks of No 4 group delivery line, whenever the No 4 group wing booster pumps are running. In addition, the tank is supplied from the refuelling line. A float valve in the tank shuts off the supply when the tank is full.

Tank Pressurisation and Venting Each tank group can be pressurised with air from its associated engine. The system maintains a pressure of 1.82 to 2.3 PSI above ambient in the tanks throughout the altitude range of the aircraft, so as to prevent loss by boiling off fuel at high altitude and high fuel temperatures. Pressurisation also prevents negative differential pressure in the tanks, thus preventing risk of tank collapse. The bomb bay tanks are not pressurised.

Pressurisation of the main tanks is controlled by a switch on the air-to-air refuelling panel; below the switch are four magnetic indicators, one for each tank group, which show black when the tanks are pressurised. A switch on the centre console for bomb bay tank pressurisation is inoperative.

Combined inward/outward relief valves are fitted in all tanks and float valves in the wing tanks. The float valve closes if the fuel level rises, to prevent fuel flowing back into the pressurisation lines. The inward relief valve is set at ¼ PSI and the outward valve at ¾ to 1 PSI. Two vent valves for each tank group, one in the bomb bay roof and one under the mainplane, give atmospheric venting when tank pressurisation is not in operation; when pressurisation is switched on, the valve is adjusted by a master control valve which, in conjunction with an air valve, maintains a pressure of 1.82 to 2.3 PSI above ambient. In the event of overpressurisation an outward relief valve in the vent valve relieves at 2.65 to 3.0 PSI.

The AAPP tank is vented to the main system in No 4 tank, No 4 group.

The bomb bay tanks are vented into the fuselage tank lines.

a. When tank pressurisation is selected on initially, the pressure indicators may remain white until RPM reach approximately 80%; they may similarly revert to white after the landing run.

b. Normally, with power on and pressure off, the pressure indicators show white. If electrical load shedding takes place, the tanks are pressurised regardless of selection and the indicators show black.

c. During descent, with pressurisation on, and after landing when it is selected off, rumbling noises maybe heard; this is normal.

Recuperators A 6-gallon recuperator for each tank group supplies fuel to the engines if there is a pressure drop in the fuel supply. Each recuperator is supplied with fuel from its own tank group and with air from its own engine. If the fuel pressure drops, the air pressure (at 6 to 10 PSI) forces the fuel into the engine feed lines. Sufficient fuel is available to supply the engines for approximately 10 seconds at full power at sea level, and up to 2 minutes at altitude at cruising RPM. When negative g is removed, normal fuel flow is resumed and the booster pumps recharge the recuperator.

Refuelling and Defuelling

Air-to-Air Refuelling Fuel from the probe flows aft on either side of the cabin, through non-return valves, to join the main refuelling lines. All tanks are refuelled at the same time, the rate of flow being approximately 4000 lb/min.

Probe lighting is provided by two lamps in the nose supplied through separate circuits.

Refuelling on the Ground Pressure refuelling of the aircraft is via two refuelling points in each main wheelbay. These two points supply a common refuelling line on each side, running to a refuelling valve in the sump plate of each tank. Refuelling instructions are detailed in the Flight Reference Cards.

During refuelling, each tank is filled to the same percentage of its capacity in order to maintain a central CG position. A selector in the port main wheelbay allows selection of quantities from 0 to 100% and operates through the electrical output of the contents gauge amplifiers.

A control panel at each refuelling point carries the switches for the system and indicator lights to show the progress of refuelling.

Only one tank in each group is filled at a time, automatic changeover to the next tank taking place when the first tank is filled to the selected percentage. The order of filling is 1, 4, 5 and 7 in the outboard groups and 2, 3 and 6 in the inboard groups.

Bomb bay tanks

a. The bomb bay tanks are filled from the port refuelling point. A double-level float switch is fitted in each tank. The bomb bay refuelling panel is in the port wheelbay and carries a master switch and low and high level indicator lights for each tank. With the master switch *ON*, the refuelling valves open and the indicator lights come on. When the tank is almost full, the lower float switch partially closes the refuelling valve, reducing the rate of flow and extinguishing the green light. The high level switch completely closes the refuelling valve when the tank is full and extinguishes the red light.

b. The main tanks must be refuelled before the bomb bay tanks.

c. The bomb bay refuelling master switch must be selected off when refuelling is complete.

Fuel System Controls and Indicators

Fuel Control Panels

Retractable console. The fuel panel on the retractable console carries a mimic diagram of the system, including the bomb bay tanks. Forward of the diagram are three CG control switches, two FWD/AFT transfer pump switches, one for each side of the system, and one *PORT/STBD* switch for use during air-to-air refuelling. On each side of the diagram are two *AUTO/MANUAL* switches, one for each group; these switches control sequence timing . In each tank on the diagram is on OFF/ON pump switch (which controls both main and auxiliary pumps) and a *CONT* pushbutton for contents reading. The crossfeed cocks are represented in the diagram by three magnetic indicators, with OPEN/close cock switches to the rear of them. Four pushbuttons, marked *NO-ENG*, are provided for flowmeter selection. The bomb bay system diagram has two *BOMB BAY/MAIN* switches, two *ON/OFF* pump switches for each tank and a pressurisation switch (inoperative).

Starboard console. The air-to-air refuelling controls are grouped on a panel on the starboard console and consist of two probe lighting dimmer switches, a nitrogen switch, a main tanks pressurisation switch, four tank pressurisation magnetic indicators, an *ON/OFF* split double-pole master switch, a refuelling indicator and a refuelling gallery pressure gauge.

Gauge panels. The contents gauges for the main tanks, one per group, are on a panel forward of the throttles, while that for the bomb bay tanks is on a panel attached to the inboard guide rail of the 1st pilot's seat, with a pushbutton for individual tank selection.

Fuel Cocks

HP cocks. The four HP cocks are opened by the initial movement of the throttle levers forward from the fully closed position. The sleeves on the levers must be held up to permit movement between the *HP COCK SHUT* position and the *IDLING* gate.

LP cocks. The four LP cocks are electrically controlled by four guarded *ON/OFF* switches on the underside of the coaming above the pilots' centre panel. Each cock is fitted with a bypass through a non-return valve, which acts as a thermal relief for fuel trapped between the engine and the LP cock, when the cock is closed. The LP cocks are supplied with power from the vital busbar.

Crossfeed cocks and indicators

a. There are two wing crossfeed cocks, each connecting the tank groups on that side, and a centre crossfeed cock between Nos 2 and 3 groups. The cocks are electrically operated by 28V essential power.

b. Three 3-position magnetic indicators show continuity with the diagram lines when the cocks are open, discontinuity when the cocks are shut and cross-hatch when the cocks are at intermediate position or when no power is available.

Bomb bay tank cocks. Shut-off cocks are provided in the delivery lines from the bomb bay tanks. These cocks are opened together if any bomb bay tank pump switch is selected on.

GROUND SERVICING COCKS. A manually operated cock in the delivery line from each tank is used during ground servicing. The cock-operating levers are so designed that the cover plates cannot be fitted into place unless the cocks are in the open position.

Fuel Pumps

BOOSTER PUMPS AND AUXILIARY PUMPS

a. Each wing tank contains both a booster pump and an auxiliary pump; the fuselage tanks have a single booster pump. The booster pumps are attached to the sump plate at the bottom of each tank and, in the case of the wing tanks, are inside the reservoir.

b. Starvation of the booster pumps with change of aircraft attitude is prevented by the auxiliary pumps at the inboard end of each wing tank. These pumps run whenever the booster pumps are switched on and supply fuel to the reservoir, thus maintaining a head of fuel for the booster pumps.

BOMB BAY TANK PUMPS

a. Each saddle-type (A and E) bomb bay tank has four booster pumps, one pair supplying each feed from the tank. The pumps run in parallel and each pump switch controls one port and one starboard pump in its tank.

b. Each cylindrical tank has three booster pumps, feeding into a common line. The same controls are provided, the right-hand pump switch for each tank controlling the forward pump and the left-hand switch controlling the other two pumps. The tanks are labelled FWD and AFT instead of A and E.

c. When the *BOMB BAY/MAIN* switches are set to *BOMB BAY*, the main tank sequence timers are isolated and the main tank pumps run at reduced speed, provided also that the main tanks are selected to *AUTO*.

TRANSFER PUMPS

a. Transfer pumps in Nos 1 and 7 tanks on each side allow the fuel to be transferred in either direction between these tanks, if it is necessary to adjust the fuel CG position. As both tanks are in the same group, transfer does not affect the group contents. Transfer is via the refuelling lines.

b. With a transfer pump switch at FWD, the refuelling valve of No 1 tank opens and No 7 tank pump starts and transfers fuel to No 1 tank; placing a switch to AFT opens the refuelling valve of No 7 tank and starts the No 1 tank pump. The rate of fuel transfer is approximately 100 lb/min when transferring from No 1 to No 7 and approximately 50 lb/min when transferring from No 7 to No 1; approximately 300 lb of fuel must be transferred to alter the slide rule index by 1.2. After transfer, check that the desired amount of fuel has been transferred.

c. If, when transferring fuel, the receiving tank is full when the transfer pump is still running, a float switch closes the refuelling valve.

d. The function of these switches is altered during air-to-air refuelling.

FUEL PRESSURE WARNING INDICATORS

a. Four magnetic indicators on the pilots' centre panel below the JPT gauges, show black when the fuel delivery pressure to the engine is satisfactory, white when the pressure downstream of the filter falls below 5 PSI and black when there are no power supplies.

b. The two bomb bay fuel indicators show black when the fuel pressure is sufficient *and* the cocks are open. They show white if the fuel pressure falls below 10 PSI.

c. If it is necessary to close the LP cock after shutting down an engine in flight, the magnetic indicators do not always turn white immediately. The time taken for fuel pressure beyond the LP cock to fall below 5 PSI depends on the rate of decay of pressure through the LP cock bypass valve.

Sequence Timers Because of the configuration of the aircraft, the fuel tanks are disposed forward and aft of the aircraft centre of gravity. It is therefore essential that fuel should be used at approximately the same rate from all tanks, in order to maintain the fuel CG position.

An electrically operated sequence timer on each side of the aircraft ensures even fuel distribution, by causing the main pumps in each tank to run alternately at full speed and reduced speed (the auxiliary pumps run continuously). The quantity of fuel pumped from any one tank during one cycle of the sequence timer (five minutes) is proportional to the tank capacity; the distribution of fuel is thus maintained throughout the tanks. The sequence timer motors use 200 volt AC.

The sequence of tank feeding is as follows:

Period No	*Outboard engine tanks*	*Inboard engine tanks*
1	1	6
2	7	2 or 6
3	4	3
4	5	2

It will be seen that No 2 tank feeds twice in each cycle, as it is the largest tank.

With all booster pumps *ON* and the *AUTO/MANUAL* switches at *AUTO*, sequence timing is in operation; to interrupt the sequence timing in any group, put the appropriate switch to *MANUAL* and, if it is desired to use fuel from any particular tank in the group, switch *OFF* all booster pumps which are not required. The *AUTO/MANUAL* switches should be put to *MANUAL* after flight, to de-energise the relays.

Fuel Contents Gauges and Flowmeters

MAIN TANKS CONTENTS GAUGES

a. A capacitor-type system provides indication of fuel contents. The four gauges, one for each tank group, are on a panel forward of the throttle levers. Each gauge is calibrated with two concentric scales, reading in pounds x 1000. Normally, each gauge reads the contents of its appropriate group, on the inner scale. An individual tank reading is obtained on the outer scale by pressing the pushbutton in the appropriate tank position on the mimic diagram.

b. In no circumstances should two gauge pushbuttons in the same group be pressed simultaneously, as this damages the instrument.

c. Four group contents gauges are at the navigator/plotter's position; there is no means of reading individual tank contents on these gauges.

d. The contents magnetic indicator for the AAPP is at the AEO's station.

e. An accurate 28 volt supply is needed to ensure correct fuel readings.

BOMB BAY TANKS CONTENTS GAUGE. The fuel gauge of the bomb bay tanks is on the 1st pilot's seat guide rail, facing towards the co-pilot. The total contents of both tanks are normally shown; individual tank contents can be obtained by pressing the appropriate pushbutton below the gauge.

FLOWMETERS

a. A Mk 3 flowmeter system is installed. This system is designed to give the following approximate indications:

(1) Fuel consumption by individual engines (lb/min)

(2) Total fuel consumption by all four engines (lb/min)

(3) Total amount of fuel gone (lb)

b. Two indicators, one giving total flow and pounds gone and the other giving instantaneous flow for individual engines, are on the co-pilot's instrument panel, together with a *FUEL FLOW/RESET/NORMAL* switch for resetting the total flow indicator. Selection of an individual engine flow is obtained by pressing the appropriate engine pushbutton on the fuel system mimic diagram. The instrument continues to indicate the flow to that engine until another engine is selected.

CG Indicator and Slide Rule A fuel CG position indicator, on the pilots' centre panel, indicates the CG of the fuel system (not of the aircraft). The instrument registers automatically when air-to-air refuelling is in operation but readings can be taken in other flight conditions by pressing the CG *CHECK* button. This button can also be used, when air-to-air refuelling is in progress, to regain contents gauge readings.

The instrument face has two arcs, one for each side of the fuel system; each arc is divided into three sectors, a central green sector to indicate the safe range and red outer sectors marked *NOSE HEAVY* and *TAIL HEAVY*. The needles should be on or near the zero position if the fuel is correctly proportioned. The green sector coves a range of 60,000 lb ft, 30,000 lb ft forward of zero and 30,000 lb ft aft. If, for example, both needles were on the forward limit of the green sector, the fuel CG would be 60,000 lb ft forward of the zero position with equally proportioned fuel.

The instrument can be checked before flight by pushing the CG pushbutton and observing any slight movement of the needles. If no movement is observed, it may be because of exact fuel proportioning. This can be checked by transferring fuel from Nos 1 or 7 tanks and checking the indicator for movement while pressing the *CHECK* button.

The bomb bay tank fuel is not included in the CG indication.

CG SLIDE RULE. A slide rule for calculating aircraft CG is provided and stowed below the starboard console.

NOTE: The CG limitations take into account the shift caused by undercarriage retraction.

Air-to-air Refuelling Controls The air-to-air refuelling indicator consists of the outline of the aircraft, with numbered lights in the approximate position of each tank. The lights in the indicator can be adjusted for day or night use by revolving the ring round the indicator. The lights come on when the valves open and go out individually as the tanks fill.

The master switch must be put *ON* before drogue engagement and must not be put off until contact has been broken. With either half of the switch *ON*, the refuelling valves (in all tanks which are not full) are opened, tank pressurisation is switched off, the fuel contents gauges are isolated and read zero, all lights in the indicator come on (except for full tanks) and the CG indicator registers automatically. As each tank is filled, a double float switch closes the refuelling valve and the appropriate light in the indicator goes out.

100% refuelling may be carried out, provided that the fuel system is depressurised. If pressure remains in the tanks, refuelling may be carried out provided that the tanker main pump is switched off. Contact must be broken immediately if the fuel gallery pressure exceeds 10 PSI.

The master switch must not be set OFF until contact is broken. The nitrogen purge switch is then set ON; this action opens the nitrogen cock and the No 2 tanks refuelling valves and nitrogen pressure at 30 PSI forces fuel from the probe lines into the No 2 tanks. Contents gauging is regained when the master switch is OFF.

CG CONTROL

a. The aircraft CG can be controlled during air-to-air refuelling by three switches on the fuel control panel: the two switches which normally control the transfer pumps, for fore-and-aft control, and the *PORT/STARBOARD* switch at the top of the panel, marked *FR RECEIVER CG CONTROL*, for lateral control.

b. When the refuelling master switch is *ON*, the transfer pump switches are disconnected from the transfer pumps; setting them to *FWD* closes the refuelling valves in tanks 6 and 7, while setting them to AFT closes the refuelling valves in tanks 1 and 2. In each case, the refuelling valves remain open in all other tanks. If the lateral control switch is moved to *PORT* or *STBD*, the refuelling valves in the Nos 6 and 7 tanks on the *opposite* side are closed.

Air-to-air Refuelling CG Control The fuel CG indicator must be monitored throughout the refuelling sequence, especially in the initial stages. If a tank refuelling valve fails to open, especially in a tank with a large moment arm, the appropriate needle moves quite rapidly forward or aft; this is the only indication of a valve failing to open. As movement of the needle towards the limit of the green sector becomes apparent, move the appropriate *FWD/AFT* switch on the fuel panel in the opposite direction from needle movement. Refuelling may be continued for as long as it is possible to keep the needles in the green sector; if it becomes impossible, contact must be broken immediately.

Normally, if all tanks are accepting fuel, the needles move to and fro within the green sector and no action need be taken apart from monitoring. If contact is broken before all tanks are full, the subsequent tank contents check, with the master switch *OFF*, may show considerable variations in tank percentages. *MANUAL* use of the fuel system then becomes necessary to balance the tanks.

Even if it is known that the tanks are only partially to be filled, monitoring of the tanks-full indicator is still necessary; in practice, Nos 7, 5 and 1 tanks are the first to fill, in that order, and the other tanks may lag behind by as much as 25%. Any method of acjusting the fuel in individual tanks, in an attempt to make all tanks fill simultaneously, reduces the safety margin provided by this lag and increases the possibility of rupturing a tank if its valve remains open when all the others have closed. Such a failure could be catastrophic.

If the bomb bay tanks refuelling master switch in the port wheelbay is inadvertently left on or an electrical fault produces the same effect, the bomb bay tanks refuelling valves open in flight as the fuel contents decrease. This results, during air-to-air refuelling, in fuel entering the bomb bay tanks; a careful watch must be kept on their contents gauges in order to keep the CG within limits.

AIR-TO-AIR REFUELLING SYSTEM

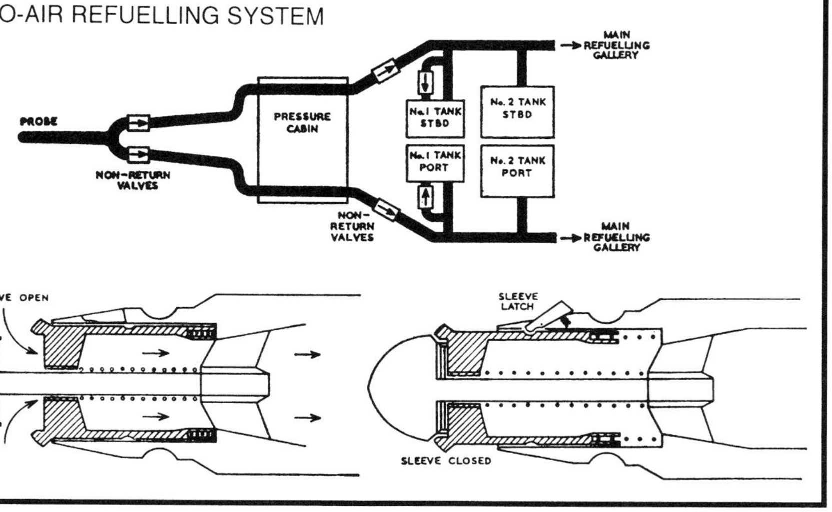

PART 7: GENERAL AND EMERGENCY EQUIPMENT AND CONTROLS

ENTRANCE DOOR, LADDERS AND CANOPY

Entrance to the Aircraft The aircraft is entered by the door on the underside of the fuselage, below the crew compartment. The door is hinged at the forward end and opens downwards. Door opening can be operated either mechanically or pneumatically; door closing is pneumatically operated.

DOOR OPENING MECHANISM

a. The door can be opened from outside by a handle near the rear edge of the door. Operation of the handle deflates the door seal and withdraws the door bolts; the door then opens under gravity.

b. Door opening from the inside is by a lever in a gated quadrant on the port side of the door, at the forward end. Movement of this lever to the gate deflates the door seals and withdraws the locking bolts. If the aircraft is on the ground, the door then opens under gravity. To select the *EMERGENCY* door opening position it is nec-

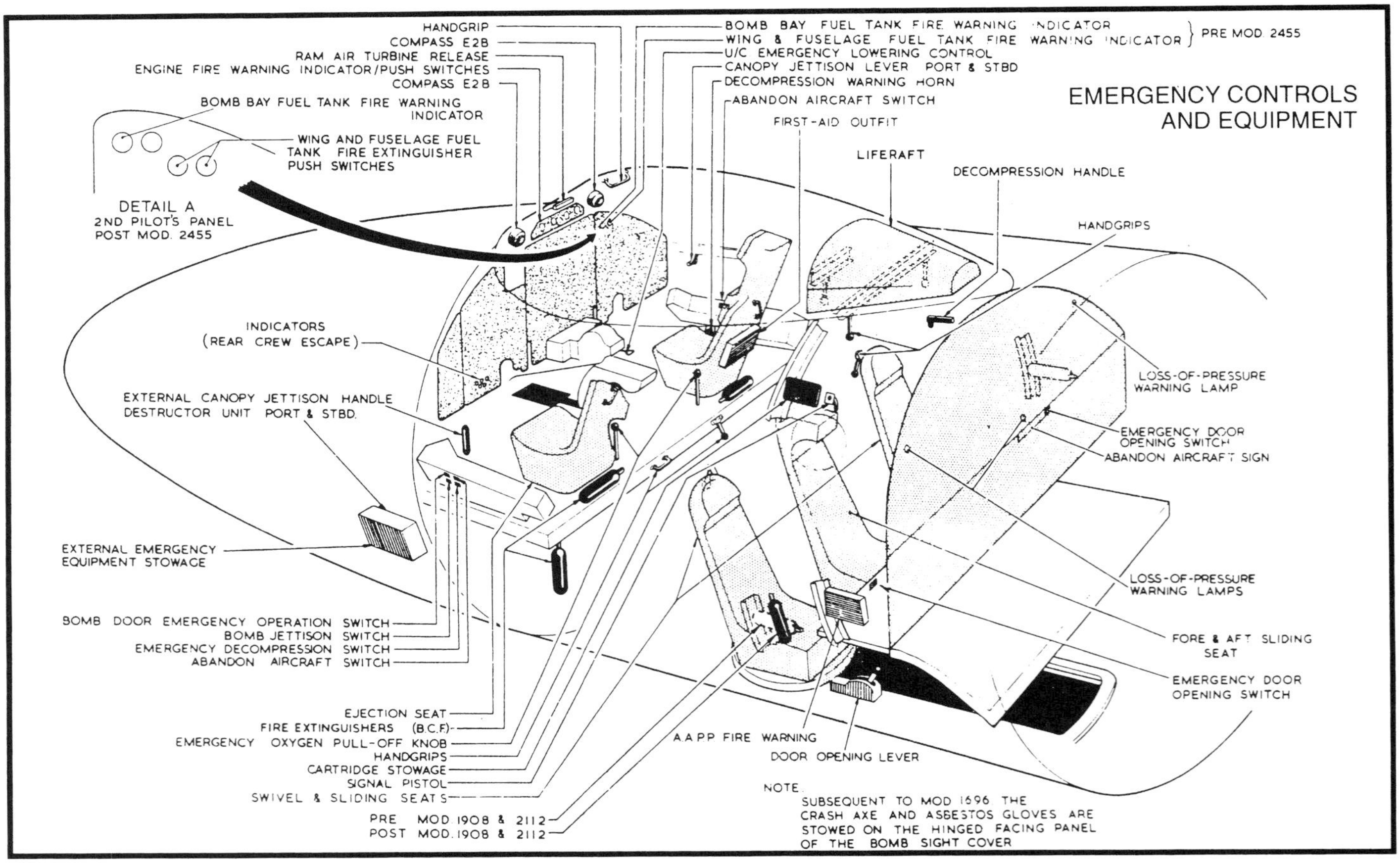

EMERGENCY CONTROLS AND EQUIPMENT

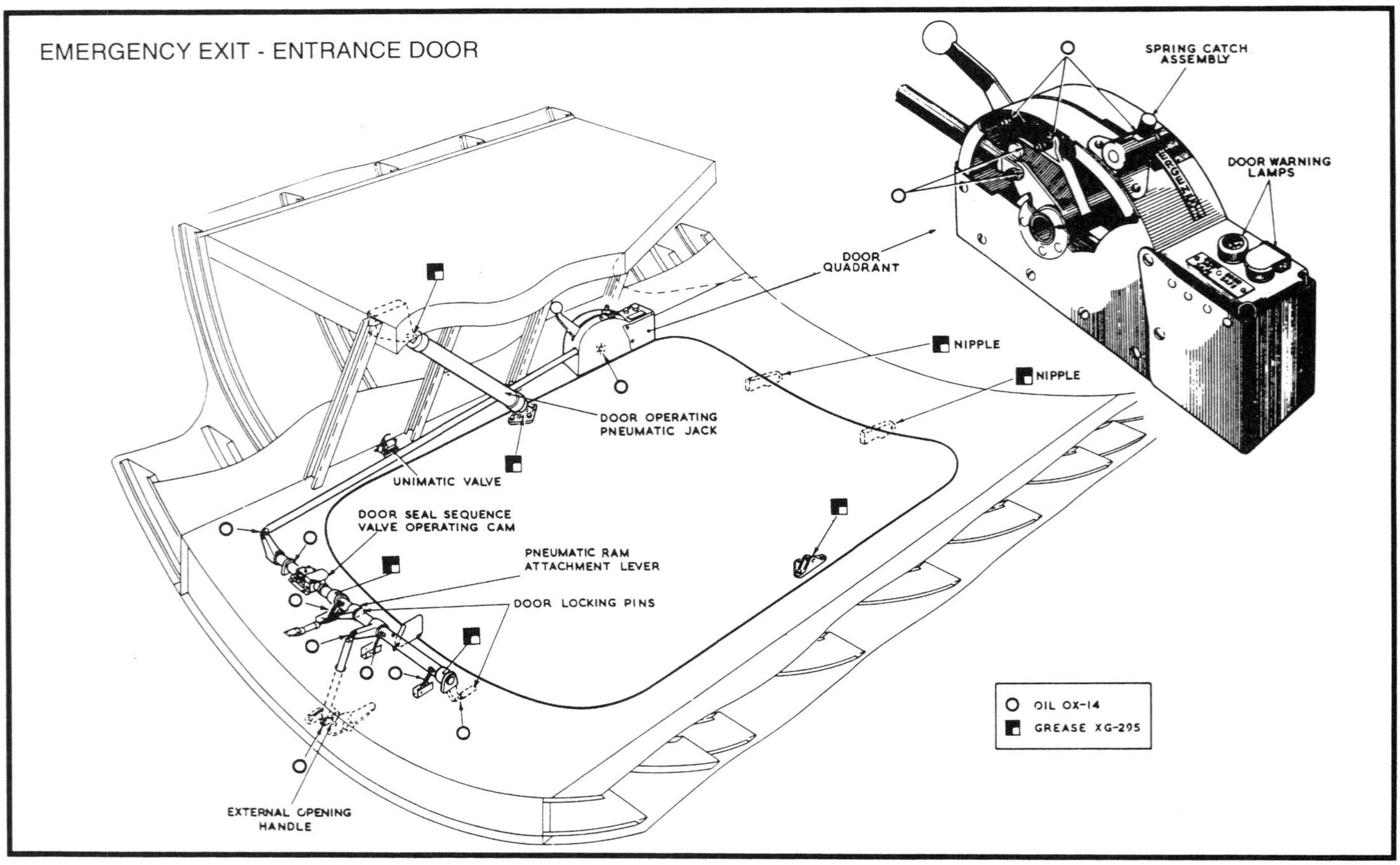

EMERGENCY EXIT - ENTRANCE DOOR

essary to move the lever to the fully forward position, in the aircraft sense, via the quadrant gate. The gate is negotiated by moving the lever outwards towards the port side of the aircraft, then continuing forward. In an emergency, the door may also be opened by a switch at the navigator/plotter's position.

An additional door-opening switch is provided, recessed into the edge of the table between the navigator/plotter and the AEO and covered by a flap. The switch has three positions ON/OFF/ON, and either ON position opens the door through the same circuits as the navigator's switch.

The main door may jam closed if the seal deflation valve plunger is out of alignment. The seal can be deflated by pulling the door inflation pipe from its rubber connector on the starboard side of the seal, or by cutting the rubber connection.

DOOR CLOSING MECHANISM

a. The door may be closed from the outside by operation of a pushbutton to the rear of the door.

b. The door is closed from inside by a toggle mechanism, the handle of which is below a cover on the crew's floor, between the navigators' seats. The door is closed by pneumatic pressure at 400 PSI and, when the door is closed and locked, the door seal is automatically inflated by nitrogen at a reduced pressure of 25 PSI.

DOOR INDICATORS. On the door operating quadrant there are two lights, one red and one green. The green light, marked DOOR SAFE, comes on when the door is locked; the red light, marked DOOR NOT SAFE, comes on whenever the door is unlocked. In addition, there is a magnetic indicator above the pilots' centre instrument panel, which shows white when the door is unlocked. In the nosewheel bay is a green light which comes on when the door is locked.

Ladders A folding ladder is attached to the entrance door. Before flight it is to be removed and strapped to the stowage on top of the bomb aimer's window cover. On the occasions when this position is covered by extra equipment the ladder should be carried in the pannier.

WARNING: Due to the hazard it presents to evacuating the cabin in an emergency, the ladder must not be left in position on the entrance door.

A ladder, which can be stowed by lifting and sliding to port, provides access to the pilots' cockpit.

Canopy, Decription The canopy, of double skin construction, is attached to the fuselage nose section by six attachment points. A seal, inflated by pnematic pressure, ensures an airtight fit. A schrader valve allows the seal to be inflated by handpump, for weather proofing, when the pneumatic system is being serviced.

CANOPY LOCKING INDICATORS

a. Two pointers, one on either side of the cockpit, indicate against an arc whether the canopy is locked or unlocked. The locked position is indicated by a small white segment, while the UNLOCKED range is indicated by a larger, red segment.

b. A magnetic indicator, at the top of the pilots' centre panel, shows white when the canopy is unlocked.

Canopy Jettison Two yellow/black wire-locked canopy jettison levers are provided, one on each side of the cockpit, above the consoles. A pip-pin is provided to lock each lever in the safe position and, when on the ground, the pins are inserted through the hole in the coaming rail to prevent inadvertent operation. The pins must always be removed before flight.

A yellow external release handle is on the port side of the nose. When this handle or either of the jettison handles is pulled, mechanical linkages open the canopy attachment jaws and operate a torque tube to fire the jettison gun.

The canopy is also jettisoned when any of the seat handles are pulled. In this case, pulling the handle operates the following sequence:

a. A pneumatic valve is opened, which allows air pressure at 1200 PSI to pass to a jack.

b. The jack operates a torque tube to open the canopy attachments and fire the jettison gun.

c. As the canopy clears the aircraft, it operates a time delay unit which fires the ejection seats 1 second later.

CANOPY JETTISON GUN SAFETY-PIN

a. A safety-pin, with pip-pin attached, is provided for the jettison gun sear at the rear of the canopy, in the cabin. The pin must be inserted in the sear after flight. Before flight, the pin must be removed from the sear and the pip-pin must be inserted in the adjacent jettison lever mechanism, to link the manual mechanism to the gun.

b. Instructions on the use of these pins is given on two tablets on the perspex cover of the gun, together with a diagrammatic arrangement of the devices. The pins are inserted through sliding panels in the perspex.

WARNING: Canopy jettison lever pip-pin must be removed and a check made that the canopy indicator remains black, before the jettison gun is made live.

WINDSCREEN AND ASSOCIATED EQUIPMENT

Windscreen and DV Panels The laminated windscreen, embodying gold film heating, is divided into three sections.

DV PANELS. A triangular DV panel at each end of the windscreen is hinged at the lower edge and opens inwards. The panel is released by pressing a catch in the handle at the top, then depressing the handle, pulling it inwards and sliding it back. No stowages are provided. When replacing the panel, care must be taken to ensure that the balls at the base are fitted into the guide tube correctly, otherwise a serious cabin pressure leak can occur.

Windscreen Wipers Windscreen wipers are provided for each pilot's windscreen panel and for the centre panel. The wipers are electro-hydraulically operated and the blades are of the parallel-motion type and are self-parking. The wipers for the 1st pilot's and centre windscreen share a common hydraulic system and electrical motor, while the co-pilot's has an independent system.

The wipers are controlled by two double-pole, 3-position OFF/FAST/SLOW switches, one for the 1st pilot's and centre windscreen panel wipers and one for the co-pilot's panel wiper. The 1st pilot's switch is on the left of his panel. The co-pilot's switch is on the right of his panel. The wipers must never be used on a dry windscreen.

The wipers are operated by 28V DC.

Sun Visors and Anti-Flash Screens

SUN VISORS. Sun visors are provided for the windscreen and side panels; the side visors are sliding and the front ones are hinged at the top. They are attached to the lower edge of the canopy.

ANTI-FLASH SCREENS. Anti-flash screens are provided for the windscreen, side screens and crew windows. Those for the windscreens have slide fasteners; when not in use, they are rolled down and stowed. The screens for the side windows are sliding shutters.

LIGHTING

Internal Lighting

COCKPIT LIGHTING

a. PANEL LIGHTING. The pilots' instrument panels and the consoles are lit by a mixture of red flood, white flood (fluorescent) and U/V lighting, while the E2B compasses have red lamps. Pillar lamps are built into the front instrument panels. The red lamps are controlled by a series of dimmer switches on the cockpit walls, forward of the port and starboard consoles. One U/V dimmer switch is on each side console. The white flood lighting is controlled by two switches, one on the outboard side of each pilot's instrument panel.

b. ANTI-DAZZLE LIGHTING. Anti-dazzle lighting is provided and is controlled by a BRIGHT/off/DIM switch on the port of the fuel contents panel; an additional OFF/BRIGHT switch is provided at the nav/plotter's position.

c. WANDER LAMP. A wander lamp, with its own integral switch, is attached to the canopy, above the pilots' position.

CREW'S LIGHTING. Both panel lighting and anglepoise lamps are provided for the crew members. This lighting is controlled by a series of *ON/OFF* switches and dimmer switches at the crew positions.

SERVICING LAMPS. Servicing lamps are provided in the bomb bay, wheelbays, power compartment and rear fuselage. The master switch for these lamps is in the starboard side of the nosewheel bay. In addition, there are sockets for inspection lamps, one on the front spar bulkhead and one on the rear spar bulkhead, in the bomb bay. The lamps are only operative while an external 28V DC supply is connected.

ELECTRICAL SUPPLIES. The U/V and fluorescent lighting uses 115V 3-phase AC from the main transformers; the red flood and anti-dazzle lighting is 28V DC operated.

External Lighting

MASTER SWITCH. Before any of the external lighting (except the servicing lights) can be used, the *EXTERNAL LIGHT* master switch must be put *ON*. This switch is on the inboard side of the starboard console.

NAVIGATION AND ANTI-COLLISION LIGHTS. Steady navigation lights are provided together with red rotating lights, one on the upper fuselage and two on the underside, below the engine air intakes. The control switch is marked *NAV LIGHTS-STDY/FLASH*. When *FLASH* is selected, the navigation lights are steady and the rotating lights operate.

IDENTIFICATION LIGHT. The downward identification light is controlled by a single-pole, *STEADY*/off *MORSE* switch, on the inboard side of the starboard console. The switch is spring-loaded from *MORSE* to off.

LANDING AND TAXYING LAMPS. There is a combined landing/taxying lamp under each wing, the lamp being extended further for the taxying position than for landing. The lamps are individually controlled by two double-pole, 3-position, *RETRACT/LANDING/TAXI* switches on the inboard side of the starboard console. The landing lamps incorporate a slipping clutch mechanism and blow in if the airspeed exceeds 180 knots. Once the lamps have blown in, the control switches must be reselected to *RETRACT* and then to *LANDING* (with the airspeed below 180 knots) before the lamps will re-extend.

PROBE LIGHTING. Two lamps in the nose of the aircraft light the probe for air-to-air refuelling. They are controlled by individual dimmer switches on the starboard console.

ELECTRICAL SUPPLIES. The external lighting uses 28V DC and the navigation and anti-collision lights are essential loads, the remainder of the external lighting is non-essential.

MISCELLANEOUS EQUIPMENT

Sextant A pressure-tight sextant mounting is provided on each side of the canopy coaming. The sextant is held in either the retracted or the operating position without loss of pressure. A lever in the mounting allows the sealing plate to be opened only when the sextant has been inserted in the carrier tube. The sextant must not be removed until the sealing plate is closed.

Ration Heaters There are five ration heaters, one at each crew position. The 28V DC non-essential supplies are controlled by two switches at the AEO's position on panel 50P. One switch controls the pilots' heaters, the other the rear crew's heaters. Sealed food tins are not to be inserted in the heaters; no tin is to be heated continuously for more than two hours.

Periscope The rearward-facing periscopes are controlled by a handle below the AEO table, raised to select the upper periscope, lowered to select the lower one, and moved sideways to rotate the selected periscope. The periscopes are heated by a 115V 1600 Hz, single-phase supply from No 2 frequency changer, controlled by an *ON/OFF* switch on the AEO's upper panel.

Rapid Start External Connections The aircraft is fitted with external pull-off connections, so that the air conditioning hoses, the electrical supply cables, the telescramble line and the static vent plugs are all removed automatically as the aircraft moves forward.

ELECTRICAL SUPPLIES. The 28V, 200V and true earth plugs are on a sloping bracket on the port side of the power compartment, accessible through a spring-loaded access panel in the underside of the port mainplane.

TELESCRAMBLE. A telescramble and mic/tel socket are on the starboard side of the power compartment, accessible through a spring-loaded access panel. Only the telescramble socket is used for rapid take-off, a further socket being introduced to this line for use of the crew chief. The telescramble system feeds into the intercom station boxes.

AIR CONDITIONING. The cabin conditioning hose connection is on the starboard side of the cockpit and the ventilated suit connection is below the engine intakes on the port side.

STATIC VENT PLUGS. The static vent plugs are pulled out by a cable.

EMERGENCY EXITS AND EQUIPMENT

Entrance Door and Static Lines The entrance door below the fuselage is the escape exit for the rear crew except in a crash landing. It can be operated by either the *EMERGENCY* position of the lever on the port side of the door, or by a switch at the navigator/plotter position marked *EMERGENCY DOOR OPEN*, or by the switch at the edge of the table, or by a combination of these controls. The door can be safely opened in flight at speeds up to 220 knots.

WARNING: If the door is opened by either switch, the normal lever may not pass through the emergency gate. If it does not and there is a failure of the 28V supply, the door will close again under the action of the slipstream. The first man at the door must check that the lever is gated in the *EMERGENCY* position.

After decompression, when the door has been opened, the crew swing themselves out of the opening, using the handle on the back of the nav/plotter's seat.

Static lines for the rear crew and 6th and 7th crew members' parachutes are fitted in the aircraft oxygen hose assemblies. One end of each line is connected to a strong point on the floor beside the oxygen point, while the other end carries the parachute attachment link. Within each hose assembly, connected to the static line, is a switch and associated electrical wiring. As each crew member abandons the aircraft in an emergency, the pull on the static line operates the switch, illuminating one of the five blue 'crew gone' lights on the bottom of the 1st pilot's instrument panel.

Canopy Jettison The canopy can be jettisoned by pulling back either of the jettison levers (one beside each pilot). If possible, pull both levers simultaneously. The canopy is automatically jettisoned when any ejection seat firing handle is pulled. It can also be jettisoned on the ground from outside, by pulling the yellow painted handle on the port side of the nose.

First-Aid Kit A first-aid kit is stowed at the rear of the co-pilot's seat.

Crash Axe and Asbestos Gloves A crash axe and asbestos gloves are stowed on the cover of the bomb aimer's window.

Life Raft In addition to the individual life rafts carried by each crew member, a life raft Type MS5 complete with survival equipment, is stowed at the rear of the canopy, below the fairing, outside the pressure cabin. The *DINGHY RELEASE* handle on the forward face of the stowage container is inaccessible unless the canopy has been jettisoned. Pulling the handle releases and inflates the life raft, which remains attached to the aircraft by a painter.

Signal Pistol and Cartridges A pressure-tight mounting for the signal pistol on the cabin port wall, above and forward of the AEO seat, has a stowage beside it for 12 cartridges.

External Emergency Equipment A compartment on the port side of the nose, opened from the outside, carries a first-aid kit, a crash axe, a pair of asbestos gloves and a BCF hand fire-extinguisher. Break-in markings, for access to the cabin and to the emergency equipment, are painted in yellow on the outside of the fuselage.

PART 8: HYDRAULIC SYSTEM AND UNDERCARRIAGE EMERGENCY LOWERING SYSTEM

General

The main hydraulic system provides pressure for:

a. Undercarriage raising and lowering and bogie trim.

b. Nosewheel centring and steering.

c. Wheelbrakes.

d. Bomb doors opening and closing.

e. AAPP air scoop closing.

An electrically-operated hydraulic power pack (EHPP) may be used for operation of the bomb doors and for recharging the brake accumulators.

A nitrogen system is provided for emergency undercarriage lowering.

Separate self-contained electro-hydraulic systems operate the powered flying control units and the windscreen wipers.

MAIN SYSTEM SUPPLIES

Reservoir The main system contains 12 gallons of fluid of which 2¼ gallons are contained in a spherical tank set in the roof of the bomb bay, at mid-position on the port side. The combined filling of the main and EHPP reservoirs is through a combined charging point on the inboard wall of the starboard undercarriage bay. For replenishment the undercarriage must be down, bomb doors open, parking brake off, and the accumulators charged with nitrogen and hydraulic fluid. Indications of a full system are given by excess fluid spilling from the overflow adjacent to the charging point and correct level indications on the sight glasses of the main and EHPP reservoirs.

To ensure that a positive head of pressure is maintained at all altitudes, the reservoir is pressurised with air from Nos 1, 2 and 3 engines. A pressure reducing valve reduces the engine air pressure from 105 PSI to 15 to 18 PSI, while a blow-off valve opens at 22 to 27 PSI and closes at 16 PSI. Mod 2321 replaces the engine air pressure with nitrogen pressure from the radio pressurisation system.

Engine-Driven Pumps Three engine-driven pumps, one on each of Nos 1, 2 and 3 engines, draw fluid from the reservoir via filters. The pumps incorporate an automatic cut-out and, when idling, circulate fluid back to the reservoir through the main return line. The pumps are low pressure spur gear, high pressure radial piston pumps.

From the pumps, fluid is delivered via non-return valves to the main gallery, at a pressure of 3600 to 4250 PSI. In addition to supplying the various services, this pressure is used to charge the wheelbrakes accumulators.

Test points for the suction, delivery and return lines are in the port main undercarriage wheelbay.

Hydraulic Pressure Gauge A triple pressure gauge is on the pilots' centre instrument panel. The left-hand arc shows the pressure in the main gallery, while the two right-hand arcs

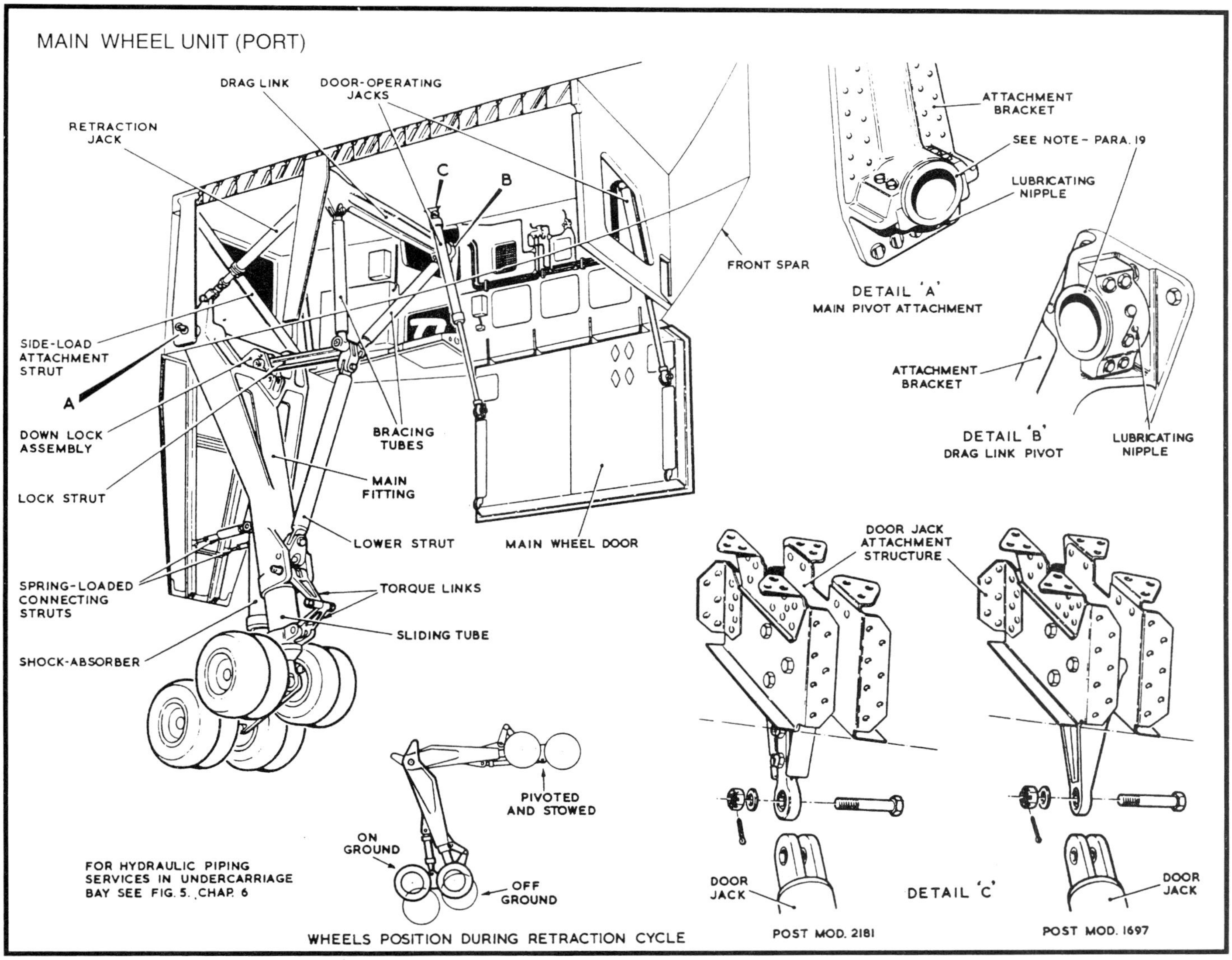

show the pressure in the two brake accumulators. Each needle is separately wired and fused and has its own pressure transmitter.

Undercarriage System

General The undercarriage mainwheel units are fourwheel, eight-tyred bogies; the nosewheel unit is twin-tyred and steerable. When undercarriage retraction is selected, the bogies pivot, to lie parallel to the main oleos.

Hydraulic pressure operates the undercarriage doors, extension mechanism, bogie trimmers and down locks, through electrically-controlled selector valves; sequencing of the operation is controlled by microswitches. Each main wheel is fitted with a hydraulically operated down lock, the nosewheel has a mechanically operated down lock. All down locks are of the over-centre type and will remain in the locked position should hydraulic pressure be subsequently lost.

Undercarriage raising and lowering is controlled by an *UP* and a *DOWN* button on the pilots' centre panel.

WARNING: To ensure that the electrical contacts are made when the landing gear selector is operated, the UP or DOWN button must be pressed fully in.

When the weight of the aircraft is on its wheels, a micro-switch on each bogie is held

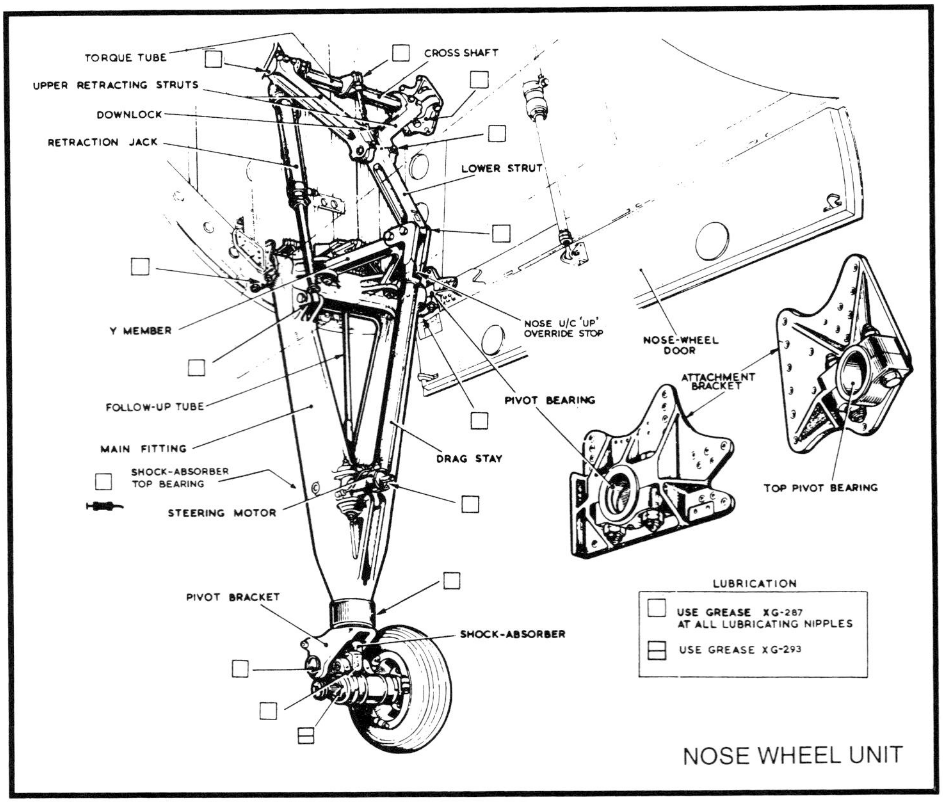

NOSE WHEEL UNIT

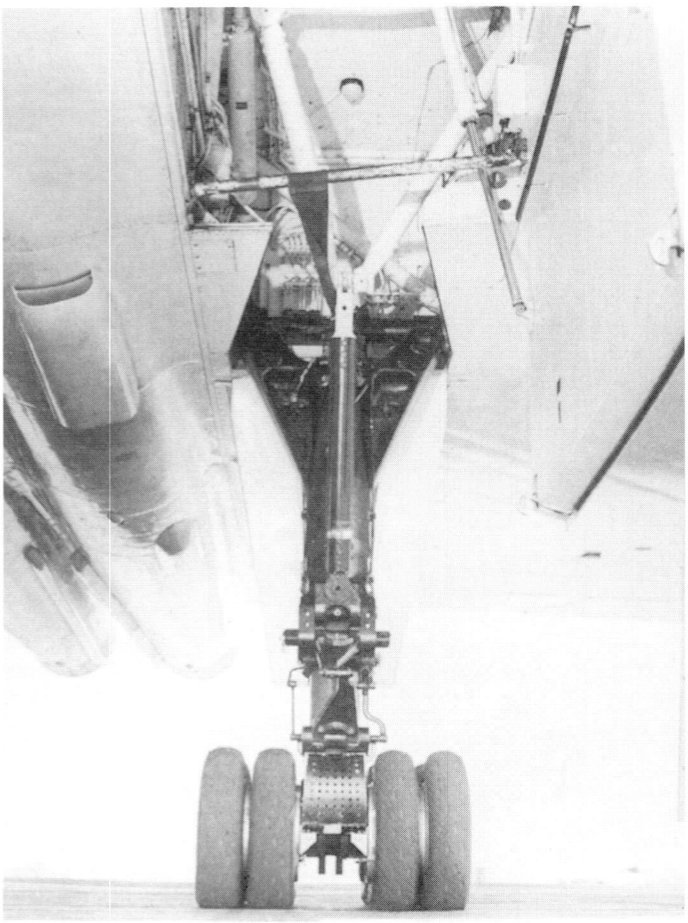

open and an interruptor pin behind the UP button prevents it from being pushed in. When the weight is off the wheels, the bogies trail and both micro-switches (in series) close. Power is then applied to a solenoid which withdraws the pin, allowing the UP button to be depressed. This device may be overriden however, by rotating the flange of the UP button slowly and gently clockwise, through approximately 60°, at the same time exerting positive forward pressure.

WARNING: In spite of this safety device, the *UP* button must always be regarded as operative, as the protective devices may not function.

The undercarriage position indicator is on the pilots' centre panel and indicates as follows:

All wheels up and doors locked closed	No lights
Wheels unlocked	Three red lights
Wheels locked down	Three green lights

A flag indicator, marked U/C, is incorporated in the co-pilot's ASI and shows if the speed is reduced below 160 knots when the undercarriage is not locked down. The absence of the indicator must not be taken as proof that the undercarriage has locked down.

Undercarriage Emergency Nitrogen System The emergency nitrogen supply for the main and nosewheels is contained in two separate bottles in the nosewheel bay. The bottles are charged to a pressure of 3000 PSI via charge points adjacent to two gauges on the starboard rear wall of the nosewheel bay. The two controlling valves are mechanically linked and are operated by a single handle on the right of the throttle quadrant. The handle is guarded and wire-locked.

When the handle is pulled to its full extent, nitrogen from the bottles passes to shuttle valves and jettison valves, expelling hydraulic fluid from the lines and allowing nitrogen to pass to the jacks. The undercarriage then lowers, regardless of the position of the normal selector.

Selection of emergency nitrogen also isolates the normal selector solenoids, so that the undercarriage cannot again be retracted once the emergency selector has been operated. Nosewheel steering, however, is still available. The alternator CSDU oil system and engine bay (zone 2B) ground cooling system is inoperative when the undercarriage has been lowered by emergency nitrogen. In these circumstances after landing, a maximum individual alternator load of 20 kW may be maintained for a maximum period of 15 minutes subject to CSDU oil temperature, and engine speeds must be kept at idling so far as is practicable.

__Left:__ Close-up of the Vulcan B.2's nose gear assembly. (John Hale)

__Far left:__ Close-up of the Vulcan B.2's port undercarriage (front), showing four beautiful un-worn tyres, the gloss black legs and strut, and the gloss white gear bay, and linkages – a pristine finish which did not last for long. (British Aerospace)

Nosewheel Centring and Steering

NOSEWHEEL STEERING

a. Nosewheel steering is hydraulically operated and electrically controlled. The nosewheel can move through 47¼° on either side of centre and movement is controlled by a pushbutton on the pilots' control column and by movement of the rudder pedals.

b. With the steering pushbutton depressed, rudder pedal movement causes the nosewheel to move in the appropriate direction; the operation of a drum switch cuts off the electrical supply to the selector valve when the selected angle is achieved.

c. As the nosewheel leaves the ground, a microswitch de-energises the stop valve in the steering circuit. This allows a bypass valve to open, permitting flow from one side of the steering jack to the other. The centring jack is now the only unit exerting any force and the nosewheel is automatically centred.

d. A *NOSEWHEEL STEERING EMERGENCY OVERRIDE – EMERGENCY/NORMAL* wire-locked switch is on panel 3P. If steering is not restored after landing, the switch can be put to *EMERGENCY* to override the microswitch referred to in sub-para c. If the switch is used on the ground, it must be set to *NORMAL* before the undercarriage is raised after take-off and returned to *EMERGENCY* when the undercarriage is locked down for landing.

NOSEWHEEL CENTRING. Nosewheel centring is hydraulically operated, the main delivery pressure passing through a pressure regulator valve direct to the centring jack. The centring system operates automatically when nosewheel steering is not in use, when the nosewheel is off the ground, or if the main hydraulic system fails.

WHEELBRAKES

General A maxaret unit in the brake unit of each double-tyred wheel temporarily relieves pressure at the brake if a skid is detected on that wheel. The eight maxaret units operate independently of each other and only operate when the wheels are rotating. The following points must be remembered:

a. If brakes are applied before a wheel touches the ground, the wheel locks and the maxaret unit cannot operate.

b. To stop rotation of the wheels after take-off, it is necessary to apply brake pressure for at least 4 seconds.

c. When landing with a reduced amount of hydraulic fluid (after a line leak) maxaretting must be avoided, as fluid under pressure would be bled rapidly to the return lines.

The brake units are hydraulically operated, the main system pressure being reduced to 2500 PSI at the brakes. Two accumulators, charged to main line pressure provide instant response and a reserve of pressure for brake operation. These accumulators can be recharged by the hydraulic power pack. A failure of one accumulator does not prevent the other from supplying pressure to both sets of wheels. A drop in nitrogen pressure in one or both accumulators would be disguised as long as the main hydraulic pressure remains normal.

The pressure at the brakes is shown on two dual pressure gauges in the nosewheel bay and the pressure at the hydraulic accumulators is shown on the triple pressure gauge on the pilots' centre panel. The accumulator nitrogen pressure gauges and charging points are also in the nosewheel bay, together with two manually-operated pressure release valves, for releasing any residual hydraulic pressure in the accumulators.

A parking brake is provided, which operates through a Bowden cable to open simultaneously all the hydraulic valves in the brakes control valve.

Operation Brake selection is controlled by toe-buttons on the rudder pedals. The pressure delivered to the brakes is proportional to the force applied to the toe-buttons; when this pressure is released, the relay in the brakes control valve closes and the fluid from the brakes is returned to the reservoir.

The parking brake is applied by turning and pulling the lever on the left of the throttle quadrant.

BOMB DOORS

Bomb Door Operation The bomb doors are hydraulically operated. For normal operation, supplies from the main system are fed through dual selector valves to the four door jacks, via a shuttle valve which forms part of the door locking assembly. If the normal supply fails, the doors can be operated from the EHPP through the emergency selector valve, and the main system is isolated by movement of the shuttle valve in accordance with the power selection.

CONTROLS AND OPERATION

a. The 1st pilot has two switches on the port console, labelled *BOMB DOOR CONTROL NORMAL* and *EMERGENCY*[The *NORMAL* switch is a rotary type with three positions: *OPEN/AUTO/CLOSE*. When *OPEN* or *CLOSE* are selected, the bomb doors operate at the time of selection. When *AUTO* is selected the bomb doors are under the control of the NBS and do not open until they receive the appropriate signal.

b. The *EMERGENCY* switch is a guarded double-pole three-position switch, labelled *OPEN/NORMAL/CLOSE*. When this switch is operated, the doors are opened or closed by supplies from the hydraulic power pack and the electrical supplies are cut off from the normal selector. This switch is inoperative if the power pack is being used to charge the brake accumulator.

c. The nav/radar has a single-pole *BOMB DOORS OPEN/CLOSED* switch. Operation of either this or the pilot's switch opens the doors but, to close them both switches must be operated. The bomb doors can also be operated by the emergency bomb jettison switch.

INDICATOR. The bomb door indicator is to the right of the alternator warning light. Either a round 2-position or a square 3-position magnetic indicator may be fitted. The 2-position magnetic indicator shows black when the bomb doors are closed and white at all other times. The 3-position magnetic indicator shows black when the bomb doors are closed, white when they are fully open and cross-hatch when they are at an intermediate position or when there is no electrical supply.

AAPP Scoop

Operation The AAPP scoop is controlled by the AAPP master switch and operated by a spring-loaded jack. When the master switch is *OFF*, main line pressure reduced to 1800 PSI closes the scoop and holds it closed against the spring pressure. When the master switch is selected to *ON*, a solenoid-operated valve is de-energised opening the hydraulic return line so that the spring pressure opens the scoop. If the 28V DC supply to the solenoid fails, the scoop opens. If the main hydraulic pressure reduces below 1800 PSI, pressure to the jack is maintained by an NRV. Eventually (approximately 90 minutes), the hydraulic pressure decays and the scoop opens. The circuits are so arranged that the scoop does not close until the AAPP has run down.

PART 9: PNEUMATIC SYSTEMS

There are five, separate, pneumatic storage systems in the aircraft as follows:

a. Emergency door opening and canopy jettison.

b. Entrance door closing, door and canopy seal inflation and bomb aimer's window de-icing.

c. H2S scanner and NBS.

d. Undercarriage emergency lowering

e. Engine starting

The engines supply compressed air for the following systems:

a. Bomb bay seal inflation.

b. Hydraulic reservoir and power pack pressurisation (pre-mod 2321).

c. Fuel tank and recuperators pressurisation.

d. Equipment in rear fuselage.

e. Anti-icing.

Entrance Door System

Entrance Door System Supplies Three storage cylinders, charged to 2000 PSI from an external supply, are on the port side of the crew compartment. Their charging points and pressure gauges are on the front bulkhead in the nosewheel bay. The forward cylinder supplies pressure for emergency door opening and canopy jettison; the remaining two bottles supply door closing, door and canopy seal inflation and pressurisation of the bomb aimer's window de-icing tank.

A ground servicing cock, on the underside of the crew's floor, is normally locked in the open position by a red cover. When turned off, it isolates the services supplied by the rear cylinder.

Emergency Door Opening Pressure at 1200 PSI for operating the door jacks is controlled by the *EMERGENCY* position of the door opening lever, on the forward end of the door frame on the port side. With the undercarriage down, the nitrogen passes through a restrictor, to control the rate of movement.

The rear crew switches allow nitrogen to pass to a jack. The jack rotates a layshaft which withdraws the bolts and moves the lower portion of the door handle to the emergency position. This operates the emergency door opening valve, allowing nitrogen to pass to the jacks. The cabin should be depressurised first. Loads on the door bolts are such that, using the switches alone, the door cannot open until the differential pressure has dropped to 1.5 PSI (30 seconds at 43,000 feet, 9.5 seconds at 27,000 feet); if the manual control is used at the same time, the door opens at 2.65 PSI (20 seconds at 43,000 feet, 5.5 seconds at 27,000 feet). However, unless escape in the minimum time is essential, the manual control should not be used simultaneously with either of the switches.

When the door has been opened by either switch, the door opening lever is carried to the gate while mechanism below the lever moves further to operate the emergency door-opening valve. A 28 volt fault could result in the door closing again under slipstream pressure. To protect against this, the first man at the door must ensure that the lever is gated in the emergency position. The emergency door opening switch is on the vital busbar.

NOTE: A worn gate may allow the lever to pass to the emergency position.

If the door locking pins become scored, the door may fail to open when the navigator's switch is used. In this case, use the manual control; closing the cabin air switches may assist by reducing the time required to depressurise the cabin.

Canopy Jettison The canopy jettison pneumatic valve is operated by pulling any one of the pilots' ejection seat firing handles. When the valve is operated, nitrogen at 1200 PSI passes to a ram which opens the jaws of the canopy attachment and operates the jettison gun.

Door Closing The door closing valve is operated either by a toggle handle or, externally, by a pushbutton near the door handle. Either selection must be held until the door is locked closed, otherwise nitrogen pressure is lost from the jacks. The toggle handle is stowed under a hinged panel on the starboard side of and below the centre crew seat.

When the valve is operated, nitrogen at 400 PSI is fed to the up side of the door jacks.

Door and Canopy Seals The door and canopy seals are supplied with nitrogen from the rear cylinder at 25 PSI. The door seal is inflated automatically when the entrance door is closed. The canopy seal is permanently inflated to 25 PSI by a mushroom valve which is held open when the canopy is locked. The seal deflates when the canopy starts to move during jettison.

De-Icing Tank Pressurisation The de-icing tank is pressurised with nitrogen at 14 to 15 PSI. A pressure-maintaining valve in the line cuts off the supply when the pressure in the main system falls to 150 PSI. The supply is also fed to the probe de-icing tank but this system is inoperative. The ground servicing cock must be closed before filling the tank and the residual pressure of 14 to 15 PSI must be relieved by pressing the pressure release valve on top of the tank.

PART 10: TERRAIN FOLLOWING RADAR

The TFR system is designed to enable the pilot to follow approximately the contours of the terrain at a height selected in flight. The components of the system are:

a. A radar pod in the nose (TFRU), containing a transmitter/receiver, an adjustable antenna, a pitch rate gyro and computing curcuits. The pod is cooled by air from the H2S radome.

b. Airstream direction detectors (ADD). Two slotted probes, protruding horizontally from each side of the nose, measure the angle of attack.

c. An airspeed transducer, supplied from the aircraft starboard pitot-static system.

d. A control unit, on the 1st pilot's console.

e. Indicator and warning lights.

The system is used in conjunction with the following items of aircraft equipment:

a. MFS port vertical gyro

b. MFS pitch computer

c. Glide path pointer of the director horizon

d. Radio altimeter Mk 7B

Description

TFRU The radar pod measures the slant range forward of the aircraft against a preset datum. The antenna angle is adjusted by the height selector and the angle of attack measured by the ADD. Dive demands are initiated when range exceeds the datum and climb demands when the range is less than the datum. Computers in the unit analyse and compare the various signals and pass them to the pilots' instruments as dive or climb signals.

Range Loop. The measured slant range is fed to a range computer which feeds a pitch rate demand signal, proportional to the range error, to the majority circuit.

Height Loop. Over flat terrain or calm water, radar returns may be insufficient to activate the range loop. To prevent this apparent loss of range initiating a dive command, height information from the Rad Alt 7B is modified by aircraft attitude and antenna angle signals, to provide a pitch rate command to the majority circuit.

When intending to use the TFR below 500 feet the Rad Alt 7B should not be selected to the 500 feet scale until below 500 feet to avoid spurious climb demands. When the aircraft reaches the set TFR height, Rad Alt 7B can be selected to the 500 feet range to provide improved accuracy when the height loop is in operation.

Programme (Attitude Hold). As the aircraft climbs towards the summit of a hill, the radar beam clears the crest. To prevent a dive signal being given before the aircraft is over the summit, a delay computer demands a steady attitude computed from the speed, pitch angle, angle of attack and last measured range. After this delay, other sub-systems take command and, in practice, the most positive pitch rate command is a minus 0.5g (applied) dive rate limit known as the pushover. A programme is not initiated if the signals increase progressively through the maximum range as opposed to disappearing instantly. This prevents inadvertent programme being caused by aircraft pitch-up.

Pitch Rate Control. Signals from the range loop, the programme, the dive rate limiter and the fail-safe system are fed into a majority circuit computer, which selects the highest climb demand of these signals. The majority circuit output goes to a comparator as a pitch rate demand for comparison with the output from the pitch rate gyro; any difference is the final pitch rate command fed to the MFS director horizons via the MFS pitch computer when the MFS/TFR switch is selected to TFR. Demands are shown on the pitch director (the GP pointer during non-TFR operations), and the pitch scale is in continuous fast-chase mode.

Climb High Function. If for any reason the aircraft pitch angle is greater than 4° nose-up, the antenna is off-set downwards, thus tending to shorten the range returns and causing the aircraft to fly higher, the effect increasing in proportion to the gradient. This prevents ballooning on the far side of a summit and gives a greater safety margin over steeply rising ground.

Acceleration Limiters. To limit acceleration to between +0.75g and minus 0·5g (applied), airspeed signals are fed into two acceleration limiters. Signals from the limiters limit the pitch rate demands from the height loop to +0·75g (applied) and from the dive rate limiter to minus 0·5g (applied).

Safety Devices. Fourteen internal monitors continuously check range loop, antenna servo loop, pitch and pitch rate circuitry, as well as the monitoring system itself. If any monitor detects a failure the green light goes out, the red FAIL light comes on and a pitch up of 1·89°/second is demanded. Those circuits which cannot be monitored are duplicated, both operating simultaneously and either one capable of operating the system. Failure of the radio altimeter activates the fail-safe circuit.

ADD. The ADD provide angle of attack information by rotating two slotted probes to maintain equal pressure either side of internally mounted vanes. This rotation is measured by a potentiometer and passed to the TFRU, where antenna angle is correspondingly adjusted. To compensate for airflow distortion the ADD outputs are paralleled and a mean signal taken. The ADD probes are electrically heated via the pressure head heater switches.

A discrepancy between the two ADD brings on the ADD MONITOR amber light at the AEO's position and initiates TFR failure indications. If the fault has cleared the warnings may be cancelled; the AEO's by pressing the ADD monitor light and the pilots' by selecting RESET/A/TEST/NORMAL switch on the ADD trim panel below the pilots' floor must be at NORMAL before flight. It should be noted that any yaw or sideslip may give an ADD warning and that the ADD warning is operative whether TFR is in the standby condition or on.

Electrical Supplies The TFRU uses 200V, 3-phase, 400 Hz AC from No 4 busbar via panel 75P. The system also uses 28V DC from panel 4P. The ADD probes are heated by 28V DC, via the pressure-head heater switches. The warning lights use 28V DC from the TFRU while their press-to-test facility is supplied from the main aircraft system. The radio altimeter uses 115V AC from the port main transformer. If No 1 or No 4 alternator fails or is switched off, the TFR may fail but can be reset immediately.

PART 11: AIRFRAME LIMITATIONS

The Vulcan B Mk 2 is designed for manoeuvres appropriate to the role of a medium bomber, in worldwide conditions. Aerobatics, stalling and spinning are prohibited. Speed must not be reduced below that for the onset of pre-stall buffet and in any case not below the threshold speed for the weight less 5 knots. In manoeuvres at altitude, acceleration should not be increased beyond that for the onset of buffet where this occurs before maximum g is attained.

Height limitations. There is no height restriction on the aircraft because of airframe limitations. However, the maximum operating altitude is limited by the oxygen equipment, as follows:

Regulator	*Pressure Jerkin*	*Anti-g Suit*	*Max Cabin Alt*	*Remarks*
Mk 17F	No	No	50,000ft	–
Mk 21A or B	Yes	Yes	56,000ft	Oxygen contents more than 3/8 of total
Mk 21A or B	Yes	No	52,000ft	–
Mk 21A or B Mk 2 or 2A	No	No	45,000ft	Above this altitude, oxygen pressure is above 30 mm Hg (max lungs can stand in comfort)
Mk 3 or 3A	No	No	50,000ft	–
Mk 2 or 2A	Yes	Yes	56,000ft	–

Note: In the worst case, eg following loss of the canopy, or if the entrance door opens, aerodynamic suction can cause the cabin altitude to exceed the aircraft altitude by up to 5000 feet.

Arresting gear. The aircraft has unrestricted clearance to trample the following runway arresting gears, provided that the configuration has not been altered by modifications later than mod 2240:

a. SPRAG.

b. CHAG.

c. RHAG Mk 1.

d. PUAG Mk 21.

e. Bliss BAK 9, BAK 12, 500S.

Speed and Mach Number Limitations (see also Release to Service)

a. *With all PFC working and all autostabilisers operative*: Maximum speed above 15,000 feet–330 knots or 0.93M (0.92 with Mk 301 engines), whichever is less. (Elevator forces are not to be trimmed out above 0.90M.)

b. *With one or more PFC inoperative*–0.90M.

c. *With one or both servos of the mach trimmer inoperative*–0.90M unless specifically authorised. If specifically authorised, 0.93M (0.92M Mk 301 engines).

d. *With one pitch damper inoperative*–0.93M (0.92, Mk 301 engines).

e. *With two or more pitch dampers inoperative*–0.90M.

f. *With feel relieved or failed*–250 knots or 0.90M, whichever is less. Extreme care is necessary to avoid overstressing the aircraft.

MAXIMUM SPEEDS FOR OPERATION OF THE SERVICES.
The speed for operating a service also applies to flight with the service extended.

a. Airbrakes	No restriction
b. Bomb doors	Up to the normal limiting speed of the aircraft.
c. Undercarriage	270 knots (0.90M above 40,000 feet).
d. RAT	330 knots or 0.93M (0.92, Mk 301 engines).
e. Tail parachute streaming	145 knots (max). Any parachute streamed above 135 knots is to be examined before re-use.

f. The tail parachute must be jettisoned at speeds between 50 and 60 knots. In an emergency the parachute may be retained until the aircraft has stopped.

FOR LOW LEVEL LIMITATIONS, see Release to Service.

Crosswind Limitations *Maximum crosswind component for take-off, landing or streaming brake parachute*: 20 knots.

G Limitations The following accelerometer readings are not to be exceeded:

AUW (lb)	*IMN*	*Max Indicated g with Aileron Angle* — *Negligible Angle*	*Large Angle*
Up to 160,000	Up to 0.89	2.0	1.8
	0.89 to 0.93	1.8	Prohibited
160,000 to 190,000	Up to 0.89	1.8	1.5
	0.89 to 0.93	1.5	Prohibited
Above 190,000	Up to 0.93	1.5	Gentle manoeuvres only

NOTE 1: Full aileron maybe applied up to the indicated Mach numbers quoted, but aileron is not to be applied rapidly. NOTE 2: Manoeuvres involving simultaneous application of large aileron angles and normal acceleration are not to be executed at indicated Mach numbers greater than 0.89. NOTE 3: Manoeuvres under zero or negative g conditions are prohibited.

Weight Limitations

Maximum for take-off and emergency landing	204,000 lb
Normal landing	140,000 lb

If, in emergency, the aircraft is landed at 195,000 lb or more, the rate of descent at touch-down must be kept to a minimum and the angle of bank on the approach must not exceed 15°.

Simulated asymmetric flying is not permitted at weights above 195,000 lb.

CG Limitations The CG limitations (undercarriage down) are:

a. At weights up to 195,000 lb	142 to 156.9 inches aft of datum
b. At weights above 195,000 lb	148 to 151.3 inches aft of datum

Aircraft Approach Limitations The aircraft approach limitations are:

	True Height (Above Touch-down)
a. PRECISION RADAR	250 feet
ILS, Auto or Manual* (in-line localiser)	250 feet
ILS, Auto or Manual*(off-set localiser)	270 feet

*It is advisable that all ILS approaches should be radar monitored.

b. VISUAL COMMITTAL HEIGHTS (VCH)

	True Height
One engine inoperative	150 feet
Two engines inoperative	200 feet

c. ENGINE OUT ALLOWANCE (EOA)

One engine out	0 feet
Two engines out (up to 185,000 lb)	50 feet
Two engines out (above 185,000 lb)	100 feet

Autopilot Limitations The autopilot limitations are:

a. *Speeds*
Maximum airspeed 350 knots
MAXIMUM MACH NUMBER

Mach trimmer operative	0.90M
Mach trimmer inoperative	0.87M

Maximum airspeed with *TRACK* and *LOC & GP* selected (ie feel partially relieved) 180 knots

b. *Minimum altitude* (except during ILS approach) 1500 feet AGL

c. The artificial feel must be functioning correctly.

With the autopilot engaged, the following conditions must be observed:

a. Longitudinal trim is to be maintained so that the autopilot trim indicator is within the safe range.

b. One pilot is to be strapped into his seat at all times.

c. The autopilot may be used with the elevator channel disengaged (if operationally essential); in the ILS mode the elevator channel must be engaged. Neither the aileron, nor the rudder channel may be disengaged separately.

Air-to-Air Refuelling Limitations Although the aircraft is cleared for air-to-air refuelling to the following standard, there is no operational requirement at present and therefore it is not to be practised.

The aircraft is cleared for air-to-air refuelling by day and by night, using Victor tankers and by day only using Boeing KC-135 tankers, with Mk 8 equipment, subject to the following conditions:

a. SPEED. The speed of the tanker at and during contact should be:

(1) KC-135	260 to 275 knots (at heights up to 30,000 feet)
(2) Victor maximum speed	300 knots up to 31,000 feet 0.80M between 31,000 feet and 35,000 feet
Minimum speed	220 knots
Maximum altitude	35,000 feet

b. AIRBRAKES. *MEDIUM* drag airbrakes are recommended for contact.

c. FUEL TRIM. The CG control switches may be used to maintain the fuel CG. Contact must be broken if either needle of the CG indicator goes into the red sector. The A and E tank gauges are monitored during refuelling to ensure that a spurious EMF has not opened the refuelling valves.

d. NIGHT CONTACTS (Victor). Before flights involving night contacts, the probe lighting must be correctly focused on the forward third of the probe.

Only one transfer pump in the KC-135 is to be used.

All the necessary flight refuelling system modifications must be embodied in the aircraft, including the Mk 8 probe and probe lighting, and the modification which ensures the ground refuelling master switch is off.

Airframe Anti-Icing Limitations Subject to the embodiment of all necessary modifications, the wing anti-icing system may be used at all levels but the fin system must remain inoperative.

Bomb Bay

BOMB BAY TANKS. The bomb bay tanks may be used in the following configurations:

a. Two cylindrical tanks

b. One cylindrical tank in forward position

c. One A tank in forward position and one cylindrical tank in rear position

d. One A tank in the forward position of the two forward locations

e. One A tank forward and one E tank aft.

BOMB BAY PANNIERS. 750 lb and 4000 lb panniers may be carried with bomb bay fuel tanks to the following configurations:

Forward	*Centre*	*Aft*
Cylindrical Tank	750 lb Pannier	Cylindrical Tank
A Tank	750 lb Pannier	E Tank
4000 lb Pann	"	–
4000 lb Pannier	"	750lb Pannier
Cylindrical Tank	4000 lb Pannier	
A Tank	4000 lb Pannier	

OPENING OF BOMB DOORS IN FLIGHT. The bomb doors may be opened in flight:

a. When the tanks have been emptied of all usable fuel.

b. During an operational emergency with fuel in the tanks.

c. Provided no panniers are fitted in the bomb bay.

d. Provided that time with the bomb doors open is kept to a minimum.

The weapons simulator must not be used on the ground if there are any signs of fuel leaks and may not be switched on in the air until the tanks are empty of all usable fuel.

PART 12: ENGINE LIMITATIONS

RPM and JPT Limitations, Olympus Engines

Mk 200/Mk 301 Series Engines. RPM and JPT for Mk 301 engines are shown in brackets, where different.

Condition	*Time Limits*	*Engine Speed % RPM*	*Max JPT °C*
Maximum for take-off and operational necessity	10 mins	101 (100)	670 (625)
Maximum continuous	Unlimited	97.5	610 (570)
Ground idling minimum (alternator on load)	Unlimited	29.5 (24.5) (minimum ISA, SL)	610 (570)
Overspeed	20 secs	104 (107)	–
During start	–	–	700

Relighting the Mk 200 series or Mk 301 engines should not normally be attempted above 35,000 feet.

To avoid resonant frequencies which could affect engine fatigue life, the RPM band 95% ± 1½% is to be avoided up to FL300 Furthermore, on the Mk 301 engines the RPM band 78% to 85% is also to be avoided below 5000 feet. The engine handling procedures recommended in this Manual meet the restrictions placed on 200 series engines. For Mk 301 engines, whenever 80% RPM (below 5000 feet) is recommended, 78% RPM should be used if the OAT is 15° or below and 85% RPM if the OAT is above 15°C.

Oil System Limitations, Olympus Engines

MK 200 SERIES ENGINES

a. Normal at 90% RPM and above	55 to 60 PSI
b. Mimimum at 90% RPM and above:	
Sea level to 20,000 feet	50 PSI
Above 20,000 feet	45 PSI
c. Maximum consumption rate	1½ pt/hr
d. Minimum oil temperature for starting	minus 26°C

MK 301 ENGINES

a. Normal at 90% RPM and above	55 to 65 PSI
b. Minimum at 90% RPM and above	
Sea Level to 20,000 feet	50 PSI
Above 20,000 feet	45 PSI
c. Maximum consumption rate	1½ pt/hr
d. Minimum oil temperature for starting	minus 26°C

AAPP JPT Limitations The following maximum JPT limitations apply to flight and ground running under any load:

a. For max of 5 minutes	715°C
b. For max of 1 hour	690°C
c. Continuous	680°C
d. During AAPP start	High transient for 10 seconds max

When ground running, the AAPP must be stopped every 10 hours for an oil check.

AAPP Oil Limitations The minimum oil pressure is 4 PSI. The pressure varies rapidly with temperature and should not be less than 12 PSI after a cold start.

Engine Anti-Icing If icing conditions are met, the anti-icing must be used.

PART 13: MISCELLANEOUS LIMITATIONS

Navigational, Operational and Radio Limitations

NBS MK1A. The NBS Mk 1A is cleared for use as a navigational and bombing system.

RADIO COMPASS. The radio compass is cleared for unrestricted use.

HRS. The HRS is cleared for use, subject to the following conditions:

a. During start-up, with fast erection, HRS is to be switched on at least 2½ minutes before taxying.

b. If airborne starting, the MRG is not to be switched on until initial take-off acceleration is over. The aircraft is to be kept on a steady heading for at least 2½ minutes while the MRG runs up.

c. Unless it fails, the MRG is not to be switched off until the aircraft is stationary.

DECCA DOPPLER. Decca doppler is cleared for unrestricted use. With the undercarriage down it will operate only in the memory mode. It is compatible with the autopilot when operating normally in the track steering mode. However, prior to doppler unlock spurious drift signals may cause the aircraft to take up a false heading.

ECM. The ECM installation is cleared for use up to 55,000 feet in temperate climates.

MFS. The MFS is cleared for Service use.

IFF. IFF/SSR is installed and is cleared for unrestricted use.

TACAN. Tacan is cleared for use.

RADIO ALTIMETER. The following limitations apply to the radio altimeter:

a. Mk 7B

High range	100 to 5000 feet
Low range	0 to 500 feet.

b. Mk 6A Unrestricted use above 5000 feet

RADIO COMMUNICATION

a. The PTR 175 is cleared for unrestricted use.

b. The ARC 52 is cleared for unrestricted use.

c. The HF/SSB is cleared for unrestricted use.

Electrical System Limitations

The maximum continuous load per alternator is 32 kW, subject to a maximum continuous CSDU oil temperature of 120°C. This oil temperature must not be exceeded and, if necessary, height or loading must be reduced to keep the oil temperature within limits.

AAPP

a. Operating altitude: ground level to 30,000 feet, undercarriage up; ground level to 5000 feet, undercarriage down

b. There is no guarantee of a successful start above 30,000 feet. The alternator must never be put on load above 30,000 feet.

c. *Maximum Loads*

Altitude feet	*Load kW*	*Time mins*
10,000 to 30,000,		

undercarriage up	17	30
0 to 10,000, undercarriage up	32	30
0 to 5000, undercarriage down	23	4
Ground running	32 (up to 45°C OAT)	

d. *Air Bleed.* Maximum electrical load for AAPP with airbleed is 10 kW.

RAT

Operating altitude	20,000 to 60,000 feet
Max load	17 kW
Speed range	Maximum speed 0.93M Minimum speed 0.85M/ 250 knots, whichever is greater
Time limit	10 minutes on load above 30,000 feet 10 minutes off load above 50,000 feet

PART 14: STARTING, TAXYING AND TAKE-OFF

Throughout, it must be remembered that the recommended limitations must be observed, and that the relevant checks in the Flight Reference Cards must be made at the appropriate times.

The air supply required for starting main engines may be obtained from an external source (Palouste) or by crossbleed from a running engine. Alternatively, engines may be started individually or simultaneously using air from the rapid start compressed air installations. As any one, or a combination of more than one of these sources of starting air may be used to start the main engines, the starting order may be varied as required. However, the airflow patterns into the combined main engine air intakes make it advisable to use an outboard rather than an inboard engine to supply air for starting the remaining engines.

Starting a Main Engine Using an External Air Supply

When using an external air supply, the engines may be started in any order. If it is intended to start the remaining engines using air supplied by the running engine, this must be No 1 or No 4 engine. After completing the relevant internal checks in the Flight Reference Cards, confirm with the crew chief that the external air supply is connected and that it is clear to start engines.

The checks before starting are given in the Flight Reference Cards.

Press the starter button and check that the indicator light in the button comes on, showing that the air control valve has opened. Wait for 10 seconds, checking that the oil pressure and RPM are rising, then move the HP cock lever towards the idling gate until a fuel flow of 8 to 10 lb/min is achieved. When the JPT rises pause for one second and then move the HP cock lever slowly to the idling gate. During starting, the JPT normally rises to 300°C to 400°C and then falls to approx 250°C as the engine accelerates. If the rate of rise of the JPT indicates that 600°C may be exceeded, meter the fuel supply by moving the throttle lever slightly behind the idling gate until the JPT decreases and then slowly advancing it to the normal idling position. If the JPT continues to rise rapidly above 600°C and it appears likely that 700°C will be exceeded, close the HP cock and isolate the starter motor by switching OFF the engine master switch. After a normal start, the RPM may stabilise below the correct ground idling speed; in order to achieve the correct idling speed, advance the throttle slightly and then return it to the idling gate. The starting cycle is terminated by the overspeed switch. The light in the starter button goes out when the air control valve has closed.

The checks during starting are given in the Flight Reference Cards.

STARTING THE REMAINING ENGINES

a. The three remaining engines may be started individually and in the same manner using air supplied by the Palouste.

b. The Palouste may be removed and the three remaining engines may be started individually using air crossbleed from the running engine, provided that its speed is set to 70% RPM.

Starting the Remaining Engines Individually Using Air Crossbleed The checks before starting are given in the Flight Reference Cards.

Set the RPM of the running engine to 70% and check that its engine air switch is open. Open the engine air switch of the engine to be started, and then start it in the manner described. The AEO should check the voltage and frequency of each alternator and switch on as required, noting that when three alternators are on line the pilots' red ALT FAIL light is steady and when the fourth alternator is switched on the pilots' ALT FAIL light goes out.

If, for any reason (eg sandy airfield, confined space), it is desirable to restrict RPM, when two engines are running their speed may be set to 60% RPM to start the remaining engines as an alternative to one engine at 70% RPM.

Quick Starting of Engines

After starting No 1 or No 4 engine, the three remaining engines may be started simultaneously using air from the running engine, provided that its speed is set to 93% RPM. Carry out the checks in the Flight Reference Cards.

Start the three remaining engines simultaneously, using the techniques described. As the fuel flow can only be monitored for one of the engines the HP cock levers for the other two must be moved forward carefully using the lever of the monitored engine as a guide. Each engine should start in the normal manner. Because of the number of indicators to be watched, it is essential that both pilots monitor the fire warning lights and indications of oil pressure, RPM and JPT. If any engine malfunctions, close its HP cock independently of the other engines but leave the engine master switch ON until the starting cycles of the other engines are complete. When all engines are running satisfactorily, the AEO switches on alternators in the normal manner.

Rapid Starting of Engine

a. 200 volt AC and 28 volt DC electrical supplies are required while starting the engines and are normally obtained from an external source. Electrical supplies *may* be obtained from the AAPP when starting engines individually but this source must not be used when starting all engines simultaneously.

b. The rapid-start compressed air installation, when fully charged, should provide sufficient air for three individual engine starts on each side. If the engines are started simultaneously, sufficient air should remain in the system for one individual start per side (minimum pressure 1100 PSI). Not more than two combuster starts on any one engine are to be attempted in any one 30-minute period.

c. Owing to the risk of high JPT's and the difficulty of monitoring and adjusting four engines at the same time, simultaneous rapid starting must not be attempted at temperatures below minus 15°C. In such temperatures, No 1 or No 4 engines should be started by the combuster starter and the remaining engines started by using air crossbleed.

SIMULTANEOUS RAPID STARTING

a. In order to gain full benefit from the rapid start installation, a complete combat readiness check should be carried out before engine starting. On completion of the combat readiness check, leave all systems selected as required for take-off. Carry out the checks in the Flight Reference Cards.

NOTE: The gyro hold-off button relay is only energised when RAPID is selected on the air selector switch and the master switch is OFF.

b. Before starting the engines, at least one booster pump per group must be on. To start the engines, move all throttles to the 50% RPM position, select the master switch ON and press the master RAPID START button. Combuster ignition is indicated by each individual starter button light coming on. Engine light-up is indicated by rising jet pipe temperature after approximately five seconds. As each engine accelerates, its starter disengages (indicated by the starter button lights going out) on overspeed-trip or on timer control after 12 seconds. During acceleration, check the indications of oil pressure, RPM, JPT and fire warning. The JPT should rise to between 400°C and 550°C in approximately 18 seconds and then begin to fall. When the JPT on any engine has stopped rising, wait a further two seconds and then close all throttles to the idling position; if the JPT on any engine reaches 600°C, all throttles must be closed immediately to the idling position. In either event the throttles, having been closed, can be reset immediately to give the required RPM.

c. During the start, the alternators come on line as engine RPM increase and, in addition, the flying control motors start automatically, the rudder first, followed by the ailerons and elevators together. All flying control motors should be started within 13 to 15 seconds of pressing the engine start button. The MFS gyros also start automatically as soon as the master start switch is selected ON.

INDIVIDUAL RAPID STARTING

a. The rapid start installation permits individual starting of engines, provided that the air temperature is above minus 26°C, without the automatic starting of PFC, etc. One or more engines may be started as required by using the individual start buttons. It must be remembered that, if the remaining engines are to be started using air crossbleed, an outboard engine should be started first.

b. The checks for a single rapid start are given in the Flight Reference Cards.

c. The remaining engines may be started in a similar manner. Alternatively, they may be started by using air crossbleed from the running engine. Select NORMAL on the air selector switch and start.

Taxying Ensure that the parking brake is fully off before taxying.

As visibility from the cockpit is restricted, it is advisable to inspect the area before entering the aircraft, especially if it is intended to taxy in confined spaces. Take particular note of objects likely to be blown by the jet efflux.

Before taxying, the scanner must be stabilised or secured and the relevant checks in the Flight Reference Cards carried out.

The thrust required to overcome the inertia of the aircraft and tyre set varies with the AUW and the surface but large amounts of thrust are rarely needed. Once the aircraft is in motion, sufficient thrust for normal taxying is obtained with all engines idling. At light weights, it is difficult to keep the speed down with all engines running. It is recommended, therefore, that on the completion of a sortie, the outboard engines are shut down to reduce the brake load.

As soon as convenient after moving, the brakes and nosewheel sterring should be checked. To operate the nosewheel steering, press the selector button at the base of the control handle and offset the rudder by the required amount. Very little is achieved by using asymmetric thrust in turns. Differential braking however, can be used to assist in tight turns but care should be taken not to turn too slightly by this method, otherwise the steering and centring jacks may be damaged. It is possible to complete a 180° turn fairly comfortably on a 50 yard runway.

a. In emergency, it is possible to taxy using only differential braking to turn; the pilot should always be ready to steer by this method should the nosewheel steering fail.

b. Do not operate the bomb doors while taxying, as the nosewheel steering becomes ineffective until their operation has ceased (approximately six seconds).

c. The brakes are very efffective but it is possible to use them unevenly and thus to overheat one side by inadvertent differential braking, when taxying or during the landing run.

Take-off Complete the checks before take-off before entering the runway. Align the aircraft with the runway and, with the brakes applied, open the throttles to 80% RPM, making sure that the brakes hold. Check for significant discrepancies between individual engine indications. When the engines are stabilised, switch on airframe anti-icing if required (30 seconds maximum before take-off). Ensure that the parking brake is off, release the brakes and then open up the throttles to full thrust. If the brakes are released suddenly, the nose tends to rise but it is unlikely that the nosewheel will leave the runway. If, in emergency, the JPT limiter is set to OFF, the RPM must be restricted during take-off (according to the table below) in order to avoid exceeding the JPT limits.

Olympus 200 Series		*Olympus 301 engines (but see Limitations)*	
Ambient Temp °C	*% RPM Limit*	*Ambient Temp °C*	*% RPM Limit*
–10	99	–5 and below	102
–5	98.5	0	101.5
0	98	5	101
5	97.5	10	101
10	97.5	15	100.5
15	97	20	100
20	96.5	25	99.5
25	96.5	30	99.5
30	96	35	99
35	96	40	98.5
40	95.5	45	98
45	95.5		

There is no tendency to swing and any small deviations in the early stages can be corrected by nosewheel steering. The rudder starts to become effective above 60 to 80 knots. Care must be taken when using either nosewheel steering or rudder to prevent over-controlling in the early part of the take-off run. Acceleration is good, even at high weights, and is very rapid if full power is used at lighter weights (below 160,000 lb AUW). Above 100 knots, nosewheel steering is almost ineffective unless weight is maintained on the nosewheel, therefore the stick should be held well forward of the central position if nosewheel steering is used continuously throughout the take-off run.

At the rotation speed (see table), ease the control column back so that the aircraft becomes airborne. (As weight is reduced below 170,000 lb, correspondingly less backward movement of the control column is required). Apply the brakes for 4 seconds and select undercarriage up; allow the aircraft to accelerate to the initial climb speed as the undercarriage is retracting and continue to accelerate to climbing speed.

Rotation and Initial Climb Speeds (knots)

AUW (lb)	*Rotation speed*	*Initial climb speed*
150,000 and below	135	148
160,000	139	148
165,000	141	149
170,000	143	151
180,000	148	156
190,000	153	160
195,000	155	163
200,000	157	165
204,000	162	170

After Take-off Keep slip and skid to a minimum while the undercarriage is travelling, in order to reduce stresses on the undercarriage door brackets. The undercarriage retracts in 9 to 10 seconds and no difficulty is experienced in achieving a clean aircraft before the undercarriage limiting speed of 270 knots is reached. Whenever possible, the undercarriage should be completely retracted before exceeding 200 knots. There is no appreciable trim change during take-off or undercarriage retraction but, as speed increases, a steadily increasing push-force on the control column is necessary, because of the rapid increase in speed. This push-force can be trimmed out easily in increments as the aircraft is accelerated to its climbing speed. Make a visual inspection of the undercarriage after UP selection, using the periscope.

At a safe height, throttle the engines to 93% and select *CRUISE* on the *TAKE-OFF/CRUISE* selector. Carry out the after take-off checks as soon as possible after take-off. Engine RPM creep in the climb, and 93% must be maintained by use of the throttles up to FL 300. Above FL 300 set and maintain 95% until top of climb is reached. 95% is the maximum permitted RPM for day-to-day operation in order to prolong engine life. Under operational conditions, or when specifically authorised, open the throttles fully and climb at maximum continuous power.

During take-off, yaw damper malfunction does not noticeably affect handling characteristics but, as speed increases to about 170 knots, the effects become apparent. Select the other channel immediately or, if both are defective, switch *OFF*.

Aborted Take-off Procedure In all instances where the take-off run has to be aborted the following actions are to be taken:

a. Warn crew aborting.

b. Close the throttles.

c. Select airbrakes to *HIGH DRAG*.

d. Stream the tail brake parachute if speed is between 75 knots and 145 knots.

e. Apply maximum continuous braking at or below normal maximum braking speed.

f. Carry out engine fire/failure drills as appropriate.

g. Inform ATC "Aborting".

h. Clear runway if feasible.

i. Carry out brake fire drills before further taxying.

After an aborted take-off using NMBS it may be possible to clear the runway. In which case the aircraft should be taxied slowly with minimum application of toe brakes; the parking brake should not be used to hold the aircraft stationary during checks, or for parking.

WARNING: If maximum continuous braking is used above NMBS, the aircraft should be stopped and evacuated as soon as practicable. Because of the high risk of tyres bursting the aircraft should not be approached for at least 2 hours unless it is necessary to extinguish any fire.

Climbing The recommended climb speed is 250 knots to 20,000 feet and then 300 knots up to a height where this speed coincides with 0.86M.

If the JPT limiters have been overriden because of unserviceability, the JPT must be watched very carefully if the limits are not to be exceeded during the climb.

Between 10,000 feet and 15,000 feet, the pressurisation failure warning horn may blow because the aircraft rate of climb is greater than the rate of increase of cabin pressure but, by 15,000 feet, the selected pressure should have been achieved. If cabin pressure surging occurs, check that the duct relief flap is in the closed position; if surging persists, close one of the in-use engine air switches and leave closed until the top of climb.

PART 15: HANDLING IN FLIGHT

Engine Handling Engine life is affected by the frequency and extent of temperature changes caused by increasing and decreasing thrust; therefore, to prolong engine life and maintain performance, throttle movement should be smooth and changes in thrust as few as possible. Slam decelerations to *IDLING* may be made at all altitudes. With 301 engines, care should be taken to ensure that the inboard throttles are not inadvertently closed beyond the detent position when above 15,000 feet. Slam accelerations should be avoided but, in an emergency, can be made from any throttle setting at all altitudes. It is recommended that throttles should not be opened from *IDLING* to *OPEN* in less than 3 seconds.

Engine RPM Thrust should not be reduced from *TAKE-OFF* by means of the *TAKE-OFF/CRUISE* selector switch alone. Before moving the switch to *CRUISE*, reduce the engine speed to 93% RPM. Then, after setting the switch to *CRUISE*, maintain 93% up to FL300 then set 95% and maintain until top of climb is reached. If maximum cruise thrust is required, open the throttles fully.

Similarly, when increasing thrust from the *CRUISE* setting to take-off, close the throttles until the RPM begin to fall before selecting the *CRUISE/TAKE-OFF* selector switch to *TAKE-OFF*. The throttles can then be opened fully.

The selector switch must be set to *TAKE-OFF* (200 series only) before entering the circuit, to ensure that full power is available for overshoot.

JPT The JPT limiters must always be switched ON, unless they are proved to be defective. Each is capable of keeping the JPT within ±5°C of the selected limitation, when controlling, but regular checks should be made for excessive temperatures, especially when taking off in high ambient temperatures, climbing and changing power at high altitudes. The JPT limiters do not prevent excessive turbine temperature during rapidly changing engine conditions with *CRUISE* selected but, at *TAKE-OFF*, their suppressed datum prevents overswing of turbine temperature during acceleration at all ambient conditions.

Under varying ambient conditions and with the JPT limiters working properly, each engine does not necessarily indicate the same RPM and JPT as the others. An engine may reach its governed RPM before reaching the JPT limit or vice versa. However, to be within the limits in steady conditions with all engines at full throttle, no engine should be more than 30°C hotter than the mean of the others, or more than 2% RPM slower than the mean of the others.

Engine Idling Speeds Idling speed varies with altitude and forward speed. The characteristics of the 200 series engines may be different on the incorporation of Mod 1785. They may result in undershoots of idling RPM after a deceleration, or a downward idling reset following a period of idling conditions, both of the order of 5% LP RPM. Engine response from these conditions will be normal in that movement of the throttle will give immediate engine acceleration, but the time to maximum RPM could be extended by as much as 1 second. The idling speeds under varying conditions are listed below:

	% RPM	
Condition	*200 Series Engines*	*301 Engines*
Static sea level idling (ISA)	32 no load 29.5 full load on alternators	27 no load 24.5
Approach idling	37 to 41	31 to 35
Idling at 50,000 feet (0.86M)	76 to 78	78 to 81
Windmilling at 0.88M	15 to 20	16 to 19

General Flying The elevator stick force varies as the square of the speed but it is possible to overstress the aircraft during manoeuvres in the pitching plane at high airspeeds. At high mach numbers, the elevator stick forces become heavier. Longitudinal stability is noticeably reduced with the CG at the aft limit. For low altitude training the CG should be kept forward of the mid-position to reduce the possibility of overstressing the aircraft in pitch.

The rudder forces are very heavy except in the low speed range when the use of rudder is necessary for correctly balanced turns.

The ailerons are very light and effective and some experience may be needed before a tendency to overcontrol at higher speeds can be avoided. The stick force is constant over the speed range but the maximum deflection is limited progressively from 150 knots onwards.

a. Coarse use of aileron produces large amounts of adverse yaw and, with the undercarriage down, the resulting sideslip can cause the load limits of the undercarriage doors to be exceeded.

b. Adverse yaw is most marked at 200 knots and heavy, co-ordinated rudder application is required to counteract it. When changing the direction of roll, large angles of sideslip are produced and co-ordination is particularly difficult. During manoeuvres, the slip indicator tends to under-read due to the heavy damping of the ball.

Trimming Care is needed to trim the aircraft accurately. The best results are achieved if small increments of trim are applied and time is given for them to take effect before any further adjustments are made.

CHANGE OF TRIM	
Raising and lowering UC	Negligible
Airbrakes (medium drag)	Slight nose-down
Airbrakes (high drag)	Further nose-down
Airbrakes (in)	Nose-up
Bomb doors	Negligible

Airbrake Characteristics At high airspeeds at lower altitudes, the airbrakes are very effective and cause only mild buffet in the *HIGH DRAG* position, with a marked nose-down change of trim. At higher altitudes, close to the limiting mach number, the *HIGH DRAG* position produces marked buffet, accompanied by severe airframe vibration, as well as the nose-down change of trim. If the limiting mach number is exceeded, this vibration makes cockpit instruments unreadable. At low airspeeds, the airbrakes are much less effective but do assist during the approach and landing. The airbrakes take approximately 5 seconds to move from *IN* to *MEDIUM DRAG* and a further 2 seconds from *MEDIUM DRAG* to *HIGH DRAG*.

Bomb Doors When bomb doors are opened at high airspeeds and mach numbers, moderate buffet occurs. Buffet is correspondingly less at lower airspeeds and mach numbers. With the bomb doors open, a slight increase in engine RPM is necessary to maintain a given airspeed in level flight.

If the aircraft is flown at altitude for more than 30 seconds with the bomb doors open, temperature effect on the control runs may result in gradual but noticeable changes in trim, particularly in the aileron sense.

High Speed Flight

WARNING: When flying at high indicated airspeeds or mach numbers, frequent comparisons must be made between the readings of the 1st pilot's, co-pilot's and navigator's ASI and between the pilots' machmeters.

AT LOW LEVEL/HIGH AIRSPEEDS. It is easy to exceed the speed limitations. When approaching the limiting speed, because of reducing longitudinal stability, pitch control becomes extremely sensitive and out-of-trim forces are very small with any change of speed. Extreme care is required to avoid overstressing the airframe.

AT HIGH LEVEL/HIGH MACH NUMBERS

a. MACH TRIMMER INOPERATIVE. Unless specifically authorised, the speed should be restricted to a maximum of 0.9M if the mach trimmer is inoperative. The aircraft readily accelerates to maximum mach number in level flight, except at high AUW when a slight descent is necessary. Very little change of trim occurs from 0.85M to 0.88M but, beyond this, a nose-down trim change develops which requires a substantial pull-force at 0.93M. At higher mach number, the nose-down trim change increases rapidly and there may be very little control left for recovery above 0.94M. If mach number increases further, the nose drops even with the stick fully back. If control is lost, recovery is effected by closing the throttles (leaving the airbrakes IN) and holding the stick fully back until, with decreasing height and attendant drop in mach number, control is regained. The trimmer can be used, if necessary, to relieve the pull-force but do *not* relieve the elevator feel; over-trimming must be avoided, otherwise there is a strong tightening of the pull-out as mach number is reduced. If the elevator feel does become inoperative, extreme care must be taken during the recovery phase to prevent serious overstressing of the airframe.

b. MACH TRIMMER OPERATIVE. No difference in handling is noted from 0.85M until the mach trimmer comes into operation at about 0.87M. Beyond this point, a steadily increasing nose-up change of trim develops (due to the progressive up elevator applied by the mach trimmer), which should not be trimmed out above 0.9M. The maximum permitted mach number is 0.93M (0.92M for 301 engines), at which speed a substantial push-force may be required, dependant on CG position. The mach trimmer still operates above 0.93M (0.92) until full extension of the servos occurs at about 0.95M at which speed the elevators have reached the almost fully up position. The aircraft now behaves, and recovery from above the limiting mach number is effected, in exactly the same manner as described in the last sub-paragraph. However, overcontrolling is more likely to occur. This is due to the extension and retraction of the mach trimmer with changing speed on recovery.

c. ENGINE HANDLING. Disturbances in air intake flow during recovery from high speed runs may lead to engine surge or flame-out particularly with 301 engines. If surge occurs, partially close the HP cock; if surge symptoms persist, close the HP cock fully and take normal cold relight action. If flame-out occurs, attempt a hot relight; if unsuccessful, close the HP cock and take cold relight action.

Pitch and Yaw Dampers Inoperative

PITCH DAMPER. The loss of one channel of the pitch damper is almost unnoticeable and no restriction is imposed but speed must be restricted to 0.90M if more than one pitch damper channel becomes inoperative.

YAW DAMPERS. The loss of the yaw damper is most noticeable when accurate course keeping is necessary or during an instrument approach. No limitation is imposed if the yaw dampers become inoperative.

Approach to the Stall Stalling is not permitted. Speed must not be reduced below the pre-stall buffet and in any case not below the threshold speed for the weight less 5 knots.

a. As speed is reduced, with airbrakes in and depending on weight, pre-stall buffet may be experienced at the corresponding threshold speed.

b. At high angles of attack the rudder is masked by the mainplane. This results in a reduced rudder response and larger than normal rudder movement is required to maintain directional control.

c. As speed is further reduced, a rate of sink develops which increases rapidly and may exceed 4000 ft/min.

d. At 115 knots all controls are light and effective but rudder response is greatly reduced. In the landing configuration with approach power, any buffet is masked by the airbrakes.

At speeds below 115 knots at aft CG and with the stick fully back, directional instability may occur, causing considerable yawing and rolling. If this is allowed to develop, it is impossible to control until the stick is pushed forward. During recovery, the direction of yaw and roll reverse. Excessive height is lost before recovery is complete.

Stalling in Turns It is not possible to stall this aircraft in turns unless either the g limitations are exceeded or airspeed is extremely low. However, at high altitudes the loading in the turn should not be increased after the onset of the initial buffet.

Flight in Turbulent Air Flight in turbulent air should be avoided but, if this is not possible, the speed should be maintained between 180 and 300 knots, preferably at 220 knots.

Flight with the Entrance Door Open The entrance door may safely be opened in flight at speeds up to 220 knots and higher in emergency. Above 220 knots there is a danger of the forward bulkhead collapsing. Below 220 knots, the handling qualities are not materially affected. There is a slight nose-up change of trim.

The noise level is very high at all speeds and intercommunication is difficult; therefore it is advisable that the captain's orders and intentions are made clear before the door is opened.

PART 16: CIRCUIT AND LANDING PROCEDURES

Circuit Speeds

AUW (lb)	*Pattern Speed (knots)*	*Approach Speed (knots)*	*Threshold Speed (knots)*
120,000 and below	155	135	125
130,000	160	140	130
140,000	165	145	135
150,000	169	149	139
160,000	173	158	143
170,000	177	162	147
180,000	181	166	151
190,000	185	170	155
200,000	189	174	159
210,000	193	178	163

Landing If it is necessary to land at an AUW greater than 140,000 lb, a runway of 9000 feet or more should be used. The tail brake parachute (TBC) may be streamed at 135 knots (145 knots maximum) and should be jettisoned between 50 and 60 knots. In emergency, it maybe retained until the aircraft has stopped and then removed by ground servicing personnel. However, if it is essential that the TBC be removed before the aircraft has been finally shut down the inboard engines may be opened up to approximately 40% and jettison selected, or the TBC jettisoned while the aircraft is taxying (if appropriate). Jettisoning the TBC with the aircraft stationary and shut down is permissible when absolutely necessary but some minor damage to the rear fuselage may result.

a. Fly the circuit and approach at the speeds recommended for the weight. A safe margin for control of the aircraft is allowed with up to 30° of bank angle at pattern speeds and 20° bank angle at approach speeds (15° at approach speed above 195,000 lb). During the later stages of the approach, (approx 200 feet), but not before decision height on an instrument approach, *HIGH DRAG* airbrake may be selected and speed reduced so as to cross the threshold with power on at the recommended speed. Maintain the correct approach speed by careful use of the throttles. At 195,000 lb and above, the rate of descent at touch-down must be kept to a minimum.

b. When the mean surface wind strength is 25 knots or above, irrespective of direction, the threshold speed should be increased by one-third of the mean wind strength. If the threshold speed then exceeds the approach speed, the latter should be increased to equal the former.

NORMAL LANDING. Aerodynamic braking may be used at all weights. After touch-down, when both bogies are firmly on the ground, raise the nose progressively as speed is reduced, until the control column is fully back. Because of the small ground clearance at the wing tips and the high angles of incidence associated with aerodynamic braking, any mishandling in the lateral sense may result in damage to the wing tips. Bank angles in excess of 3½° are significant in this respect. Aerodynamic braking must not be continued below 85 knots if the headwind is greater than 25 knots, since there is a possibility of the tail being scraped. Two red lights, on the coaming in front of the 1st pilot, come on when the tail of the aircraft is too close to the runway. With headwind components of less than 25 knots, aerodynamic braking may be continued down to 80 knots. Lower the nosewheel onto the runway and apply the brakes as required.

OVERWEIGHT LANDINGS: At weights below 140,000 lb, normal approach and landing techniques should be employed. At weights above 140,000 lb the speed at touch-down may be higher than the normal maximum braking speed (NMBS) and the maximum permissible speed for streaming the TBC. In such cases hold the nose as high as possible after touch-down and use aerodynamic braking until the speed falls to 145 knots. At 145 knots stream the TBC and when it deploys, lower the nose. Start braking when the nosewheel is on the runway and the speed is at NMBS. Provided that the AEO has been warned, the outboard engines may be shut down. Under favourable conditions of runway length, headwind or AUW, the pilot may, at his discretion, delay streaming the TBC until 135 knots. (Any parachute streamed above 135 knots may be scrapped).

SHORT LANDING. Cross the runway threshold at the lowest safe height and at the calculated threshold speed. Provided that the speed is below 145 knots, stream the TBC as soon as the main wheels are on the runway. Use aerodynamic braking until the TBC has developed and the speed is 5 knots above NMBS, then lower the nose. When the nosewheel is on the runway and the speed is at NMBS apply maximum continuous braking.

Braking Both front and rear wheels of the mainwheel units must be firmly on the ground before the wheelbrakes are applied, as the maxaret units do not operate until the wheels are rotating. As a safeguard against locking the wheels during a bounce after landing, the maxaret units remain inoperative for a few seconds. Apply brake pressure smoothly and progressively when the speed is below the braking speed for the weight. On dry surfaces, the maxaret units normally prevent the wheels from locking when excessive brake pressure is applied but, unless the shortest possible landing run is required, more gentle use of the brakes is recommended.

On wet surfaces, braking action may be severely reduced according to the degree of wetness of the surface. Use light intermittent brake application initially. As speed is reduced, brake application may be progressively increased and held continuously. If slip or skid is suspected, release the brakes momentarily and then re-apply them gradually.

A drastic reduction in braking action must be expected on flooded or icy surfaces; whenever possible, avoid these conditions. If a landing has to be made on a flooded or icy runway, the TBC is to be used, crosswind conditions permitting. If the use of the brake parachute is not possible, aim for a firm touch-down using aerodynamic braking down to at least 90 knots. Braking action must not be taken until the nosewheel is firmly on the ground; care should be exercised during braking to avoid wheel locking.

To prevent possible damage, it is necessary to limit the speed at which continuous braking is applied. This speed is referred to as the Normal Maximum Braking Speed (NMBS). It is defined as the maximum airspeed from which maximum continuous braking can be applied and the aircraft brought to rest without damage to the brakes. However, heavy braking will markedly reduce brake effectiveness as the heat absorption limit of the brakes is approached; even moderate braking at light weight and slow speed can have the same effect if prolonged, eg, lengthy taxying using brakes against power. Following any such cases of excessive braking, sufficient cooling time should be allowed to restore the brakes to full capacity.

WARNING: If maximum continuous braking is used from NMBS or speeds approaching NMBS, to avoid subsequent damage to the brakes the aircraft should not normally be brought completely to rest. The aircraft should be taxied slowly to dispersal with the minimum use of brakes and parked without applying the parking brake. If it is necessary to stop before reaching the dispersal, the minimum application of toe brakes should be used; the parking brake should not be used.

The emergency maximum braking speed (EMBS), defined in the *Take-off* Section of the Operating Data Manual, does not apply to landing. Tests have shown that the use of EMBS does not give a corresponding reduction in the landing run.

If the brake parachute fails to deploy, the appropriate NMBS must be used.

BRAKE COOLING TIMES (*Training Case Below* 140,000 lb AUW). If an intermediate landing is made during a sortie, the following conditions are to be observed:

a. On the intermediate landing, brakes must not be applied above 80 knots.

b. Great care must be taken during taxying to minimise any further heating of the brakes.

c. A minimum of 15 minutes is to elapse between the end of the landing roll and the start of the take-off run.

d. On the subsequent take-off, the undercarriage must not be retracted for a minimum period of 5 minutes after unstick.

e. If the subsequent take-off is aborted, the TBC must be streamed but the brakes should not be applied until the speed has fallen to the NMBS without parachute figure. If practicable brake application should be delayed until the speed is below 80 knots.

Landing With CG Outside Recommended Range The recommended CG index range for landing is +2 to -2 landing gear down. At low fuel states it may not be possible to maintain the CG within these limits. At any fuel state, if the non-essential loads are not reset after load shedding, the CG will move rapidly aft if the No 1 and 2 tank booster pumps are feeding. An aft movement of about 5 units of index can be experienced during a normal low level instrument circuit. The tail proximity warning lights are inoperative with non-essential loads shed.

LANDING WITH AFT CG. Landing with the CG at the aft limit presents no undue difficulty. On the approach to land, sufficient elevator control is available and speed stability is not markedly affected. When the CG index is aft of +4, it is recommended that the threshold speed is increased by 10 knots and that the aircraft is flown gently onto the runway rather than flared. Aerodynamic braking should not be attempted but the TBC may be used as required.

LANDING WITH FORWARD CG. When the CG index is forward of minus 4, it is recommended that the approach to land is slightly shallower than normal, and that the threshold speed is increased by 10 knots to improve elevon effectiveness for the flare. After touchdown it may not be possible to maintain aerodynamic braking attitude down to 80 knots.

Crosswind Landing A crosswind landing, using the crab technique, presents no special difficulty in crosswind components up to the limitation of 20 knots. When yawing the aircraft into line with the runway prior to touchdown, there is a marked tendency for the into-wind wing to rise; this tendency may be countered by prompt application of aileron. Aerodynamic braking may be used within the limits imposed by the tendency of the into-wind wing to rise. Lower the nose to allow braking below NMBS. The braking parachute may be used after the nosewheel has been lowered; any swing which develops due to the use of the braking parachute is best controlled by using nosewheel steering and brakes. If any difficulty is experienced in maintaining control, jettison the parachute. Avoid landing on very wet or icy runways in strong crosswinds; if the crosswind component in these conditions exceeds 7 knots, it is inadvisable to stream the parachute.

Landing Without Using Airbrakes When landing without airbrakes, use the normal procedure but a longer approach is advisable. To avoid high sink rates developing if the engines are throttled back to the slow response range, any necessary increase in power must be anticipated.

Overshooting Overshooting from any height presents no difficulties. Engine response is rapid on the approach but is comparatively slow (approximately 5 seconds to maximum RPM in normal temperatures, up to 13 seconds in tropical temperatures) when going round again from the runway. Open the throttles as necessary and climb away. At a safe height, if leaving the circuit, complete the overshoot checks. Under normal conditions, an overshoot from ground level followed by a visual circuit and landing requires 1200 to 1500 lb of fuel, and an overshoot from ground level followed by a low level instrument approach and landing requires 2000 to 2500 lb of fuel. At low AUW, the aircraft accelerates rapidly if full power is applied on overshoot. To avoid an extremely steep climb-away and to prolong engine life, it is recommended that power is restricted to 80% RPM.

Roller Landings When making a roller landing, hold the nosewheel close to the runway. Retract the airbrakes and open the throttles smoothly to a minimum of 80% RPM, being prepared for some difference in response from each engine. Avoid any tendency to overcontrol on the rudder. During acceleration, avoid a high nose-up attitude and any tendency to take off below the rotation speed (135 knots up to 150,000 lb).

When making a roller landing after an asymmetric approach, lower the nosewheel onto the runway. Before the throttles are opened for take-off they must all be in the idling position; it is essential that RPM on all engines are equal.

PART 17: ASYMMETRIC FLYING

Engine Failure During Take-off

SINGLE ENGINE FAILURE. Single engine failure on take-off presents no handling problems. However, in cases of mechanical failure it may result in double failure and should be treated as such.

DOUBLE ENGINE FAILURE

a. If the failure occurs before the decision speed is reached, abandon the take-off, using the appropriate FRC drill.

b. If failure occurs above the decision speed and the take-off is continued, maintain directional control, using rudder or a combination of rudder and nosewheel steering until rotation speed is reached. Rotate the aircraft, aiming to reach the initial climb speed at 50 feet. Apply rudder to keep the aircraft straight and, on becoming airborne, apply up to 5° of bank towards the live engines, accepting a slip indication of half a ball's width towards the live engines; the use of coarse aileron must be avoided, as the adverse yaw induced affects directional control. At rotation, be prepared for the aircraft to move sideways towards the dead engines.

Shutting Down or Failure of an Engine in Flight If an engine fails or is being shutdown in flight, close the throttle to the HP cock *SHUT* position, close the appropriate *ENGINE AIR* switch, adjust the relevant booster pumps and crossfeed cocks as necessary and inform the AEO. The LP cock should be closed if the situation demands it.

If an engine fails in flight when it is unlikely to have suffered, and is not showing symptoms of mechanical damage, and is windmilling at a steady and reasonable speed, an attempt may be made to relight it. During relighting, keep a careful watch on the engine indicators and, at any sign of malfunction or difficulty, shut the HP cock immediately; do not relight.

a. The buried wing root installation of the Olympus engines makes the adjacent engine of a pair liable to mechanical damage should one engine suffer structural failure. To minimise damage to the airframe, containment shields are fitted outboard of the outer engines to protect the wing, inboard of the inner engines to protect the bomb bay. They are *not* fitted between each engine and captains must always be aware of the possibility of damage occurring to the adjacent engine whenever fire or failure indications for one engine are received.

b. The following points should be considered whenever engine fire or failures occur in flight.

(1) FIRE/FAILURE INDICATIONS FOR BOTH ENGINES. Both engines should be closed down and the appropriate fire/failure drills carried out.

(2) FIRE/FAILURE INDICATIONS FOR ONE ENGINE. The failed engine should be closed down and the appropriate fire/failure drills carried out. Consideration should then be given to the following:

(a) If accompanied by obvious signs of *engine* structural failure (eg marked vibration, explosion or ruptured aircraft skin) and circumstances permit, the adjacent engine of the pair should be shut down as a precaution.

(b) If there are no obvious signs of structural failure, the other engine should be left at cruise power and monitored carefully for symptoms of malfunction. It is emphasised that there is no benefit to be gained in this situation from throttling the adjacent engine to flight idle.

Relighting in Flight If two engines fail simultaneously, relight the outboard first.

Relighting is progressively more certain with reduction in altitude and should always be possible at heights below 35,000 feet, and at airspeeds of 0.9M or less if practicable (preferably below 200 knots). 'Hot relights' may be achieved at any height, provided that relight action is taken within a few seconds of flame-out; hot relights are not recommended if the cause of flame-out is not known, except in the case of a multi-engine flame-out.

a. If, during a cold relight, a rapid rise in JPT occurs, without an accompanying rise in RPM, follow the recommended procedure.

b. If no relight is obtained after 30 seconds, release the button and *SHUT* the HP cock. A further attempt can be made at a lower altitude, after allowing the engine a minimum of 3 minutes to drain out.

c. Do not make more than three attempts to relight any one engine in the same sortie.

d. With Olympus 301 engines, severe buffeting can occur with an inboard engine windmilling. Relighting under such circumstances can be impossible. Buffeting can be reduced by decreasing airspeed and/or reducing RPM on the adjacent outboard engine.

e. Relighting is facilitated by throttling back to idling RPM the adjacent engine of the pair.

After the engine has been relit, inform the AEO.

Whenever an engine is relit in flight, a JPT/RPM comparison check between the engines must be carried out.

General In asymmetric flight conditions, above 200 knots, there is little difficulty in controlling the aircraft, even with two engines failed on the same side. At and below 200 knots, care is required to co-ordinate aileron and rudder movements to reduce the effects of adverse yaw caused by aileron drag and to maintain accurate control of the aircraft.

If asymmetric, with bomb bay loads of 21,000 lb and above, only gentle manoeuvres are to be carried out; rapid and/or full movement of the controls is not to be made.

When flying with one inboard engine windmilling, some airframe buffet may be experienced at speeds above 0.85M. In aircraft powered by Olympus Mk 200 series engines, this buffet is very pronounced at around 40,000 feet and enough to shake the instrument panels vigorously as speed is increased above 0.91M. At altitudes around 50,000 feet the buffet is less marked and changes little with change of mach number. Aircraft powered by Olympus Mk 301 engines are affected in a similar manner, although the buffet is even more pronounced and becomes most severe if the adjacent outboard engine is set at high power. When flying at 0.85M at 30,000 feet, the vibration becomes excessive if the RPM of the outboard engine are increased to 88%, while at 48,000 feet/0.85M severe vibration is felt with this engine set at 100% RPM. As height is increased above 55,000 feet, the vibration becomes much less marked and at all altitudes a setting of 80% in the outboard engines reduces the vibration to negligible proportions.

Asymmetric Landing and Overshoot

a. One engine inoperative. The technique and procedure used for approach using the three engines are the same as for a normal approach, except that the power settings are increased by approximately 3%. The visual committal height (VCH) for a three engine approach is 150 feet.

b. Two engines on one side inoperative. The minimum approach speed during a two engine asymmetric approach down to VCH must not be below the calculated approach speed for the weight or 145 knots, whichever is higher. High drag airbrake must not be selected until a decision to land has been made at the VCH of 200 feet above touch-down.

If the thrust available is marginal, it is recommended that a landing without airbrakes is carried out.

When an asymmetric overshoot is made it must be initiated at or above the VCH and the approach speed. The following procedure will allow an asymmetric overshoot on two engines to be made at any AUW within the WAT limits:

a. Level the wings.

b. Increase the power required, counteracting yaw with rudder.

c. Airbrakes IN.

d. Select landing gear up if required. To avoid undue stress on the landing gear door assemblies, only raise the landing gear if any of the following apply:

(1) Rear crew must escape
(2) At weights above 140,000 lb
(3) Leaving the circuit
(4) It is essential for safe control
(5) The AAPP operation must be considered

e. Allow the aircraft to accelerate to pattern speed before climbing away. Rudder must be applied to counteract the yaw and up to 5° of bank may be applied towards the live engines; coarse use of aileron must be avoided.

At normal landing weights, the power should be increased initially to 93% RPM (full power can be used if required).

Warning: The throttles must be opened carefully so that increase in power is simultaneous with throttle movement. Too rapid throttle movement which entails a lag in power response must be avoided.

PART 18: AIR-TO-AIR REFUELLING (FROM VICTOR AIRCRAFT)

Initial Approach

Warning: When a red or green light, or no lights are showing on the hose drum unit, contacts must not be attempted. Contacts are only permissible if amber light(s) are showing. If, when in contact, a red light comes on or all lights go out, contact must be broken immediately.

The recommended tanker speed is 220 to 300 knots up to 31,000 feet and 0.8M above 31,000 feet.

The recommended relative closing speed is two to three knots (maximum of five knots); use this speed approaching from below and dead astern, keeping the signal lights in view at all times.

When waiting to start an approach, position the receiver behind and to the starboard of the tanker in case the hose becomes detached while being trailed or wound in.

Turbulence reduces the chances of successful contact. It is advisable to attempt contact at a different altitude, free from turbulence. If severe turbulence is encountered while in contact, make an emergency break, as there is a danger of the nozzle breaking through hose whip.

When necessary use airbrakes and maintain power between 80 and 90% RPM, where the best throttle response occurs. Do not, however, operate the airbrakes while in contact.

If, during the initial approach, there is any unserviceability of the tanker drogue or floodlights, night refuelling is at the discretion of the receiver captain.

Prior to contact, the following radio and radar checks are to be made:

a. H2S off (NBS left on).

b. HF to standby or receive.

c. Active ECM to standby.

d. Warning receivers off.

e. IFF to standby.

Final Approach and Contact Make the final approach from dead astern and below the drogue, so that the pilot is looking along the line of the hose. Set power to maintain the correct closing speed and, from about 40 feet, adjust speed by visual judgment rather than by reference to the ASI. Careful engine handling and accurate flying are required and over-controlling must be avoided. To this end, it is important that the seat is adjusted to a comfortable position so that the pilot does not have to lean forward to get an adequate view of the probe. When about 5 to 10 feet short of the drogue, a moderate buffet is felt; at this point a small increase of power may be needed to maintain the closing speed. As the probe enters the drogue, mild buffeting is experienced, accompanied by considerable noise. When buffeting is experienced, considerable fluctuation of the pressure instruments may occur and the main and feel button warning lights may flash.

Once contact has been made and the probe is positively coupled to the drogue, fly the aircraft gradually up the line of the hose until the refuelling position is reached; keep the curve of the hose concave to the receiver. A slight reduction of power is then needed to maintain the refuelling position.

The recommended refuelling position is achieved when the forward end of a 10 foot long yellow band on the hose is just entering the serving carriage of the HDU. 7 feet of the hose must be wound in before the tanker fuel valve opens. When the valve is open, the tanker lights change from amber to green and the fuel gallery pressure gauge in the receiver starts to indicate. Continue the approach until the recommended position is reached.

The line of trail of the hose makes it difficult to see the yellow band unless it has been freshly painted; the correct refuelling position is reached when the hose is wound in until the serving carriage of the HDU is one-third of its travel from the right-hand side.

In Contact Once in contact, make small control movements to hold the correct station, dead astern of the tanker, with the yellow hose markings showing and the signal lights visible; guard against any tendency to over-correct. Avoid carrying the hose excessively downwards or sideways or probe damage may occur. It is difficult to achieve a permanent in-trim condition. Coarse throttle movement may be necessary to hold station but, normally, make small movements only. With the throttle friction damper fully off, throttle movement is comfortable; always ensure that the throttles are moved together.

Breaking Contact

Normal procedure

a. To break contact, reduce power slightly and allow the aircraft to fall astern gradually. Hose unwinding should be controlled at a slow rate by throttle movement. When the last 7 feet of the hose is coming off the drum, the signal lights change to amber if the tanker valve has not already been closed. Aim to break contact with the drogue in its natural position so that it can be watched as it draws away. If contact is broken in any other position, the drogue oscillates over a wide area about its normal position.

b. To ensure a positive break and to prevent the receiver being stuck by an oscillating drogue, when the last few feet of the hose (marked with red and white stripes) are being unwound close the throttles to the idling gate. This ensures a swift deceleration once contact has been broken but (provided that it is not done too soon) should not cause the hose drum brake unit to operate.

c. If the red and white stripes are difficult to see, it should be noted that the serving carriage of the HDU is at the left-hand end of its travel when the last few feet of the hose are being unwound.

EMERGENCY PROCEDURE. If a red light comes on, or if all lights go out, or if it is necessary to break contact quickly for any other reason, close the throttles fully and select airbrakes out to ensure that the deceleration rate from the hose is sufficient to reach a speed of 5 ft/sec, when its brake is automatically applied and contact is broken. This method should only be used in emergency conditions or for training purposes, as it throws a heavy load on the hose drum unit.

CLEARING THE TANKER. When contact is broken, some fuel splash occurs. This should normally be no more than a momentary mist but may be greater following an emergency break. Clear the tanker downwards and to starboard, so that the tanker can be kept in view all the time. The H2S is to be left off until 10 minutes after contact has been broken.

Incorrect Contact If the probe misses the drogue, close the throttles and withdraw to a safe distance along the approach path as the aircraft decelerates.

If the probe hits the outer rim of the drogue, the hose may wind in. If this occurs, withdraw behind and to starboard of the tanker while the hose is retrailed.

If the probe penetrates the canopy or spokes of the drogue, withdraw along the approach path to break contact with the drogue in the natural position; if necessary, wait for the hose to be retrailed.

If the probe appears to enter the drogue but fuel does not flow, a soft contact may have occurred because the closing speed was too low in the final stages of the approach; the hose may wind in. Withdraw and, if necessary, wait for the hose to be retrailed.

If speed is too high at contact, the hose loops upwards and the nozzle weak link breaks. A fast approach must be recognised at an early stage and, unless speed can be reduced before contact, the approach must be discontinued. Contact should not be made with the throttles at idling RPM, as no power control is then available for decelerating on contact.

a. If the nozzle is broken through mishandling, the windscreen becomes completely obscured by fuel from the probe body for a few minutes. The pilot of the receiver aircraft must clear well to starboard and astern of the tanker immediately. Loss of the probe nozzle does not affect aircraft handling but speeds in excess of normal cruising speeds should be avoided.

b. In some cases the fuel splash may be sufficient to flame-out an engine. If this occurs, the alternator of the affected engine must be switched off, to reduce the fire risk, and the cabin air isolation cock must be closed to prevent fuel contamination of the cabin air. Exceptionally, the engine or airframe may have been damaged by debris from the broken probe and consideration should be given to this before an attempt is made to relight the engine. Unless an immediate relight is necessary for safety reasons, allow a 5-minute period to elapse before relighting, so that the windmilling engine can scavenge the excess fuel. After relighting, the alternator must be left off for a further 5 minutes, to ensure that its cooling system is scavenged of fuel.

PART 19: EMERGENCIES

Crash Landing The following considerations are recommended if a crash landing becomes necessary:

a. BEFORE LANDING
(1) Reduce weight as much as is practicable.
(2) Have the nav/radar make the ejection seats safe. The pip pin for the canopy jettison gun must *not* be removed.
(3) If crash landing on an airfield, request foam on the runway as early as possible.
(4) If, in the opinion of the captain, there may be a danger of the navigators and AEO being trapped in the aircraft after the landing, they should be ordered to abandon the aircraft. Ensure that the undercarriage is in the up position.
(5) A check should be made for obstructions, bearing in mind the direction of expected swing, ie one mainwheel up condition.
(6) If crash vehicles are available check their positions.
(7) If possible, check that a long ladder is available to expedite the crew's escape.
(8) Ensure that all unnecessary navigational and electrical equipment is switched off.
(9) Uncover the rear cabin windows prior to crash landing.

b. APPROACH
(1) Make a normal approach with the undercarriage up or down according to circumstances. The advantages of reducing impact load with the undercarriage down, however, should be carefully considered.
(2) Jettison the canopy and close the HP cocks just before touchdown.

Landing with Undercarriage in Abnormal Positions
GENERAL

a. If, after using the emergency system, only one leg is lowered, it is recommended that the aircraft is abandoned. In other cases, if a landing is considered feasible, then the general principle is that all crew stay with the aircraft.

b. Where practicable, make the landing at an airfield equipped with foam-laying apparatus. When landing with one main unit unlocked, the foam strip should be laid along the side of the runway that the wing tip is expected to strike. The foam acts as a lubricant and so delays the start of the ground loop, which imposes a heavy strain upon the undercarriage.

c. The possibility of major damage is also reduced if, after touchdown, the unsupported wing or nose is lowered at a controlled rate while the flying controls are still effective, rather than be allowed to drop on to the runway.

LANDING TECHNIQUES
a. BELLY LANDING. If, after the use of the emergency system, all units of the undercarriage remain retracted, it is recommended that the aircraft be belly-landed, as follows:
(1) Reduce weight as much as practicable and switch off all unnecessary equipment.

(2) Have the nav/radar make the ejection seats safe. The pip-pin for the canopy jettison gun must not be removed.
(3) Ensure that the bomb doors and entrance door are closed.
(4) Ensure all loose objects are stowed, that all crew have their harnesses tight and locked, protective helmets on, with 100% and emergency oxygen selected and flowing correctly.
(5) Make a normal approach.
(6) Jettison the canopy while still on the approach.
(7) Make a normal landing, keeping the wings level and the rate of descent to a minimum.
(8) Close the HP cocks. As soon as possible, operate the fire extinguishers and switch off all electrics.

b. NOSEWHEEL UP, BOTH MAINWHEELS DOWN
(1) Move the CG as far aft as possible, within permitted limits of the available fuel.
(2) Carry out a low overshoot, to check wind conditions.
(3) Ensure all loose objects are stowed, that all crew have their harnesses tight and locked, protective helmets on, with 100% and emergency oxygen selected and flowing correctly.
(4) Carry out a normal circuit. Open the entrance door. Jettison the canopy on completion of final turn. Switch on the landing lamps at night.
(5) Touch down normally at the correct speed.
(6) When firmly on the main wheels, stream the tail parachute (crosswind permitting) and cut the outboard engines.
(7) AEO to switch off Nos 1 and 4 alternators.
(8) Hold the nose up until speed drops to 80 knots, runway length permitting.
(9) While elevator control is still available, lower the nose on to the ground.
(10) As soon as the nose touches, cut the remaining engines; the co-pilot switches off all LP cocks; the AEO switches OFF all alternators and operates the battery isolating switch.
(11) When the nose is firmly on the ground, apply the brakes gently and evenly.
(12) When the aircraft stops, the co-pilot leaves first, followed by the nav/radar, AEO, nav/plotter and 1st pilot in that order. If 6th and 7th seat members are carried they should leave the aircraft after the co-pilot in the order 6th, then 7th.
c. NOSEWHEEL DOWN, ONE MAINWHEEL DOWN
(1) Move the CG as far aft and as far away from the failed mainwheel as possible.
(2) Carry out at least one low overshoot, to check wind conditions.
(3) Ensure all loose objects are stowed, that all crew have their harnesses tight and locked,

protective helmets on, with 100% and emergency oxygen selected and flowing correctly.
(4) Carry out a normal circuit and jettison the canopy on completion of the final turn. Switch on the landing lamps at night.
(5) Touch down normally at the correct speed.
(6) On touchdown, cut the outer engines and lower the nosewheel onto the ground.
(7) AEO switches off Nos 1 and 4 alternators.
(8) Hold the wing up, using aileron, rudder and nosewheel steering.
(9) Before control effectiveness is lost, lower the wing and cut the remaining engines; hold the aircraft straight for as long as possible. The co-pilot switches off the LP cocks; the AEO switches off all the alternators and operates the battery isolating switch.
(10) When the aircraft stops, the co-pilot leaves first followed by the nav/radar, AEO, nav/plotter, and 1st pilot in that order. If 6th and 7th seat members are carried they should leave the aircraft after the co-pilot in the order 6th, then 7th.

d. Nosewheel down, both mainwheels up. In these circumstances, it is recommended that the aircraft be abandoned, as it is considered that the hazards for the rear crew escaping past the nosewheel are less than the danger to the whole crew of the nose section breaking off and the main fuselage overrunning the cabin. If, for any reason, a landing is imperative, the following technique is recommended:
(1) Reduce weight to the minimum practicable.
(2) Insert the pins in the ejection seats but not in the canopy jettison gun. Switch off all unnecessary equipment. Ensure all loose objects are stowed, that all crew have their harnesses tight and locked, protective helmets on, with 100% and emergency oxygen selected and flowing correctly.
(3) Make a normal approach. Jettison the canopy at the end of the final turn. Switch on the landing lamps at night.
(4) Make a normal landing, keeping the wings level; avoid a high nose-up attitude and land with minimum drift. Do not stream the brake parachute.
(5) As soon as the nosewheel drops to the ground, cut all engines and switch off all services.

Abandoning the Aircraft

General

a. Ejections may be initiated in straight and level flight, at any height from ground level upwards. However, runway ejections should only be made when the speed of the aircraft is above 90 knots. At low altitude the aircraft should be straight and level or climbing; any significant rate of descent or nose-up attitude at the instant of ejection reduces the seat performance.

b. Rear crew members can leave the aircraft down to a minimum height of 250 feet at a maximum speed of 250 knots. Whenever possible, speed should be reduced to 200 knots and the aircraft be in a shallow climb with undercarriage raised, prior to escape.

To minimise the possibility of injury by air blast or by loss of equipment, it is recommended that, if circumstances permit, speed is reduced as much as possible before attempting to escape. Escape is made easier if no personal survival pack is worn.

The following amplifies the drills in the Flight Reference Cards:

a. Escape for rear crew members—general
(1) Whenever possible, altitude should be reduced to below 40,000 feet. Above 40,000 feet the aircraft should only be abandoned in an extreme emergency. Crew members should initiate the demand emergency oxygen set and then disconnect from the aircraft system. Post-Mod 2393 a combined static line, oxygen hose and mic/tel release coupling is fitted for rear crew members. Speed should be reduced as much as possible. It is most important that the exit is made by sliding cleanly down the door, in a bunched-up attitude. Ground tests also show that rear crew members can clear an extended nose-wheel on escape at speeds up to 180 knots.
(2) Move the abandon aircraft switch rearwards to the EMERGENCY position and confirm on the intercom. Post-SEM 027, operation of the abandon aircraft switch automatically illuminates the cabin light.
(3) Nav/plotter and AEO operate the door opening switches. Above 20,000 feet, the normal door opening lever should only be operated in addition to and simultaneously with the switches when escape in the minimum time is essential. Below 20,000 feet, the switches and door opening lever may both be used. Whichever method has been used to open the door, the first rear crew member to reach the door should ensure the door opening lever is in the gated *EMERGENCY* position. Ensure that static lines are connected.
(4) When giving the order to abandon the aircraft, the pilot should normally indicate to the rear crew members that the static lines are to be used. However, below 1000 feet and 200 knots he should order the manual overrides to be used.
(5) The nav/radar's last action before sliding down the door must be to ensure that his oxygen hose passes behind his PSP.
(6) Navigators and AEO leave the aircraft in the order, nav/radar, AEO and nav/plotter. If an experienced 6th seat crew member is carried he will be first to leave the aircraft. In the case of an inexperienced 6th member he will leave after the nav/radar. When an inexperienced 7th member is carried, the 6th member must be an experienced aircrew member or a crew chief. The 7th member is not to be given any task other than leave the aircraft when instructed. The order of abandoning will be 6th, 7th, nav/radar, AEO and nav/plotter. The co-pilot, if possible, should watch the rear crew members leave the aircraft and inform the 1st pilot when the nav/plotter has left. The crew gone lights indicate to the pilot that the rear crew members have left the aircraft.

b. Escape for rear crew members—undercarriage raised
(1) Sit on the floor at the front end of the door aperture facing aft.
(2) Grasping the handle at the bottom of the centre seat, swing forward onto the door and slide down it. At speeds above 200 knots it is advisable to adopt and hold a bunched-up attitude to minimise the possibility of injury from limb flailing. Below 200 knots an extended attitude with the legs straight out and rigid probably gives an easier exit. An upward pull with the arms is necessary to ensure that the PSP is lifted clear of the door edge.

c. Escape for rear crew members—undercarriage lowered. If the undercarriage cannot be raised, the following technique is recommended:
(1) Grasping the handle at the bottom of the centre seat, swing the legs onto the door facing aft. Slide down the door with the legs apart until the feet can be braced against the door-operating jacks. An upward pull with the arms is necessary to ensure that the PSP is lifted clear of the door edge.
(2) Releasing the grip, lean forward with bent knees and grasp the right-hand (port) jack with both hands, as low as possible, thumbs uppermost, right hand on top.
(3) Withdrawing both feet inwards from the jacks, keeping the knees bent and the body close to the port jack, swing down and round the port jack and over the port side at the bottom of the door. Release the hold on the jack as the body swings completely clear. Try to maintain a compact position with the arms close to the body after letting go. Keeping close to the port jack decreases the risk of the PSP fouling the starboard jack.

d. Escape for rear crew members at low altitudes Note: Whenever possible, convert speed to height. If it is necessary to abandon the aircraft at very low altitude (below 1000 feet), reduction of the time interval between the moment at which the order to abandon aircraft is given and the moment at which the parachute deploys can be of overriding importance and the following points should be borne in mind:
(1) The time taken to open the door can be reduced to a minimum by operating either rear crew switch immediately then, if necessary, operating the manual door control.
(2) The static line arms a barostat, which then withdraws the parachute pack pins after a delay of 2 seconds. Therefore, whether a static line is connected or not, the parachute release handle should be pulled as soon as possible after clearing the door.

The pilots should escape, using their ejection seats, after the rear crew members have escaped.

If the ejection seat automatic system fails after ejection, proceed as follows:

a. When forward speed is sufficiently low, discard the face screen.

b. Pull the manual separation lever outwards and then up.

c. Fall clear of the seat and pull the rip-cord handle.

Ditching Model tests indicate that the ditching qualities of the aircraft are good, there being no tendency to nose under after impact.

a. The following considerations and actions amplify the drill given in the FRC:
(1) Assessment of sea state. Whenever possible, fly low over the water and study its surface before ditching. It is important to establish correctly the direction of the swell and of the surface wind.
(2) Direction of approach. The aircraft should always be ditched into wind if the surface of the water is smooth or there is a very long swell. However, ditching into the swell or large waves should be avoided because of the danger of nosing under. In practice a direction of approach which is a compromise between swell, wave and wind direction, may be the best choice.
(3) Judgment of height. As judgment of height over water can be difficult, the Alt 7 or Alt 6 should be used if possible. The landing lamps should also be used at night.
(4) Fuel weight. Fuel weight should be reduced as much as practicable prior to ditching. Excess fuel may be used to position the aircraft in a more favourable location, eg closer to ships or land, but it is essential that the ditching is carried out while engine power is still available.

b. Ditching drill
(1) Ensure all loose objects are stowed, that all crew have their harnesses locked and tight, protective helmets on, 100% and emergency oxygen selected and flowing correctly. Uncover the rear cabin windows.
(2) Have ejection seat pins replaced.
(3) Disconnect PSP and lanyards, leg restraint, emergency oxygen and parachute harnesses as appropriate to crew position.
(4) On the approach, stow the fuel console and jettison the canopy.

c. Touchdown
(1) Touchdown should be made in a tail-down attitude at the lowest practicable speed commensurate with the minimum rate of descent. Touching down at high speed and low angle of attack should be avoided due to the likelihood of the aircraft bouncing and the probable collapse of the bomb-aimer's blister with subsequent flooding of the cabin. In any event the control column should be held hard back after impact.

Aborted Take-off Procedures

a. If an emergency occurs before decision speed, take-off is to be aborted in accordance with the FRC drill. The following emergencies constitute mandatory reasons for abandoning take-off, unless otherwise authorised.
(1) Engine failure.
(2) Any fire warning light coming on.
(3) Double alternator failure.
(4) PFC failure (main warning not accompanied by a white reminder MI).

b. The Captain is to warn the crew "Aborting".

c. The pilot flying the aircraft is to:
(1) Close the throttles.
(2) Select *HIGH DRAG* airbrake.
(3) Apply maximum continuous braking at NMBS or below.

d. The non-flying pilot is to:
(1) Stream the tail braking parachute (75 knots to 145 knots).
(2) Carry out engine failure/fire drills as ordered.

e. The AEO calls "Aborting, Aborting" on the frequency in use.

f. The nav/plotter calls airspeeds down to 50 knots.

Emergency Evacuation on the Ground The following considerations for evacuating the aircraft in an emergency on the ground amplify the drills given in the Flight Reference Cards:

a. Undercarriage position. The direction of exit depends on the emergency and whether the undercarriage is raised or has collapsed during the emergency. If the nosewheel has collapsed, it may be possible to leave the aircraft through the door; if, however, all the undercarriage legs are retracted, exit will have to be via the canopy aperture. The route from the canopy to leave the aircraft will depend upon the condition of the aircraft and whether a fire exists.
b. Canopy jettison. It will be necessary to leave via the canopy aperture if exit through the door is not possible. When the canopy is jettisoned, if the aircraft is stationary, the possibility exists that the canopy will fall back on to the cockpit and may injure one or other of the pilots.

c. Ejection seat pins. If exit through the entrance door is feasible, the pilots should replace the seat pan firing handle safety pin prior to leaving their seats. If the exit has to be made via the canopy aperture, and time permits, the main gun sear pins are to be inserted to make the ejection seats safe.
d. Crew ladder. If speed of exit is essential and exit through the door is feasible the crew should slide down the door and clear the vicinity of the aircraft as quickly as possible. Only replace the door ladder when the degree of emergency allows.

e. Battery. If conditions permit the AEO should switch off the aircraft battery prior to evacuating the aircraft. It should be borne in mind that with the battery off all cabin lighting is lost. However, if the battery was left on, when it is safe and if it is feasible, the AEO should return to the aircraft to switch off the battery in order to make the aircraft electrically safe.

Engine Failure Above Decision Speed

a. If engine failure or other serious emergency occurs above decision speed, the take-off is normally to be continued and the recommended drill followed.

b. When the aircraft is safely airborne, the pilot flying the aircraft is to close the HP cock(s) of the affected engine(s), simultaneously ordering the non-flying pilot to select undercarriage up. The flying pilot is then to order the non-flying pilot to carry out the drill required, eg "Engine Failure Drill, No 3 Engine".

c. The non-flying pilot is to complete, from memory, the engine fire/failure drill as ordered: the immediate actions listed in the FRC as far as 'Fuel Pumps' are to be completed.

d. The AEO declares an emergency on the frequency in use.

e. Once the aircraft is fully under control (pattern speed attained) the FRC checks for engine failure/fire are to be completed.

f. A turn on to the downwind leg is not to be initiated below 1000 feet above ground level, and until pattern speed is attained. Bank is to be restricted to a maximum of 25° in the turn. It is recommended that an instrument pattern is flown following double engine failure.

g. When the aircraft is established on the downwind leg, the 'Resetting' checks are to be carried out (if required) followed by the 'Prelanding' checks. The undercarriage is not to be lowered until approaching the glide path.

PART 20: FIRE PROTECTION SYSTEMS

Engine Fire Protection

Olympus Power Plant Fire Extinguishing System Each engine bay is divided into three zones: Nos 1, 2A and 2B. Zone 1, which holds the LP compressor, has no fire protection. Zone 2A, which holds the HP compressor, has six flame detectors and Zone 2B has five. Each detector consists of one shrouded and one unshrouded thermocouple; a temperature differential of 250°C induces sufficient current to operate the control unit relays and give fire warning. Fire warning indication cancels when the temperature differential drops below 250°C.

There are two methyl-bromide extinguisher bottles on each side of the bomb bay. The forward one of each pair serves the inboard engine and the rear one the outboard engine. The bottles feed through spray pipes on the sides of the engine bays.

CONTROLS AND INDICATORS

a. Four guarded fire-extinguisher pushbuttons, one for each engine, are on the coaming above the centre instrument panel; each button incorporates a red warning light. The lights may be tested by gently pulling out the pushbuttons, when the light should come on. The buttons return by spring action but they must not be allowed to snap back and they must not be pushed back. The action of the buttons is very sensitive and they must be treated with care. The fire warning is inoperative while gyro hold-off is engaged.

b. A test switch is provided at the top panel 4P for testing the whole fire-warning circuit. All four circuits are tested simultaneously and all four warning lights should come on. A ground test facility is provided in the nosewheel bay. The test facility is supplied from the essential busbar.

OPERATION

a. If an engine fire is indicated by a fire warning light coming on, the drill in the FRC must be carried out without delay.

b. The warning light goes out when the fire is extinguished and the temperature differential drops below 250°C. On no account make an attempt to relight the engine, as no extinguisher is available if another fire occurs.
Note: The fire warning light could also go out as a result of a damaged thermocouple, as they are wired in series.

AAPP Fire Extinguishing System Four flame detectors provide fire detection in the AAPP, three on the rear panel and one on the top rail. The flame detectors are set to operate at a temperature difference of 185°C. The methyl-bromide extinguisher bottle is on the outside of the AAPP fireproof bulkhead and operates through two spray rings.

CONTROLS AND INDICATORS. A guarded fire-extinguisher button, embodying a warning light, is on panel 70P. Below it is a *FIRE TEST* pushbutton, which is used to test the warning system. When the extinguisher button is pressed, the LP cock is closed automatically.

OPERATION

a. If the fire warning light comes on, take the following actions:
Extinguisher button Press
Master switch *OFF*
Subsequently, set the LP cock switch to *OFF*.

b. The warning light goes out when the fire is extinguished and the temperature differential drops below 185°C. The AAPP cannot be restarted once the extinguisher button has been pressed.

FUEL TANK FIRE PROTECTION

Fuel Tank External Fire Protection The fuel tank and leading edge fire protection system is operated automatically by fire-wire sensing elements, installed around the tank bays. When any part of the sensing element is heated to approximately 250°C, the circuit is made to the appropriate extinguisher bottles. Triple-F-D fire detector units are provided, two for the fuselage tanks, four for the wing tanks and one for the bomb bay tanks.

MANUALLY OPERATED SYSTEM. Post SEM 012, the wings and fuselage automatic system is made inoperative, the indicator deleted and the bomb bay fire warning indicator repositioned. Two manually operated flap-guarded push switches on the co-pilot's panel give independent control of the port and starboard extinguisher systems, the switches are labelled *'WING/FUSELAGE, FIRE EXTINGUISHERS, PORT-STARBOARD'*. Operation of these switches will discharge all fuselage, wing and leading edge fire extinguishers but the wing tank fire extinguishers will be discharged to the inboard fuel tank bay only.

FUSELAGE TANKS. The No 1 and No 2 tanks are protected by four methyl-bromide fire-extinguisher bottles, two for each pair of tanks. The contents of the bottles are discharged into the appropriate tank bays through spray pipes.

WING TANKS. Tanks Nos 3, 4 and 6, in the inboard tank bay, and tanks Nos 5 and 7, in the outboard bay, are protected by six dual-head fire-extinguisher bottles in each wing. The bottles can supply either the outboard or the inboard bay but cannot supply both bays simultaneously. The firing of either operating head discharges the total contents of the bottle.

LEADING EDGE INSTALLATION. Three extinguisher bottles in each wing, forward of the main wheel units, supply a spray pipe inside the anti-icing ducting in the leading edge. The extinguishers are actuated by the wing tank sensing units.

BOMB BAY FUEL TANKS. When provision is made for bomb bay fuel tanks, eight methyl-bromide extinguishers are installed, four on each side of the bomb bay. The extinguishers are automatically operated by fire-wire sensing elements, or by the inertia switches.

INDICATORS. Two red warning lights, on the co-pilot's instrument panel, one for the wings and fuselage and one for the bomb bay, indicate if a fire in the fuel tanks has caused the extinguishers to operate. The lights go out when the temperature falls below 250°C. Fuse-type indicators on the rear face of the front spar, on the port side of the bomb bay, show if the bomb bay extinguishers have operated. A test switch light is on a panel on the starboard side of the nosewheel bay. A relay in the circuit prevents inadvertent operation of the extinguishers when the test switch is operated. Post SEM 012, only one red warning light for the bomb bay fire warning is fitted to the co-pilot's panel.

HAND FIRE EXTINGUISHERS AND INERTIA SWITCHES

Hand Operated Fire Extinguishers Five bromochlorodifluoromethane (BCF) hand-operated fire extinguishers are in stowages in the crew's compartment:

a. Behind each pilot's seat (2)

b. Outboard of the nav/radar's seat (1)

c. Behind the AEO's seat on the forward and rear wall of the HRS crate (2).

A BCF fire extinguisher is provided for external use and is stowed in the external emergency equipment compartment.

BCF extinguishers are a universal type of extinguisher which may be used on any type of fire without restriction.

FIRE IN THE CABIN. The majority of fires in the cabin are electrical in origin and can usually be controlled by switching off all equipment in the vicinity. If the fire still persists, the hand extinguishers may be used. As circumstances permit and once the fire is extinguished, reduce cabin pressure by selecting *COMBAT* or *NO PRESSURE* (depending on altitude), to flush out the fumes more rapidly. Oxygen regulators should be selected to 100% and emergency and care taken not to get any BCF in the eyes.

Inertia Switches Inertia switches, on the lower forward face of the rear pressure bulkhead, automatically discharge the engine, AAPP, fuel tank extinguishers (wing extinguishers to inboard tank groups) and bomb bay extinguishers in a crash landing, when deceleration exceeds 4½g. At the same time, the alternators are automatically switched off, the AAPP (if in use) is automatically stopped and the 24 volt battery is disconnected from the essential busbar. By automatically switching off all the electrical supplies in the aircraft (except for the vital busbar supplies), risk of fire is minimised.

PART 21: ELECTRICAL SYSTEM

Introduction The main electrical system is AC operated; 200 volt, 3-phase, 400 Hz power is supplied by four 40 kVA alternators, one on each engine. Each alternator is driven from its appropriate engine via a hydro-mechanical constant-speed unit and a frequency control circuit which maintains the alternator speed at 6000 RPM ± 1% under steady state input speed and load conditions.

From each alternator, current is fed to an individual busbar which can be connected to a synchronising ring main busbar for load sharing purposes.

From the individual busbars, a number of transformer rectifier units (TRU), transformers and frequency changers provide the secondary power supplies.

Provision is made for standby supplies in the event of a major AC failure. A ram air turbine (RAT) supplies power primarily at high altitude and an airborne auxiliary power plant (AAPP) supplies power at lower altitudes.

The distribution feeders are triplicated as a safety measure and all circuits except the ground supply are fused. No distribution fuses are accessible in flight.

The main controls for the electrical system are grouped on the alternator control panel (10P), the secondary supplies panel (50P) and the AAPP panel (70P), all at the AEO's station. The controls for the frequency changers are on panel 12P at the navigator/radar's station.

200 Volt AC Supplies

Alternators Each alternator provides 3-phase power at 200 volts, 400 Hz. Automatic protection is provided against:

a. Over-voltage.

b. Under-voltage or incorrect phase sequence.

c. Line-to-line and line-to-earth faults up to but not including the busbars.

d. Underspeed.

e. Overspeed.

Alternator supplies are controlled by two circuit breakers. With the alternator (A) breaker closed, the alternator feeds its own busbar. With the synchronising (S) breaker and the A breaker closed, the alternator supplies its own busbar and the synchronising busbar. The A and S breakers are so arranged that, if the A breaker is opened, the S breaker is normally closed, thus ensuring an alternative power supply to the individual busbar via the synchronising busbar. The S breaker normally opens before the A breaker is closed; S breakers can be closed in order to parallel two or more alternators on the synchronising busbar.

When two alternators or more are connected in parallel, real load sharing (distribution of load between alternators) is controlled by magnetic amplifiers, which adjust the torque of the constant speed unit. Reactive load sharing is controlled by automatic adjustment of the voltage regulator settings. The load sharing limitations are ± 3 kW (real) ± 2½ kVAR (reactive) of the mean values.

The alternators are cooled by ram air ducted into the front end of the alternator and exhausted to atmosphere at the rear. Provision is made for induced cooling using bleed air from each engine to augment the air flow when the undercarriage is selected DOWN. If the undercarriage is selected down using emergency air, this induced cooling is not available.

Each load busbar supplies approximately a quarter of the total loads and the PFC loads are divided between the four busbars.

Alternator Controls and Operation

WARNING: In flight, the alternators must not be run in parallel, except as directed by the Flight Reference Cards.

The alternator control panel (10P) is at the AEO's station and carries the following controls and indicators:

a. A voltmeter and frequency meter for the selected INCOMING alternator.

b. RAT and AAPP test pushbuttons, used to obtain the readings for these supplies on the meters in a. above.

c. An alternator selector switch, incorporating a pushbutton to facilitate synchronisation of alternators.

d. An EXTRA SUPPLIES TRIP pushbutton, used to trip any extra supply (RAT, AAPP, 200 volt ground supply) from the synchronising busbar.

e. A mimic diagram of the 200 volt system. The diagram incorporates a voltmeter and a frequency meter to show supplies at the synchronising busbar, magnetic indicators which show continuity when an S breaker is closed and amber lights to show when an alternator is not connected to its own busbar. Magnetic indicators for the RAT and AAPP show continuity when they are connected to the synchronising busbar. Placed centrally on 10P is a red alternator failure warning light (duplicated on the pilots' centre panel) which shines steadily if one alternator fails and flashes if two or more fail. Beside the AAPP magnetic indicator is an AAPP ON pushbutton, beside each S breaker indicator is an alternator ISOLATE button and beside each amber light is an alternator RESET button.

f. A NON-ESSENTIAL SUPPLIES, TRIP/RESET switch, spring-loaded to the central (guarded) position, is on panel 10P. This switch can be used to trip non-essential supplies without releasing the RAT and to reset non-essential supplies once power has been restored.

g. Four kW/kVAR meters, one for each alternator, normally read kW; a button, placed centrally, is labelled PUSH FOR KVAR.

h. Four ON/OFF switches, one for each alternator.

CSDU oil temperature gauges are provided at the AEO's station. The maximum permitted load for each alternator is 32 kW, provided that the CSDU oil temperature remains below 120°C. This oil temperature must not be exceeded and, if necessary, height or loading must be reduced to keep the oil temperature within limits.

When an engine is running, its alternator is brought on line as follows:

a. Check, by means of the alternator selector switch, that the alternator voltage and frequency are within 115 ± 5 volts, 400 ± 4Hz.

b. When the alternator is running correctly, set its alternator switch ON. Check that the S breaker opens, the A breaker closes (amber light out) and the kW/kVAR meter registers the load, indicating that the alternator is feeding its busbar.

Whenever there is no supply on the synchronising busbar, it is arranged that No 2 alternator S breaker closes automatically.

To connect an alternator to the synchronising busbar, select the appropriate alternator on the selector switch and then press in the switch until the magnetic indicator shows continuity. When available, No 2 alternator should be used as the medium for switching supplies to the synchronising busbar. Failure to do so can, under certain circumstances, cause involuntary and simultaneous connection of No 2 alternator and the selected alternator and could lead to failure of both. To take an alternator off the synchronising busbar, press its ISOLATE button.

Before flight, the synchronisation and isolation, together with the real and reactive load sharing, of all four alternators must be checked. For take-off, the AAPP is connected to the synchronising busbar and is normally closed down at 20,000 feet. If the climb is continued, No 4 alternator is connected to the synchronising busbar but, for low level flight or descent below 20,000 feet, No 3 alternator is substituted for No 4 on the synchronising busbar. On airfield recovery, the AAPP is connected to the synchronising busbar at 5000 feet.

CSDU Tolerances Although, in steady flight conditions, alternator frequences must be within 400 ± 4 Hz and the real load sharing of alternators in parallel must be within ± 3 kW, transient deviations are permissible in the circumstances quoted below:

a. CHANGE OF ENGINE SPEED. During engine acceleration and deceleration (including taxying and ground running conditions) frequency deviations of up to ± 30 Hz are permissible. With alternators paralleled, these may also cause real load swings outside the normal load sharing limits. Recovery to normal conditions should be accomplished within 2 seconds of completing the engine speed change.

b. LOAD SWITCHING. When load switching, frequency deviations of up to ± 30 Hz are acceptable. Recovery to normal should be within 2 seconds on completion of load switching.

c. RANDOM LOAD OSCILLATIONS. With a new CSDU, low system load or low CSDU oil temperature, random load oscillations between paralleled alternators are permissible up to ± 2 kW beyond the normal variation. These oscillations are erratic, of a low frequency and normally in opposition to each other (one alternator taking up the load shed by another); the oscillations should not occur at full system load conditions.

Ram Air Turbine A ram air turbine (RAT) in the underside of the port air intake can be lowered into the airstream to provide power for electrical services in an emergency. The RAT drives a 22 kVA alternator which supplies 3-

phase, 200V 400 Hz to the synchronising busbar. No protective features are included. The electrical supplies should not be used below 20,000 feet.

When the pilot pulls the RAT release toggle, a Bowden cable operated bomb slip releases the RAT into the airstream and, at the same time, all the non-essential loads are shed automatically. A function of the non-essential loads being shed is that a cartridge start is preselected for the AAPP. Also, a circuit is made to provide RAT field initiation from the vital busbar to ensure a rapid build-up of alternator voltage. The RAT should be ready to supply the loads within 2 seconds; to maintain its output, speed must be maintained above 0.85M or 250 knots (0.88M optimum) at higher altitudes and suitably adjusted during descent to lower altitudes. The output can be checked on the alternator control panel either by pressing the RAT TEST pushbutton or, if the RAT is on the synchronising busbar, by reading the voltage and frequency direct from the synchronising busbar meters.

The RAT output cannot be connected to the synchronising busbar unless No 2 alternator A breaker is open, the RAT voltage is above 180 volts and there is no supply on the synchronising busbar. The RAT is automatically disconnected from the synchronising busbar if No 2 alternator of the AAPP is brought on line.

Once the RAT has been released, it cannot be retracted again in flight. However, in the event of over-voltage when the RAT is in use, a RAT FIELD switch, NORMAL (mid)/OFF (down), is fitted at the AEO's panel 10P by Mod 2503. Selection to OFF energises the coil of relay RL3 in the voltage control protection unit (VCPU), which connects the RAT field to earth and reduces the RAT voltage output to near zero.

Airborne Auxiliary Power Plant (AAPP) The AAPP consists of a gas turbine driving a 40 kVA alternator in a bay immediately aft of the starboard wheelbay. It can provide a 200V supply for use in emergency or for use on the ground when an external power unit is not available. On the ground, an air-bleed facility may be used for air ventilated suits.

The AAPP supplies 200V 400Hz, 3-phase AC as a standby electrical supply and may be connected to any individual busbar via the synchronising busbar. Attempts must not be made to start the AAPP above 30,000 feet. During an electrical emergency involving the use of the RAT, the AAPP must be started and connected to the synchronising busbar above 20,000 feet.

Automatic protection is provided against line-to-earth faults and field overload.

The AAPP may be started electrically or by a cartridge. Whenever the non-essential services are tripped, either by operation of microswitches as the RAT is released or by selection of the NON-ESSENTIAL SUPPLIES TRIP/RESET switch to TRIP, a cartridge start is pre-selected for the AAPP. Following RAT release, the non-essential services may be RESET, in which case the electrical method of starting the AAPP is restored. Cartridge starting of the AAPP must not be used on the ground.

SECONDARY POWER SUPPLIES

Secondary Power Supplies, General The secondary power supplies required to operate the aircraft equipment are provided by transformer rectifier units, transformers and frequency changers, all fed from the primary 200 volt AC busbars.

The controls and indicators for the main secondary supplies are grouped on the secondary supplies panel (50P), which embodies a mimic diagram.

115 Volt, 3-Phase, 400 Hz Four transformers supply 115 volt, 3-phase, 400 Hz power: an NBS transformer (1kVA); a standby artificial horizon transformer (40VA) and two main transformers (each 3kVA) which supply the remainder of the 115 volt, 400 Hz services. The two main transformers are above panels 27P and 28P on the front wall of the bomb bay; the NBS transformer is on the port side of the nosewheel bay and the standby artificial transformer is adjacent to panel 75P in the cabin.

Each main transformer normally supplies its own services but, if one transformer fails, its loads are automatically transferred to the other transformer. Two ON/OFF/COUPLE switches on 50P control the transformers and indications are provided by two three-position magnetic indicators, adjacent to the switches. When the transformers are ON and serviceable, the indicators show line continuity. If one transformer fails and automatic coupling takes place, or if COUPLE is selected, its indicator shows discontinuity. When automatic coupling has taken place, select manual COUPLE in order to disconnect the 200 volt input from the failed transformer. When OFF is selected, the loads have no supply and the indicator shows crosshatch.

The NBS transformer is fed from No 1 or No 4 200 volt busbar, depending on whcih 1600 Hz frequency changer is supplying the NBS.

115 Volt, Single-Phase, 1600 Hz Two rotary 3kVA frequency changers provide the 1600 Hz supplies. All loads are normally fed from No 2 frequency changer, with No 1 switched off. No 1 frequency changer is used if No 2 fails. The frequency changers are on the port side of the nosewheel bay.

Each frequency changer is controlled by START and STOP pushbuttons on 12P and individual magnetic indicators show black normally and white if a failure occurs. A FREQUENCY CHANGER FAILURE switch, mounted centrally on 12P, enables the loads of a failed machine to be transferred to the serviceable frequency changer. When No 1 FAIL is selected the 1600 Hz supply for the NBS is taken from No 2 frequency changer and the NBS transformer input is transferred from No 4 busbar to No 1 busbar.

28 Volt DC Four busbars, interconnected by fuses and circuit breakers, are used to distribute the 28 volt power from two 7.5 kW transformer rectifier units (TRU) whose outputs are paralleled, either being capable of supplying the total 28 volt system load. The TRU are one on each side of the nosewheel bay.

The 28 volt loads are supplied from battery, vital, essential and non-essential busbars. The battery busbar is connected directly to the positive terminal of the battery, the only loads being the AAPP starter motor and the battery test socket. The vital busbar is supplied, via 30 amp fuses and diodes, from both the battery and essential busbars, and feeds those loads which must be guaranteed a supply at all times. The essential busbar obtains its supply from either the battery, via the battery isolation contactor, the normal 28 volt plug from the GPU or the 28 volt TRU. The loads connected to this busbar are those required for the safe flying of the aircraft. The non-essential busbars are fed via the port and starboard load shedding contactors from the essential busbar. These loads are not essential to the safe flying of the aircraft but without them the aircraft cannot fulfil its operational role.

An additional 0.75 kW TRU provides ripple free 28 volt DC supplies for the cartridge discharger. A POWER, ON/OFF switch is on the selector control unit at the AEO's station.

A 24 volt 40 amp/hour type K2 (nickel cadmium) battery, located on the starboard side of the nosewheel bay, is connected to the battery busbar but supplies the vital busbar at all times via a fuse and diode. When the battery switch is put to ON (50P), the battery busbar is connected to the essential busbar for limited general use and for battery charging.

The controls for the 28 volt system are on the secondary supplies panel (50P) and consist of two guarded ON/OFF/RESET switches for the TRU and a guarded ON/OFF switch, which is spring-loaded to the centre position, for the battery. Ammeters are provided in the lines. Three-position indicators between the essential and non-essential busbars show continuity between these busbars normally, show discontinuity when automatic load shedding (either by release of RAT or operation of the TRIP/RESET switch) has taken place and show override (continuity on background of cross-hatch) when RESET is selected after RAT release. The non-essential TRIP/RESET switch on 10P sheds and restores the non-essential loads independently of RAT operation.

It must be remembered that 28 volt DC is required for the operation of all contactors and relays for AC services. The TRU and battery, once switched ON, should be left on for the duration of the flight. Only in the case of a double TRU failure should they be switched OFF, as directed by the Flight Reference Cards.

When the RAT handle is pulled and the RAT lowered into the slipstream, micro-switch contacts trip the load shedding contactors. All non-essential loads are then shed. To regain these loads, reference to the FRC must be made and all non-essential loads physically switched off. Following this procedure prevents shock loads to the aircraft electrical system.

Failure of 28 Volt TRU If one of the TRU fails in flight, the other TRU supplies the 28 volt services satisfactorily.

If both TRU fail, all the aircraft DC loads are taken by the battery and, unless immediate action is taken to reduce them, the battery only lasts for an extremely short period. With all possible DC loads shed, the battery should last for approximately 30 minutes. Therefore, if a landing is not possible within this period, the battery must be switched off.

The drill given in the Flight Reference Cards must be actioned immediately.

112 Volt DC 112 volt DC for the H2S scanner is supplied through a TRU. The supply to the TRU is controlled automatically when the H2S is brought into operation. The TRU is in the roof of the scanner compartment.

External Power Supplies

200 Volt AC Ground Power Units For ground servicing and aircraft generation purposes, a 60 kVA diesel driven or electrical ground power unit (GPU) may be plugged into the aircraft. The 6-pin snatch-disconnect plug is in the port wing root. During a scramble, the socket is snatched out by the initial forward movement of the aircraft.

With American type ground power units, the GPU contactor is closed by a pushbutton adjacent to the 6-pin ground supply plug on the aircraft.

The external supply from the GPU may be disconnected from the aircraft system by pressing the extra supplies trip button on 10P, by pressing the AAPP ON button, or by pressing the stop button on the GPU. The 200 volt ground supply is automatically isolated from each main busbar when its alternator is switched on. Alternators cannot be synchronised until the ground supply is disconnected from the synchronising busbar. A phase sequence unit to protect against incorrect phase sequence of GPU supplies is fitted.

If the GPU supply fails, it must not be reconnected until all those services which were being supplied by the GPU have been physically switched off, otherwise fuses in the distribution network may rupture, necessitating a comprehensive check of this fuse sytem.

28 Volt DC Ground Supply A 28 volt, quick-disconnect ground supply plug is in the port wing root, angled rearwards. This supply feeds all ground service lighting, all normal 28 volt services and, if the battery switch is ON, charges the battery. During a scramble, the socket is snatched out by the initial forward movement of the aircraft.

For ground refuelling only, a separate 28 volt supply may be plugged in on the starboard side of the nose. This isolates the ground refuelling circuits from the normal 28 volt system, which remains de-energised during refuelling.

An aircraft earthing point, for use during refuelling and ground servicing (but not during undercarriage retraction tests) is provided in the nosewheel bay and a snatch-disconnect earthing point is in the wing root.

115 Volt Supplies

a. 115 Volt,. 3-phase 400 Hz

(1) Port main transformer

Vital, Essential and Non-Essential Loads

Vital loads
(supplied direct from battery)
Engine fire extinguishers
Fuel tank fire extinguishers
LP fuel cocks
Battery isolation
Crash switches
Engine relighting
28 volt DC control
RAT excitation
AAPP control circuits
Pressurisation control
Emergency door opening
Cabin decompression
Abandon aircraft sign
Crew escape lights
Panel 9P illumination

Battery busbar loads
AAPP starter motor
Battery test socket

Essential loads
(remaining after RAT has been lowered)
PFC motors (except rudder auxiliary)
PFC warning
Artificial feel and trimmers
Autostabilisers
Nos 1 and 2 fuel pumps, port and starboard
Fuel pressure warning, crossfeed cocks
RT1, RT2
HF, IFF/SSR
Intercom
MFS and standby artificial horizon
General instruments
Pressure-head heating control
Windscreen wipers
Pressurisation warning horn and lights
Cabin lighting
Fire detection and warning
Battery charging
28 volt DC control
115 volt 400 Hz control
Bomb jettison, bomb doors
Undercarriage operation, indication and nosewheel steering
Tail parachute
Canopy and entrance door warning
AAPP indication, sump and cartridge heaters, cartridge start and 200 volt AC controls
Gold film, low heat
Engine fire-warning test
Air-to-air refuelling
RPM governor
Navigation and anti-collision lights
Vibration unit for Mk 29B altimeter

Non-essential loads
(shed by operation of RAT or by AEO)
External lighting, except navigation and anti-collision lights. (Non-essential cabin lighting to be switched off if restoring loads).
Air temperature indication
Pressurisation underheat control, bomb bay conditioning and temperature indication
Ventilated suits
Ground refuelling, fuel transfer pumps, flowmeter selection, fuel contents and nitrogen
*Bomb bay fuel pumps (if fitted). Fuel tank pressurisation, hold-off supply
*Wing tank fuel pumps and sequence timers
Autopilot
*ILS
VG recorder and fatigue meter
Airbrakes (switch corresponding to airbrakes position before restoring loads)
Hydraulic power pack
Rudder auxiliary motor
Alternator failure warning
Frequency changers
Wing and engine anti-icing control
Normal engine starting
ADF, sextant heater, air mileage unit
Radar altimeter Mk 6A
*Bomb gear, NBS, HRS, Doppler, ECM, tail warning, calculator type 7, window launching
*Ration heaters
*Tacan
*TFR
*Radio altimeter Mk 7B
Gold film, medium and high heat
*Auxiliary AVS and face blowers
Tail skid proximity warning lights

**These loads must be selected OFF manually before restoring non-essential loads.*

Bomb fusing and release
NBS (TAS unit)
Autopilot
Port MFS (port compass, port gyro vertical, port comparator, variation setting unit)
U/V lighting
JPT limiters (Nos 1 and 4 engines)
Oil pressure gauges (Nos 1 and 2 engines)
Fire detection (port wing and fuselage tanks)
Radio altimeter Mk 7B
Autostabilisation (mach trimmer, pitch and yaw dampers)
ADF
Vibration unit for Mk 19F altimeter
IFF/SSR (blower motor only)

(2) STARBOARD MAIN TRANSFORMER
Bomb fusing and release
De-icing
Fluorescent lighting
Cabin heating (magnetic amplifier)
Starboard MFS (stbd compass, stbd gyro vertical, stbd comparator, variation setting unit, computer)
Tacan
JPT limiters (Nos 2 and 3 engines)
Oil pressure gauges (Nos 3 and 4 engines)
Fire detection (stbd wing and bomb bay tanks)
Fuel flowmeters
IFF (fan supplies)
Autostabilisation system (as for port transformer)
(3) NBS TRANSFORMER
H2S
NBC
HRS
GP16
GSR

(4) STANDBY ARTIFICIAL HORIZON TRANSFORMER
Standby artificial horizon

b. 115 VOLT, SINGLE-PHASE, 1600 Hz
(1) NO 1 FREQUENCY CHANGER
NBC
H2S
(2) NO 2 FREQUENCY CHANGER
Radar altimeter
Periscope heater

c. 115 VOLT, SINGLE-PHASE, 400 Hz
Mk 30 A altimeter

DC Supplies

a. 28 VOLT DC
NBS, calculator type 7, bomb gear and bomb jettison
Radio altimeters Mks 6A and 7B, radio compass, ILS, Tacan
IFF/SSR, RT1, RT2, intercom
Window launchers, tail warning, ECM
MFS, TASU, VG recorder and fatigue meter.
Pressure-head heater control
Artificial feel, trimmers, PFC warning, autostabilisers
Autopilot
General instruments, fuel contents, LP cocks, crossfeed cocks, fuel pressure warning
JPT gauges
AAPP gauges
Bomb bay cold air valve, cabin heating, pressurisation and warning
De-icing, de-misting, windscreen wipers
Red flood and white lighting, external lighting
Ration heaters
Tail parachute, UC operation, indication and nosewheel steering
Canopy and entrance door warning
Relighting, AAPP starting, fire extinguishers, crash switches
Load shedding, relays, battery charging and isolation, frequency changer excitation
F95 camera
Vibration unit for Mk 29B altimeter

b. 112 VOLT DC
H2S scanner

PART 22: ICE PROTECTION

A thermal anti-icing system provides protection for the leading edges of the wings and for the engine air intakes. Hot air from the engines and cold air from individual intakes are mixed and pass along the inside of the skin and are then exhausted to atmosphere.

In the engine, thermal anti-icing is provided for the compressor entry guide vanes, intake struts and bullet by means of hot air from the HP compressor through an on/off electrically-operated valve. This anti-icing air exhausts into the LP compressor on 200 series engines and overboard on 301 engines.

Gold film heating is provided for the pilots' windscreen.

The air intake for the ECM air scoop has an electrically powered anti-icing system for the vapour cycling cooling pack (VCCP).

ANTI-ICING SYSTEMS

Airframe Anti-icing System Hot air, branched from each half of the supplies to the cabin heating system, is fed to a hot air valve at the root of each wing. An electrically-operated flap varies the area of the cold air intakes below each engine air intake to control the amount of cold air mixed with the hot air. The mixed air is passed along ducts inside the skin, round the engine air intake leading edges and separator, and along the leading edge of the wing.

The heating air from the engine air intakes is exhausted through an electrically-operated extractor flap on the lower skin of the air intake, while the air from the wing duct flows rearwards through the wing, to exhaust through a louvre on the underside of the outer wing.

An overheat switch operates at 165 ± 5°C to close the hot air valve. When the ducting temperature drops to 160°C, the hot air valve returns to its original setting.

Fin Anti-icing System Fin anti-icing is inoperative, apart from the temperature gauge used to detect any hot air leak.

Anti-icing Controls The anti-icing controls are grouped together on a panel at the rear of the starboard console. One group is for the port wing and engines and one for the starboard wing and engines. The 'fin anti-icing' switch controls the heating for the ECM ram air intake via two operative positions, *ON* (outboard) and *OFF* (centre). The ECM intake heater must not be used for more than 60 seconds on the ground and must always be selected ON when the airframe system is switched on. Anti-icing controls include:

a. An *AUTO/OFF/MANUAL* double pole switch.

b. A temperature gauge, reading from 0 to 200°C.

c. A manual heat control switch, labelled INC/DEC, spring-loaded to the central neutral position.

The thermal anti-icing system is designed to prevent the formation of ice and must, therefore, be switched on before entering icing conditions, whenever icing conditions are anticipated or forecast, or if a rapid build-up of ice is seen on the windscreen or windscreen wipers. The system must be used for 301 engines before and during flight in cloud even if there is no visual evidence of icing. The wing system must not be used on the ground, except during take-off and on the landing run. The *ENGINE AIR* switches must be *OPEN* before hot air can be supplied to the airframe systems.

a. With the *AUTO/OFF/MANUAL* switch at *AUTO*, the hot air valve is under the control of a wing leading edge temperature sensing element set to maintain a skin temperature of 10°C, and the cold air intake and extractor flaps move to the fully open position. After a 10 second thermal delay, the cold air intake flap is placed under the control of a duct sensor set to maintain a duct temperature of 150°C.

b. When *MANUAL* is selected, the cold intake and extractor flaps open fully. The manual heat control switch must first be held to INC until the temperature reaches 140 ± 5°C, and subsequently adjusted to maintain the correct temperature.

c. When *AUTO* or *MANUAL* is selected, engine anti-icing is also switched on, irrespective of *ENGINE AIR* switch settings. Engine anti-icing must be used on the ground in conditions of cold, damp weather (temperature +3°C or below *and* the humidity is 90% or more *or* it reduces visibility to less than 1000 metres).

Two separate guarded *ON/OFF* switches, one on either side of the manual heat control switches, enable engine anti-icing to be used when the wing anti-icing is not in use.

DE-ICING SYSTEMS

Windscreen De-icing System The pilots have gold film windscreen heating designed to operate at 40°C; an overheat control cuts off the electrical supply when the windscreen temper-

AIRFRAME ANTI-ICING SYSTEM

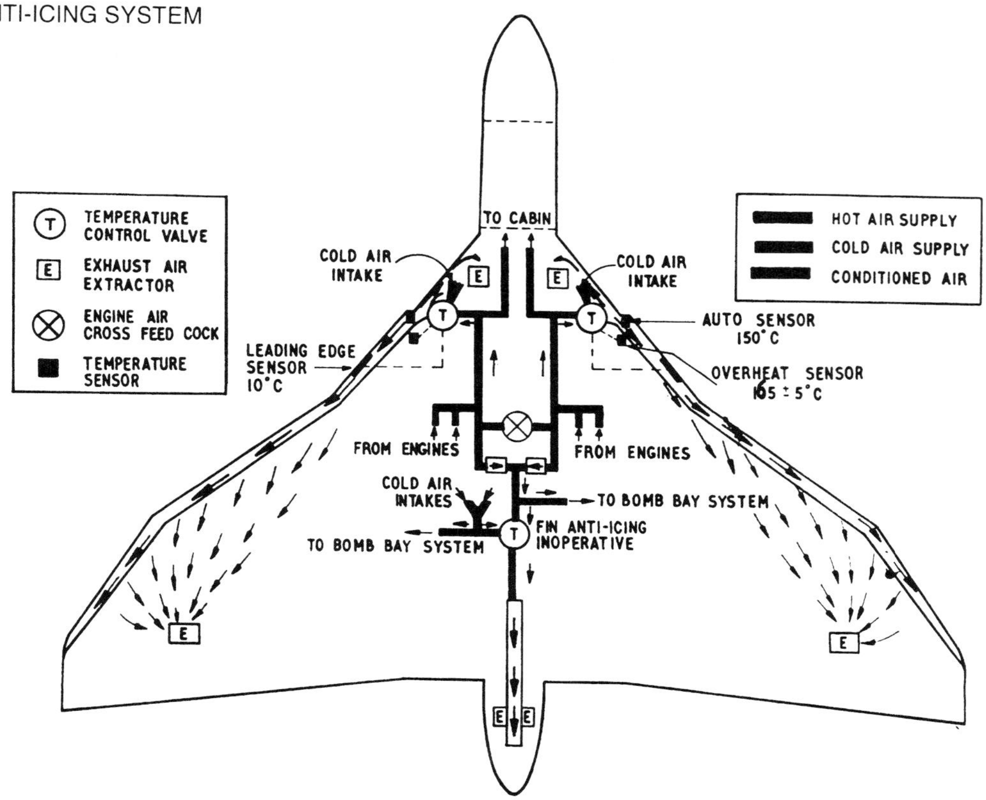

THERMAL DE-ICING INSTALLATION

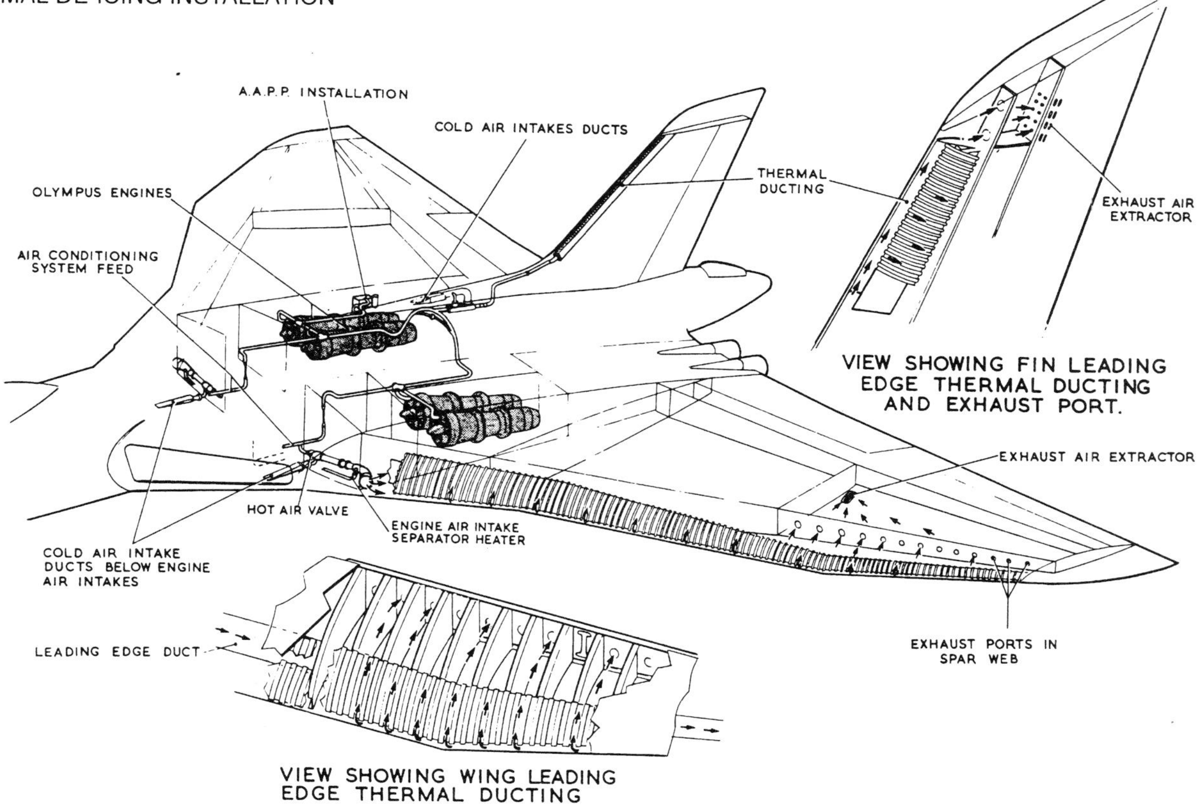

ature reaches 55° ± 5°C, and switches it on again when the temperature drops by 15°C.

a. A 3-position switch on the co-pilot's panel allows selection of three levels of heat: *LOW* (250 watts/sq ft), *MEDIUM* (500 watts/sq ft) and *HIGH* (750 watts/sq ft). A press-to-test warning light beside the switch gives warning of overheat. On the starboard console, three 3-position magnetic indicators, one for each windscreen, show *NORMAL* when the windscreen heating is operating satisfactorily, O/H when a windscreen is overheating and cross-hatch when windscreen heating is off or isolated. Isolation switches for individual windscreens are on the rear face of panel 4P (nav/radar position).

b. If the warning light comes on, switch off the appropriate isolation switch. Check that the magnetic indicator shows cross-hatch and that the light goes out.

c. If the windscreen is damaged (other than damage to the inner laminations) select *COMBAT* pressure immediately and *LOW* on the heat control. If overheat warning is also indicated, or if a higher setting is required on the serviceable screens, isolate the affected windscreen.

NOTE: When the ambient temperature exceeds +30°C, *HIGH* should be selected during the **Pre-Take-Off** checks and *MEDIUM* at the top of the climb, to prevent windscreen cracking.

Above: *An air sampling pod attached to a Vulcan's port wing; unusually, the forward shroud is half-painted. The pods were reportedly manufactured from aircraft drop tanks (probably from Sea Vixens). The filter section is just visible inside the pod's intake. (British Aerospace)*

Refuelling Probe De-icing Provision for de-icing the refuelling probe may be in some aircraft but the system is inoperative and the controlling switch must be off at all times.

ELECTRICAL SUPPLIES

Electrical Supplies The anti-icing system uses 115V AC from port and starboard main transformers and 28V DC. The de-icing systems are 28V DC and 200V AC from No 2 busbar. If load shedding occurs, the supplies to the anti-icing are cut off and gold film reverts to low heat.

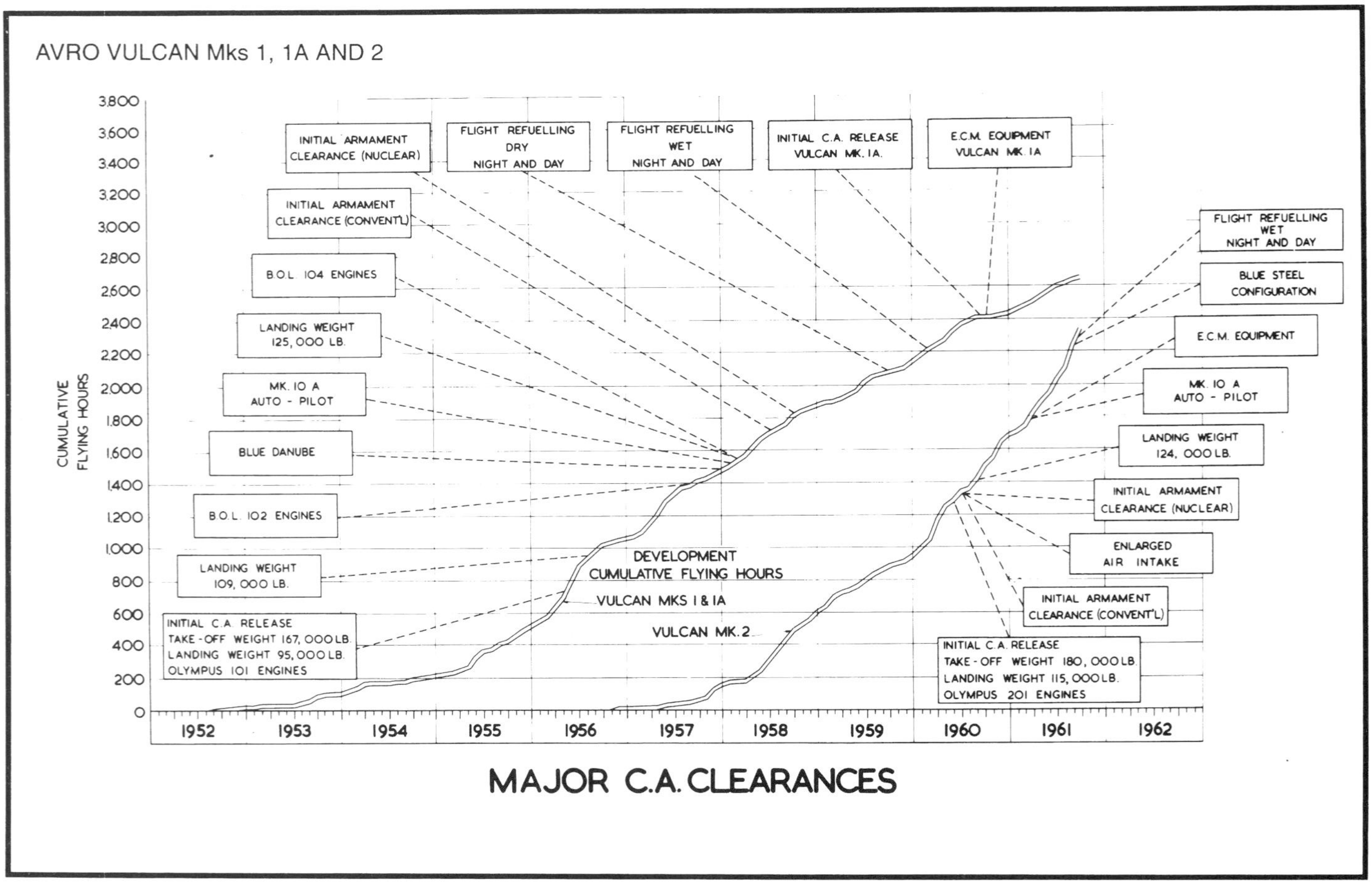

ENGINE AND FUEL SYSTEM CONTROLS

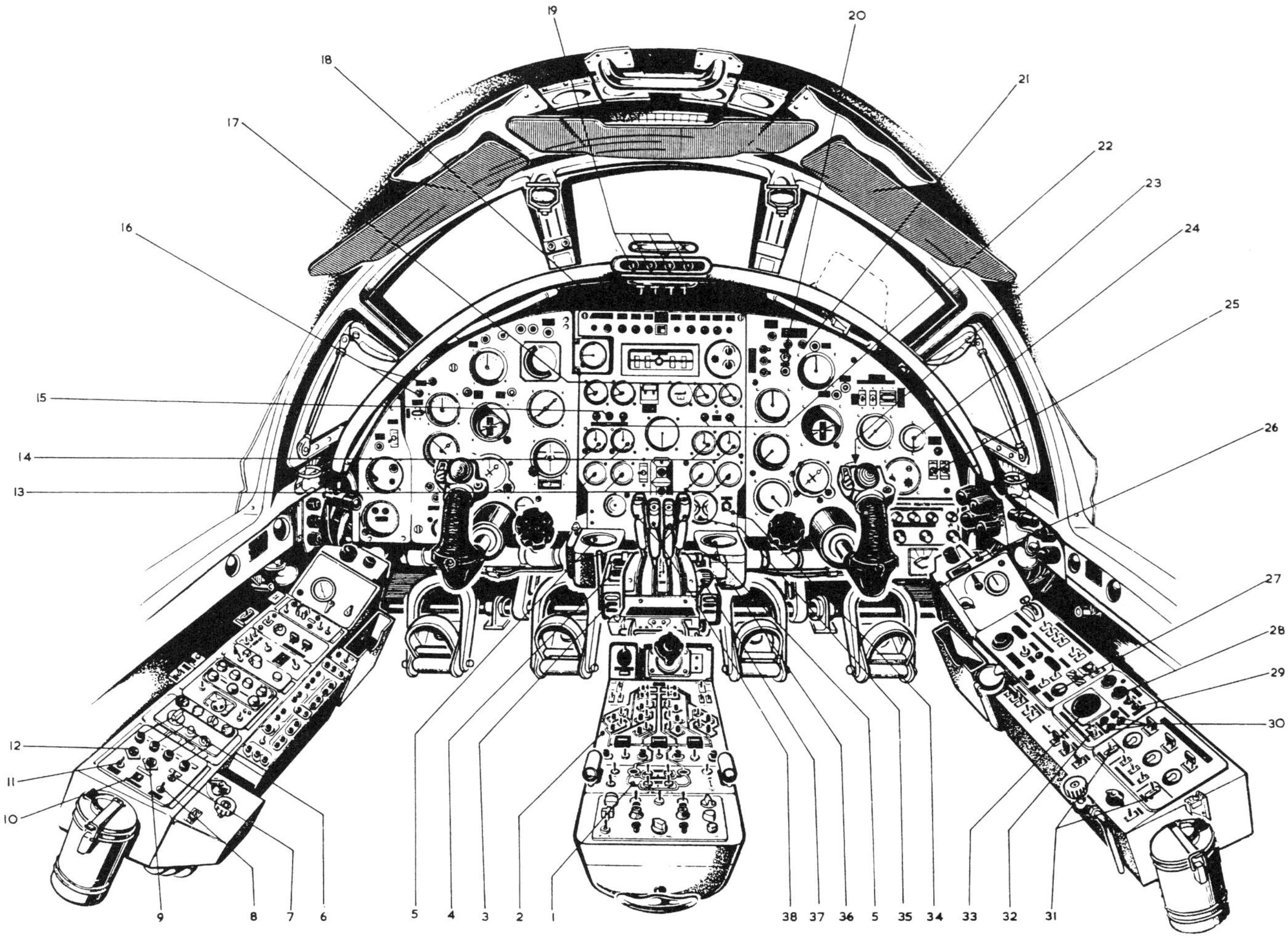

1. BOMB BAY TANKS system control panel.
2. FUEL SYSTEM control panel (Refer to Sect.4, Chap.2).
3. Jet pipe temperature limiter switch (guarded).
4. R.P.M. governor switch (guarded).
5. FUEL TANK CONTENTS panel. Houses four contents gauges (Refer to Sect.4, Chap.2).
6. Individual engine start press switches. PRESS AND RELEASE to start engine.
7. NORMAL/RAPID start selector (lift toggle to select).
8. ON/OFF MASTER switch.
9. Simultaneous RAPID start push button.
10. AIR CROSS-FEED indicator.
11. IGNITION ON/OFF switch.
12. GYRO HOLD-OFF press switch.
13. OIL PRESSURE gauges.
14. Engine R.P.M. indicators.
15. R.P.M. governor indicator - BLACK take-off – WHITE cruise.
16. AUTO-THROTTLE failure indicators. (inoperative).
17. ENGINE TEMPERATURE indicators.
18. L.P. fuel cock switches (guarded). forward - ON, rearward - OFF.
19. Engine FIRE indicator/operating switches. Illuminate RED when engine temperature becomes excessive; press to operate, pull to test filament.
20. FUEL FIRE warning indicator - BOMB BAY TANKS.
21. FUEL FIRE warning indicator - FUSELAGE AND WING TANKS.
22. FUEL LOW PRESSURE WARNING indicators.
23. TOTAL FUEL FLOW indicator.
24. FUEL FLOW indicator. Indicates rate of flow for any engine when relevant switch is selected on fuel control panel.
25. FUEL FLOW indicator switch.
26. TEST switch-flight idling detent, spring-loaded to OFF (Sect.4, Chap.1A).
27. FLIGHT REFUELLING PRESSURE gauge.
28. NITROGEN PURGE - flight refuelling.
29. TANK PRESSURISATION switch.
30. TANK PRESSURE indicators.
31. ENGINE ANTI-ICING system control switches (guarded)
    Forward switch - PORT ENGINE
    Aft switch - STARBOARD ENGINE.
32. MASTER SWITCHES (2), flight refuelling ON/OFF.
33. TANKS FULL INDICATOR - flight refuelling.
34. FUEL C. of G. indicator switch.
35. FUEL C. of G. indicator.
36. T.F.R. RESET switch PRESS to break.
37. Throttle friction adjuster.
38. Throttle control levers - Re-light press switch in handles.

NAVIGATIONAL, SIGNALLING AND LIGHTING EQUIPMENT

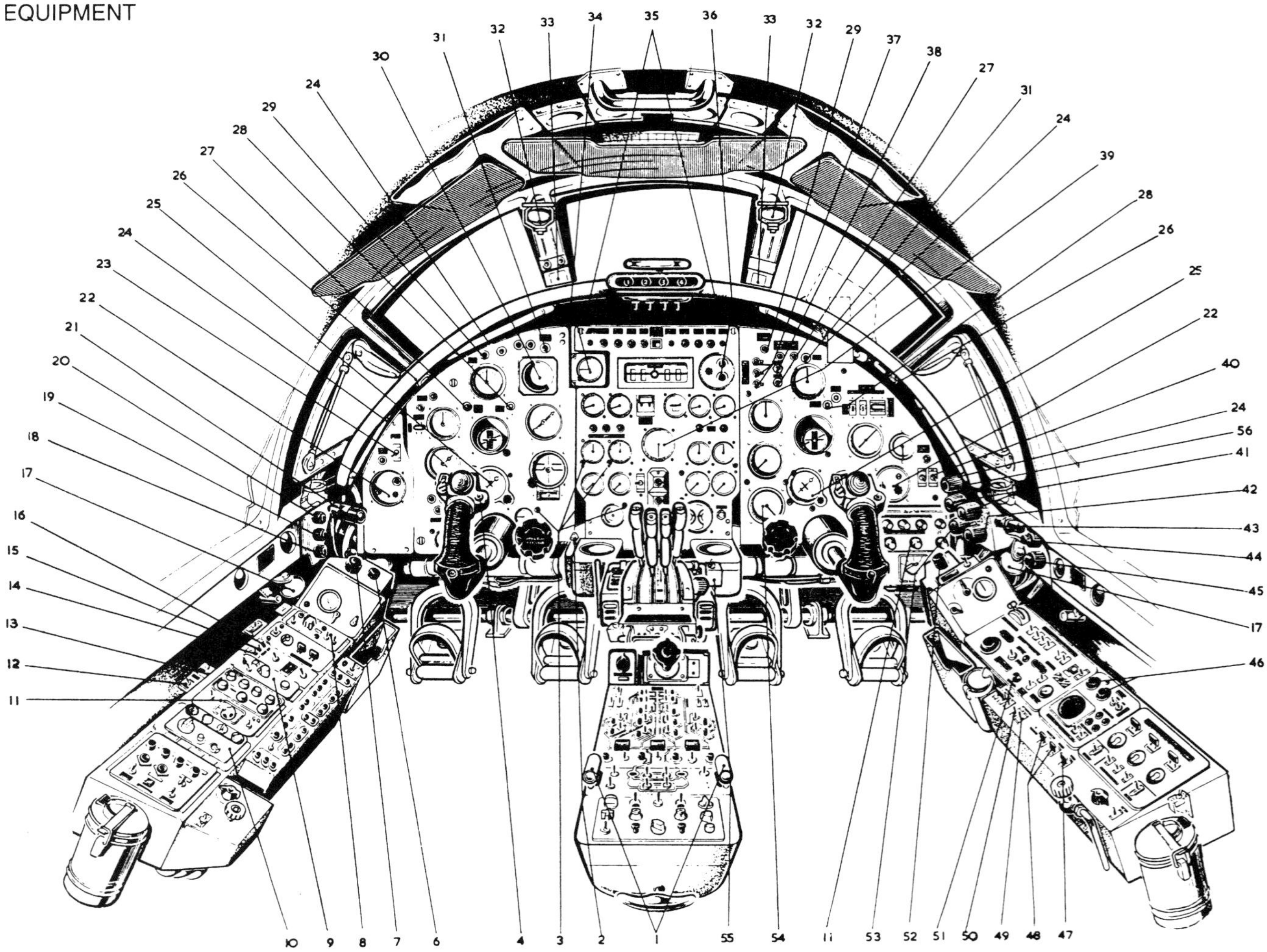

NAVIGATIONAL

5. DELETED
8. CONTROL UNIT TYPE 10695 (A.R.I. 23061).
9. CONTROL UNIT PART NO.T6654 (A.R.I.5959).
14. AUDIO – I.L.S. TACAN A.D.F. CHANGEOVER SWITCH.
22. ANNUNCIATOR UNIT – M.F.S.
25. BEAM COMPASS.
27. T.F.R. VIDEO INDICATOR (A.R.I. 5959).
28. T.F.R. FAIL INDICATOR (A.R.I.5959).
29. T.F.R. WARNING INDICATOR (A.R.I. 5959).
30. ALTITUDE AND AUTO-LAND PHASE INDICATOR.
31. I.L.S. MARKER LAMP (A.R.I.18011).
32. E.2.B. COMPASS.
33. HEAD UP INDICATOR (A.R.I.5959).
34. ACCELEROMETER.
36. M.F.S. SELECTOR UNIT.
37. SELECTED ALTITUDE INDICATOR LAMPS.
    Top – AMBER – above selected altitude.
    Centre – GREEN – selected altitude.
    Bottom – RED – below selected altitude.
38. SELECTOR SWITCH.
    Up – M.F.S.
    Down – T.F.R.
39. TACAN INDICATOR.
54. A.D.F. BEARING COMPASS.
55. READ-OUT HEADING SELECTOR SWITCH.
    Forward – H.R.S.
    Rearward – M.F.S.

SIGNALLING

4. INTERCOMM. PRESS-TO-TRANSMIT SWITCH.
10. CONTROL UNIT 5821-99-942-8543 (A.R.I.18124).
11. INTERCOMM. CONTROL UNIT.
12. R./T.1 TONE SWITCH.
    Forward – ON.
    Rearward – OFF.
13. AUDIO WARNING PRESS-TO-TEST SWITCH.
15. R./T.2 TONE SWITCH.
    Outboard – ON
    Inboard – OFF.
16. AERIAL CHANGEOVER SWITCH.
    Outboard – R./T.1 UPPER.
    Inboard – R./T.2 UPPER.

LIGHTING

1. RED FLOOD LAMPS.
2. ON/OFF SWITCH – HIGH-INTENSITY ANTI-DAZZLE LAMPS.
3. PILLAR LAMPS (TYPICAL LOCATION)
6. DIMMER SWITCH – U./V. LAMPS.
7. DIMMER SWITCH – U./V. LAMPS FOR OXYGEN PANELS.
17. U./V. LAMP.
18. DIMMER SWITCH – FIRST PILOT'S KNEE PAD LAMP.
19. DIMMER SWITCH – E.2.B. COMPASS LIGHT.
20. DIMMER SWITCH – PILOTS' PANEL PILLAR LIGHTS.
21. FIRST PILOT'S KNEE PAD LAMP.
23. ON/OFF SWITCH – WHITE FLOOD LAMPS.
24. U./V. LAMPS.
26. RED FLOOD LAMPS.
35. HIGH INTENSITY ANTI-DAZZLE LAMPS.
40. ON/OFF SWITCH – WHITE FLOOD LAMPS.
41. DIMMER SWITCHES – RED FLOOD ON CENTRE CONSOLE.
42. DIMMER SWITCH – RED FLOOD ON STARBOARD CONSOLE.
43. SECOND PILOT'S KNEE PAD LAMP.
44. DIMMER SWITCH – SECOND PILOT'S KNEE PAD LAMP.
45. DIMMER SWITCH – E.2.B. COMPASS LIGHT.
46. DIMMER SWITCHES – PROBE ILLUMINATION LAMPS.
47. STEADY/FLASH SWITCH – NAVIGATION LIGHTS.
48. LANDING LIGHT SWITCHES – PORT AND STARBOARD – RETRACT, LANDING TAXI.
49. IDENT. LIGHT SWITCH – STEADY, MORSE.
50. EXTERNAL LIGHT SWITCH.
51. DIMMER SWITCH – U./V. LIGHTS.
52. DIMMER SWITCH – U./V. LIGHT-OXYGEN PANEL.
53. DIMMER SWITCH – RED FLOOD ON STARBOARD COAMING.
56. DIMMER SWITCH – S.F.O.M. GUNSIGHT AND PILLAR LAMP.

FLYING CONTROLS AND INSTRUMENTS

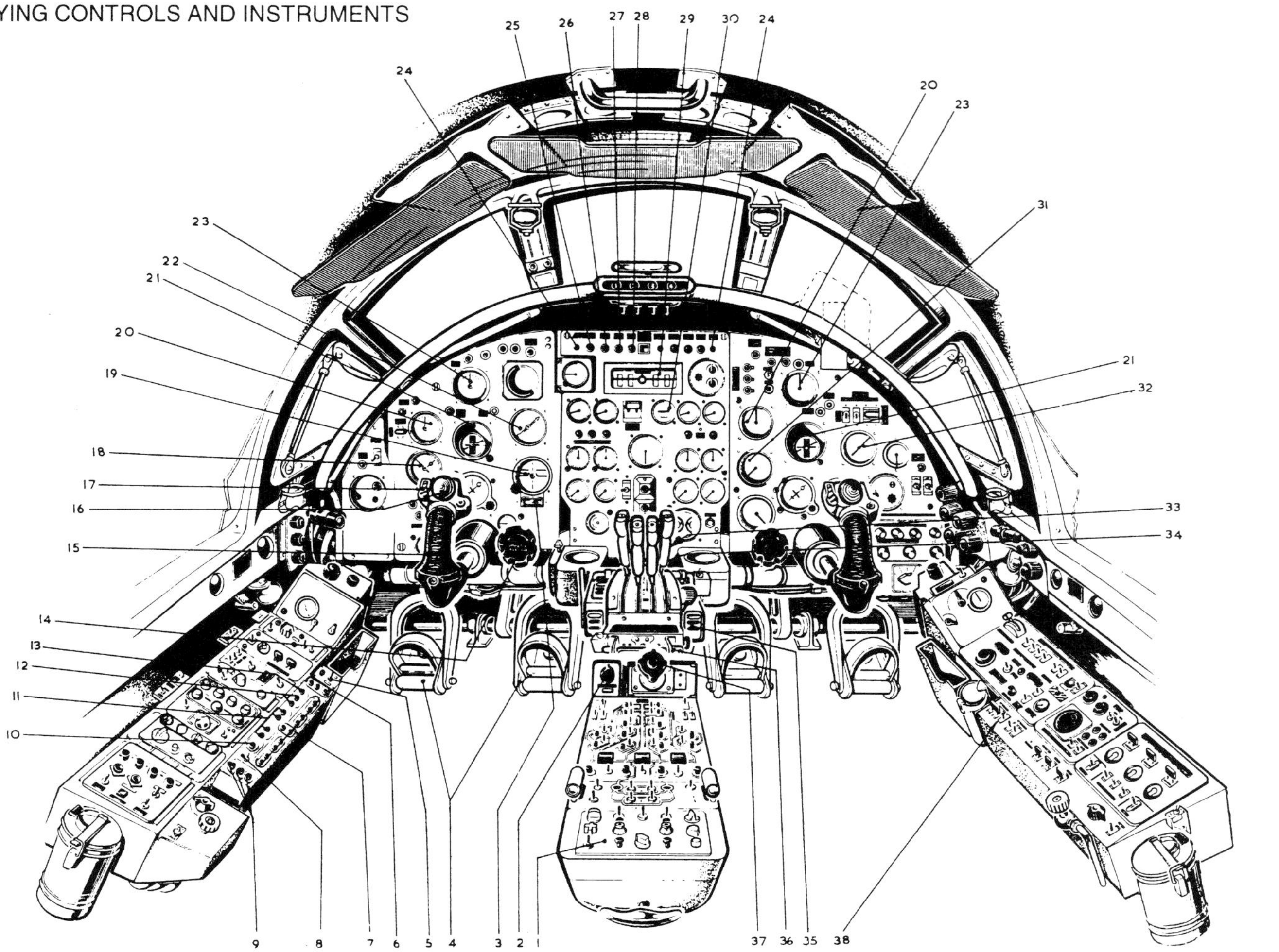

CONTROLS - MANUAL

4. Rudder pedals - incorporating brake master cylinders.
14. Adjuster - rudder pedals.
15. Control handle - elevons.

CONTROLS AND INDICATORS - ELECTRICAL

5. FEEL RELIEF system isolation lock-in switch and indicator. Switch labelled NORMAL-LOCK.
6. ARTIFICIAL FEEL Failure indicator/push switches. Illuminate AMBER when failure occurs. PRESS to isolate failed unit.
7. P.F.C. MOTOR - failure indicator/push switches. Illuminate AMBER for motor failure. PRESS to isolate failed motor.
8. YAW DAMPER - 2 position toggle switch.
   No.1 - rearward - No.1 system engaged.
   No.2 - forward - No.2 system engaged.
9. P.F.C. START - Groups start push switches.
   A. push to start outboard elevon units.
   R. push to start rudder main unit.
   E. push to start inboard elevon units.
10. COMPARATOR RESET - push to reset.
11. PITCH DAMPER - failure indicator push switches. Illuminate AMBER when failure occurs. PRESS to disengage failed system.
12. AUTO-mach - TRIM - individual channel indicators. Illuminate BLUE when failure occurs. PRESS to disengage.
13. AUTO-mach-TRIM - indicator push/pull switch. Illuminates AMBER when failure occurs.
    PUSH to disengage.
    PULL to engage.
16. Elevon trim - 4-way double-pole switch. Operate in natural sense.
17. ARTIFICIAL FEEL RELIEF cut-out switch (guarded). PRESS to disengage system.
24. MAIN WARNING system indicators. Illuminate AMBER for flying control system or unit failure.
25. P.F.C. UNIT failure - magnetic doll's eye indicator.
    BLACK - normal functioning.
    WHITE - displayed when faulty unit is disengaged. Remains white to remind pilot that fault exists after 24 (amber) is extinguished.
26. ARTIFICIAL FEEL failure - magnetic doll's eye indicator.
    BLACK - normal functioning.
    WHITE - displayed when fault occurs in system. Remains white to remind pilots that fault exists after 24 (amber) is extinguished.
27. AUTO-STABILISERS - system failure magnetic doll's eye indicator.
    BLACK - normal functioning.
    WHITE - displayed when fault occurs in system. Remains white to remind the pilots' that fault exists when 24 (amber) is extinguished.
28. AIR BRAKES - magnetic doll's eye indicator.
    BLACK - airbrakes IN.
    WHITE - airbrakes OUT.
33. RUDDER FEEL RELIEF - push switch.
    Press to disengage system.
34. RUDDER FEEL TRIM switch.
    P - lift - trims rudder to port.
    S - right - trims rudder to starboard.
35. AIR BRAKES EMERGENCY switch (guarded)
    UP - NORMAL
    Down - EMERGENCY - energises stand-by motor.
36. AIR BRAKES selector switch (with locking bar).
    UP - IN - air brakes stowed in main plane.
    Centre - MEDIUM DRAG - partial extension of pillars with slats at 35 deg.
    Down - HIGH DRAG - full extension of pillars with slats at 80 deg.
37. EMERGENCY TRIM control
    Press to energise - operate in natural sense.
38. AUTO-PILOT RESET SWITCH (Mod. 2305,2306). Operate to reset d.c. supply.

INSTRUMENTS AND INDICATORS

1. AUTO-PILOT control panel
2. AUTO-PILOT control
3. SIDE SLIP indicator
18. ALTIMETER Mk.19
19. ARTIFICIAL HORIZON (stand-by)
20. AIR SPEED INDICATOR
21. DIRECTOR HORIZON (Beam and G.P.).
22. RATE OF CLIMB INDICATOR
23. MACHMETER
29. CONTROL SURFACE INDICATOR
30. AUTO PILOT TRIM INDICATOR
31. 100,000 ft. ALTIMETER
32. CLIMB AND DESCENT INDICATOR

MISCELLANEOUS CONTROLS AND EQUIPMENT - CREW STATIONS (BLUE STEEL ROLE)

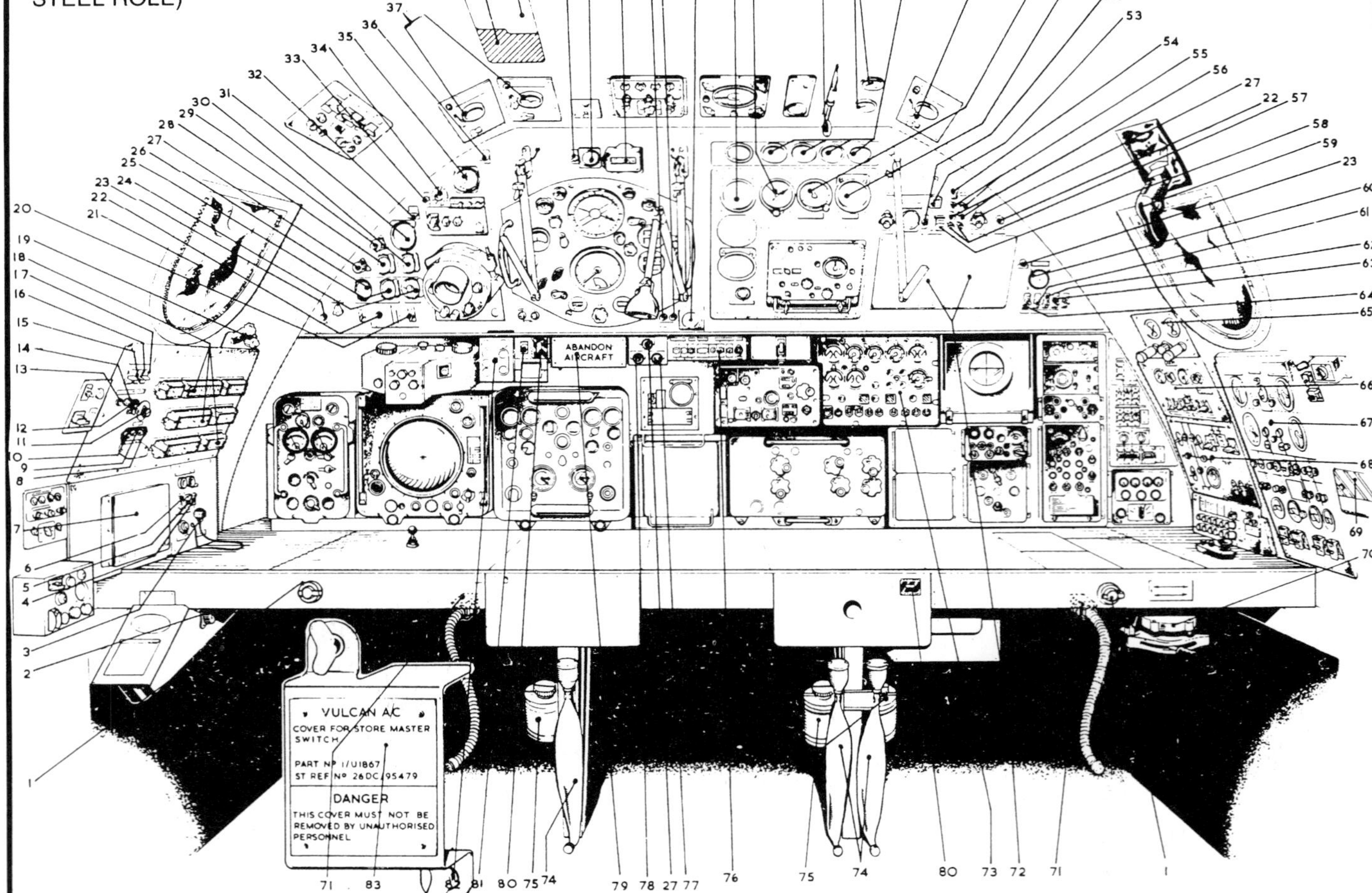

1. A.V.S. MANUAL TEMPERATURE CONTROL
2. DIMMER SWITCH - PANEL PILLAR LIGHTS
3. BOMB FIRING SWITCH
4. SWITCH - LIGHT AT AIR BOMBER'S PRONE POSITION
5. BOMB RELEASE SWITCH
6. BOMB DOORS SWITCH
7. MOUNTING PANEL FOR E.Q. CONTROL UNIT
8. PRESS TO TEST INDICATOR - OVERRIDE BREAK UP
9. PRESS TO TEST INDICATOR - COMMAND BREAK UP
10. PRESS TO TEST INDICATOR - SHUTTERED DETONATOR
11. DIMMER SWITCH - E.Q. PANEL LIGHT
12. D.C. SUPPLIES SWITCH - SINGLE POLE, GUARDED
13. RELEASE PRESSURE INDICATOR - ILLUMINATES AMBER - PRESS TO TEST
14. STORE GONE INDICATOR - ILLUMINATES AMBER
15. E.Q. POWER SUPPLIES EMERGENCY OVERRIDE - DOUBLE POLE SWITCH, GUARDED
16. ON/OFF SINGLE POLE SWITCH - RELEASE UNIT HEATER
17. BOMB SELECTOR SWITCH, BALLISTIC - POWER - DOUBLE POLE-GUARDED
18. FUSE BLOCK
19. DIMMER SWITCH AND LAMP
20. STORE HEATING CONTROL
21. ANTI-FLASH SCREEN
22. WARNING INDICATOR - LOSS OF CABIN PRESSURE
23. OXYGEN PRESSURE INDICATOR
24. STORE EXCHANGER OUTLET TEMPERATURE SELECTOR
25. STORE BAY TEMPERATURE SELECTOR
26. STORE ENGINE TEMPERATURE GAUGE
27. DIMMER SWITCH - CHARTBOARD LIGHTS
28. STORE BAY TEMPERATURE GAUGE
29. DIMMER SWITCH - PANEL LIGHTS
30. STORE-EXCHANGER OUTLET TEMPERATURE SELECTOR
31. BOMB BAY TEMPERATURE INDICATOR
32. BOMB BAY HEATING CONTROL SWITCH
33. BOMB BAY HEATING MANUAL CONTROL SWITCH
34. BOMB BAY TEMPERATURE SELECTOR
35. N.B.S. AIR SUPPLY PRESSURE INDICATOR
36. N.B.S. AIR SUPPLY ON/OFF SWITCH
37. OXYGEN REGULATORS
38. ACCESS DOOR - STORE RELEASE HANDLE
39. ACCESS DOOR - SAFETY LOCK REMOVAL HANDLE
40. H.2.S. PRESSURISATION ON/OFF SWITCH
41. H.2.S. PRESSURE GAUGE
42. AIR NAUTICAL MILES COUNTER
43. OXYGEN 'ON' INDICATOR
44. COMPASS DEVIATION CARD HOLDER
45. AIR SPEED INDICATOR
46. ALTIMETER
47. CABIN DECOMPRESSION HANDLE
48. OXYGEN PRESSURE GAUGES
49. FUEL CONTENTS GAUGES - NO.1, 2, 3 & 4 ENGINE
50. FORWARD THROW INDICATOR
51. OUTSIDE AIR TEMPERATURE INDICATOR
52. FIN GAP DOORS SWITCH - NORMAL
53. FIN GAP DOORS - MAGNETIC INDICATOR
54. REFRIGERATION HEATER ON/OFF SWITCH
55. E.P.C.U. START PUSH SWITCH & PRESS TO TEST INDICATOR
56. START/STOP PUSH SWITCH - A/C HYDRAULIC UNIT
57. START/STOP PUSH SWITCHES - A/C REFRIGERATION
58. FIN GAP DOORS EMERGENCY SWITCH-GUARDED
59. SIGNAL PISTOL
60. E.C.M. COOLANT TEMPERATURE INDICATOR
61. CABIN LIGHT SWITCH
62. BELOW TABLE LIGHT SWITCH
63. PERISCOPE HEATER SWITCH
64. PORT ROOF LIGHT SWITCH
65. C.S.D.U. OIL TEMPERATURE GAUGES WITH DIMMER SWITCH AND LAMPS
66. A.A.P.P. CONTROL PANEL - 70P (SECTION 6, CHAP.5)
67. ALTERNATOR CONTROL PANEL - 10P (SECTION 6, CHAP.2)
68. SECONDARY SUPPLIES PANEL - 50P (SECTION 6, CHAP.4)
69. TIME DELAY EMERGENCY JETTISON PANEL
70. PERISCOPE CONTROL HANDLE
71. A.V.S. FLOW CONTROL
72. WINDOW LAUNCH AND/OR TELEMETERING CONTROL PANEL
73. STORE CONTROL PANEL - OPERATING & MONITORING
74. SANITARY CONTAINERS
75. RATION HEATERS
76. STARBOARD ROOF LIGHT SWITCH
77. DIMMER SWITCH - STORE PANEL LIGHT
78. DIMMER SWITCH - INSTRUMENT PANEL LIGHT
79. ABANDON AIRCRAFT SIGN
80. EMERGENCY DOOR OPENING SWITCHES (2 OFF)
81. ANTI-DAZZLE LIGHTS SWITCH
82. WIND INDICATOR UNIT
83. COVER FOR STORE CONTROL SWITCHES

RADAR, RADIO AND ASSOCIATED EQUIPMENT - CREW STATIONS (BLUE STEEL ROLE)

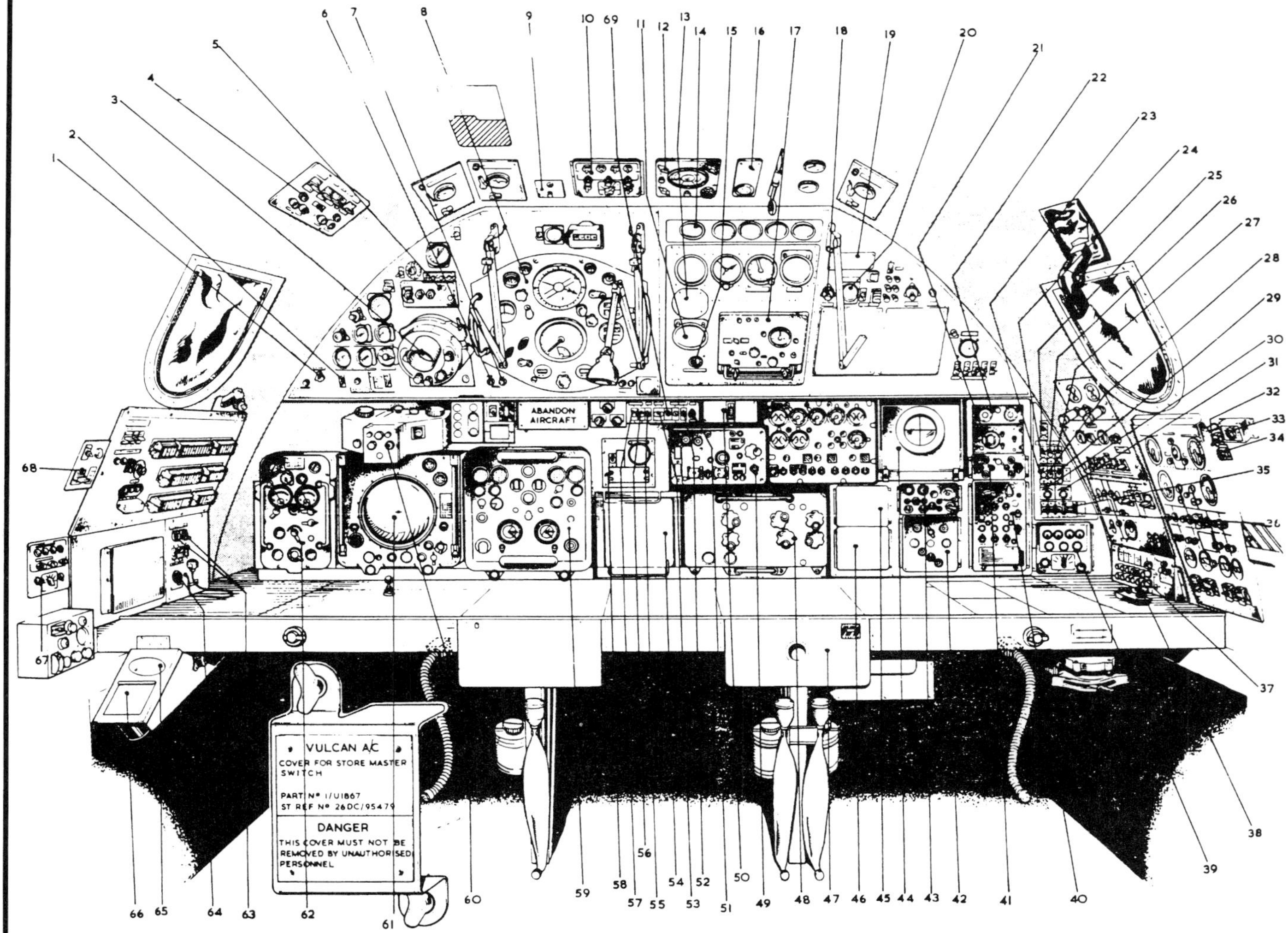

1. SCANNER STABILISATION SWITCH (A.R.I.5928)
2. SCANNER ROTATION CONTROL SWITCH (A.R.I.5928)
3. PULSE ALTIMETER
4. RADIO CONTROL PANEL 12P (SECT.6, CHAP.7)
5. TRUE AIRSPEED CONTROL PANEL
6. POWER SUPPLIES INDICATOR - N.B.C.
7. POWER SUPPLIES INDICATOR - H.2.S.
8. NAVIGATION PANEL
9. VARIABLE AIRSPEED UNIT
10. INTERCOMM. CONTROL PANEL - NAV./RADAR OP.
11. RADIO ALTIMETER
12. CONTROL UNIT, TYPE 1274 (A.R.I.23023)
13. COMPASS REPEATER - TRUE TRACK MAGNETIC HEADING
14. A.D.F. - D.F. BEARING INDICATOR (A.R.I.23023)
15. STEERING SIGNAL TEST SOCKET
16. LOOP CONTROLLER (A.R.I.23023)
17. TRACK CONTROLLER UNIT - M.F.S.
18. DIMMER SWITCH - AUTO LAND AND T.C.U. LIGHTS
19. CONTROL UNIT, TYPE 160501 (Inoperative when Mod.2263 embodied)
20. TEST METER (Inoperative when Mod.2263 embodied)
21. I.F.F. CONTROL UNIT (A.R.I.5848)
22. S.I.F. CONTROL UNIT (A.R.I.5848)
23. PRESS-TO-TRANSMIT SWITCH
24. H.F. SUPPLIES SWITCH (A.R.I.5874)
25. I.F.F. SUPPLIES SWITCH (A.R.I.5848)
26. H.F. OUTPUT SWITCH (A.R.I.5874)
27. A.D.F. SUPPLY SWITCH (A.R.I.23023)
28. CONFERENCE INTERCOMM. MASTER SWITCH
29. MONITOR - ALARM SWITCH (A.R.I.18105)
30. DIMMER SWITCH - CONTROL UNIT DIAL LIGHTING (A.R.I.18105 AND 18076)
31. DIMMER SWITCH - CONTROL UNIT DIAL LIGHTING
32. I.L.S. SUPPLY ON/OFF SWITCH
33. CONTROL UNIT TYPE 705
34. AUTO-THROTTLE ON/OFF SWITCH (Inoperative when Mod.2263 embodied)
35. INTERCOMM. MASTER CONTROL SWITCH
36. EXTERNAL INTERCOMM. SWITCHES
37. E.C.M. POWER SUPPLY CONTROL PANEL
38. MORSE KEY
39. INTERCOMM. CONTROL PANEL A.E.O.
40. CONTROL UNIT, TYPE 9422 (A.R.I. 18076)
41. CONTROL UNIT, TYPE 7812 (A.R.I. 18074)
42. CONTROL UNIT, TYPE 9562 (A.R.I. 18105)
43. CONTROL UNIT, TYPE 9456 (A.R.I. 18075)
44. INDICATOR UNIT, TYPE 6935 (A.R.I. 5919)
45. CONTROL UNIT, TYPE 7216 (A.R.I.5874) (Pre-Mod.2300) CONTROL TRANSMITTER/RECEIVER, TYPE M53 (A.R.I.23090) (Post Mod.2300)
46. CONTROL UNIT, TYPE 4189 (A.R.I.5874) (Pre-Mod.2300) ANTENNA CONTROL UNIT, Ref.10L 951 4615 (A.R.I.23090) (Post Mod.2300)
47. I.N. MONITORING UNIT
48. G.P.I. MK.6
49. I.N. CONTROL PANEL
50. SHORTING PLUG PLATE (A.R.I. 23023)
51. EVENT MARKER - PUSH SWITCH
52. RECORDER - ON/OFF SWITCH
53. ON/OFF SWITCH - GEE or (subsequent to MOD.1291) CONTROL UNIT, TYPE 7780)
54. INDICATOR CONTROL UNIT, TYPE 9869 (A.R.I.5972)
55. ON/OFF SWITCH - DOPPLER (A.R.I.5972)
56. COMPASS ISOLATION SWITCH (STBD.)
57. COMPASS ISOLATION SWITCH (PORT)
58. CONTROL UNIT TYPE 7750 (A.R.I. 18107/13)
59. CONTROL UNIT TYPE 585 (A.R.I.5928)
60. CAMERA TYPE RX.88 (A.R.I.5928)
61. INDICATING UNIT TYPE 301 (A.R.I. 5928)
62. CONTROL UNIT TYPE 595 (A.R.I. 5928)
63. N.B.C. ISOLATION INDICATORS
64. N.B.C. SIMULATOR SOCKET
65. BOMBING SELECTOR SWITCH
66. CONTROL UNIT TYPE 12580
67. INTERCOMM. CONTROL UNIT-NAV./AIR BOMBER
68. SIMULATED BOMBING PANEL
69. T.F.R. FAILURE WARNING LIGHT

MISCELLANEOUS CONTROLS AND EQUIPMENT - CREW STATIONS (FREE FALL ROLE)

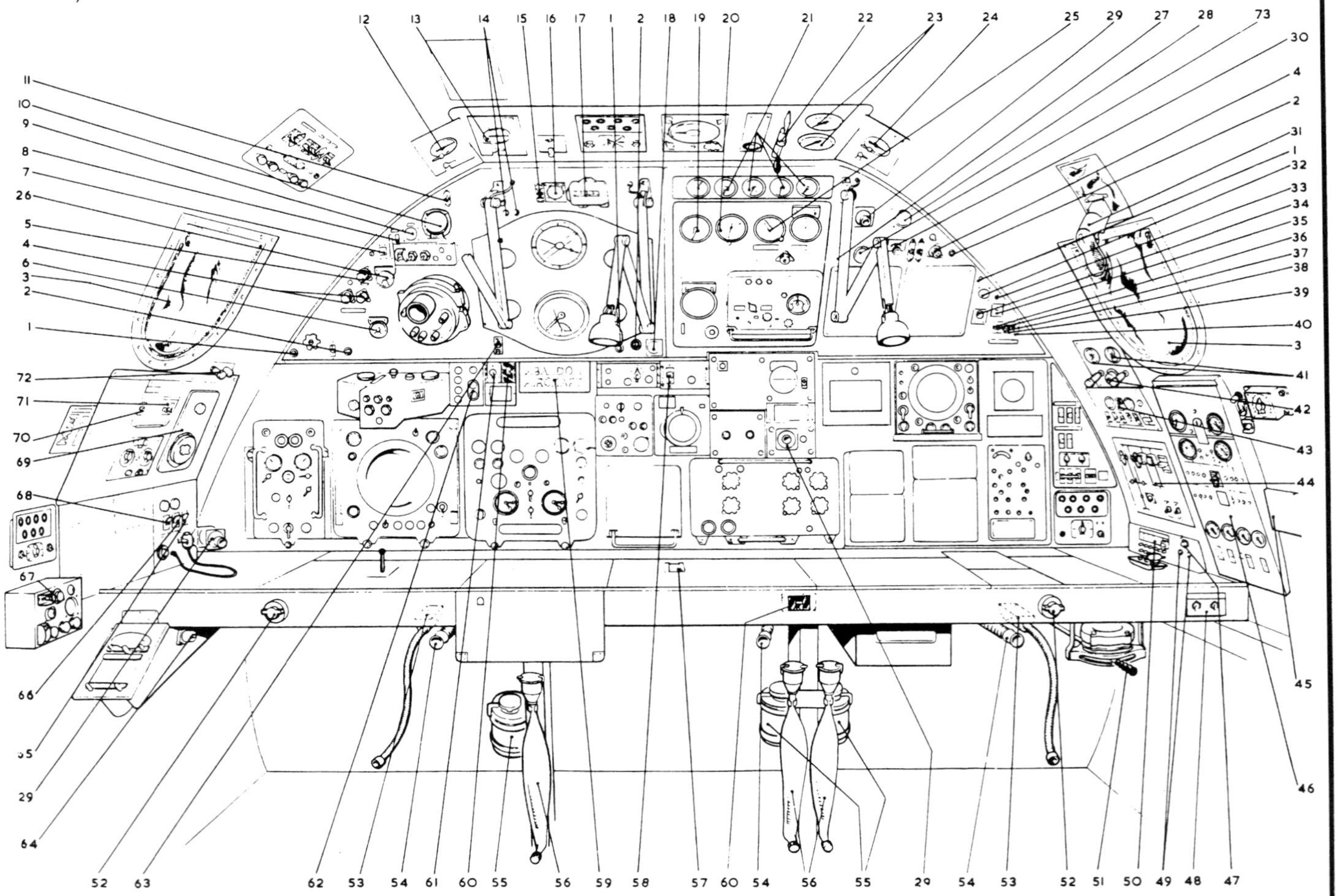

1. OXYGEN PRESSURE INDICATOR
2. LOSS OF PRESSURE WARNING LAMP
3. ANTI FLASH SCREEN
4. DIMMER SWITCHES CHARTBOARD LIGHTS
5. DIMMER SWITCH PANEL LIGHTS
6. BOMB BAY TEMPERATURE INDICATOR
7. BOMB BAY HEATING SWITCH - AUTO-OFF-MANUAL
8. MANUAL HEATING CONTROL SWITCH, INC, -OFF, -DEC.
9. BOMB BAY TEMPERATURE SELECTOR
10. N.B.C. AIR SUPPLY - DIFFERENTIAL PRESSURE GAUGE
11. N.B.C. PRESSURISATION CONTROL - ON/OFF SWITCH
12. OXYGEN REGULATOR - NAV/BOMBER
13. OXYGEN REGULATOR - NAV/RADAR OP.
14. N.B.C./H.2.S. SUPPLIES - BLACK WHITE DOLLS EYES
15. H.2.S. PRESSURISATION CONTROL SWITCH
16. H.2.S. PRESSURE GAUGE
17. AIR NAUT. MILES COUNTER
18. COMPASS DEVIATION CARD HOLDER
19. AIR SPEED INDICATOR
20. ALTIMETER MK.19F
21. FUEL CONTENTS GAUGE No.1, 2, 3 and 4 ENGINE
22. CABIN DECOMPRESSION HANDLE
23. OXYGEN PRESSURE INDICATORS
24. OXYGEN REGULATOR A.E.O.
25. FORWARD THROW INDICATOR
26. OUTSIDE AIR TEMPERATURE INDICATOR
27. DIMMER SWITCH – AUTO LAND INSTRUMENT LIGHTS
28. E.C.M. COOLANT TEMPERATURE GAUGE
29. PUNKAH LOUVRE
30. DIMMER SWITCH, INSTRUMENT PANEL
31. SIGNAL PISTOL
32. ELECTRO MAGNETIC COUNTER WINDOW INSTALLATION
33. WINDOW INSTALLATION SWITCH
34. SWITCH FATIGUE METER
35. R.B.W. CONTROL PANEL, LIGHTS – DIMMER SWITCH
36. STBD. ROOF LIGHT SWITCH
37. PORT ROOF LIGHT SWITCH
38. CABIN LIGHT SWITCH
39. UNDER TABLE LIGHT SWITCH
40. PERISCOPE HEATER SWITCH
41. OIL TEMPERATURE GAUGES C.S.D. UNITS
42. DIMMER SWITCH AND LIGHTS
43. A.A.P.P. CONTROL PANEL 70P (SECT.6)
44. SECONDARY SUPPLIES PANEL 50P (SECT.6)
45. BOMB TIME DELAY EMERGENCY JETTISON PANEL
46. ALTERNATOR CONTROL PANEL 10P
47. EXPLOSION PROTECTION RESET BUTTON (MOD.1744)
48. AUXILIARY A.V.S. SWITCHES
49. EXPLOSION PROTECTION INDICATOR LAMPS PORT AND STBD. (MOD.1744)
50. E.C.M. POWER SUPPLY PANEL
51. PERISCOPE CONTROL HANDLE
52. A.V.S. TEMPERATURE CONTROL
53. A.V.S. FLOW RATE CONTROL
54. AUXILIARY A.V.S. QUICK-RELEASE CONNECTOR
55. RATION HEATERS
56. SANITARY CONTAINERS
57. A.S.I. CORRECTION CARD HOLDER
58. CONTROL SWITCH (A.R.I.5972)
59. ABANDON AIRCRAFT SIGN
60. EMERGENCY DOOR OPENING SWITCHES (2 OFF)
61. ANTI-DAZZLE SWITCH
62. WIND INDICATOR UNIT
63. BOMB DOOR SWITCH
64. DIMMER SWITCH PANEL PILLAR LIGHTS
65. LIGHT SWITCH – AIR BOMBER'S PRONE POSITION
66. BOMB RELEASE SWITCH
67. CAMERA CONTROL UNIT TYPE 551
68. BOMB DOOR CONTROL SWITCH
69. BOMB SPACING UNIT PANEL
70. LIVE JETTISON SWITCH
71. V.T. FUZING SWITCH
72. DIMMER SWITCH AND PANEL LIGHT
73. REMOTE FATIGUE INDICATOR, TYPE M2372

RADAR, RADIO AND ASSOCIATED EQUIPMENT - CREW STATIONS (FREE FALL ROLE)

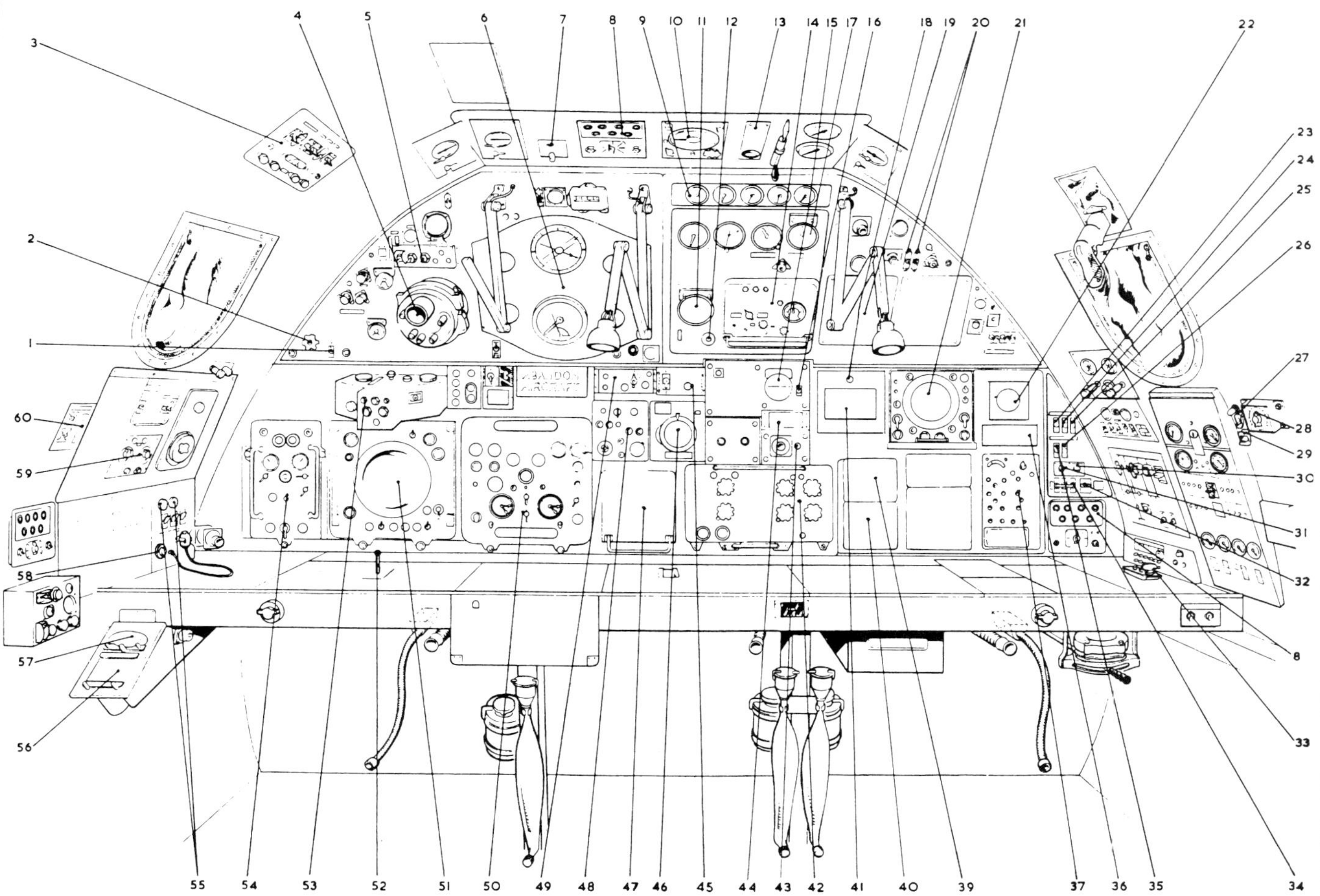

1. SCANNER STABILISATION SWITCH (A.R.I.5928)
2. SCANNER ROTATION CONTROL SWITCH (A.R.I.5928)
3. PULSE ALTIMETER
4. RADIO SWITCH PANEL
5. CONTROL PANEL – TRUE AIR SPEED
6. POWER SUPPLIES INDICATOR – N.B.C.
7. POWER SUPPLIES INDICATOR – H.2.S.
8. NAVIGATION PANEL
9. VARIABLE AIRSPEED UNIT
10. COMPASS ISOLATION SWITCH (PORT)
11. COMPASS ISOLATION SWITCH (STBD.)
12. ON/OFF SWITCH (A.R.I.5972)
13. CONTROL UNIT (A.R.I.23023)
14. D.F. BEARING INDICATOR (A.R.I. 23023)
15. COMPASS – REPEATER – TRUE TRACK MAGNETIC HEADING
16. LOOP CONTROLLER (A.R.I.23023)
17. RADIO ALTIMETER
18. STEERING SIGNAL TEST SOCKET
19. TRACK CONTROLLER UNIT – M.F.S.
20. DIMMER SWITCH – AUTO LAND AND T.C.U. LIGHTS
21. PILOTS DIRECTION INDICATOR
22. WINDOW LAUNCH OR TELEMETERING CONTROL PANEL
23. FAIL INDICATOR (A.R.I.23134/5/4)
24. TEST POINT (G.P.I. Mk.6)
25. INDICATOR, TYPE 6935 (A.R.I.5919)
26. INDICATOR, TYPE 17171 (A.R.I. 18228/1)
27. SUPPLIES SWITCH (A.R.I.5874)
28. OUTPUT SWITCH (A.R.I.5874)
29. SUPPLY SWITCH (A.R.I.23023)
30. PRESS-TO-TRANSMIT SWITCH
31. CONFERENCE INTERCOMM. – MASTER SWITCH
32. ON/OFF SWITCH (A.R.I.18011)
33. CONTROL UNIT, TYPE 705 (A.R.I. 18011)
34. AUTO-THROTTLE ON/OFF SWITCH (Inoperative)
35. DIMMER SWITCH – CONTROL UNIT DIAL LIGHTING
36. DIMMER SWITCH – CONTROL UNIT DIAL LIGHTING (A.R.I.18076)
37. INTERCOMM. MASTER CONTROL
38. EXTERNAL INTERCOMM. SWITCHES
39. MORSE KEY
40. INTERCOMM. CONTROL UNIT (A.E.O.)
41. CONTROL UNIT, TYPE 17172 (A.R.I. 18228/1)
42. CONTROL UNIT, TYPE 9422 (A.R.I. 18076)
43. DELETED (Mod.2501)
44. BLANKING PLATE
45. CONTROL TRANSMITTER/RECEIVER TYPE M53 (A.R.I.23090)
46. ANTENNA CONTROL UNIT, (A.R.I. 23090)
47. CONTROL UNIT, TYPE 16929 (A.R.I. 23134/5/4)
48. NOT ALLOCATED
49. GROUND SPEED SELECTOR UNIT
50. H.R.U. POWER FAILURE INDICATOR
51. G.P.I. MK.6
52. NAV. HEADING UNIT (H.R.S.)
53. H.R.S. CONTROL UNIT
54. EVENT MARKER PUSH SWITCH
55. RECORDER – ON/OFF SWITCH
56. FAILURE WARNING LIGHT (A.R.I. 5959)
57. INDICATOR CONTROL UNIT, TYPE 9869 (A.R.I.5972)
58. CONTROL UNIT, TYPE 7750 (A.R.I. 18107/13)
59. CONTROL UNIT, TYPE 585 (A.R.I. 5928)
60. CONTROL UNIT, TYPE 626 (A.R.I. 5928)
61. INDICATING UNIT, TYPE 301 (A.R.I. 5928)
62. CAMERA, TYPE RX.88 (A.R.I.5928)
63. CONTROL UNIT, TYPE 595 (A.R.I. 5928)
64. N.B.C. ISOLATION INDICATORS
65. CONTROL UNIT, TYPE 12580
66. BOMBING SELECTOR SWITCH
67. N.B.C. SIMULATOR SOCKET
68. BOMBING SELECTOR PANEL
69. SIMULATED BOMBING PANEL

MISCELLANEOUS CONTROLS AND EQUIPMENT - CREW STATIONS

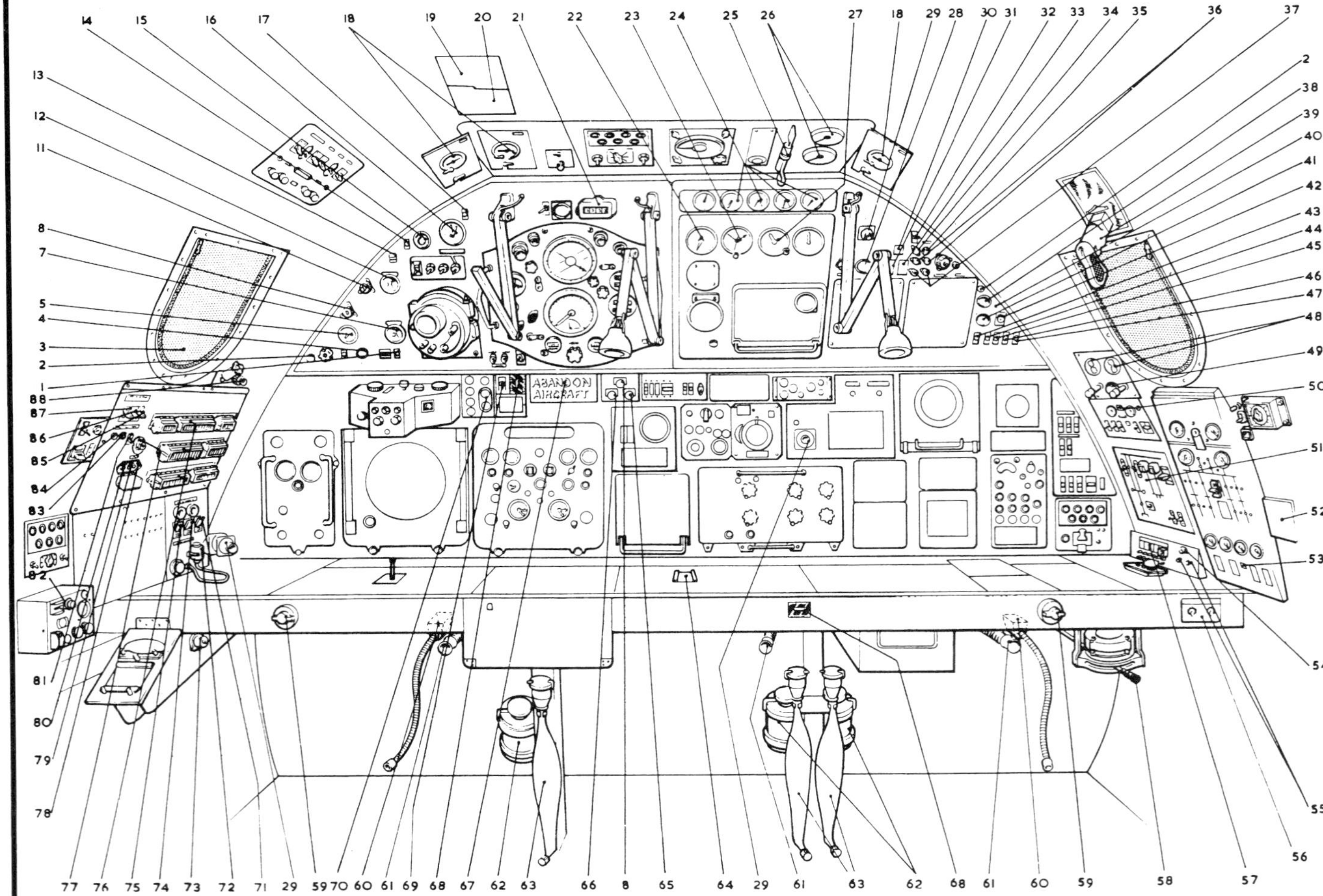

1. STORE HEATING CONTROL
2. OXYGEN PRESSURE INDICATOR
3. ANTI-FLASH SCREEN
4. LOSS OF CABIN PRESSURE WARNING LAMP
5. STORE ENGINE TEMPERATURE GAUGE
6. DELETED
7. OUTSIDE AIR TEMPERATURE INDICATOR
8. DIMMER SWITCH – CHARTBOARD LIGHTS
9. DELETED
10. DELETED
11. DIMER SWITCH PANEL LIGHTS
12. BOMB BAY TEMPERATURE INDICATOR
13. BOMB BAY HEATING CONTROL SWITCH
14. BOMB BAY HEATING MANUAL CONTROL SWITCH
15. BOMB BAY TEMPERATURE SELECTOR
16. N.B.C. AIR SUPPLY PRESSURE INDICATOR
17. N.B.C. AIR SUPPLY ON/OFF SWITCH
18. OXYGEN REGULATORS
19. ACCESS DOOR – STORE RELEASE
20. ACCESS DOOR SAFETY LOCK REMOVAL HANDLE
21. AIR NAUTICAL MILES COUNTER
22. AIR SPEED INDICATOR
23. ALTIMETER
24. FUEL CONTENTS GAUGES No.1, 2, 3 and 4 ENGINE GROUPS
25. CABIN DECOMPRESSION HANDLE
26. OXYGEN PRESSURE GAUGES
27. FORWARD THROW INDICATOR
28. REMOTE FATIGUE INDICATOR TYPE M2372
29. PUNKAH LOUVRE
30. FIN GAP DOORS - MAGNETIC IND.
31. FIN GAP DOORS - SWITCH - NORMAL
32. REFRIGERATION HEATERS SWITCH
33. FIN GAP DOORS - EMERGENCY SWITCH - GUARDED
34. E.P.U.C. START PUSH SWITCH
35. PRESS TO TEST INDICATOR
36. START/STOP PUSH SWITCHES - A/C HYDRAULIC UNIT
37. START/STOP PUSH SWITCHES - A/C REFRIGERATION
38. ELECTRO MAGNETIC COUNTER WINDOW INSTALLATION
39. SIGNAL PISTOL
40. WINDOW INSTALLATION SWITCH
41. E.C.M. COOLANT TEMPERATURE GAUGE
42. R.B.W. CONTROL PANEL LIGHTS SWITCH
43. FATIGUE METER - SWITCH
44. PORT ROOF LIGHT - SWITCH
45. CABIN LIGHT - SWITCH
46. BELOW TABLE - LIGHT SWITCH
47. PERISCOPE HEATER - SWITCH
48. C.S.D.U. OIL TEMPERATURE
49. DIMMER SWITCH WITH LIGHTS
50. A.A.P.P. CONTROL PANEL 70P
51. SECONDARY SUPPLIES PANEL
52. TIME DELAY EMERGENCY JETTISON PANEL
53. ALTIMETER CONTROL PANEL
54. EXPLOSION PROTECTION RESET
55. EXPLOSION PROTECTION INDICATOR LAMPS PORT AND STBD. (MOD.1744)
56. AUXILIARY A.V.S. SWITCHES
57. E.C.M. POWER SUPPLY CONTROL PANEL
58. PERISCOPE CONTROL HANDLE
59. A.V.S. TEMPERATURE CONTROL
60. A.V.S. FLOW RATE CONTROL
61. AUXILIARY A.V.S. QUICK-RELEASE CONNECTOR
62. RATION HEATERS
63. SANITARY CONTAINERS
64. A.S.I. CORRECTION CARD HOLDER
65. DIMMER SWITCH - STORE - PANEL LIGHT
66. DIMMER SWITCH - INSTRUMENT - PANEL LIGHT
67. ABANDON AIRCRAFT SIGN
68. EMERGENCY DOOR OPENING SWITCHES (2 OFF)
69. ANTI-DAZZLE LIGHT SWITCH
70. WIND INDICATOR UNIT
71. SWITCH-LIGHT AT AIR BOMBER'S PRONE POSITION
72. BOMB FIRING SWITCH
73. DIMMER SWITCH - PANEL PILLAR LIGHTS
74. BOMB RELEASE - SWITCH
75. BOMB DOORS - SWITCH
76. FUSE BLOCKS
77. DIMMER SWITCH E.Q. PANEL
78. PRESS TO TEST INDICATOR - OVERRIDE BREAK UP
79. PRESS TO TEST INDICATOR - COMMAND BREAK UP
80. PRESS TO TEST INDICATOR - SHUTTERED DETONATOR
81. D.C. SUPPLIES SWITCH - SINGLE POLE GUARDED
82. CAMERA CONTROL UNIT TYPE 551
83. STORE GONE INDICATOR ILLUMINATES AMBER
84. RELEASE PRESSURE INDICATOR - ILLUMINATES AMBER PRESS TO TEST
85. BOMB SELECTOR SWITCH BALLISTIC - POWER - DOUBLE POLE GUARDED
86. ON/OFF SINGLE POLE SWITCH - RELEASE UNIT HEATER
87. E.Q. POWER SUPPLIES EMERGENCY OVERRIDE - DOUBLE POLE SWITCH GUARDED
88. DIMMER SWITCH AND LAMP

RADAR, RADIO AND ASSOCIATED EQUIPMENT - CREW STATIONS

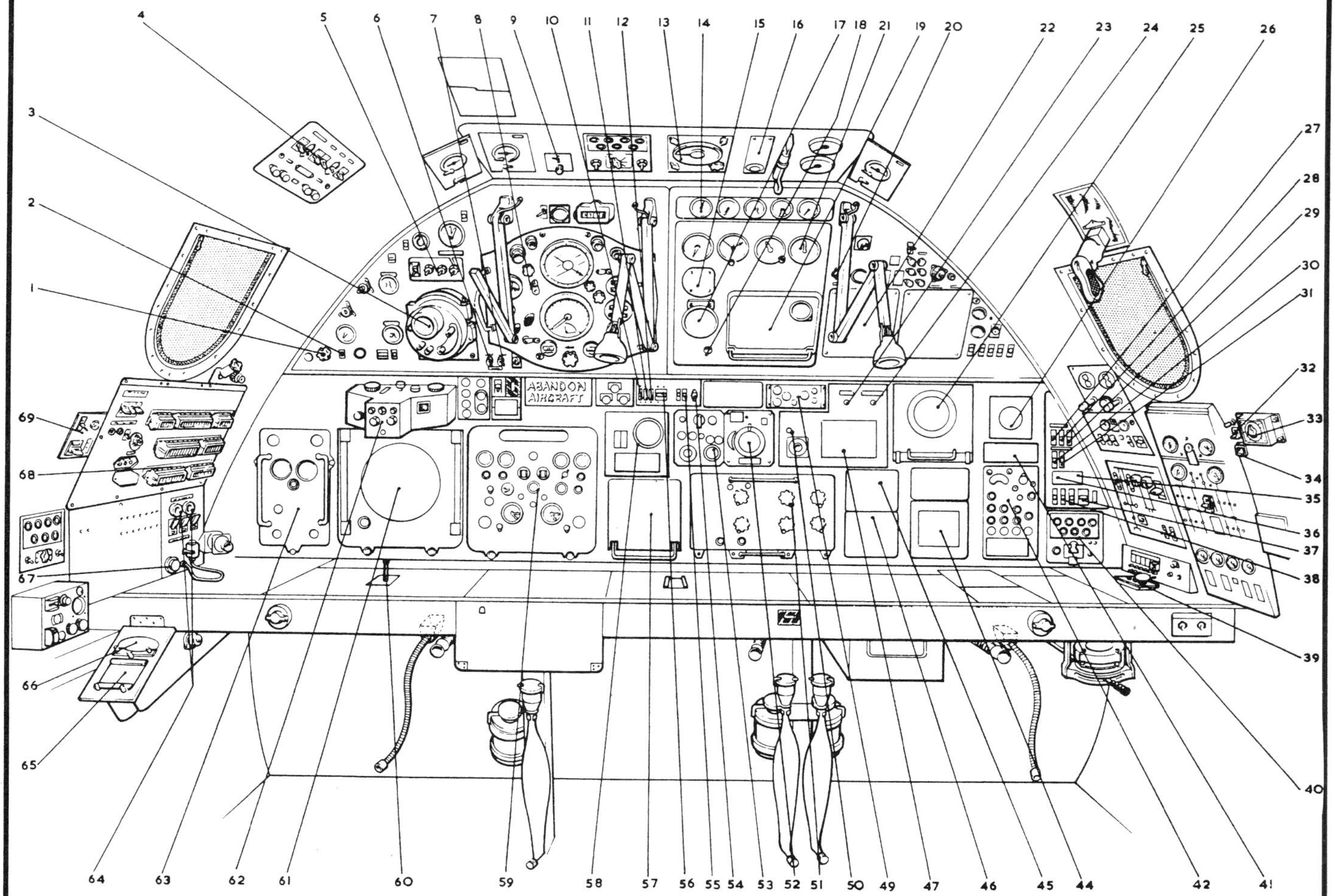

1. SCANNER STABILISATION SWITCH (A.R.I.5928)
2. SCANNER ROTATION CONTROL SWITCH (A.R.I.5928)
3. PULSE ALTIMETER
4. RADIO SWITCH PANEL
5. CONTROL PANEL – TRUE AIR SPEED
6. POWER SUPPLIES INDICATOR – N.B.C.
7. POWER SUPPLIES INDICATOR – H.2.S.
8. NAVIGATION PANEL
9. VARIABLE AIRSPEED UNIT
10. COMPASS ISOLATION SWITCH (PORT)
11. COMPASS ISOLATION SWITCH (STBD.)
12. ON/OFF SWITCH (A.R.I.5972)
13. CONTROL UNIT (A.R.I.23023)
14. D.F. BEARING INDICATOR (A.R.I. 23023)
15. COMPASS – REPEATER – TRUE TRACK MAGNETIC HEADING
16. LOOP CONTROLLER (A.R.I.23023)
17. RADIO ALTIMETER
18. STEERING SIGNAL TEST SOCKET
19. TRACK CONTROLLER UNIT – M.F.S.
20. DIMMER SWITCH – AUTO LAND AND T.C.U. LIGHTS
21. PILOTS DIRECTION INDICATOR
22. WINDOW LAUNCH OR TELE-METERING CONTROL PANEL
23. FAIL INDICATOR (A.R.I.23134/5/4)
24. TEST POINT (G.P.I. Mk.6)
25. INDICATOR, TYPE 6935 (A.R.I.5919)
26. INDICATOR, TYPE 17171 (A.R.I. 18228/1)
27. SUPPLIES SWITCH (A.R.I.5874)
28. OUTPUT SWITCH (A.R.I.5874)
29. SUPPLY SWITCH (A.R.I.23023)
30. PRESS-TO-TRANSMIT SWITCH
31. CONFERENCE INTERCOMM. – MASTER SWITCH
32. ON/OFF SWITCH (A.R.I.18011)
33. CONTROL UNIT, TYPE 705 (A.R.I. 18011)
34. AUTO-THROTTLE ON/OFF SWITCH (Inoperative)
35. DIMMER SWITCH – CONTROL UNIT DIAL LIGHTING
36. DIMMER SWITCH – CONTROL UNIT DIAL LIGHTING (A.R.I.18076)
37. INTERCOMM. MASTER CONTROL
38. EXTERNAL INTERCOMM. SWITCHES
39. MORSE KEY
40. INTERCOMM. CONTROL UNIT (A.E.O.)
41. CONTROL UNIT, TYPE 17172 (A.R.I. 18228/1)
42. CONTROL UNIT, TYPE 9422 (A.R.I. 18076)
43. DELETED (Mod.2501)
44. BLANKING PLATE
45. CONTROL TRANSMITTER/RECEIVER TYPE M53 (A.R.I.23090)
46. ANTENNA CONTROL UNIT, (A.R.I. 23090)
47. CONTROL UNIT, TYPE 16929 (A.R.I. 23134/5/4)
48. NOT ALLOCATED
49. GROUND SPEED SELECTOR UNIT
50. H.R.U. POWER FAILURE INDICATOR
51. G.P.I. MK.6
52. NAV. HEADING UNIT (H.R.S.)
53. H.R.S. CONTROL UNIT
54. EVENT MARKER PUSH SWITCH
55. RECORDER – ON/OFF SWITCH
56. FAILURE WARNING LIGHT (A.R.I. 5959)
57. INDICATOR CONTROL UNIT, TYPE 9869 (A.R.I.5972)
58. CONTROL UNIT, TYPE 7750 (A.R.I. 18107/13)
59. CONTROL UNIT, TYPE 585 (A.R.I. 5928)
60. CONTROL UNIT, TYPE 626 (A.R.I. 5928)
61. INDICATING UNIT, TYPE 301 (A.R.I. 5928)
62. CAMERA, TYPE RX.88 (A.R.I.5928)
63. CONTROL UNIT, TYPE 595 (A.R.I. 5928)
64. N.B.C. ISOLATION INDICATORS
65. CONTROL UNIT, TYPE 12580
66. BOMBING SELECTOR SWITCH
67. N.B.C. SIMULATOR SOCKET
68. BOMBING SELECTOR PANEL
69. SIMULATED BOMBING PANEL

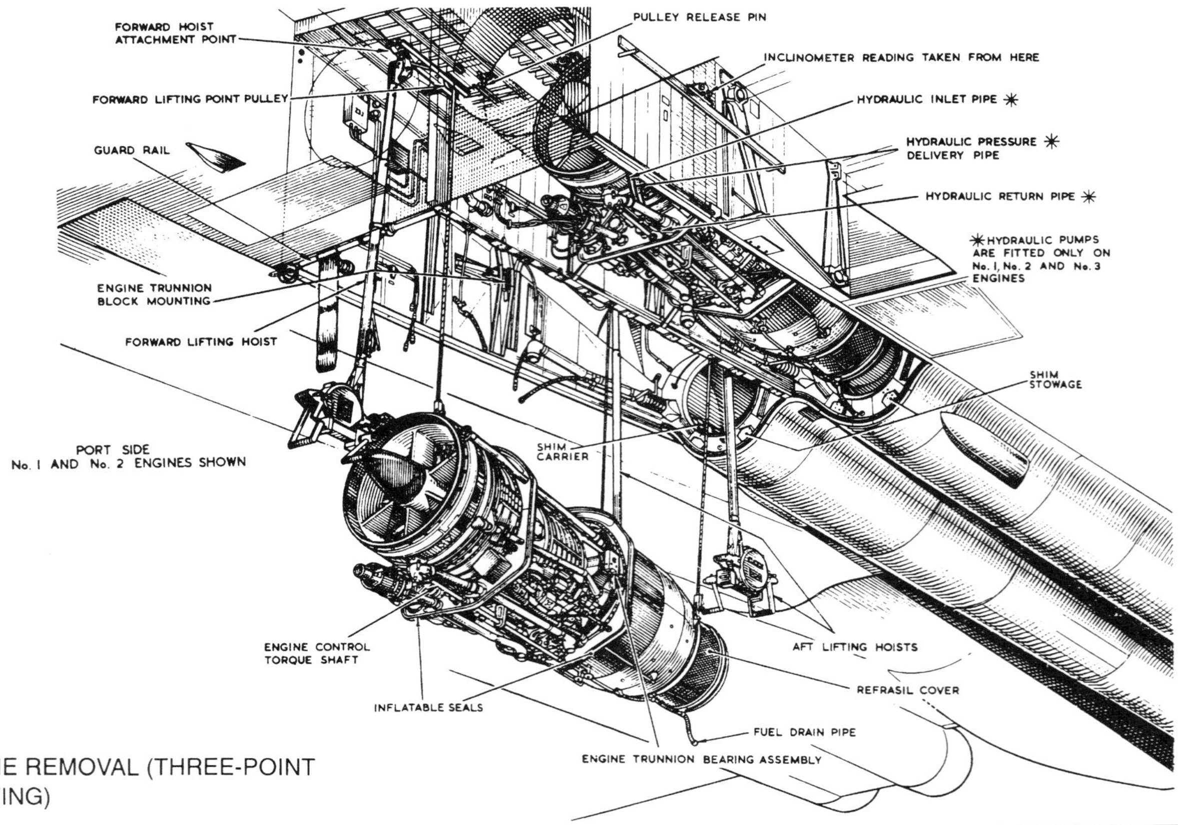

ENGINE REMOVAL (THREE-POINT HOISTING)

E.C.M. BALLAST AND STOWAGE

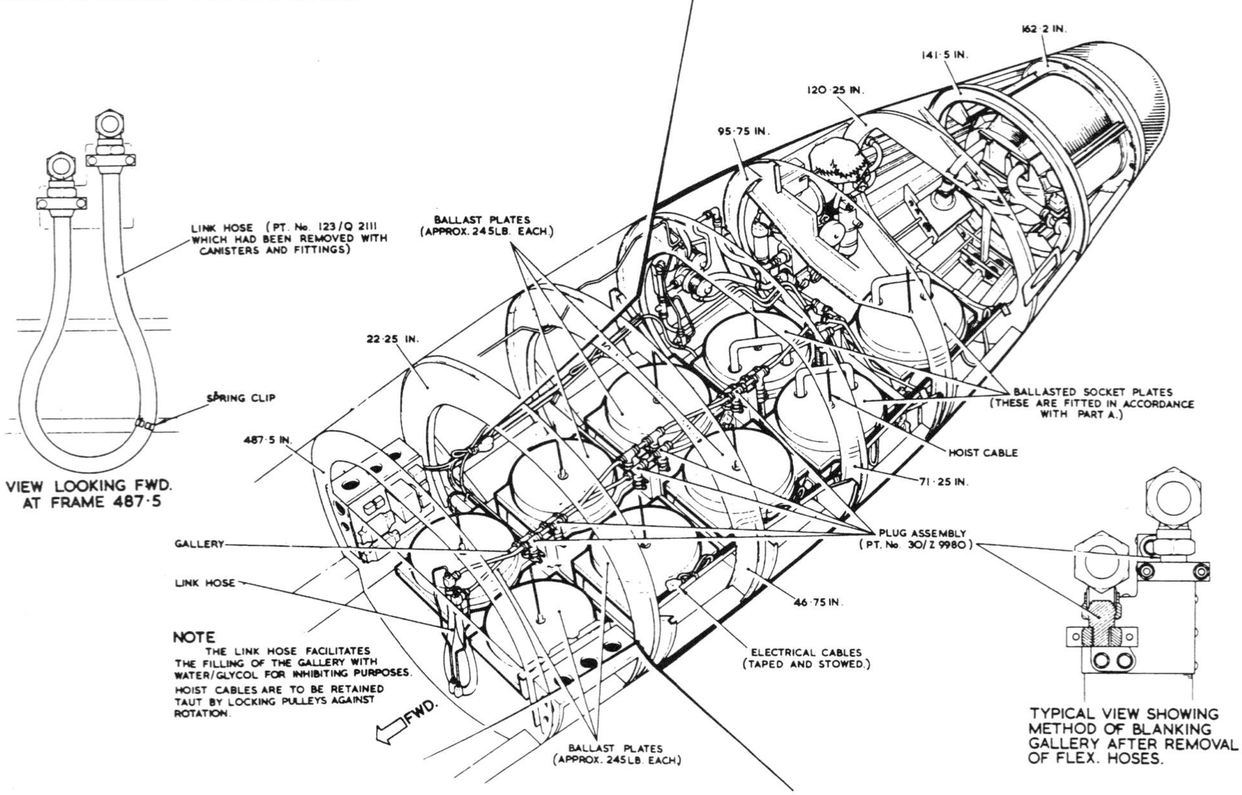

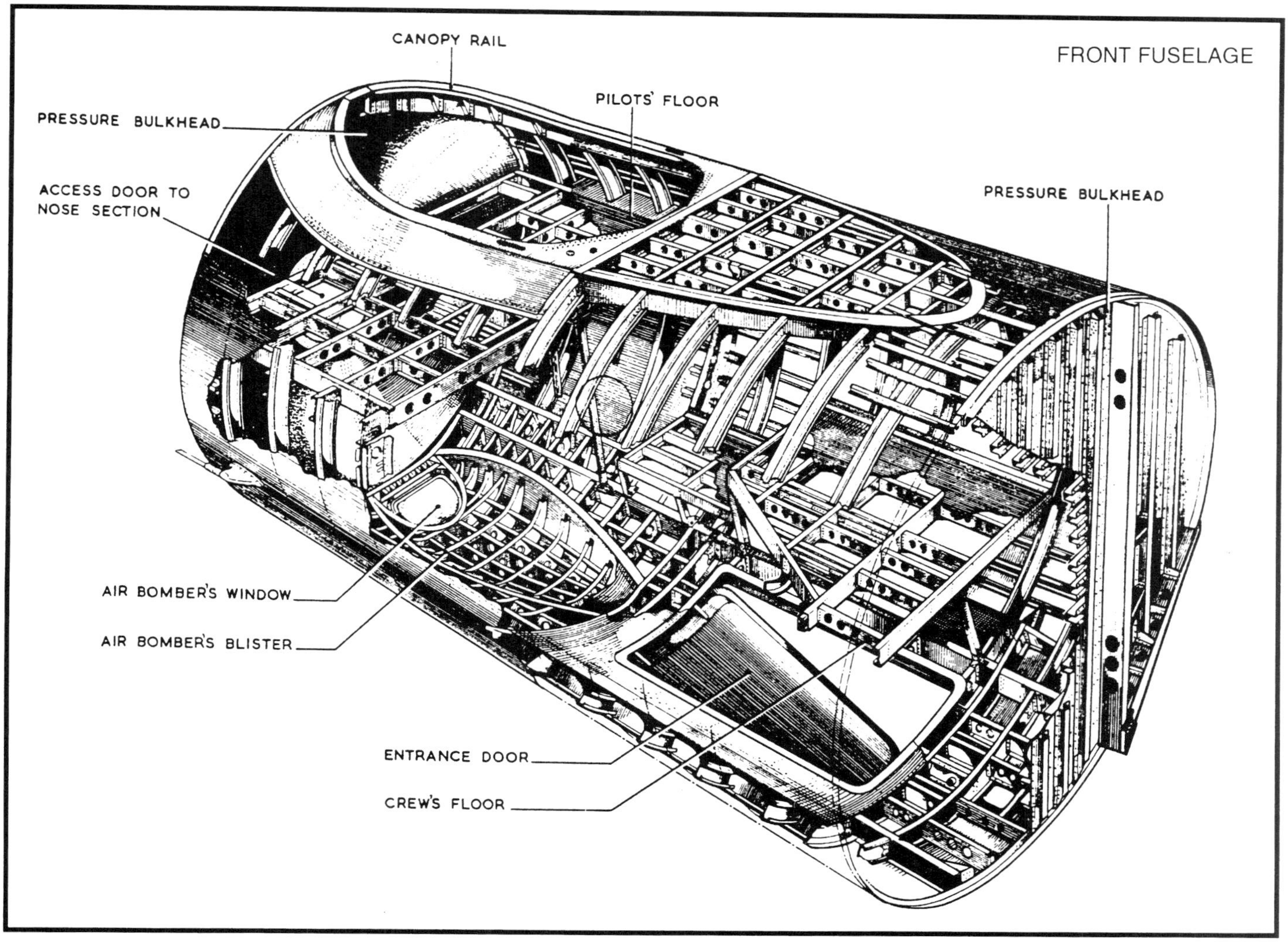
FRONT FUSELAGE
CANOPY RAIL
PRESSURE BULKHEAD
PILOTS' FLOOR
ACCESS DOOR TO NOSE SECTION
PRESSURE BULKHEAD
AIR BOMBER'S WINDOW
AIR BOMBER'S BLISTER
ENTRANCE DOOR
CREW'S FLOOR

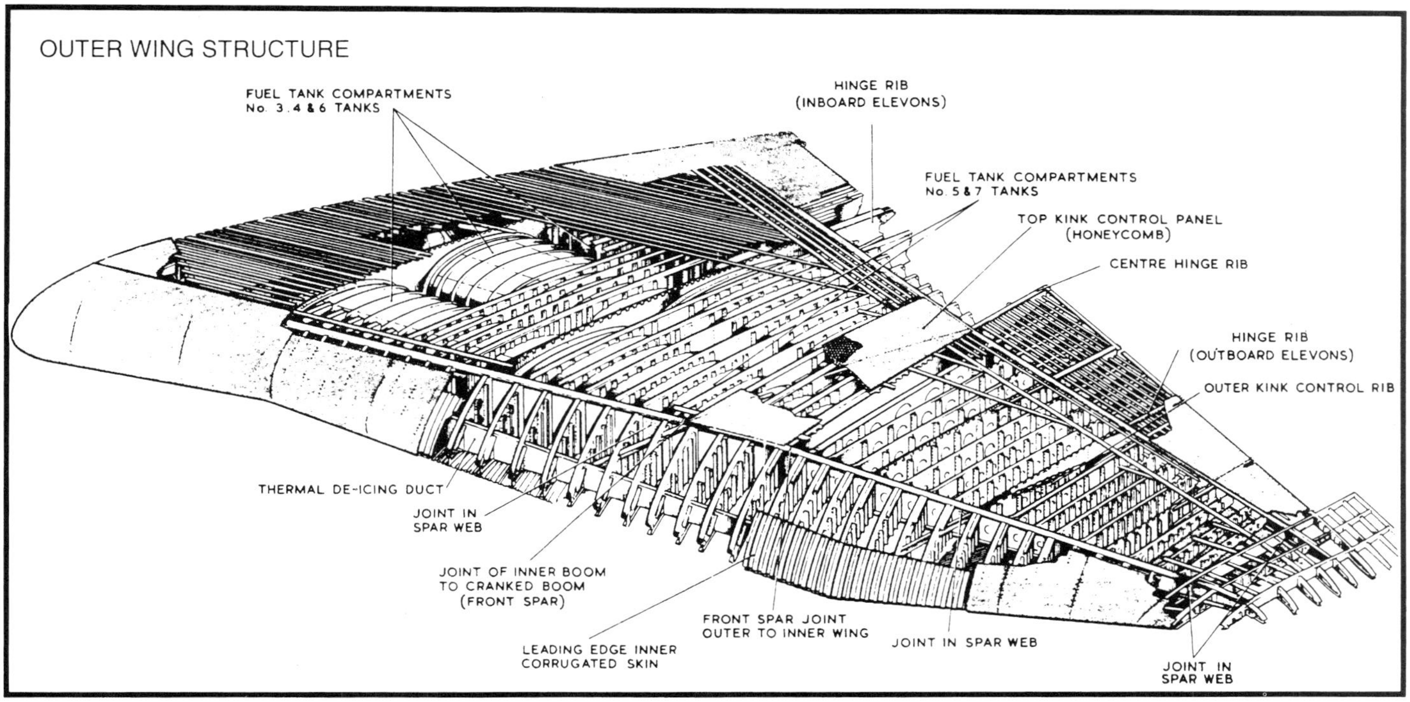
OUTER WING STRUCTURE
FUEL TANK COMPARTMENTS No. 3, 4 & 6 TANKS
HINGE RIB (INBOARD ELEVONS)
FUEL TANK COMPARTMENTS No. 5 & 7 TANKS
TOP KINK CONTROL PANEL (HONEYCOMB)
CENTRE HINGE RIB
HINGE RIB (OUTBOARD ELEVONS)
OUTER KINK CONTROL RIB
THERMAL DE-ICING DUCT
JOINT IN SPAR WEB
JOINT OF INNER BOOM TO CRANKED BOOM (FRONT SPAR)
FRONT SPAR JOINT OUTER TO INNER WING
JOINT IN SPAR WEB
LEADING EDGE INNER CORRUGATED SKIN
JOINT IN SPAR WEB

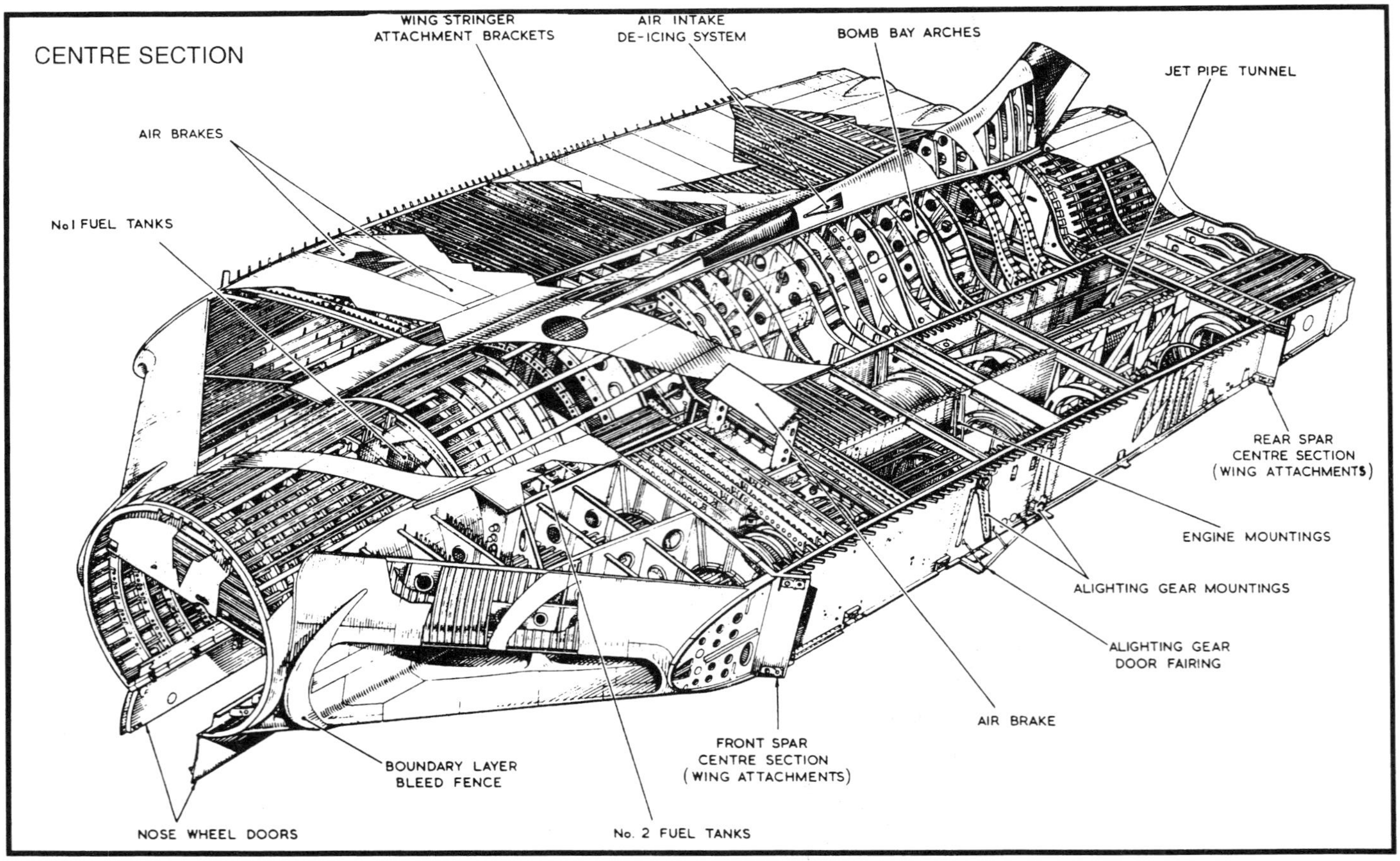
CENTRE SECTION
WING STRINGER ATTACHMENT BRACKETS
AIR INTAKE DE-ICING SYSTEM
BOMB BAY ARCHES
JET PIPE TUNNEL
AIR BRAKES
No.1 FUEL TANKS
REAR SPAR CENTRE SECTION (WING ATTACHMENTS)
ENGINE MOUNTINGS
ALIGHTING GEAR MOUNTINGS
ALIGHTING GEAR DOOR FAIRING
AIR BRAKE
FRONT SPAR CENTRE SECTION (WING ATTACHMENTS)
BOUNDARY LAYER BLEED FENCE
NOSE WHEEL DOORS
No. 2 FUEL TANKS

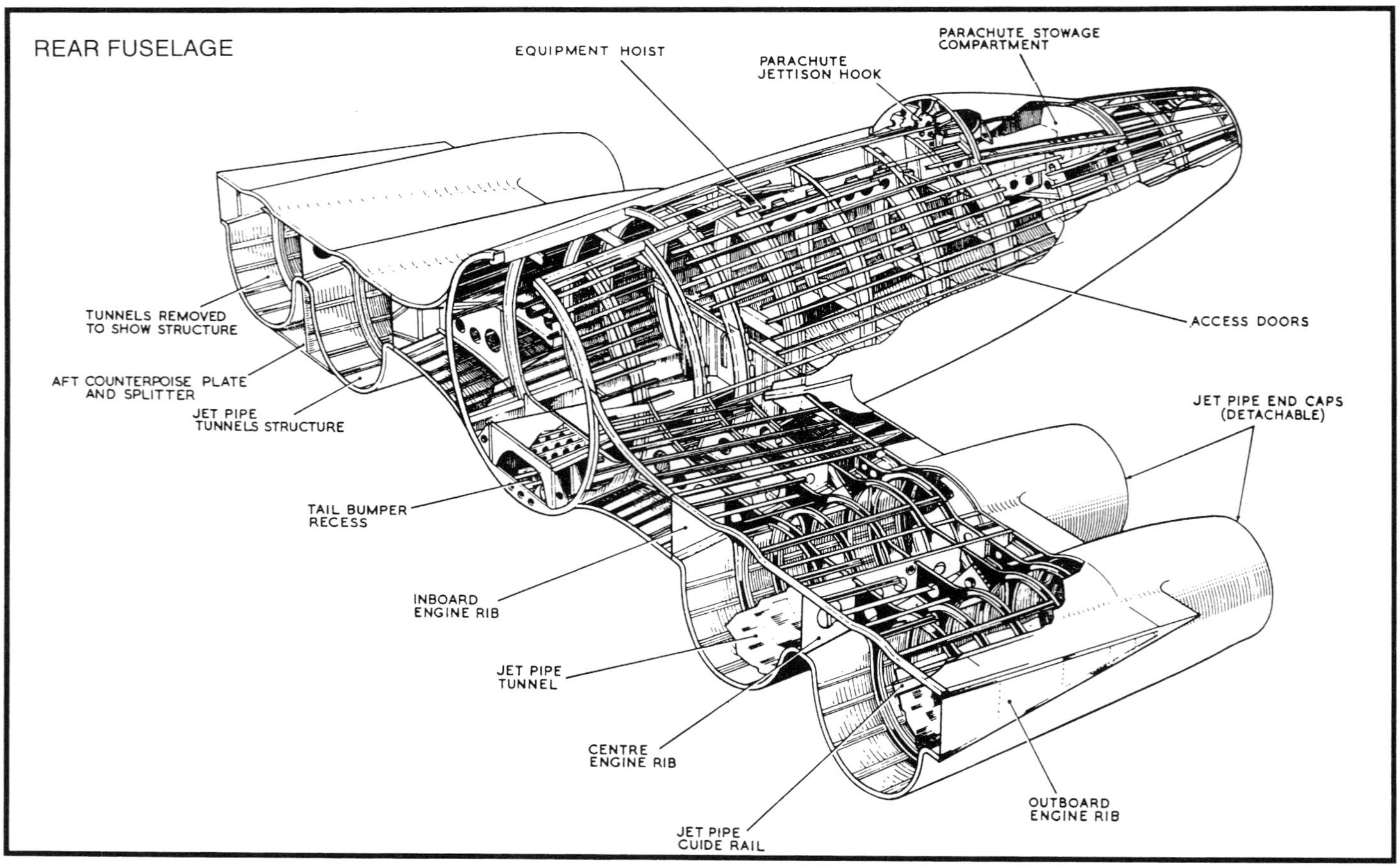
REAR FUSELAGE
EQUIPMENT HOIST
PARACHUTE JETTISON HOOK
PARACHUTE STOWAGE COMPARTMENT
TUNNELS REMOVED TO SHOW STRUCTURE
ACCESS DOORS
AFT COUNTERPOISE PLATE AND SPLITTER
JET PIPE TUNNELS STRUCTURE
JET PIPE END CAPS (DETACHABLE)
TAIL BUMPER RECESS
INBOARD ENGINE RIB
JET PIPE TUNNEL
CENTRE ENGINE RIB
OUTBOARD ENGINE RIB
JET PIPE GUIDE RAIL

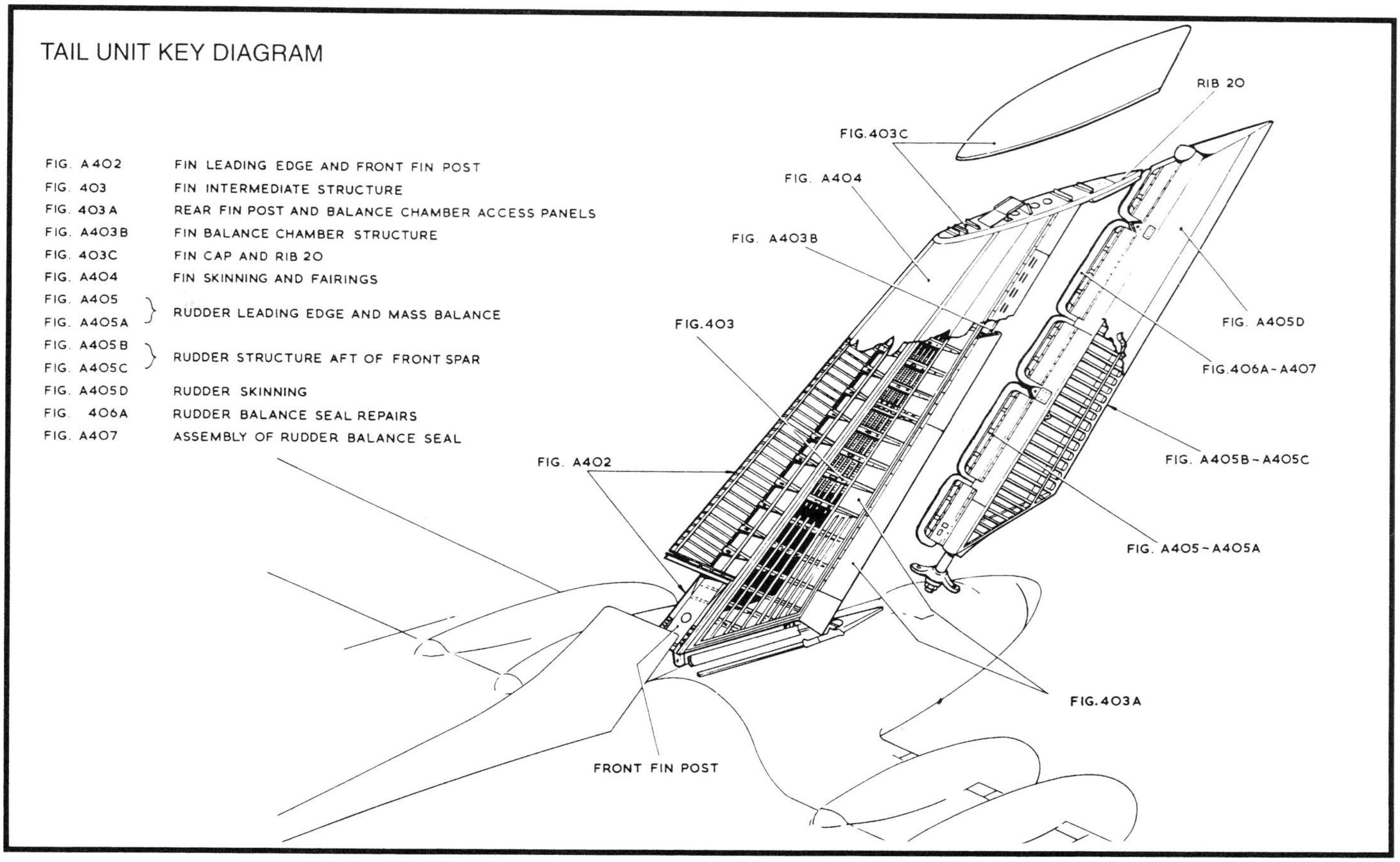
TAIL UNIT KEY DIAGRAM
FIG. A402 FIN LEADING EDGE AND FRONT FIN POST
FIG. 403 FIN INTERMEDIATE STRUCTURE
FIG. 403A REAR FIN POST AND BALANCE CHAMBER ACCESS PANELS
FIG. A403B FIN BALANCE CHAMBER STRUCTURE
FIG. 403C FIN CAP AND RIB 20
FIG. A404 FIN SKINNING AND FAIRINGS
FIG. A405 FIG. A405A RUDDER LEADING EDGE AND MASS BALANCE
FIG. A405B FIG. A405C RUDDER STRUCTURE AFT OF FRONT SPAR
FIG. A405D RUDDER SKINNING
FIG. 406A RUDDER BALANCE SEAL REPAIRS
FIG. A407 ASSEMBLY OF RUDDER BALANCE SEAL
RIB 20
FIG.403C
FIG. A404
FIG. A403B
FIG.403
FIG. A405D
FIG.406A-A407
FIG. A405B-A405C
FIG. A402
FIG. A405-A405A
FIG.403A
FRONT FIN POST

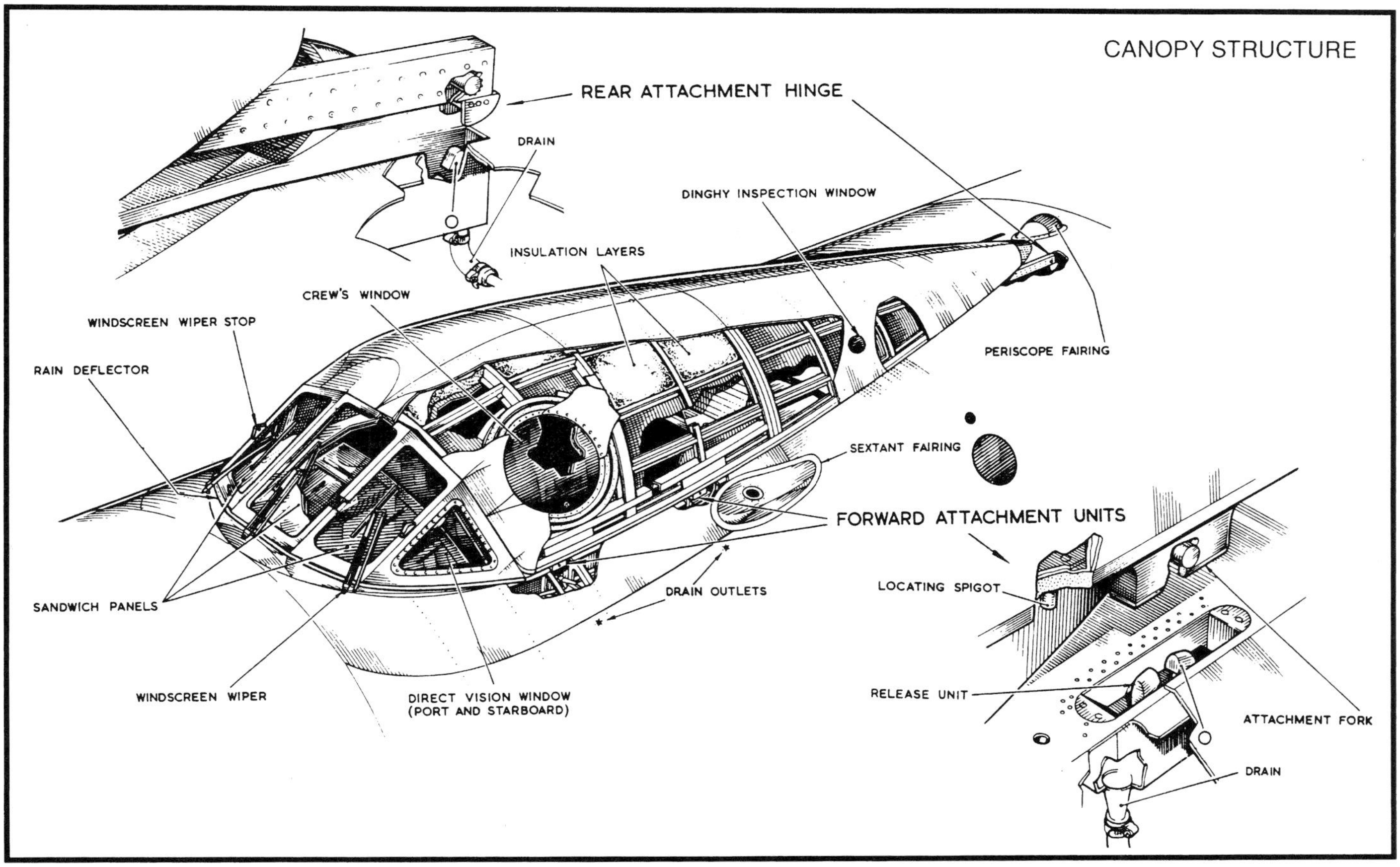
CANOPY STRUCTURE
REAR ATTACHMENT HINGE
DRAIN
DINGHY INSPECTION WINDOW
INSULATION LAYERS
CREW'S WINDOW
WINDSCREEN WIPER STOP
RAIN DEFLECTOR
PERISCOPE FAIRING
SEXTANT FAIRING
FORWARD ATTACHMENT UNITS
LOCATING SPIGOT
DRAIN OUTLETS
SANDWICH PANELS
RELEASE UNIT
ATTACHMENT FORK
WINDSCREEN WIPER
DIRECT VISION WINDOW
(PORT AND STARBOARD)
DRAIN

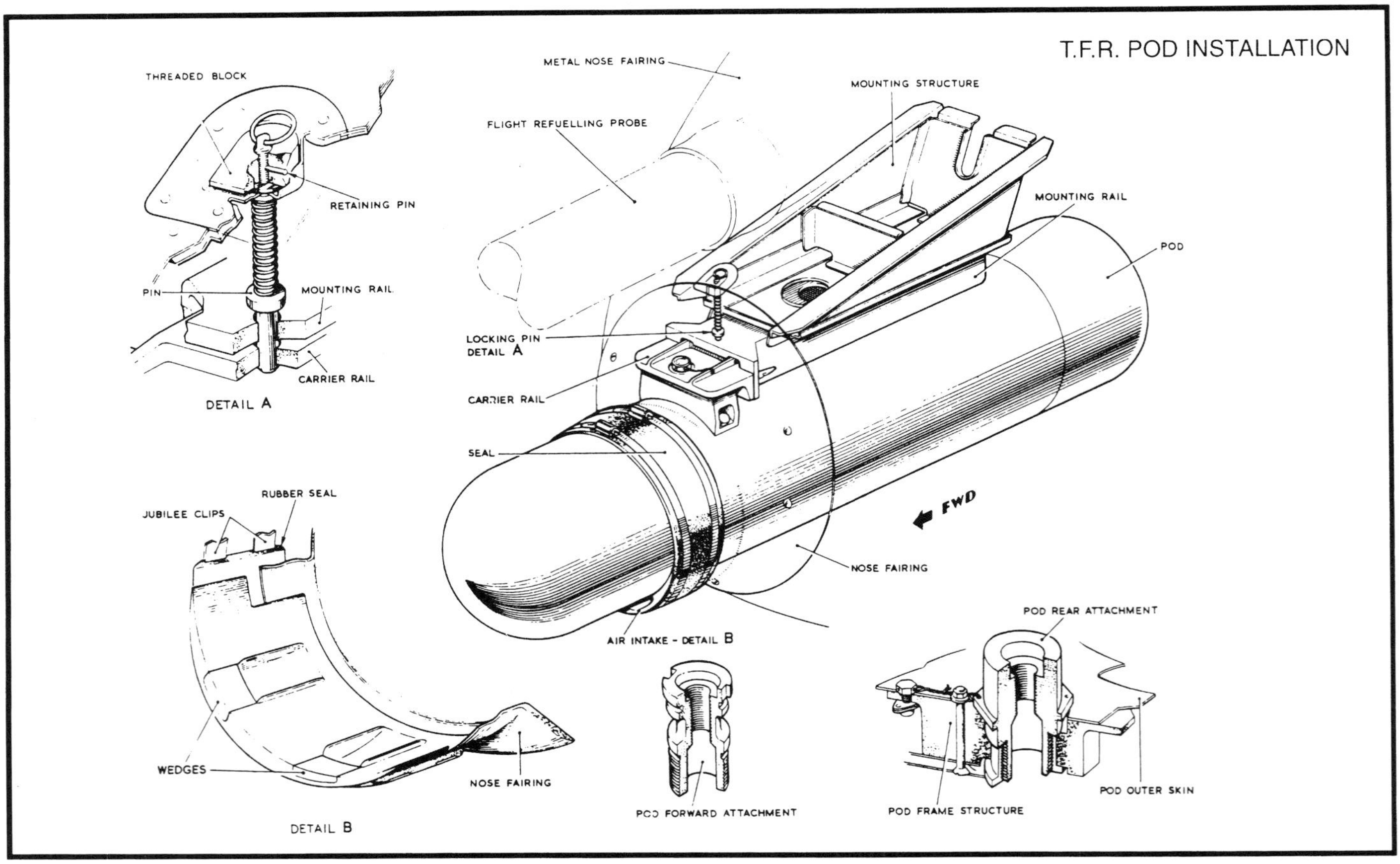
T.F.R. POD INSTALLATION
THREADED BLOCK
RETAINING PIN
PIN
MOUNTING RAIL
CARRIER RAIL
DETAIL A
METAL NOSE FAIRING
FLIGHT REFUELLING PROBE
MOUNTING STRUCTURE
MOUNTING RAIL
POD
LOCKING PIN DETAIL A
CARRIER RAIL
SEAL
FWD
NOSE FAIRING
AIR INTAKE - DETAIL B
RUBBER SEAL
JUBILEE CLIPS
WEDGES
NOSE FAIRING
DETAIL B
POD FORWARD ATTACHMENT
POD REAR ATTACHMENT
POD FRAME STRUCTURE
POD OUTER SKIN

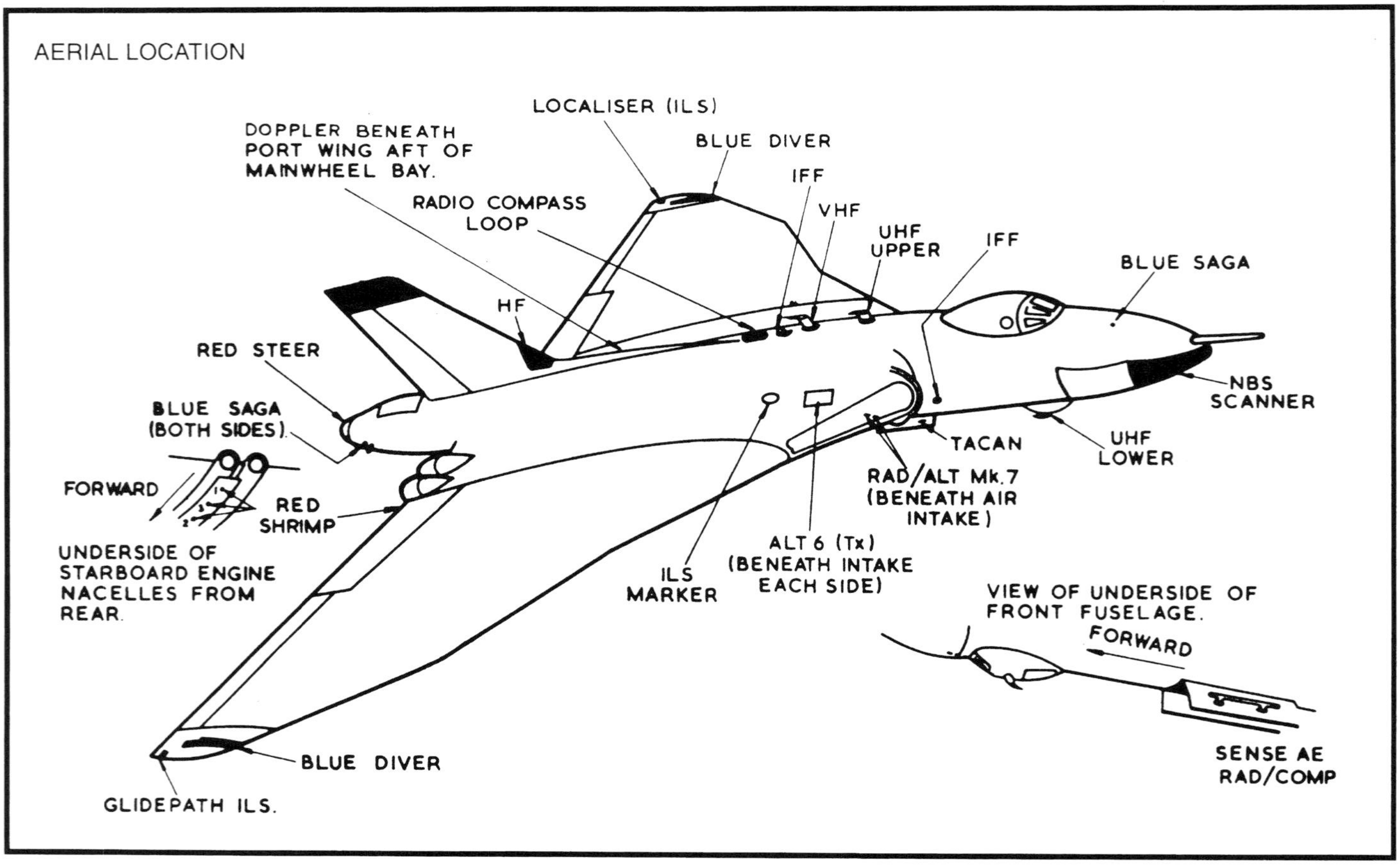
AERIAL LOCATION
LOCALISER (ILS)
DOPPLER BENEATH PORT WING AFT OF MAINWHEEL BAY.
BLUE DIVER
IFF
RADIO COMPASS LOOP
VHF
UHF UPPER
IFF
BLUE SAGA
HF
RED STEER
BLUE SAGA (BOTH SIDES)
NBS SCANNER
TACAN
UHF LOWER
FORWARD
RED SHRIMP
RAD/ALT Mk.7 (BENEATH AIR INTAKE)
ALT 6 (Tx) (BENEATH INTAKE EACH SIDE)
UNDERSIDE OF STARBOARD ENGINE NACELLES FROM REAR.
ILS MARKER
VIEW OF UNDERSIDE OF FRONT FUSELAGE.
FORWARD
BLUE DIVER
SENSE AE RAD/COMP
GLIDEPATH ILS.

ACCESS PANELS

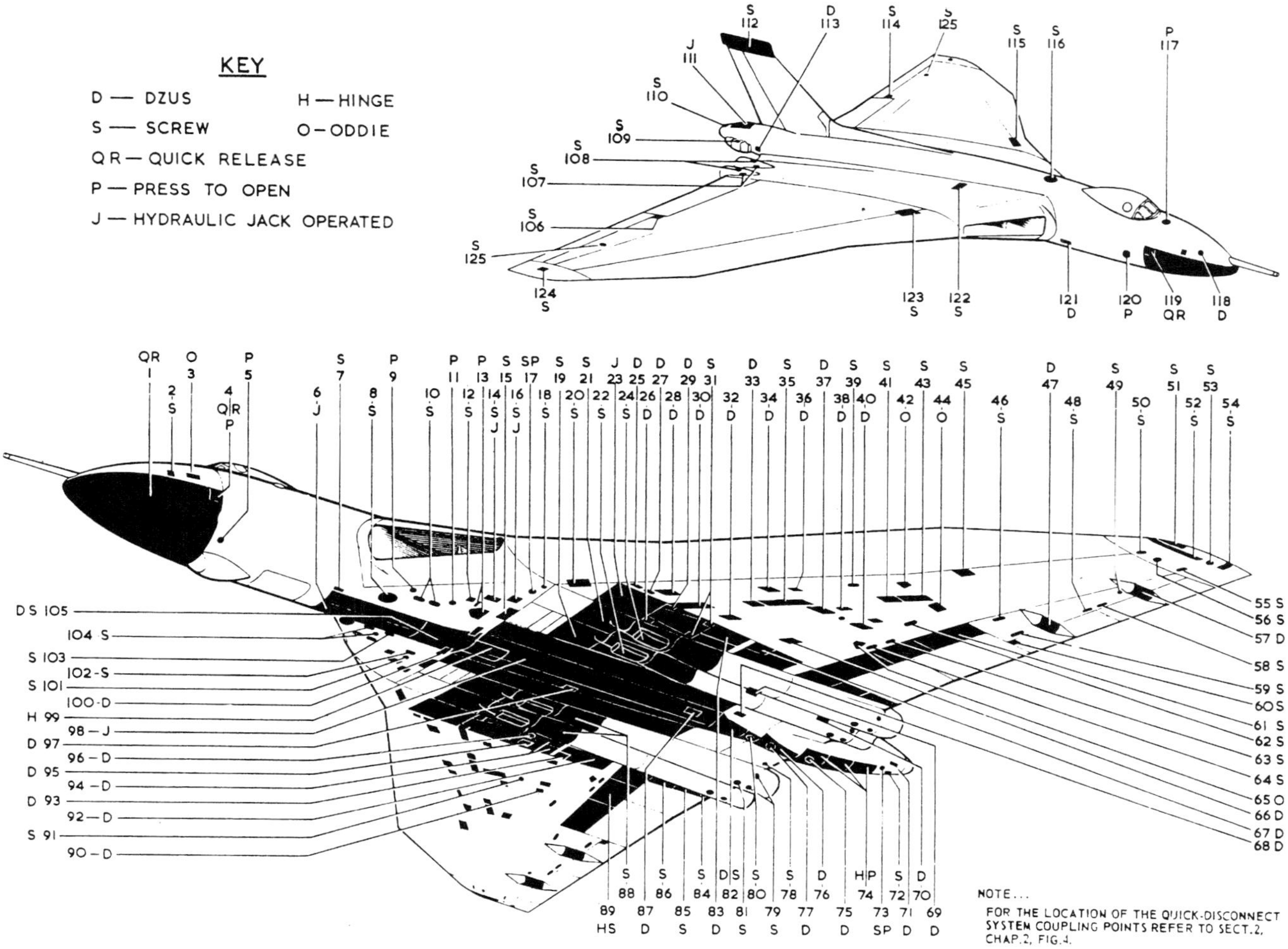

1. RADOME, H2S SCANNER
2. RADOME, HOIST ATTACHMENTS
3. H2S/NBS PNEUMATIC SYSTEM CHARGING
4. EMERGENCY EQUIPMENT AND DESTRUCTOR STOWAGE
5. GROUND COOLING CONNECTION, RADAR
6. NOSE WHEEL DOORS
7. NOSE WHEEL UNIT PIVOTS
8. AERIAL, RADIO ALTIMETER, HIGH RANGE
9. GROUND CONDITIONING CONNECTION, VENTILATED SUIT SYSTEM
10. ENGINE THROTTLE AND R.A.T. CONTROLS
11. GROUND SERVICING COCK, NO.1 TANK
12. AERIAL, RADIO ALTIMETER, LOW RANGE
13. RAM AIR TURBINE PLATFORM AND GROUND RELEASE
14. ANTI-ICING INJECTOR
15. DEFUELLING COCKS
16. ANTI-ICING EXTRACTION DOOR
17. ANTI-ICING
18. ANTI-ICING
19. ENGINE ACCESS DOOR, FORWARD INBOARD
20. FRONT SPAR SHACKLE BOLTS
21. ENGINE ACCESS DOOR, FORWARD OUTBOARD
22. ENGINE ACCESS DOOR, CENTRE INBOARD
23. MAIN WHEEL DOORS
24. ENGINE ACCESS DOOR, CENTRE OUTBOARD
25. COCKS, GROUND SERVICING, NO.4, 5 AND 7 FUEL TANKS
26. HYDRAULIC TEST (PORT) HYDRAULIC CHARGING (STARBOARD)
27. COCKS, GROUND SERVICING, NO.3 AND 6 FUEL TANKS
28. FUEL LEVEL SWITCH AND SECONDARY PUMP, NO.3 TANK
29. REFUELLING CONNECTIONS (PORT AND STARBOARD)
30. FUEL PIPE CONNECTIONS
31. MAIN WHEEL UNIT PIVOTS
32. FUEL LEVEL SWITCH AND SECONDARY PUMP, NO.4 TANK
33. FUEL PIPE CONNECTIONS (PORT AND STARBOARD)
34. SUMP, NO.3 FUEL TANK
35. FUEL PIPE CONNECTIONS
36. FUEL LEVEL SWITCH AND SECONDARY PUMP, NO.5 TANK
37. SUMP, NO.4 FUEL TANK
38. ELECTRICAL COMPONENTS
39. ELECTRICAL, EXPLOSION PROTECTION
40. SUMP, NO.6 FUEL TANK
41. FUEL PIPE CONNECTIONS
42. SUMP, NO.5 FUEL TANK
43. FUEL PIPES
44. SUMP, NO.7 FUEL TANK
45. LANDING LIGHT
46. FLYING CONTROL RODS
47. OUTBOARD ELEVON POWER UNITS
48. FLYING CONTROL RODS
49. ELECTRICAL COMPONENTS
50. WING TIP ATTACHMENT, FRONT SPAR
51. NAVIGATION LAMP CONNECTIONS
52. AERIAL, A.R.I.18075
53. AERIAL CONNECTIONS
54. AERIAL MOUNTING
55. WING TIP ATTACHMENT, REAR SPAR
56. ELECTRICAL COMPONENTS
57. OUTBOARD ELEVON POWER UNITS
58. FLYING CONTROL RODS
59. FLYING CONTROL RODS
60. ELEVON HINGE ASSEMBLY
61. FLYING CONTROL RODS
62. ELECTRICAL, EXPLOSION PROTECTION
63. ELECTRICAL COMPONENTS
64. VENT VALVE, FUEL TANK PRESSURISATION
65. P.F.C. UNIT COOLING
66. FUEL LEVEL SWITCH AND SECONDARY PUMP, NO.6 TANK
67. WINDOW LAUNCHING EQUIPMENT
68. GROUND ELECTRICAL SUPPLY PLUG, 200V A.C.
69. PNEUMATIC CHARGING – ENGINE RAPID START SYSTEM
70. FLYING CONTROLS
71. NITROGEN CHARGING POINT
72. NAVIGATION LIGHT
73. SCANNER COOLING
74. AIRBORNE EQUIPMENT, FRONT, CENTRE AND REAR DOORS
75. GROUND CONDITIONING CONNECTION
76. RUDDER POWER UNITS
77. NITROGEN CHARGING POINT
78. JET PIPE ATTACHMENT
79. JET PIPE THERMOCOUPLES
80. DOWNWARD IDENTIFICATION LAMP
81. JET PIPE ADJUSTMENT
82. BOMB BAY CONVERSION FAIRINGS
83. A.R.I. 5851
84. FLYING CONTROL RODS
85. FLYING CONTROLS
86. FLYING CONTROLS
87. BOMB CONDITIONING OUTLET LOUVRE
88. ENGINE ACCESS, REAR DOORS
89. POWER CONTROL UNITS, INBOARD ELEVONS
90. FUEL LEVEL SWITCH AND SECONDARY PUMP, NO.7 TANK
91. ELECTRICAL COMPONENTS
92. WINDOW LAUNCHING AND A.A.P.P. FUEL TANK
93. A.A.P.P. OXYGEN CHARGING AND SUMP TEMPERATURE GAUGE
94. AUXILIARY AIRBORNE POWER PLANT
95. A.A.P.P. OIL FILLER AND STARTER CARTRIDGES
96. ENGINE START, GROUND CONNECTION
97. BOMB HEATING, GROUND CONNECTION
98. BOMB BAY
99. SERVICING DOORS
100. SUMP, NO.1 AND 2 FUEL TANKS
101. COCK, GROUND SERVICING, NO.1 FUEL TANK
102. HYDRAULIC SYSTEM
103. AERIAL
104. AIR MILEAGE UNIT
105. BOMB BAY CONVERSION FAIRING
106. ELEVON HINGE ASSEMBLY
107. ELECTRICAL COMPONENTS
108. JET PIPE ADJUSTMENT
109. FREON CONDENSER
110. NAVIGATION LIGHT
111. BRAKE PARACHUTE
112. AERIALS U.H.F. AND GEE
113. GROUND INTERCOMMUNICATION CONNECTION
114. ELEVON HINGE ASSEMBLY
115. FRONT SPAR SHACKLE BOLTS
116. AERIAL DISHPAN
117. DE-ICING TANK
118. NITROGEN REPLENISHING, (FLIGHT REFUELLING)
119. EMERGENCY EQUIPMENT STOWAGE
120. CABIN CONDITIONING, GROUND CONNECTION
121. GROUND ELECTRICAL SUPPLY PLUGS, 28V D.C.
122. EMERGENCY DEFUELLING
123. FRONT SPAR SHACKLE BOLTS
124. DETECTOR UNIT M.F.S.
125. REAR SPAR INSPECTION

COMPONENT WEIGHTS AND DIMENSIONS

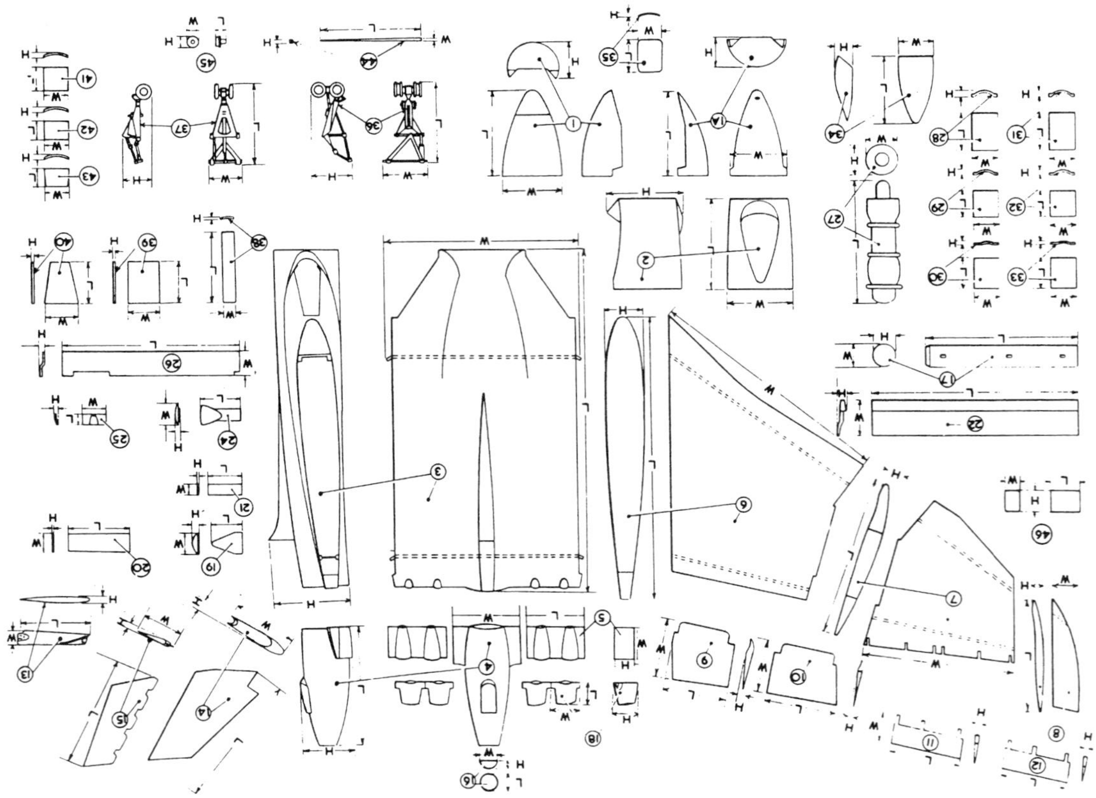

Item	Component	Length (ft.)	Width (ft.)	Height (ft.)	Structure tare weight (lb.)
1	NOSE (lower portion, composite)	13·5	8·75	5·5	290
1a	NOSE (upper portion, metal)	13·5	8·7	4·25	230
2	FRONT FUSELAGE	16·75	9·2	10·25	2,081
3	CENTRE SECTION	52·85	28·85	12·0	17,979
4	REAR FUSELAGE	18·5	10·6	6·33	962
5	REAR FUSELAGE FAIRING	8·25	5·0	3·33	258
6	WING INNER (Starboard)	50·0	35·5	5·0	6,457
6a	WING INNER (Port)	50·0	35·5	5·0	6,446
7	WING OUTER (Port and starboard)	24·5	20·5	2·5	1,708
8	WING TIP (Port and starboard)	14·8	3·75	0·79	107
9	ELEVON INNER (Inboard, port and starboard)	9·75	10·6	1·66	326
10	ELEVON INNER (Outboard, port and starboard)	10·25	8·75	1·5	323
11	ELEVON OUTER (Inboard, port and starboard)	9·75	4·25	1·6	210
12	ELEVON OUTER (Outboard, port and starboard)	9·75	4·25	1·6	203
13	FIN CAP	11·33	2·25	1·41	100
14	FIN	21·0	10·0	1·87	919
15	RUDDER	19·25	6·0	1·0	305
16	TAIL RADOME	2·47	2·47	1·54	14
17	JET PIPE	22·98	2·63	2·63	492
18	JET PIPE CAP	3·25	4·25	2·87	97
19	FAIRING (counterpoise plate, each)	4·0	3·58	0·5	17
20	COUNTERPOISE PLATE, FRONT (each)	7·6	3·08	0·08	39
20a	COUNTERPOISE PLATE, REAR (each)	5·75	3·25	0·08	31
21	SPLITTER PLATE FRONT (each)	3·87	1·75	0·16	10
21a	SPLITTER PLATE REAR (each)	5·75	2·54	0·16	23
22	BOMB BAY DOORS (each)	29·25	5·2	0·66	713
23	(DELETED)				
24	BOMB BAY FAIRING, REAR	6·33	3·25	1·0	23
25	BOMB BAY FAIRING, FRONT	6·0	7·0	0·75	4·8
26	BOMB BAY FAIRING, PORT	29·0	4·75	1·5	444
26a	BOMB BAY FAIRING, STARBOARD	29·0	5·75	1·6	520
27	ENGINE (Olympus 20101) (including oil and starter)	13·68	3·75	4·35	4,761
28	ENGINE DOOR, FORWARD)	5·29	4·08	0·5	54
29	ENGINE DOOR, CENTRE)Inboard, port and stbd.	4·85	4·04	1·33	80
30	ENGINE DOOR, REAR)	5·83	4·79	1·25	68
31	ENGINE DOOR, FORWARD)	5·29	4·08	0·5	52
32	ENGINE DOOR, CENTRE)Outboard, port and stbd.	4·83	4·08	1·33	82
33	ENGINE DOOR, REAR)	5·83	4·79	1·25	73
34	CANOPY	10·5	4·66	1·4	284
35	MAIN ENTRANCE DOOR	5·0	2·75	1·0	100
36	MAIN WHEEL UNIT (each)	12·75	5·0	6·0	2,485
37	NOSE WHEEL UNIT	13·5	3·5	3·08	990
38	NOSE WHEEL DOOR (each)	10·75	1·75	0·33	48
39	MAIN WHEEL DOOR	6·5	4·75	0·75	164
40	MAIN WHEEL FAIRING	5·25	4·0	0·41	32
41	REAR FUSELAGE ACCESS DOOR (front)	4·27	4·04	0·79	27
42	REAR FUSELAGE ACCESS DOOR (centre)	3·29	4·08	0·79	23
43	REAR FUSELAGE ACCESS DOOR (rear)	3·25	4·0	0·87	22
44	REFUELLING PROBE	9·7	0·5	0·5	38
45	RAM AIR TURBINE	1·3	1·16	1·25	94
46	AIRBORNE AUXILIARY POWER PLANT	4·5	2·0	3·16	420

Vulcan Production, Service and Disposals

Prototypes
Contract 6/Air/1942/CB.6(a). (Dated 6 July 1948)

VX770: Delivered August 1952. Avon/Sapphire/Conway engines. A & AEE and manufacturer trials, suffered a mid-air explosion due to structural failure, at Syerston, 20.9.58, and was destroyed.

VX777: Delivered September 1953. Olympus 100 engines. Trials aircraft, converted to prototype B.Mk.2, making a first flight in this configuration 31.8.57. Further trials in new configuration, before being used for non-flying runway trials with the RAE. Last flight 27.4.60. Broken-up at Farnborough 7.63.

Vulcan B.Mk.1.
Contract 6/Air/8442/CB.6(a). 25 off—14.8.52.

1/ XA889: Delivered 4.2.55. Olympus 104 engines. A & AEE trials, Bristol Siddeley trials at Patchway. Withdrawn and scrapped at Boscombe Down in 1971.

2/ XA890: Delivered 1955. Olympus 104 engines. A & AEE trials. RAE Farnborough and Thurleigh trials. Manufacturer trials. Radio and radar trials, blind landing trials, and ballistics research. Withdrawn and scrapped at Bedford in 1971.

3/ XA891: Delivered 1955. Olympus 104 engines. A & AEE trials. Bristol Siddeley trials at Patchway (Olympus 200 series), RAE trials at Farnborough. Manufacturers trials. Crashed on a test flight 24.7.59. near Hull, due to electrical failure.

4/ XA892: Delivered 1955. Olympus 104 engines. Manufacturers trials and A & AEE armament trials. Delivered to Halton for ground instruction (became 7746M), and scrapped in 1972.

5/ XA893: Delivered 1956. Olympus 104 engines. A & AEE electrical trials, connected with B.Mk.2 variant. Broken up at Boscombe Down in 1962, nose section transferred to 71 Maintenance Unit at Bicester.

6/ XA894: Delivered 1957. Olympus engines. A & AEE trials, engine development trials. Operated by Bristol Siddeley at Patchway, used as engine test bed for Olympus 22R, as part of the TSR-2 trials programme. Destroyed during a ground fire whilst ground running at Patchway, 3.12.62.

7/ XA895: Delivered 16.8.56. Olympus 104 engines. Converted to B.Mk.1A. 230 Operational Conversion Unit, Bomber Command Development Unit. A & AEE

Below: *XA894 was used as a development aircraft for the Bristol Olympus engine, and following service with the A & AEE a test pod was attached under the bomb bay to accommodate an Olympus engine which was being developed for the TSR-2. Seen over Filton, the Vulcan's twin air intakes are feeding an Olympus 320. (Rolls-Royce)*

Right: *A five-engined Vulcan! XA894 at the 1962 SBAC Show, thundering in at low level during an era when airshow organizers were rather less paranoid about exciting aerial demonstrations. XA894 was later destroyed in a ground fire accident at Patchway. (R. L. Ward)*

Above: *Operated by Rolls-Royce on various engine trials, XA902 is seen touching-down at Hucknall while fitted with Spey engines. Note the unusual blister fairings above the engines. (Rolls-Royce)*

ECM trials. Withdrawn 13.1.67. Sold for scrap (Bradbury Ltd.) 19.9.68.

8/ XA896: Delivered 7.3.57. Olympus 104 engines. 230 OCU, 83 Squadron, 44 Squadron. Bristol Siddeley test bed for BS100 vectored-thrust engine, intended for Hawker P.1124. Partially converted for this role until fighter development was abandoned. Withdrawn during 1966 and scrapped at Patchway.

9/ XA897: Delivered 20.7.56. Olympus 104 engines. 230 OCU, A & AEE trials. Crashed during approach to Heathrow Airport 1.10.56, and was destroyed.

10/ XA898: Delivered 3.1.57. Olympus 104 engines. 230 OCU. Used exclusively by the OCU before being delivered to Halton 25.8.64, for use as an instructional airframe (7856M). Scrapped 1971.

11/ XA899: Delivered 28.2.57. Olympus 104 engines. A & AEE trials, RAE trials at Thurleigh, blind landing experiments. Auto pilot development. Delivered to Cosford as an instructional airframe (7812M). Scrapped 1973. Nose section retained by Cosford Museum.

12/ XA900: Delivered 25.3.57. Olympus 104 engines. 230 OCU, 101 Squadron. Delivered to Cosford as an instructional airframe (7896M) 28.2.66. Withdrawn from use and transferred to Cosford Museum as last intact Vulcan B.Mk.1. Scrapped during 1986.

13/ XA901: Delivered 4.4.57. Olympus 104 engines. 230 OCU, 44 Squadron, 83 Squadron. Delivered to Cranwell as an instructional airframe (7897M) in 1964. Scrapped 1972.

14/ XA902: Delivered 10.5.57. Olympus/Conway/Spey engines. 230 OCU. Damaged in a landing accident 28.2.58. Engine trials (Conway and Spey) with

Below: *During night flying operations on 1 March 1961 XA904 ran out of fuel and made a crash landing at Waddington. The aircraft was then allocated to ground instruction duties. In March 1958 XA904 had been displayed as a static exhibit during the official opening of Nairobi's new airport. (British Aerospace)*

Above: *Vulcan XA911 at Luqa, Malta, in September 1964. Note the nose-up attitude of the B.1 due to the nosewheel leg which was longer than that fitted to the B.2. (R.C.B. Ashworth)*

Rolls-Royce. Scrapped 1963.

15/ XA903: Delivered 31.5.57. Olympus 101 engines. A & AEE, RAE Farnborough. Blue Steel trials aircraft. Delivered to Rolls-Royce as test bed for Concorde Olympus and Tornado RB199 engines. Experimental 27mm cannon fit at A & AEE. Last flight by B.1 at Farnborough 22.2.79. Scrapped 1980.

16/ XA904: Delivered 16.7.57. Converted to B.1A standard 1960. Olympus 104 engines. 83 Squadron, 44 Squadron. Damaged in crash landing at Waddington 1.3.61. Disposed as instructional airframe (7738M) and later scrapped.

17/ XA905: Delivered 11.7.57. Converted to B.1A standard 1960. Olympus 104 engines. 83 Squadron, 44 Squadron, 230 OCU, Waddington Wing. Delivered to Newton as an instructional airframe (7857M). Scrapped 1974.

18/ XA906: Delivered 12.8.57. Converted to B.1A standard 1962. Olympus 104 engines. 83 Squadron, 44 Squadron, Waddington Wing. Stored at St. Athan 10.3.67. Sold as scrap to Bradbury & Co. 6.11.68.

19/ XA907: Delivered 29.8.57. Converted to B.1A standard 1961. Olympus 104 engines. 83 Squadron, 44 Squadron, Waddington Wing, BCDU. Withdrawn from use 3.11.66. Sold as scrap 20.5.68.

20/ XA908: Delivered 18.9.57. Olympus 104 engines. 83 Squadron. Crashed in Michigan, USA, 24.10.58.

21/ XA909: Delivered 1.10.57. Converted to B.1A standard 1962. Olympus 104 engines. 101 Squadron, 50 Squadron, Waddington Wing. Crashed in Anglesey 16.7.64, following engine explosion.

22/ XA910: Delivered 31.10.57. Converted to B.1A standard 1962. Olympus 104 engines. 101 Squadron, 230 OCU, 50 Squadron, 44 Squadron. Became instructional airframe (7995M) and later scrapped.

23/ XA911: Delivered 1.11.57. Converted to B.1A standard 1962. Olympus 104 engines. 83 Squadron, 230 OCU, Waddington Wing. Delivered to St. Athan 2.2.67, sold as scrap 8.11.68.

24/ XA912: Delivered 2.12.57. Converted to B.1A standard 1960. Olympus 104 engines. 101 Squadron, Waddington Wing.

25/ XA913: Delivered 19.12.57. Converted to B.1A standard 1961. Olympus 104 engines. 101 Squadron, Waddington Wing. Stored St. Athan 21.12.66, sold as scrap 20.5.68.

Vulcan B.Mk.1.
Contract 6/Air/11301/CB.6(a). 37 off—30.9.54.

26/ XH475: Delivered 11.2.58. Converted to B.1A standard 1962. Olympus 104 engines. 101 Squadron, Waddington Wing. Became instructional airframe (7996M) 20.11.67. Scrapped 7.6.69.

27/ XH476: Delivered 4.2.58. Converted to B.1A 1962. Olympus 104 engines. 101 Squadron, 44 Squadron, Waddington Wing. Withdrawn from use 4.5.67, sold as scrap 21.1.69.

28/ XH477: Delivered 17.2.58. Converted to B.1A standard 1960. Olympus 104 engines. 83 Squadron, 44 Squadron, 50 Squadron. Crashed in Scotland 12.6.63.

29/ XH478: Delivered 31.3.58. Converted to B.1A standard 1962. Olympus 104 engines. Ministry of Aviation (in-flight refuelling trials), Waddington Wing. Delivered to Akrotiri as instructional airframe (MC8047M) 3.69. Later scrapped.

30/ XH479: Delivered 28.3.58. Converted to B.1A standard 1961. Olympus 104 engines. Waddington Wing. Delivered to Halton as instructional airframe (7974M), scrapped 1973.

31/ XH480: Delivered 22.4.58. Converted to B.1A standard 1962. Olympus 104 engines. 83 Squadron, 44 Squadron, Waddington Wing. Delivered to St. Athan 10.11.66, sold as scrap 30.9.68.

32/ XH481: Delivered 30.4.58. Converted to B.1A standard 1960. Olympus 104 engines. 101 Squadron, Waddington Wing. Delivered to Cottesmore fire dump 11.1.68, scrapped 1977.

33/ XH482: Delivered 5.5.58. Converted to B.1A 1962. Olympus 104 engines. 617 Squadron, 50 Squadron, 101 Squadron,

Waddington Wing. Delivered to St. Athan 13.10.66, scrapped 19.9.68.

34/ XH483: Delivered 20.5.58. Converted to B.1A standard 1961. Olympus 104 engines. 617 Squadron, 50 Squadron, Waddington Wing. To Manston fire dump 3.8.67, scrapped 1977.

35/ XH497: Delivered 29.5.58. Converted to B.1A standard 1962. Olympus 104 engines. 617 Squadron, 50 Squadron, Waddington Wing. Withdrawn from use 17.5.66, scrapped 1969.

36/ XH498: Delivered 30.6.58. Converted to B.1A standard 1962. Olympus 104 engines. 617 Squadron, 50 Squadron, Waddington Wing. Became instructional airframe (7993M), later scrapped.

37/ XH499: Delivered 17.7.58. Converted to B.1A standard 1962. Olympus 104 engines. 617 Squadron, 50 Squadron, 44 Squadron, A & AEE. Withdrawn from use 11.65, scrapped later at Bitteswell.

38/ XH500: Delivered 15.8.58. Converted to B.1A standard 1959. Olympus 104 engines. 617 Squadron, BCDU, 50 Squadron, Waddington Wing. Became instructional airframe (7994M), to Waddington fire dump, scrapped 1977.

39/ XH501: Delivered 3.9.58. Converted to B.1A standard 1961. Olympus 104 engines. 617 Squadron, 44 Squadron, 44/50 Squadron. Delivered St. Athan 3.11.66. Sold as scrap 8.11.68.

40/ XH502: Delivered 10.11.58. Converted to B.1A standard 1962. Olympus 104 engines. 617 Squadron, 50 Squadron, Waddington Wing. To Scampton fire dump 1.68, nose section to Waddington for instructional duties.

41/ XH503: Delivered 30.12.58. Converted to B.1A 1963. Olympus 104 engines. 83 Squadron, 44 Squadron, Waddington Wing. To St. Athan 6.12.66, sold as scrap 8.11.68.

42/ XH504: Delivered 30.12.58. Converted to B.1A 1961. Olympus 104 engines. 230 OCU, Waddington Wing. Delivered to Cottesmore fire dump 4.1.68, later scrapped.

43/ XH505: Delivered 13.3.59. Converted to B.1A standard 1960. Olympus 104 engines. 230 OCU, 617 Squadron, 50 Squadron, Waddington Wing. Delivered to Finningley fire dump 9.1.68, later scrapped.

44/ XH506: Delivered 17.4.59. Converted to B.1A standard 1960. Olympus 104 engines. 101 Squadron, 617 Squadron, 50 Squadron, Waddington Wing. Withdrawn from use 10.1.68, sold as scrap 8.11.68.

45/ XH532: Delivered 31.3.59. Converted to B.1A standard 1962. Olympus 104 engines. Last production B.1. 230 OCU, 101 Squadron, Waddington Wing. Delivered to St. Athan 17.5.66, sold as scrap 8.11.68.

VULCAN B.MK.2.

Contract 6/Air/11301/CB.6(a). 17 off—30.9.54.

1/ XH533: First flight 19.8.58. Olympus 200 engines. A & AEE 26.3.59. St. Athan Engineering Squadron (8048M). Sold to Bradbury & Co as scrap 15.10.70.

2/ XH534: Completed 17.7.59. Olympus 201 engines. Manufacturers trials 4.3.60, A & AEE, 230 OCU 6.12.66. Manufacturers for storage 7.4.72. Converted to B.2(MRR) 8.73. 27 Squadron 14.8.74, St. Athan 7.4.81. Sold to Harold John & Co as scrap 16.2.82.

3/ XH535: Completed 27.5.60. Olympus 201 engines. A & AEE 27.5.60. Crashed near Andover 11.5.64.

4/ XH536: Completed 17.7.59. Olympus 201 engines. A & AEE 31.5.60, Waddington Wing 24.11.65. Crashed in Wales 11.2.66 during TFR trials.

5/ XH537: Completed 27.8.59. Olympus 201 engines. Manufacturers trials 31.8.60, 230 OCU 31.5.65, St. Athan 14.2.78. Conversion to B.2(MRR), 27 Squadron 8.5.78. Abingdon 24.3.83 instructional/exhibition airframe (8749M).

6/ XH538: Completed 23.9.59. Olympus 201 engines. Manufacturers/A & AEE trials 30.1.61, Scampton Wing 14.5.69, Waddington Wing 29.4.70, 230 OCU 21.4.71, 27 Squadron 3.12.73, 230 OCU 15.1.75, 35 Squadron 28.7.77, Waddington Wing 16.8.78, 35 Squadron 23.11.79, St. Athan 11.3.81, sold to W. Harold & Co as scrap 31.8.81.

7/ XH539: Completed 30.9.59. Olympus 201 engines. Manufacturers/A & AEE trials 25.5.61. Withdrawn from use 12.71, to Waddington fire dump 7.3.72, later scrapped.

8/ XH554: Completed 29.10.59. Olympus 201 engines. 83 Squadron 10.4.61, 230 OCU 1.11.62, Firefighting School Catterick 9.6.81 (8694M), later scrapped.

Left: *XH535 was operated by the A & AEE until 11 May 1964 when the aircraft entered a spin while returning to Boscombe Down and crashed. All four rear crew were killed although the pilots managed to eject. Some recognizable components can still be seen among the wreckage, including the immensely strong undercarriage. (A & AEE)*

Above: *Used for weapons trials with the A & AEE, XH539 carried black calibration markings along the lower edges of the bomb bay doors, as illustrated during a rare public demonstration at Boscombe Down on 19 March 1971. A year later the aircraft was delivered to Waddington for fire fighting practice. (R. L. Ward)*

9/ XH555: Completed 6.61. Olympus 201 engines. 27 Squadron 14.7.61, 230 OCU, Manufacturers for fatigue tests, St. Athan for structural integrity tests. Scrapped 1971.

10/ XH556: Completed 9.61. Olympus 201 engines. 27 Squadron 29.9.61, 230 OCU. Struck off charge following undercarriage collapse 19.4.66, to Finningley fire dump, later scrapped.

11/ XH557: Completed 13.5.60. Olympus 201/301 engines. To Bristol Siddeley for engine trials 21.6.60. Fitted with Mk.301 engines in outer nacelles, later fitted with four 301s. First B.2 with enlarged intakes. Cottesmore Wing 6.12.65, Waddington Wing 8.2.66, Akrotiri Wing 19.4.74, Waddington Wing 15.1.75, 50 Squadron 3.81. Sold to Bird Group as scrap 8.12.82.

Below: *XJ781 at Benson, September 1964. The aircraft was damaged beyond repair in Iran in 1973, landing on a foam carpet with the port undercarriage leg retracted. (R. L. Ward)*

12/ XH558: Completed 30.6.60. Olympus 201 engines. 230 OCU 1.7.60, Waddington Wing 26.2.68. Conversion to B.2(MRR) 17.8.73, 230 OCU 18.10.76, 27 Squadron 29.11.76, Waddington Wing 31.3.82. Conversion to K.2 30.6.82, 50 Squadron 12.10.82, Waddington Station Flight 1.4.84, allocation cancelled Waddington 14.11.84. Conversion to B.2 4.85, 55 Squadron 9.85. Last Vulcan in RAF service. Sold to C. Walton, and delivered to Bruntingthorpe, 23.3.93. Struck off Charge 23.3.93.

13/ XH559: Completed 30.7.60. Olympus 201 engines. 230 OCU 24.8.60, St. Athan 27.5.81, sold to Harold John & Co. as scrap 29.1.82.

14/ XH560: Completed 30.9.60. Olympus 201 engines. 230 OCU 3.10.60, Manufacturers 28.11.60, 12 Squadron 26.9.62, 230 OCU 29.11.63, Cottesmore Wing 23.8.65, Waddington Wing 10.4.67, Cottesmore Wing 2.2.68, Akrotiri Wing 15.1.69, Manufacturers for storage 20.10.71. Conversion to B.2(MRR) 1.2.73, 27 Squadron 15.3.74, Waddington Wing 25.3.82. Conversion to K.2 15.6.82, 50 Squadron 23.8.82. Waddington Station Flight 4.84, Marham dump 29.11.84, later scrapped.

15/ XH561: Completed 31.10.60. Olympus 201 engines. 230 OCU 4.11.60, Waddington Wing 7.8.67, Cottesmore Wing 8.5.68, Akrotiri Wing 19.3.69, 35 Squadron 6.3.75, 50 Squadron 4.9.81. Conversion to K.2 4.5.82. 50 Squadron 18.6.82, Waddington Station Flight 1.4.84. Allocated 8809M 22.3.84. Delivered Firefighting School Catterick 14.6.84, later scrapped.

16/ XH562: Completed 30.11.60. Olympus 201 engines. 35 Squadron 1.3.63, 230 OCU 11.3.63, 35 Squadron 30.4.63, 230 OCU 19.9.63, Cottesmore Wing 1.8.65, 50 Squadron 8.3.66, Waddington Wing 10.2.67, Cottesmore Wing 24.4.68, Akrotiri Wing 15.1.69, Waddington Wing 9.5.75, 230 OCU 27.9.77, 35 Squadron 16.12.80, 9 Squadron 7.81, 101 Squadron 6.82. Firefighting School Catterick 19.8.82 (8758M). Scrapped 1984.

17/ XH563: Completed 22.12.60. Olympus 201 engines. 83 Squadron 28.12.60, 12 Squadron 26.11.62, 230 OCU 5.3.65, Waddington Wing 6.8.68, 230 OCU 18.3.69, Scampton Wing 3.5.71, 230 OCU 7.5.71. Conversion to B.2(MRR) 9.2.73. 27 Squadron 17.12.73. Allocated 8744M 31.3.82 for preservation at Scampton. Later scrapped.

VULCAN B.Mk.2.
Contract 6/Air/11830/CB.6(a). 8 off—31.3.55.

18/ XJ780: Completed 10.1.61. Olympus 201 engines. 83 Squadron 16.1.61, 12 Squadron 26.11.62, 230 OCU 16.8.63, Waddington Wing 10.10.67, Cottesmore Wing 6.12.68, Waddington Wing 18.4.69, Akrotiri Wing 12.1.70, Waddington Wing 17.1.75. Modification to B.2(MRR) standard 31.3.76. 27 Squadron 23.11.76.

Allocated for spares recovery 31.3.82. Sold to Bird Group as scrap 11.82.

19/ XJ781: Completed 20.2.61. Olympus 201 engines. 83 Squadron 23.2.61, 12 Squadron 29.10.62, 230 OCU 4.2.64, Waddington Wing 10.2.66, Cottesmore Wing 22.4.68, Akrotiri Wing 18.4.69. Damaged during landing, Shiraz, Iran 23.5.73. Struck off charge 27.5.73.

20/ XJ782: Completed 2.61. Olympus 201 engines. 83 Squadron 2.3.61, 12 Squadron 23.10.62, 230 OCU 20.12.63, Waddington Wing 25.3.66, Cottesmore Wing 9.4.68, Akrotiri Wing 19.3.69, Waddington Wing 8.1.75. Modification to B.2(MRR) standard 1.77. 27 Squadron 15.2.77. Flew last Vulcan sortie at Scampton 31.3.82. Allocated to Scampton dump 31.3.82. Re-allocated to 101 Squadron 22.5.82. To Finningley for preservation 4.9.82 (8766M). Later transferred to dump and scrapped.

21/ XJ783: Completed 6.3.61. Olympus 201 engines. 83 Squadron 13.3.61, 9 Squadron 7.11.62, 230 OCU 28.2.64, Waddington Wing 3.1.66, Cottesmore Wing 22.3.68, Akrotiri Wing 15.1.69, 35 Squadron 16.1.75, 230 OCU 11.8.76, 35 Squadron 23.8.76, 617 Squadron 23.11.78, 35 Squadron 3.4.81. Spares recovery 1.3.82. Sold to Bird Group as scrap 11.82.

22/ XJ784: Completed 30.3.61. Olympus 301 engines. A & AEE 29.3.61, 230 OCU 22.12.66, Akrotiri Wing 21.7.70, Waddington Wing 15.1.75, 9 Squadron 2.75, 44 Squadron 6.79, 101 Squadron 6.80. Spares recovery 10.9.82. Sold to Bird Group as scrap 8.12.82.

23/ XJ823: Completed 20.4.61. Olympus 201 engines. 27 Squadron 21.4.61, 35 Squadron 2.1.63, Cottesmore Wing 3.64 230 OCU 11.5.64, Waddington Wing 1.11.66, Cottesmore Wing 29.4.68, Akrotiri Wing 5.2.69, Waddington Wing 17.1.75, 9 Squadron 2.75. Modified to B.2(MRR) standard 3.77. 27 Squadron 27.4.77, 35 Squadron 2.4.81, Waddington Wing 1.3.82, 9 Squadron 3.82, 50 Squadron 4.82, Station Flight Waddington 4.1.83, sold to T. Stoddart 21.1.83, delivered to Solway Aviation Society Carlisle 24.1.83.

24/ XJ824: Complete 11.5.61. Olympus 201 engines. 27 Squadron 16.5.61, 9 Squadron 25.2.63, 230 OCU 2.12.63, Cottesmore Wing 4.7.66, Waddington Wing 4.10.66, Cottesmore Wing 19.6.68, Akrotiri Wing 5.2.69, 35 Squadron 24.1.75, 230 OCU 14.2.77, 44 Squadron 10.79, 101 Squadron 7.82. Last Vulcan to leave Bitteswell after manufacturers modifications 8.6.81. Delivered to Imperial War Museum Duxford 13.3.82.

25/ XJ825: Completed 27.7.61. Olympus 201 engines. 27 Squadron 28.7.61, 35 Squadron 4.2.63, 230 OCU 30.4.64, Cottesmore Wing 3.9.65, Waddington Wing 11.4.67, Cottesmore Wing 19.2.68, Akrotiri Wing 26.2.69, 35 Squadron 16.1.75. Modification to B.2(MRR) standard 13.1.76. 27 Squadron 15.12.76, 35 Squadron 6.4.81, 101 Squadron 1.3.82. Conversion to K.2 11.5.82. 50 Squadron 25.6.82. Allocated 8810M 22.3.84, battle damage repair duties. Struck off charge 5.4.84. Scrapped 1992.

VULCAN B.MK.2.

Contract 6/Air/13145/CB.6(a). 24 off—25.2.56.

26/ XL317: Completed 14.7.61. Olympus 201 engines. Blue Steel modifications. A & AEE 13.7.61, 617 Squadron 7.6.62, 230 OCU 24.4.74, 617 Squadron 1.5.74. To Akrotiri as 8725M for crash rescue training, delivered 1.12.81. Later scrapped.

27/ XL318: Completed 30.8.61. Olympus 201 engines. Blue Steel modifications. 617 Squadron 4.9.61, 230 OCU 22.5.72, 27 Squadron 31.1.74, 230 OCU 1.2.74, Waddington Wing 18.6.75, 230 OCU 5.8.75, Waddington Wing 7.11.79, 230 OCU 21.2.80, 617 Squadron 1.7.81. Last sortie by a 617 Squadron Vulcan 11.12.81. Assigned to RAF Museum 4.1.82 as 8733M. Transported to Hendon 12.2.82.

28/ XL319: Completed 19.10.61. Olympus 201 engines. Blue Steel modifications. 617 Squadron 23.10.61, 230 OCU 14.5.70, Scampton Wing 12.11.70, 617 Squadron 22.4.71, 230 OCU 19.9.72, 35 Squadron 16.10.78, 44 Squadron 1.3.82. Sold to North Eastern Aircraft Museum 20.1.83, delivered to Sunderland 21.1.83.

29/ XL320: Completed 30.11.61. Olympus 201 engines. Blue Steel modifications. 617 Squadron 4.12.61, 83 Squadron 6.71, 27 Squadron 9.71, 230 OCU 29.3.72. Flew 500,000th Vulcan hour 18.12.81. To St. Athan 2.6.81. Sold to W. Harold & Co. 31.8.81 as scrap.

30. XL321: Completed 10.1.62. Olympus 201 engines. Blue Steel modifications. 617 Squadron 11.1.62, 27 Squadron 1.71, 230 OCU 29.3.72, 617 Squadron 15.9.72, 230 OCU 11.10.72, 617 Squadron 13.4.73, 44 Squadron 8.6.76, 230 OCU 8.11.76, 35 Squadron 1.7.81, 617 Squadron 14.9.81, 35 Squadron 6.10.81, 50 Squadron 21.1.82. Delivered to Firefighting School Catterick 19.8.82 (8759M). Highest individual Vulcan operational flying hours (6,952.35). Later scrapped.

31/ XL359: Completed 31.1.61. Olympus 201 engines. Blue Steel modifications. 617 Squadron 1.2.62, 27 Squadron 3.71, 230 OCU 21.10.71, 35 Squadron 1.7.81. Allocated as gate guard at Scampton 1.3.81, but later dumped. Sold to Bird Group as scrap 11.82.

32/ XL360: Completed 28.2.62. Olympus 201 engines. Blue Steel modifications. 617 Squadron 2.3.62, 230 OCU 13.7.71. Waddington Wing 18.8.75, 230 OCU 21.10.75, 617 Squadron 5.12.77, 35 Squadron 31.5.78, 101 Squadron 5.1.82. Sold to Midland Air Museum 26.1.83, delivered to Baginton 4.2.83.

33/ XL361: Completed 14.3.62. Olympus 201 engines. Blue Steel modifications. 617 Squadron 15.3.62, 230 OCU 7.10.70, Scampton Wing 19.11.70, 230 OCU 30.11.70, Scampton Wing 5.4.71, OCU 12.5.71, 27 Squadron/230 OCU 14.1.74, A & AEE 7.8.75, 617 Squadron 3.9.75, 35 Squadron 3.8.77, 9 Squadron 13.4.81. Accident at Goose Bay, Canada, 13.11.81. Grounded 21.12.81, and placed on display at Happy Valley, Goose Bay, 7.6.82.

34/ XL384: Completed 30.3.62. Olympus 301 engines. Blue Steel modifications. 230 OCU 2.4.62, Scampton Wing 5.8.64, Waddington Wing 23.3.70, 230 OCU 27.11.70. Heavy landing 12.8.71, allocated 8505M on 30.9.76 as escape trainer. Later transferred to crash rescue training as

8670M 29.1.81, and struck off charge 23.5.85.

35/ XL385: Completed 17.4.62. Olympus 301 engines. Blue Steel modifications. 9 Squadron 18.4.62, Scampton Wing 9.10.64. Ground fire at Scampton 6.4.67. Struck off charge 7.4.67.

36/ XL386: Completed 11.5.62. Olympus 301 engines. Blue Steel modifications. 9 Squadron 14.5.62, Scampton Wing 16.8.65, 230 OCU 1.4.70, 44 Squadron 30.9.77, 101 Squadron 5.81, 50 Squadron 10.81. Delivered to Central Training Establishment at Manston 26.8.82 as 8760M, later scrapped.

37/ XL387: Completed 31.5.62. Olympus 301 engines. Blue Steel modifications. 230 OCU 4.6.62, Scampton Wing 5.2.65, 230 OCU 5.7.72, 101 Squadron 10.1.73, 50 Squadron 8.75. To St. Athan for crash rescue training 28.1.82. Sold to T. Bradbury as scrap 2.6.83.

38/ XL388: Completed 13.6.62. Olympus 301 engines. Blue Steel modifications. 9 Squadron 14.6.62 (Coningsby Wing), 230 OCU 19.4.71, 617 Squadron 15.9.72, 230 OCU 29.9.72, 617 Squadron 2.2.73, 230 OCU 14.5.73, 617 Squadron 1.11.73, 230 OCU 5.3.74, 617 Squadron 6.3.74, 44 Squadron 1.4.74. To Honington fire dump 2.4.82 (8750M). Sold to Swefeling Group as scrap 13.6.85.

39/ XL389: Completed 11.7.62. Olympus 301 engines. Blue Steel modifications. 230 OCU 13.7.62, Scampton Wing 20.5.65, 230 OCU 11.11.70, 617 Squadron 12.70, 230 OCU 7.4.72, 617 Squadron 30.6.72, 230 OCU 12.1.73, 617 Squadron 16.1.73, 9 Squadron 26.6.74, 44 Squadron 7.79, 101 Squadron 6.80. To St. Athan 6.4.81. Sold to W. Harold 31.8.81 as scrap.

40/ XL390: Completed 19.7.62. Olympus 301 engines. Blue Steel modifications. First production aircraft with Skybolt hardpoints. 9 Squadron 20.7.62, Scampton Wing 27.5.65, 230 OCU 30.4.71, 617 Squadron 3.6.71, 230 OCU 31.5.74, 617 Squadron 4.6.74. Crashed during air display, Glenview NAS, USA, 12.8.78.

41/ XL391: Completed 22.5.63. Olympus 301 engines. Blue Steel modifications. A & AEE 22.5.63, BCDU 15.6.65, A & AEE 6.1.66, Cottesmore Wing 31.7.68, Akrotiri Wing 5.2.69, 9 Squadron 17.1.75, 101 Squadron 6.80. Selected for 'Black Buck' modifications, but not used operationally. 44 Squadron 21.6.82. Sold to Manchester Vulcan Bomber Society 11.2.83. Delivered to Blackpool 16.2.83.

Above: *Resplendent in the markings of No. 617 Squadron, Vulcan XL425 is seen shortly after terrain-following radar was installed. The RWR (radar warning receiver) modification to the tail fin had yet to be made. In the distance are two Hastings T.5s, part of No. 230 OCU's fleet, which were used for training the Vulcan's rear crew. (MoD)*

42/ XL392: Completed 31.7.62. Olympus 201 engines. Blue Steel modifications. 83 Squadron 2.8.62, 230 OCU 11.12.70, Scampton Wing 21.12.70, 230 OCU 12.1.73, 617 Squadron 15.1.73, 35 Squadron 4.1.82. Delivered to Valley for crash rescue training as 8745M 24.3.82, later scrapped.

43/ XL425: Completed 30.8.62. Olympus 201 engines. Blue Steel modifications. 83 Squadron 31.8.62, Scampton Wing, 617 Squadron 30.11.72, 27 Squadron 1.11.73, 617 Squadron 1.4.74. Grounded 4.1.82. Sold to Bird Group as scrap 4.82.

44/ XL426: Completed 7.9.62. Olympus 201 engines. Blue Steel modifications. 83 Squadron 13.9.62, Scampton Wing, 230 OCU 29.3.72, 617 Squadron 7.4.72, 230 OCU 28.6.72, 617 Squadron 4.7.72, 230 OCU 11.7.72, 617 Squadron 1.8.72, 230 OCU 13.4.73, 617 Squadron 16.4.73, 27 Squadron 6.2.74, 617 Squadron 21.2.74, 50 Squadron 5.1.82, 55 Squadron 1.4.84. Sold to Roy Jacobsen and delivered to Southend 19.12.86. Registered as G-VJET 7.7.87.

45/ XL427: Completed 29.9.62. Olympus 201 engines. Blue Steel modifications. 83 Squadron 2.10.62, Scampton Wing, 617 Squadron 9.69, 27 Squadron 3.71, 230 OCU 29.6.72, 617 Squadron 5.7.72, 230

Below: *XL426 is now registered as a civil aircraft, G-VJET, the registration being applied to the Vulcan's RWR fairing. Maintained in good condition, the machine is potentially airworthy, if sufficient funds can be found to finance it. The Vulcan Memorial Flight Supporters Club continues to care for XL426 at Southend Airport in the hope that the aircraft will one day fly again. (VMF Supporters Club)*

OCU 25.9.72, 27 Squadron 4.1.74, 230 OCU 11.8.76, 27 Squadron 27.8.76, 9 Squadron 2.5.77, 50 Squadron 4.81, 9 Squadron 10.81, 44 Squadron 6.82. Delivered to Macrihanish for crash rescue training 13.8.82 as 8756M. Dumped 1986.

46/ XL443: Completed 4.10.62. Olympus 201 engines. Blue Steel modifications. 83 Squadron 8.10.62, Scampton Wing, Akrotiri Wing 12.4.72, 35 Squadron 24.1.75. Allocated to RAF Museum 4.1.82. Later sold to Bird Group as scrap 4.82.

47/ XL444: Completed 29.10.82. Olympus 201 engines. Blue Steel modifications. 27 Squadron 1.11.62, Scampton Wing, 230 OCU 18.6.66, Scampton Wing 19.6.67, 230 OCU 5.4.71, 27 Squadron 11.5.71, 617 Squadron 9.71, 230 OCU/617 Squadron 19.7.72, 617 Squadron 18.12.73, 35 Squadron 31.5.78, 9 Squadron 6.4.81. grounded 10.9.82. Sold to Bird Group as scrap 8.12.82.

48/ XL445: Completed 19.11.62. Olympus 201 engines. Blue Steel modifications. 27 Squadron 26.11.62, Scampton Wing, Waddington Wing 30.9.66, Cottesmore Wing 18.4.68, Akrotiri Wing 15.1.69, 35 Squadron 16.1.75, Waddington Wing 16.6.77, 35 Squadron 1.10.77, 230 OCU 16.10.78, 35 Squadron 1.7.81, 44 Squadron 18.11.81. Conversion to K.2 25.5.82. 50 Squadron 22.7.82. Allocated 8811M 22.3.84 for crash rescue training. Delivered Lyneham 1.4.84. Later scrapped.

49/ XL446: Completed 19.11.62. Olympus 201 engines. Blue Steel modifications. 27 Squadron 30.11.62, Scampton Wing, Waddington Wing 16.9.66, 230 OCU 28.12.67, Scampton Wing 18.4.72, Akrotiri Wing 31.7.72, 35 Squadron 16.1.75, Waddington Wing 24.5.78, 617 Squadron 31.10.78, 35 Squadron 4.1.82. Grounded 1.3.82. Sold to Bird Group as scrap 11.82.

VULCAN B.MK.2.
Contract KD/B/01/CB.6(a). 40 off—22.1.58.

50/ XM569: Completed 4.1.63, Olympus 201 engines. Blue Steel modifications. 27 Squadron 1.2.63, Scampton Wing, Waddington Wing 17.11.66, Cottesmore Wing 19.1.68, Akrotiri Wing 26.2.69, 27 Squadron 4.7.74, 9 Squadron 23.11.76, 50 Squadron 6.79, 101 Squadron 9.81, 44 Squadron 8.82. Sold to Wales Aircraft Museum 21.1.83. Delivered to Cardiff 2.2.83.

51/ XM570: Completed 26.2.63. Olympus 201 engines. Blue Steel modifications. 27 Squadron 27.2.63, Scampton Wing, Waddington Wing 2.1.67, Cottesmore Wing 26.1.68, Akrotiri Wing 26.2.69, 27 Squadron 8.3.74, 35 Squadron 8.12.76, 230 OCU 28.2.77, 35 Squadron 2.3.77, 617 Squadron 4.9.78, 35 Squadron 31.10.78. Delivered to St. Athan 11.3.81. Sold to Harold John & Co as scrap 29.1.82.

52/ XM571: Completed 20.2.63. Olympus 201 engines. Blue Steel modifications. 83 Squadron 22.2.63, Scampton Wing, Cottesmore Wing 20.1.67, Waddington Wing 3.7.67, Cottesmore Wing 13.9.67, Waddington Wing 15.12.67, Akrotiri Wing 19.3.69, 27 Squadron 3.1.75, 35 Squadron 9.4.75, Waddington Wing 16.6.75, 35 Squadron 3.11.75, 50 Squadron 15.6.76, 35 Squadron 15.11.76. St. Athan 9.1.79, 617 Squadron 27.3.79, Waddington Wing 20.8.79, 617 Squadron 4.12.79, 101 Squadron 8.1.82. Conversion to K.2 11.5.82. 50 Squadron 25.8.82. Waddington Station Flight 4.84. Allocated 8812M 22.3.84. Delivered to Gibraltar for preservation 9.5.84. Later scrapped.

53/ XM572: Completed 28.2.63. Olympus 201 engines. Blue Steel modifications. 83 Squadron 28.2.63, Scampton Wing, Cottesmore Wing 5.4.68, Akrotiri Wing 19.3.69, 35 Squadron 24.1.75, 9 Squadron 2.9.81. Grounded 10.9.82. Sold to Bird Group as scrap 30.11.82.

54/ XM573: Completed 26.3.63. Olympus 201 engines. Blue Steel modifications. 83 Squadron 28.3.63, Scampton Wing, Waddington Wing 25.4.67, 230 OCU 15.2.68, Akrotiri Wing 26.6.70, 27 Squadron 17.4.74, 44 Squadron 9.3.77, 230 OCU 18.12.78, 9 Squadron 7.4.81, Scampton 22.5.82. Delivered to Offutt AFB, USA, 7.6.82, presented to USAF 12.6.82.

55/ XM574: Completed 12.6.63. Olympus 301 engines. Blue Steel modifications. 27 Squadron 21.6.63, Scampton Wing, 230 OCU 3.5.71, 27 Squadron 12.5.71, 101 Squadron 3.11.71, Akrotiri Wing 24.8.73, 35 Squadron 24.1.75, 617 Squadron 14.8.75. To St. Athan 31.8.81. Sold to Harold John & Co. as scrap 29.1.82.

56/ XM575: Completed 21.5.63. Olympus 301 engines. Blue Steel modifications. 617 Squadron 22.5.63, Scampton Wing, Waddington Wing 28.7.70, Scampton Wing 27.11.70, 230 OCU 3.5.71, 617 Squadron 7.5.71, 101 Squadron 15.3.74, 50 Squadron 6.78, 44 Squadron 8.79. Sold to Leicestershire Air Museum 25.1.83. Delivered to Bruntingthorpe 28.1.83.

***Left:** An unusual nose marking is visible on XM573, presumably in recognition of the 500th Vulcan Major Servicing to have been carried out at RAF St. Athan. XM573 now belongs to Air Combat Command and resides in the Strategic Air Command Museum at Offutt AFB, Nebraska, alongside other famous nuclear bombers such as the B-36, B-47, B-58 and B-52. (British Aerospace)*

***Above:** End of the line – XM595 is slowly destroyed at Waddington and a supreme example of aerodynamic engineering becomes a pile of scrap. (via H. Hughes)*

Ferried to Castle Donington as G-BLMC. East Midlands Aeropark.

57/ XM576: Completed 14.6.63. Olympus 301 engines. Blue Steel modifications. Scampton Wing 21.6.63. Crash landed Scampton 25.5.65. Later struck off charge.

58/ XM594: Completed 9.7.63. Olympus 301 engines. Blue Steel modifications. 27 Squadron 19.7.63, Scampton Wing, Waddington Wing 24.8.72, 101 Squadron 6.75, 44 Squadron 5.77. Sold to Newark Air Museum 19.1.83. Delivered to Winthorpe 7.2.83.

59/ XM595: Completed 21.8.63. Olympus 301 engines. Blue Steel modifications. 617 Squadron 21.8.63, Scampton Wing, 27 Squadron 16.8.74, 617 Squadron 9.75, 35 Squadron 11.76, 617 Squadron 2.78, 35 Squadron 4.1.82. Grounded 1.3.82. Sold to Bird Group as scrap 11.82.

60/ XM596: Not completed. Aircraft used for static fatigue tests at Woodford, in connection with low level operations. Scrapped 1972.

61/ XM597: Completed 26.8.63. Olympus 301 engines. Blue Steel modifications. 12 Squadron 27.8.63, Coningsby Wing, Cottesmore Wing 18.12.64, Waddington Wing 18.4.68, A & AEE 29.11.71, 101 Squadron 8.73, 44 Squadron 9.75, 50 Squadron 4.76, 9 Squadron 5.79, 44 Squadron 10.81, 101 Squadron 7.82. Modified for 'Black Buck' operations. 44 Squadron 1.7.82, 50 Squadron 24.12.82. Delivered to Royal Scottish Museum of Flight, East Fortune, 12.4.84.

62/ XM598: Completed 30.8.63. Olympus 301 engines. 12 Squadron 4.9.63, Coningsby Wing, Cottesmore Wing 11.64. Waddington Wing 9.4.68, 101 Squadron 5.72, 44 Squadron 8.75, 50 Squadron 4.78, 9 Squadron 10.79, 50 Squadron 10.81, 44 Squadron 6.82. Modified for 'Black Buck' operations. Allocated 8778M 4.1.83, delivered to Cosford Aerospace Museum 20.1.83.

63/ XM559: Completed 30.9.63. Olympus 301 engines. 35 Squadron 1.10.63, Coningsby Wing, Waddington Wing 9.12.68, 101 Squadron 5.72, 50 Squadron 3.77, 44 Squadron 6.79. Delivered to St. Athan 27.5.81. Sold to H. John & Co. as scrap 29.1.82.

64/ XM600: Completed 30.9.63. Olympus 301 engines. 35 Squadron 3.10.63, Coningsby Wing, Waddington Wing 3.5.68, 101 Squadron 8.73. Crashed near Spilsby following engine bay fire 17.1.77.

65/ XM601: Completed 31.10.63. Olympus 301 engines. 9 Squadron 5.11.63, Coningsby Wing. Crashed on approach to Coningsby 7.10.64.

66/ XM602: Completed 11.11.63. Olympus 301 engines. 12 Squadron 13.11.63, Coningsby Wing, Cottesmore Wing, Waddington Wing 24.4.68, 9 Squadron 12.75, 230 OCU 19.10.76, 35 Squadron 29.10.76, Waddington Wing 1.11.76, 101 Squadron 5.80. To St. Athan 7.1.82. Transferred to St. Athan Historic Aircraft Museum 16.3.83 (8771M).

67/ XM603: Completed 29.11.63. Olympus 301 engines. 9 Squadron 4.12.63, Coningsby Wing, Cottesmore Wing, Waddington Wing 18.1.68, 50 Squadron 8.75, 101 Squadron 12.80, 44 Squadron 7.81. Sold to British Aerospace for preservation, delivered to Woodford 12.3.82. Mock-up aircraft for K.2 conversions.

68/ XM604: Completed 29.11.63. Olympus 301 engines. 35 Squadron 4.12.63, Coningsby Wing, Cottesmore Wing. Crashed near Cottesmore following loss of control during overshoot 30.1.68.

69/ XM605: Completed 17.12.63. Olympus 301 engines. 9 Squadron 30.12.63, Coningsby Wing, Cottesmore Wing, Waddington Wing 16.12.68, 101 Squadron 8.73, 50 Squadron 5.79. Delivered to Castle AFB, USA, 2.9.81. Presented to USAF 8.9.81.

70/ XM606: Completed 18.12.63. Olympus 301 engines. 12 Squadron 30.12.63, Coningsby Wing, Cottesmore Wing 18.2.65, MoA 14.6.65, Cottesmore Wing 5.4.68, Waddington Wing 13.5.68, 101 Squadron 12.75. 9 Squadron 6.79. Delivered to Barksdale AFB, USA, 7.6.82. Presented to USAF 14.6.83.

71/ XM607: 30.12.63. Olympus 301 engines. 35 Squadron 1.1.64, Coningsby Wing, Cottesmore Wing, Waddington Wing, 24.5.68, 44 Squadron 4.76, 9 Squadron 5.79, 101 Squadron 3.81, 44 Squadron 7.81. Modified for 'Black Buck' operations. 44 Squadron 14.6.82. Withdrawn from use 17.12.82, allocated 8779M 4.1.83. To static display at Waddington 19.1.83.

72/ XM608: Completed 28.1.64. Olympus 301 engines. 29.1.64, Coningsby Wing, Cottesmore Wing, Waddington Wing 23.2.68, 50 Squadron 4.75. To St. Athan 6.4.81. Sold to Bird Group as scrap 2.12.82.

Above: XM607's bomb bay, revealing a cluster of seven 1,000lb HE bombs and a pair of long-range fuel tanks. (John Hale)

73/ XM609: Completed 28.1.64. Olympus 301 engines. 12 Squadron 29.1.64, Coningsby Wing, Cottesmore Wing 3.3.65, 230 OCU 7.8.67, Cottesmore Wing 1.10.67, Waddington Wing 8.3.68, 9 Squadron 9.75, 44 Squadron 4.76. To St. Athan 12.3.81. Sold to W. Harold & Co. as scrap 31.8.81.

74/ XM610: Completed 10.2.64. Olympus 301 engines. 9 Squadron 12.2.64, Coningsby Wing, Cottesmore Wing, Waddington Wing 5.2.68. Crashed Wingate 8.1.71 following engine bay fire.

75/ XM611: Completed 12.2.64. Olympus 301 engines. 9 Squadron 14.2.64, Coningsby Wing, Cottesmore Wing, Waddington Wing 28.5.68, 101 Squadron 5.72. To St. Athan 27.1.82. Sold to T. Bradbury as scrap 2.6.83.

76/ XM612: Completed 28.2.64. Olympus 301 engines. 9 Squadron 3.3.64, Coningsby Wing, Cottesmore Wing, A & AEE 5.3.68, Waddington Wing 4.4.68, 101 Squadron 5.75, 44 Squadron 7.81. Modified for 'Black Buck' operations. 44 Squadron 23.5.82. Sold to Norwich Aviation Museum 19.1.83. Delivered 30.1.83.

77/ XM645: Completed 10.3.64. Olympus 301 engines. Coningsby Wing 12.3.64, Cottesmore Wing, Waddington Wing 15.12.67, 230 OCU 5.8.68, Waddington Wing 21.4.71, 101 Squadron 8.73, Akrotiri Wing 12.3.74, 9 Squadron 15.1.75. Crashed Zabbar, Malta, following explosion 14.10.75.

78/ XM646: Completed 7.4.64. Olympus 301 engines. 12 Squadron 8.4.64, Coningsby Wing, Cottesmore Wing, Akrotiri Wing 5.2.69, 9 Squadron 17.1.75, 101 Squadron 6.81. To St. Athan 26.1.82. Sold to T. Bradbury as scrap 29.6.83.

79/ XM647: Completed 15.4.64. Olympus 301 engines. 35 Squadron 15.4.64, Coningsby Wing, Cottesmore Wing, Akrotiri Wing 26.2.69, Waddington Wing 15.1.75, 9 Squadron 1.75, 44 Squadron 9.79, 50 Squadron 9.81. Delivered to Laarbruch 17.9.82 for ground instruction (8765M). Sold to Solair UK 25.2.85 as scrap. Scrapped 1.3.85.

80/ XM648: Completed 5.5.64. Olympus 301 engines. 9 Squadron 6.5.64, Coningsby Wing, Cottesmore Wing, Waddington Wing 25.1.68, 101 Squadron 5.72, 44 Squadron 5.75, 101 Squadron 3.77, 9 Squadron 9.80, 101 Squadron 10.81. Grounded 10.9.82. Sold to Bird Group as scrap 8.12.82.

81/ XM649: Completed 12.5.64. Olympus 301 engines. 9 Squadron 14.5.64, Coningsby Wing, Cottesmore Wing, Waddington Wing 18.1.68, 101 Squadron 8.73, 9 Squadron 4.76, 101 Squadron 8.79. To St. Athan 2.9.81. Sold to Bird Group as scrap 2.12.82.

82/ XM650: Completed 27.5.64. Olympus 301 engines. 12 Squadron 5.6.64, Coningsby Wing, Cottesmore Wing, Waddington Wing 20.12.67, 44 Squadron 5.75, 50 Squadron 1.77. To St. Athan 28.1.82. Allocated 8748M 16.3.83. Sold to Bournewood Aviation as scrap 22.3.84.

83/ XM651: Completed 19.6.64. Olympus 301 engines. 12 Squadron 22.6.64, Coningsby Wing, Cottesmore Wing, Waddington Wing 24.4.68, 101 Squadron 5.72, 50 Squadron 9.75, 101 Squadron 9.79. Grounded 10.9.82. Sold to Bird Group as scrap 30.11.82.

84. XM652: Completed 12.8.64. Olympus 301 engines. 9 Squadron 17.8.64, Coningsby Wing, Cottesmore Wing, Waddington Wing 24.12.67, 44 Squadron 9.75, 9 Squadron 10.81, 50 Squadron 10.82. Sold to Boulding Group 20.2.84. Dismantled and transported to Sheffield 7.5.84. Nose to Burntwood 2.85, rest of airframe scrapped 2.85.

85/ XM653: Completed 31.8.64. Olympus 301 engines. 9 Squadron, Coningsby Wing, Cottesmore Wing, Waddington Wing 24.1.68, 101 Squadron 5.72, 44 Squadron 5.75, 9 Squadron 9.75, 101 Squadron 10.78, 9 Squadron 5.79, 101 Squadron 7.79. To St. Athan 10.9.79. Dumped 18.12.80. Sold as scrap 28.7.81.

86/ XM654: Completed 22.10.64. Olympus 301 engines. 12 Squadron 26.10.64, Coningsby Wing, Cottesmore Wing, Waddington Wing 30.4.68, 101 Squadron 8.73, 50 Squadron 9.75, 101 Squadron 9.81, 50 Squadron 10.81. Grounded 29.10.82. Sold to Bird Group as scrap 30.11.82.

87/ XM655: Completed 19.11.64. Olympus 301 engines. 9 Squadron 23.11.64, Cottesmore Wing, Waddington Wing 12.1.68, 101 Squadron 5.72, 44 Squadron 7.81, 50 Squadron 8.82. Sold to Roy Jacobsen 11.2.84, delivered to Wellesbourne Mountford 11.2.84.

Registered G-VULC 27.2.84. Re-registered N655AV 1985. Sold to Radar Moor 1992.

88/ XM656: Completed 11.12.64. Olympus 301 engines. 35 Squadron 15.12.64. Cottesmore Wing, Waddington Wing 2.2.68, 101 Squadron 9.75, 9 Squadron 12.80. To Cottesmore for display 9.8.82, allocated 8757M. Sold to Bird Group as scrap 30.3.83.

89/ XM657: Completed 14.1.65. Olympus 301 engines. 35 Squadron 15.1.65, Cottesmore Wing, Waddington Wing 19.3.68, 101 Squadron 5.72, 50 Squadron 8.75, 101 Squadron 3.77, 44 Squadron 4.80. Allocated to Central Training Establishment 5.1.82, delivered to Manston 12.1.82. Allocated 8734M. Later scrapped. Last production Vulcan B.2.

VULCAN DEPLOYMENT

VULCAN WING DEPLOYMENT

AKROTIRI

9 Sqdn	1.69–1.75.
35 Sqdn	1.69–1.75.

CONINGSBY

9 Sqdn	3.62–11.64.
12 Sqdn	7.62–11.64.
35 Sqdn	12.62–11.64.

adopted aircraft pooling *c*.3.64.

COTTESMORE

9 Sqdn	11.64–1.69.
12 Sqdn	11.64–12.67.
35 Sqdn	11.64–1.69.

aircraft pooled throughout

SCAMPTON

27 Sqdn 4.61–3.72 and 11.73–3.82.

35 Sqdn	1.75–2.82.
83 Sqdn	10.60–8.69.
617 Sqdn	9.61–12.81.

adopted aircraft pooling *c*.4.64.

230 OCU moved in from Finningley 12.69. but remained separate from Scampton Wing for purposes of aircraft assignment.

WADDINGTON

9 Sqdn	1.75–4.82.
44 Sqdn	1967–12.82.
50 Sqdn	1966–3.84.
101 Sqdn	1967–8.82.

adopted aircraft pooling pre-B.Mk 2

VULCAN B.Mk 2 SQUADRONS

No 9 Formed Coningsby 1.3.62.; Cottesmore 7.11.64.; Akrotiri 1.69.; Waddington 1.75.; disbanded 29.4.82. (Insignia: a bat)

No 12 Formed Coningsby 1.7.62.; Cottesmore 7.11.64.; disbanded 31.12.67. (Insignia: a fox's mask)

No 27 Formed Scampton 1.4.61.; disbanded 29.3.72.; re-formed Scampton 1.11.73 in MRR role; disbanded 31.3.82. (Insignia: elephant or cartoon 'Dumbo')

No 35 Formed Coningsby 1.12.62.; Cottesmore 7.11.64.; Akrotiri 1.69.; Scampton 1.75.; disbanded 26.2.82.; (Insignia: Pegasus, later numerals '35')

No 44 Converted to B.Mk 2 at Waddington 1967 (formed with B.Mk 1 10.8.60.); disbanded 21.12.82. (Insignia: numerals '44')

No 50 Converted to B.Mk 2 1966-67 at Waddington (formed with B.Mk 1 1.8.61.); converted to K.Mk 2 1982; disbanded 31.3.84. (Insignia: two dingoes)

No 83 Transferred to Scampton 10.10.60. (previously with B.Mk 1 at Waddington 21.5.57.-10.8.60.); disbanded 31.8.69. (Insignia: an antler)

No 101 Converted to B.Mk 2 at Waddington 1967 (formed with B.Mk 1 at Finningley 15.10.57.; transferred to Waddington 6.61.); disbanded 4.8.82.; (Insignia: numerals '101')

No 617 Converted to B.Mk 2 at Scampton 9.61. (formed with B.Mk 1 1.5.58.); disbanded 31.12.81.; (Insignia: three lightning flashes; later, breached dam)

No 230 OCU Converted to B.Mk 2 at Waddington from 1.7.60. (formed with B.Mk 1.7.56.); (Insignia: Lincoln arms); Finningley 6.61. (Insignia: white Yorkshire rose); Scampton 12.69. (Insignia: sword upon white disc); disbanded 31.8.81.

Below: *No. 27 Squadron's five Vulcan B.2(MRR)s (together with another four B.2s which were modified to B.2(MRR) standard) often carried underwing air sampling 'sniffer' pods, a task taken over from No. 543 Squadron. (John Hale)*

V-BOMBER BASES

Coningsby	(Vulcan)
Cottesmore	(Vulcan/Victor)
Finningley	(Vulcan/Victor/Valiant)
Gaydon	(Valiant)
Honington	(Victor)
Marham	(Valiant/Victor)
Scampton	(Vulcan)
Waddington	(Vulcan)
Wittering	(Valiant/Victor)
Wyton	(Valiant/Victor)

(10 Airfields)

V-BOMBER DISPERSAL AIRFIELDS

Aldergrove
Bedford
Boscombe Down
Brawdy
Burtonwood
Cranwell
Elvington
Filton
Kemble
Kinloss
Leconfield
Leeming
Leuchars
Llanbedr
Lossiemouth
Lyneham
Macrihanish
Manston
Middleton St George
Pershore
Prestwick
St Mawgan
Shawbury
Tarrant Rushton
Valley
Yeovilton
(26 Airfields)

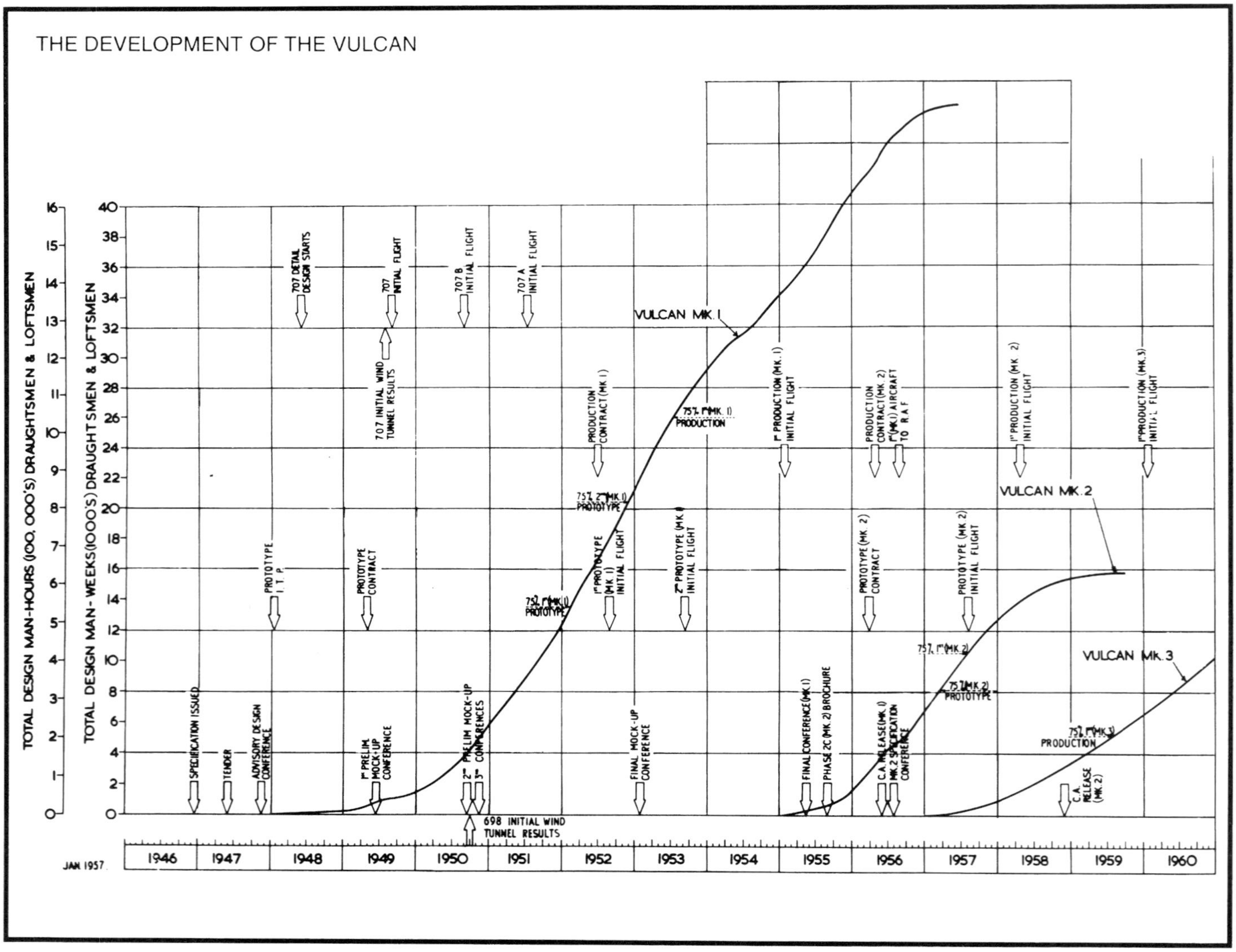

INDEX

A

Aberporth, RAE, 68, 135
Abingdon, RAF, 132
Adelaide, 81
Aden, 51, 80, 83
Advanced Bomber Projects Group, 13, 23
Airframe limitations, 181
Akrotiri, RAF, 69, 113
Amberley, RAAF, 81
Anson, Avro, 110
Argentina, 60, 132, 134, 135, 137
Argentine Air Force/Army/Navy, 132, 133
Armament, 163
Armstrong Whitworth, 13
Ascension Island, 132, 133, 134, 137, 139
Assymetric flying, 189
Attlee, C, 10
Australia, 35, 80, 82, 113
Avalon, RAAF, 41, 80
Avro, 13, 16, 35, 51, 58, 65, 81, 87, 89, 91, 101, 102, 106
Avro 698, 14, 17, 19, 23, 35
Avro 707, 14, 17, 27, 35
Avro 710, 27, 147
Avro 730, 87, 101
AW.52G, Armstrong Whitworth, 23

B

Barton, 123
Biggin Hill, 121
Blackburn B.66, 23
Blackbushe, 48
Black Buck, 82, 132, 133, 135, 137, 139
Blue Danube, 12, 23, 65
Blue Ranger, 116
Blue Sky, 101
Blue Steel, 63, 65, 68, 71, 72, 81, 87, 88, 90, 113, 116
Blue Streak, 88
Boeing B-29, 11
Boeing B-52, 81, 88, 89
Boeing 707, 83, 143
Boeing 747, 132
Boeing KC-135, 139
Boothman, Air Marshal, 34
Bomb doors, 179
Bomber Command Development Unit, 64
Boscombe Down, 28, 45, 47, 48, 63, 80, 110, 111
Boulton Paul, 43
Brazil, 60, 137, 138, 139
British Aerospace, 141, 144, 147
British Airways, 132
Brisbane, 51, 81
Bristol, 13, 23
Broadbridge, Dr. H.G., 54
Broadhurst, Sir Harry, 50, 51, 54, 55, 58, 80, 81, 108, 111
Bruntingthorpe, 147
Buccaneer, 135
Butterworth, RAAF, 80, 83, 112, 116

C

Cabin air system, 158
Cabin pressurisation, 158
Calder, Wing Commander, 104
Canada, 108
Canberra, 91, 110
Castor Oil, exercise, 85
Catterick, RAF, 144
Chadderton, 23, 45, 102, 104, 108
Chadwick, Lord, 10
Chadwick, Roy, 17, 23, 24, 26, 109
Churchill, Sir Winston, 9, 10
Christchurch, 81
Christmas Island, 65
Comet, de Havilland, 104
Coningsby, RAF, 64, 147
Convair B-58, 81, 88
Cosford, RAF, 121
Cottesmore, RAF, 64, 147
Cranwell, RAF, 122
Crew, 147
Cricklewood, 100
Crowe, Dr. Alwyn, 12
Cuban missile crisis, 65

D

Darwin, 51, 80, 81, 112, 116
Davies, Stuart, 16, 23, 24
Delta design, 16
Delta origins, 19
Detroit, 60
Dimensions, 155
Dobson, Sir Roy, 17, 29, 102
Douglas, 88
Dowty, 43
Dry Martini, exercise, 86

E

East Germany, 68
East Fortune, 141
ECM, 62, 63, 91, 132, 135, 139, 144
Eden, A, 48
Edinburgh, 81, 82, 83, 116
Eglin AFB, 88
Eisenhower, Dwight D., 88
Ejection seats, 160
Electrical systems, 195
El Adem, 116
Emergencies, 191
Engines, 164, 183
English Electric, 13
Esler, Eric, 28
Ewans, J. R., 19, 51

F

Fairey, 101
Falk, Roland, 17, 29, 45, 48, 104, 107
Falklands, 132, 133, 135, 137, 141
Farren, W., 26
Farnborough, 13, 17, 23, 25, 26, 28, 29, 43, 45, 47, 48, 63, 106, 107
Finningley, RAF, 64, 109, 147
Fire protection systems, 194
Flight Refuelling Ltd, 95, 141
Flying controls, 166
Frankenstein, 104
Frisch, O., 9
Fuel system, 169

G

Gan, RAF, 83, 113, 116
Gander, 85
General Dynamics F-111K, 90
Gibraltar, RAF, 111, 141
Grand Slam, 12
Green Palm, 62
Goose Bay, RAF, 60, 113
Guam, 85

H
Haig, Alexander, 137
Hall, Sir Arnold, 48
Handley Page, 13, 14, 26, 100, 102
Handley Page HP.80, 14, 45, 100
Handling, 186
Hardman, Sir Donald, 53
Harrison, Jimmy, 108, 109
HDU, 141, 144
Heathrow, 51, 53, 54, 107
Henlow, RAF, 100
Hercules, 132, 139
High Castor, exercise, 84
High Jupiter, exercise, 84
High Mars, exercise, 84
High Rigel, exercise, 83
High Venus, exercise, 84
High Wycombe, RAF, 51, 68
Honolulu, 85
Horten brothers, 23
Hound Dog, 89
Hucknall, 30, 108
Hurricane, 11
Hyde Park Memorandum, 10

I
Indonesia, 83
Institute of Aviation Medicine, RAF, 104
Instrument layout, 155

J
Joint Service Trials Unit, No. 4, 116

K
Karachi, 82
Kay, J. A. R., 14
Kellog Field, 60
Kennedy, J. F. K., 88, 89, 90
Kenya, 60
Khormaksar, 116
Kinloss, RAF, 144

L
Lake St. Clair, 60
Laverton, RAAF, 38
LGB, 139
Libya, 60, 83
Lincoln, Avro, 12
Lincoln Cathedral, 147
Lincoln AFB, 60
Lindley, R, 24
Lippisch, 14, 19, 23
Locking, RAF, 121
London, 68
Lone Ranger, 60, 113
Los Alamos, 10
Lossiemouth, RAF, 65
Luqa, RAF, 68, 113
Lyneham, RAF, 121, 141

M
Macmillan, Harold, 65, 88, 89, 90
MacNamara, Robert, 88
McDougal, Sqn Ldr, N., 138
McMahon Bill, 10
Malaysia, 83
Maldive Islands, 83
Mallala, RAAF, 81
Manchester Airport, 104
Manhattan Project, 10
Marham, RAF, 122, 132, 144, 145, 147
Martel, 135
Martin Baker, 108
Maud Committee, 9
Melbourne, HMAS, 37
Mildenhall, RAF, 123
Millikin, Flt Lt P., 121, 145
Minuteman, 88
Monte Bello Islands, 11
Morgan, M, 13
Moscow, 65

N
Nairobi, 113
Nasa, 100
New Zealand, 50, 60, 80, 81, 83, 112
Nicosia, 81
Nimrod, 132, 134, 137, 147
Normalair, 100, 102, 105

O
OCU, No. 230, 50, 60, 63, 64, 95, 110
Offut AFB, 85, 113
Ohakea, RNZAF, 81, 112
Opal Digger, exercise, 85
Operational Requirement 229, 12
Orrell, Jimmy, 45

P
Pearce, RAAF, 82
Peierls, R., 9
Penny, William, 11
Perth, 82, 83
Phase 2C wing, 62, 63
Phase 6, Vulcan, 89
Pneumatic systems, 180
Point Cook, RAAF, 80
Polaris, 88, 89
Port Stanley, 133, 134, 135, 137
Powers, F. G., 90

Q
Quick Reaction Alert, 113

R
RAAF, 80
Red Arrows, 145
Red Beard, 65
Red Flag, exercise, 132
Red Shrimp, 62
Red Steer, 62
Renfrew, 38
Rhodesia, 60
Richmond, RAAF, 81, 82, 83
Rio de Janeiro, 137
Rivers, Peter, 100
Rockwell B-1, 87
Roosevelt, F. D., 9, 10
Royal Aircraft Establishment, 13, 81, 100
Royal Navy, 72, 90

S
St. Mawgan, RAF, 65
Sabre, F-86, 81
Sandys, D, 87
San Fransisco, 85
Santa Monica, 88
Save the Vulcan campaign, 145
Scampton, RAF, 64, 81, 82, 85, 112, 113, 116, 147
Serial allocations, 217
Shackleton, 91
Sheffield, 141
Sherratt, J. J., 141
Sidewinder, 139
Shorts, 13, 14, 23
Short Spica, exercise, 84
Shrike, 137, 139
Singapore, 51, 80, 82
Skybolt, 88, 89, 90, 91, 132
Skyguard, 137
Slessor, Sir John, 45
Southend, 145, 147
Specification B.9/48, 23
Specification B.14/46, 14
Specification B.35/46, 12, 23, 26, 45, 62
Specification E.10/49, 29, 35
Specification E.15/48, 28, 35
Spectre, 68
Sperrin, 14, 23
Squadrons, 227
Squadrons, RAF:
  No. 9, 64, 95, 132
  No. 12, 64
  No. 27, 64, 68, 82, 85, 95
  No. 35, 64, 95
  No. 44, 64, 83, 95, 132, 139
  No. 50, 64, 83, 132, 139, 141
  No. 83, 60, 64, 68, 82
  No. 101, 60, 64, 82, 83, 95, 132
  No. 543, 72, 95

No. 617, 64, 68, 81, 82, 95
Stentor, 68, 71
Sunflower, exercise, 83
Superfuse, 134
Soviet Union, 65
Syerston, 60
SR-71, 87

T
Teddington, 101, 105
Tengah, 83
Terrain Following Radar, 91, 180
Thomas, Sqn Ldr D., 120, 145
Thompson, Flt Lt P., 120
Thor, 88
Tornado, 91, 95
Top Limit, exercise, 86
Touch, Dr. A. G., 53, 54, 58
Town House, exercise, 84
Trident, 88
Truman, Harry S., 10
TSR-2, 90
Tuxford, Sqn Ldr R., 134

U
U-2, 90
Undercarriage, 178
USA, 60, 65, 100, 137
USAF, 65, 88, 89, 139

V
Valletta, 106
V-2, 12
V-Bomber bases, 228
V-Bomber dispersal airfields, 228
VC10, 88, 132, 139, 141, 147
Valiant, 23, 45, 64, 65, 68, 72, 82, 83, 90, 113
Vickers, 23
Victor, 46, 48, 64, 65, 90, 91, 95
Vulcan Association, 145
Vulcan Display Flight, 120, 145

W
Waddington, RAF, 34, 50, 51, 63, 64, 83, 95, 110, 121, 122, 132, 133, 135, 139, 141, 144, 145, 147
Wake Island, 85
Wellington, 81, 112
Western Ranger, exercise, 113
West Freugh, 88
Westland, 100
Whiskey Sour, exercise, 85
White Waltham, 109
Wideawake, 133, 134, 137
Wing deployments, 227
Withers, Flt Lt M., 133, 134, 135
Woodford, 17, 26, 28, 29, 30, 35, 37, 45, 48, 58, 60, 68, 95, 103, 104, 141, 147
Woomera, 68, 80, 81, 90, 113
Wright Patterson AFB, 88
Wyton, RAF, 95